Computers in Art, Design and Animation

John Lansdown Rae A. Earnshaw
Editors

Computers in Art, Design and Animation

With 218 Illustrations, 68 in Full Color

Springer-Verlag
New York Berlin Heidelberg
London Paris Tokyo

John Lansdown
50-51 Russell Square
London WC1B 4JP
United Kingdom

Rae A. Earnshaw
University of Leeds
Leeds LS2 9JT
United Kingdom

On the Front Cover: Computer Sculpture by William Latham, Sculptor Software by Mike King, Ray Tracing Software by Amazing Array, Ltd., London, United Kingdom.

Library of Congress Cataloging-in-Publication Data
Computers in art, design and animation / John Lansdown, Rae A.
Earnshaw, editors.
p. cm.
ISBN 0-387-96896-2
1. Computer art. 2. Computer-aided design. 3. Computer graphics.
I. Lansdown, John. II. Earnshaw, Rae A.
N7433.8.C67 1989
760--dc19 88-38983

Typeset by Impressions, Inc., Madison, Wisconsin.
Printed and bound by Universitätsdruckerei H. Stürtz AG, Würzburg, Federal Republic of Germany.

9 8 7 6 5 4 3 2 1

ISBN 0-387-96896-2 Springer-Verlag New York Berlin Heidelberg
ISBN 3-540-96896-2 Springer-Verlag Berlin Heidelberg New York

Preface

The collection of papers that makes up this book arises largely from the joint activities of two specialist groups of the British Computer Society, namely the Displays Group and the Computer Arts Society. Both these groups are now more than 20 years old and during the whole of this time have held regular, separate meetings. In recent years, however, the two groups have held a joint annual meeting at which presentations of mutual interest have been given and it is mainly from the last two of these that the present papers have been drawn. They fall naturally into four classes: visualisation, art, design and animation—although, as in all such cases, the boundaries between the classes are fuzzy and overlap inevitably occurs.

Visualisation

The graphic potential of computers has been recognised almost since computing was first used, but it is only comparatively recently that their possibilities as devices for the visualisation of complex and largely abstract phenomena has begun to be more fully appreciated. Some workers stress the need to be able to model photographic reality in order to assist in this task. They look to better algorithms and more resolution to achieve this end. Others—Alan Mackay for instance—suggest that it is "not just a matter of providing more and more pixels. It is a matter of providing congenial clues which employ to the greatest extent what we already know." The three papers in this section perceptively examine some of the theoretical questions that arise in the use of computers and visualisation.

Computer Art

Alan Turing (1912–1954) looked forward to the day when computers could do such creative and imaginative things as write poetry and paint pictures. Even in the 1940s and early 1950s—when computers had very restricted capabilities indeed—he foresaw them being used for creative tasks which, even today, we regard as quintessentially human. Although still not able to fully realise Turing's dream, computing has intrigued artists for nearly 40 years.

Nowadays many artists use computers to help them in their work and it is no longer remarkable that they should do so. However, most artists who are concerned with the use of the machine use it to realise ideas which they have devised without computer aid: computing in this case is used as a *tool* of production or, perhaps, as a *medium*. This is by far the most popular and time-honoured role for computing in the arts. Some artists—a small few—are interested in using the computer as an *intelligent apprentice* where the computer acts more independently. Always, though, I think we will find that every artist who uses computing sees it as a *catalyst* to new, more exciting and innovative work. The ultimate possibilities, however, are only just being dimly seen.

Richard Wright tells us that "painters and sculptors rarely need to justify their choice of media," yet we think this choice sometimes needs explanation. The role that computers can play in the visual arts is often misunderstood or, perhaps, understood too narrowly. Part of the aim of this collection is to broaden the understanding and to illustrate the wide range of assistance the computer can give to the artist.

Design

The papers in this section look at both the theoretical and practical issues of using computers in the difficult process of designing artefacts. Philip Steadman encapsulates the problems of assisting the computer-aided design process (in contrast to the computer-aided drafting process) thus: "the designer works with ill-formed, tentative, ambiguous and vague ideas; this ambiguity and imprecision are carried over into the representations which the designer uses, his sketches and doodles; and these are qualities which it is notoriously difficult to embody in computer programs."

Despite these problems, assistance can be given to designers and some of our papers outline the ways in which this might be and is being done. A note of caution is sounded by Gillian Crampton Smith, however. She gives us the views of a practising graphic designer with considerable experience of computing and complains of the shortfall between the dream and the reality: "Too costly, too complex, too cryptic," she says of the available help and adds, "It is also too damn ugly."

Animation

Much of the thrust towards faster, more powerful and more photorealistic graphics computing comes from the needs of the entertainment industry: film and television. Nowadays many of the special effects in these media are achieved not by model-shooting or conventional means but by computer animation, and huge sums of money have been invested in this process. But the techniques that have been derived have more practical purposes too. The first of the papers in this section deals with one of these: the needs and methods of pilot training. John Vince, one of the pioneers of British computer animation, outlines the problems of producing, for flight simulators, high-quality imagery in real time, that is, more than a million times faster than that achieved by many conventional rendering systems. (Surprisingly—or perhaps not so surprisingly to those who have experienced a "flight" in one of these magical simulators—these are now being sold to the entertainment industry for installation in theme and amusement parks.)

At the other end of the scale of cost and speed, we have the provisions for students learning the art of computer animation, and two authors who have been engaged in teaching this subject outline their personal view of the problems. The difficult—indeed, still largely unsolved—task of modelling movement of the human body to assist in recording and animating an Indian dance form is examined, as is the modelling and animation of the human face. Something that can possibly help in this direction as well as in many others—the modelling of soft, malleable objects—is also covered here.

All the papers in all the sections illustrate something of the broad range of techniques, theory and methods for realising creative ends through computer graphics of varying levels of technological sophistication. Whether your concerns are mainly in computing, in graphics, in art or in design, we are sure that you will find much to interest you in this collection.

John Lansdown
Rae A. Earnshaw

Contents

Contributors

Ian O. Angell Department of Information Systems, London School of Economics, Houghton Street, London WC2A 2AE, UK.

Ian Angell graduated from the University College of Wales and, after taking his PhD there (in computer applications to algebraic number theory), lectured for many years in the Department of Computer Science at Royal Holloway College, London. He is now professor of Information Systems at the London School of Economics and Political Science. His research covers a wide range of applied computing topics including statistical geometry, geometric modelling, human factors and multimedia information systems. He is author of many papers and a number of books on these subjects.

Paul Brown Faculty of Art, Swinburne Institute, P.O. Box 218, Hawthorn, Victoria 3122, Australia.

Paul Brown originally trained as a painter and sculptor in the mid-1960s and has been using computers since 1974. He received a BA (Hons) in Fine Art at Liverpool Polytechnic and the HDFA (Lond) from the Slade School of Fine Art. In 1982 he co-founded the computer animation studio, Digital Pictures. From 1984 he was a Principal Lecturer in Computer Aided Art and Design and, later, Head of the Advanced Studies Centre at Middlesex Polytechnic. He took up his post as Director of the Computer Image Program at Swinburne Institute in January 1988. His work as an artist has been exhibited internationally, including shows at the 1980 Venice Biennale, SIGGRAPH 84 Electronic Theatre and the SIGGRAPH 86 Art Show.

Christine I. Brownrigg c/o Department of Computer Science, City University, Northampton Square, London EC1V 0HB, UK.

Christine Brownrigg has a DipAD from Sheffield Art College. Her work ranges from portraiture to trophy design. For some years her interest has centered on photography, with exhibitions in Jamaica, USA, UK and elsewhere during this period. Lately she has become concerned with image processing and computer graphics techniques as an extension of photographic dark room effects only realisable with the computer as a medium.

David R.K. Brownrigg Department of Computer Science, City University, Northampton Square, London EC1V 0HB, UK.

David Brownrigg has BSc, MSc and PhD degrees from Reading University, covering mathematics, computer science and galactic dynamics. His technical publications range from tunnel engineering to combinatorial geometry whilst his current research interests include the design of noise insensitive edge detectors and interpolants for fractal terrain maps. His work on computer art image processing has developed from research on nonlinear digital filters.

Peter P. Comninos Department of Communication and Media, Dorset Institute of Higher Education, Poole, Dorset BH12 5BB, UK.

Peter Comninos received a Diploma in Computer Programming from ASME, Athens, Greece, a BSc (Hons) degree in Computer Science and a PhD degree in Computer Animation from Teesside Polytechnic and is currently Reader at the Department of Communication and Media at the Dorset Institute of Higher Education. His research interests include computer animation, compilers, hidden-surface and hidden-line techniques as well as computational geometry techniques.

Rae A. Earnshaw Head of Computer Graphics, University of Leeds, Leeds LS2 9JT, UK.

Rae Earnshaw received his BSc and PhD in Computer Science from the University of Leeds, where he is now Head of Computer Graphics. He has interests in graphic algorithms, integrated graphics and text, display technology, CAD/CAM and issues of human/computer interfaces. He has been a Visiting Professor at Illinois Institute of Technology, George Washington University and Northwestern Polytechnical University, China. In the last few years he has directed a number of NATO Advanced Study Institutes and Summer Schools on graphics algorithms and techniques and has written and edited a number of books on aspects of computer graphics.

Iain Elliot National Semiconductor GmbH, Industriestrasse 10, 8080 Fuerstenfeldbruk, FRG.

Iain Elliot studied electrical and electronic engineering at Heriot-Watt University, Edinburgh, where he gained his BSc (Hons) degree. He worked on software development for graphic workstations at ICL and was seconded to ECRC at Muenchen to work on Prolog compiler and interpreter development as well as to provide an interface between prolog and graphics. He now works for National Semiconductor in NS32000 after-sales software support.

William Fawcett Cambridge Architectural Research Ltd., 6 Chaucer Road, Cambridge CB2 2EB, UK.

William Fawcett trained as an architect and gained his PhD at Cambridge University, England. After working in architectural practice and teaching at the University of Hong Kong, he recently took up a Research Fellowship at the Centre for Configurational Studies in the Open University.

Avon Huxor European Computer Industry Research Centre, Arabellastrasse 17, D-8000 Muenchen, FRG.

Avon Huxor studied architecture and town planning at University College, London, where he gained a BA degree. He received his Master's degree from the Department of Design Research at the Royal College of Art for his investigations into the application of A1 techniques in CAD. Until recently he worked at the European Computer Industry Research Centre, Muenchen, West Germany, where he was concerned with the knowledge engineering aspects for a knowledge-based economic decision-support system.

James Hennessey Industrial Design Department, University of Washington, Seattle, Washington, USA.

James Hennessey is an Associate Professor of Industrial Design and heads the Department of Industrial Design at the University of Washington. He is a visiting research fellow with Vakgroep Vormgeving, Technical University, Delft, The Netherlands, where some of the work described in his paper was carried out.

Alexander King Senior Lecturer, Department of Communication and Media, Dorset Institute of Higher Education, Poole, Dorset BH12 5BB, UK.

Alex King carried out his undergraduate studies at North-East London Polytechnic and Bristol Polytechnic and recently received his MPhil in Computer Animation at Dorset Institute, where he is also a Senior Lecturer on the Communication and Media Production Course. He has worked in industry as a programmer and analyst in London and Bristol. His interests are in computer animation on microcomputers and in user interfaces.

Mike King Research Fellow in Computer Art and Animation, John Cass Faculty of Arts, City of London Polytechnic, 100 Minories, London EC3N 1JY, UK.

Mike King gained a BSc in Physics and Chemistry at Oxford Polytechnic and taught for seven years before taking his Master's degree in Software Engineering at Oxford University and a PhD at the Department of Design Research, Royal College of Art. He has always had a strong interest in the visual arts and has painted for many years. His computer graphic images have been shown at exhibitions in London, Bristol and Exeter. He is currently engaged in developing software packages for artists and designers.

William Latham IBM Scientific Centre, Athelstan House, St. Clement Street, Winchester, Hants SO23 9OR, UK.

William Latham studied Fine Art at Christ Church, Oxford University from 1979 to 1982, where he gained a BA (Distinction) degree. He won a Henry Moore Award in 1982 to study at the Royal College of Art, where he gained his MA in 1985. He is currently researching his PhD degree at the Painting School there, although his computing work for this is carried out at the IBM Scientific Centre where he is a research fellow. His prints, sculptures and short films have been shown in exhibitions world-wide and are also in private collections.

John Lansdown Centre for Advanced Studies in Computer Aided Art and Design, Middlesex Polytechnic, Cat Hill, Barnet, Herts EN4 8HT, UK.

John Lansdown practised as an architect from 1952 to 1983, when he left architecture to devote more time to his teaching commitments and to being Chairman of System Simulation Ltd. He has used computers in creative tasks since 1960 and was one of the founders of the Computer Arts Society, an organisation of which he has been Honorary Secretary since its inception in 1968. He took up his post as professor of Computer Aided Art and Design at Middlesex Polytechnic in September 1988, where he is Head of CASCAAD and acting head of the School of Communication Design. He is the author of three books and more than 200 papers on the use of computers in art, design, architecture, animation and choreography.

Alan L. Mackay Department of Crystallography, Birkbeck College, University of London, Malet Street, London WC1E 7HX, UK.

Alan Mackay has spent his academic career in the Department of Crystallography founded by J.D. Bernal at Birkbeck College. He has now the title of professor and is engaged in generalising the concepts of classical crystallography to include the many modern developments revealed by the electron microscope and other techniques. He has tried to assimulate to this aspects of non-Euclidean geometry and of cellular automata. To this end he wishes to see the development of microcomputer graphics as a convenient element of exploratory thought. He has many papers and a preliminary book in this area. He is a Fellow of the Royal Society.

George L. Mallen Managing Director, System Simulation Ltd., 25OM Bedford Chambers, The Piazza, Covent Garden, London WC2E 8HA, UK.

George Mallen graduated in physics after combined academic and professional research training at the Royal Aircraft Establishment, Farnborough and became involved with computers in 1962 working on digital simulations of air traffic control systems. Joining Gordon Pask at System Research Ltd. he led the design, development and use of an organisational simulation methodology for crime investigation. In addition, he developed computer models of human learning and decision making. In 1977 he founded the Computing Activities Unit in the Department of Design Research at the Royal College of Art, where he was Deputy Head of Department. From 1983 to 1985 he was Head of the Department of Communication and Media at Dorset Institute of Higher Education. During this period he initiated a new, multidisciplinary degree in Communication and Media production.

Barry Martin Department of Computer Science and Applied Mathematics, Aston University, Birmingham B4 7ET, UK.

Barry Martin is a Lecturer in Mathematics in the Department of Computer Science and Applied Mathematics at the University of Aston in Birmingham. He joined Aston in 1973 and prior to that was with Rice University in the USA. He has a PhD in non-Newtonian fluid dynamics from Cambridge University, England. His interest in interation and computer graphics began in 1985.

Tom W. Maver Director, ABACUS, Department of Architecture and Building Science, University of Strathclyde, Rotten Row, Glasgow, UK.

Tom Mayer has pioneered the use of computing in architectural design and building science since the 1960s. He is professor of Computer Aided Design and Director of the ABACUS research unit at the University of Strathclyde—an organisation which has done a great deal to foster and develop the application of computer-aided architectural design in theory and practise. He is the author of many papers and a number of books on this subject. He also has a professorial appointment in CAD at the Technical University of Eindhoven.

Sumant Narayan Pattanaik Graphics and Computer Aided Design Division, National Centre for Software Technology, Gulmohar Cross Road 9, Juhu, Bombay 400 049, India.

Sumanta Pattanaik is a Staff Scientist at the National Centre for Software Technology in Bombay, India. He has a BSc and an MSc from Utkal University, and his interests include programming methodology, graphics systems, computer animation, and geometric modelling.

Gillian Crampton Smith Royal College of Art, Kensington Gore, London SW7 2EU, UK.

Gillian Crampton Smith studied at Newnham College, Cambridge, where she gained her MA degree in Philosophy and History of Art. In her professional career she has specialised in graphic design for newspapers and magazines and has worked either as Art Editor or Designer on the *Sunday Times*, the *Times Literary Supplement* and the British Film Institute quarterly, *Sight and Sound.* To assist in this work she developed a program to calculate and display text-fitting and graphics layout for the magazine spreads and has been interested in the more widespread application of computers to design ever since. She has taught at Canterbury College of Art, Central School of Art, London and, from 1982 to December 1988, at St. Martin's School of Art, where she directed the post-graduate diploma course in Graphic Design and Computers. She took up her post at the Royal College of Art in January 1989.

Cathy Sobhanpanah Department of Computer Science, Royal Holloway and Bedford New College, Egham, Surrey, UK.

Cathy Sobhanpanah is a lecturer in Computer Science at Royal College and Bedford New College. Her research includes relating geometric modelling and databases to computer graphics.

Mike Stapleton System Simulation Ltd., 250M Bedford Chambers, The Piazza, Covent Garden, London WC2E 8HA, UK.

Mike Stapleton has a BSc in Physics and Master's degrees in Computer Science from London University and in Design from the Royal College of Art. He has worked at the Computing Activities Unit at the Royal College of Art and at the Experimental Cartography Unit of the National Environment Research Council. Until recently he combined his work on software design and development at System Simulation Ltd., with the role of Reader at Dorset Institute of Higher Education. Currently he works full-time as Technical Director of System Simulation Ltd.

Philip Steadman Centre for Configurational Studies, Open University, Milton Keynes MK7 6AA, UK.

Philip Steadman studied architecture at Cambridge University, and then worked in research in architecture and planning at Cambridge before moving to the Open University in 1977. He is Lecturer in Design and Director of the Centre for Configurational Studies at the Open University. He is author of many papers and books on the subject of design, geometry and morphology.

John A. Vince Research Consultant, Rediffusion Simulation Ltd., Fleming Way, Crawley, West Sussex RH10 2JY, UK.

John Vince graduated in electronics and gained a Master's degree in Computer Science. He received his PhD in Computer Graphics from Brunel University. For some years he was principal lecturer at Middlesex Polytechnic, where he continued development of his famous PICASO computer graphics package, which was used both as a training program for artists and designers and as a production tool for a large number of television animations. He is now a Visiting Professor at Middlesex Polytechnic. For the last four or so years in his present occupation he has been dealing with research into the computer graphics aspects of flight simulators.

Keith Waters CASCAAD, Middlesex Polytechnic, Cat Hill, Barnet, Herts EN4 8HT, UK.

Keith Waters received his first class BA (Hons) degree in Graphic Design at Middlesex Polytechnic in 1985. Whilst an undergraduate there he specialised in computer graphics, which gave him the opportunity to work at the BBC on the graphics for a current affairs programme. After completing his first degree he worked for a short period in a videographics production house specialising in three-dimensional computer animation. Resisting further opportunities from industry, he returned to the Polytechnic to pursue his doctoral research into the computer synthesis of expressive three-dimensional facial character animation. He received his PhD for this work in July 1988. He has won a number of awards for the computer graphics illustrations of his works, notably both the Student and Supreme Awards at CG 86 and third place in the graduate category at NCGA. He took up his post at Schlumberger in December 1988.

Richard Wright Centre for Advanced Studies in Computer Aided Art and Design, Middlesex Polytechnic, Cat Hill, Barnet, Herts EN4 8HT, UK.

Richard Wright graduated in Fine Art from Winchester School of Art in 1986, where he first began exploring the use of mathematical systems and then computers as new media for art. After spending his final year working as a research fellow at the IBM UK Scientific Centre, he moved to the Centre for Advanced Studies in Computer Aided Art and Design at Middlesex Polytechnic, where he became their Artist in Residence. He completed his Master's degree there working on video animation and sound synthesis as well as theoretical aspects of science and art.

Brian Wyvill Department of Computer Science, University of Calgary, 2500 University Drive NW, Calgary, Alberta, Canada T2N 1N4.

Brian Wyvill received his PhD from the University of Bradford in 1975 and continued his interest in computer animation as a research fellow at the Royal College of Art. He is now a Full Professor at the University of Calgary, where he leads the Graphicsland animation research team. His current interests are in soft objects, motion control and recursive data structures for computer animation.

Geoff Wyvill Department of Computer Science, University of Otago, Dunedin, New Zealand.

Geoff Wyvill is a senior lecturer in computer science at the University of Otago, New Zealand. He graduated in physics from Jesus College, Oxford and gained MSc and PhD degrees in computer science from the University of Bradford, where he lectured in this subject from 1969 to 1978. He is on the editorial board of *The Visual Computer.*

Part 1 Visualisation

In the Mind's Eye*

Alan L. Mackay

Introduction

I have often been astonished to find that almost all books on philosophy and even most modern books on geometry are totally without pictures. Philosophy is supposed to be the study of thought and I had always believed that most people thought in pictures.

It has not always been so, and philosophers of the Middle Ages used pictures and diagrams extensively. Dante's vision of Hell is simply a dramatic geometrical classificatory system with sin as the main parameter. When we use the word hierarchy it denotes this kind of tree arrangement. One of the great inventions of Ramon Llull (1233–1316) was the tree diagram (Llull, ca. 1272). He also invented the universal buzzword generator—concentric discs of mode words which could be used in innumerable combinations. Medieval philosophy is full of diagrams of trees, matrices, mandalas, hierarchic classifications in two or three dimensions, besides personification of abstract concepts for better visualisation of relationships. Philosophers seem to think that even such rudimentary devices as the Venn diagram are beneath them. (In fact, the Venn diagram is not so rudimentary—try drawing a Venn diagram for four qualities and generalise the construction to N qualities.)

The art of memory, as taught long ago in the early universities, was entirely based on visualisation. It used the miniature theatre of the mind which we seem to have in our brains and in which we can do remarkable thought experiments. For example, when you look at a picture hanging on your living room wall, it is easy to visualise what is at the other side of the same wall. We may even ask if orthogonal Cartesian coordinates are natural or a cultural product. I think that analysing motions into rotations about three mutually perpendicular directions is natural because the semi-circular canals in the ear do it this way. Even today the prodigies

---

*This paper has been reproduced by permission of Birkbeck College, University of London.

of memory base their feats on visual images. That there is really a spatial representation in the brain can be seen from knowledge as to how the whiskers of a rat, which are used for exploring the rat-hole, are mapped into a region of the brain. If young rats are shaved and never use their whiskers, then the corresponding regions of the brain never develop properly. In recent experiments, people were asked to rotate in their minds a picture of a molecule and, by bringing it into coincidence with another picture, to say whether the two were of the same or of opposite hand. The clear result was that the time required to do this operation was directly proportional to the rotation needed. Perhaps we do indeed have a hard-wired rotation function just like the Evans and Sutherland Picture System!

I think that modern philosophy has been captured by the power of words and has forgotten the basic things to which they refer. Linguistic philosophy has long been predominant. The pre-linguistic period of the early Royal Society was satirised by Swift (1726) in *Gulliver's Travels*, where he depicted philosophers as carrying sacks of geometrical objects which they unpacked and gestured with in their discussions. "If they would, for example, praise the beauty of a woman . . . they describe it by rhombs, circles, parallelograms, and other geometrical terms." These days the images of computer-aided design are really not much more sophisticated, except that they would round off the corners with "splines"—a short and unattractive little word suggesting a combination of "whalebone stays" and "splints"—and put in shadows and highlights. I would like to see a return to this attitude in a modern form with a system which would conjure up all kinds of images and allow their combination and alteration. Having images on a disc (hard or compact) is more convenient than carrying around the actual models in a sack. Derek Price used to ask why human beings do not have a visual output organ to match the channel capacity of the eye. (The answer might be that all eyes would then be overloaded.)

Geometry, dealing as it does with real things, was a rather despised branch of mathematics and only the persistence of the greater figures like H.S.M. Coxeter, who appealed above the heads of other mathematicians to the wider audience of intelligent students and amateurs, succeeded in eventually bringing it back into the mainstream of mathematics. Gruenbaum and Shephard (1985) write: "mathematicians have long since regarded it as demeaning to work on problems related to elementary geometry in two or three dimensions, in spite of the fact that it is precisely this sort of mathematics which is of practical value."

Even Archimedes who admitted to finding his results by "mechanical methods"—essentially the computer graphics of the time—had to present them in the form of the proofs demanded by the contemporary style of logic. His computer graphics were circles in the sand, but engineers of that time could bore a tunnel through a mountain and arrange that those starting from each side met accurately in the middle, as most strikingly in the tunnel of Eupalinus on Samos.

Today the younger mathematicians are re-discovering geometry and are using computer graphics enthusiastically in this search, although the deadening classical presentations without pictures are still predominant. See, for example, the current explosion of interest in minimal surfaces (Mackay, 1985; Hoffman, 1987). Robotics has forced the development of computational three (and higher) dimensional geometry.

The geometrical representation of mathematical structures is undergoing a renaissance. We can instance the field of non-linear mechanics, which has been totally transformed by the possibilities of computation and of the display of results, for example the trajectories of representative points in parameter space. New concepts such as "strange attractors," "chaotic regimes," the "Mandelbrot set" and "fractals" gain rapid acceptance by their visibility. In chemical dynamics the demonstration of reactions periodic in time and space has deep implications for biology. The title of Arthur Winfree's (1980) book–*The Geometry of Biological Time*–is designed to provoke deep thought. The subject is incomprehensible without computer graphics. The design of biological molecules is only one of the more obvious applications. An isomorphous field, the design of robots, demands not merely the representation of situations in three dimensions but also a study of the N-dimensional parameter space of all the variables concerned.

I do not want to consider the problems of drawing patches of colour on a screen with more and more pixels. Realism is not to be obtained just by having more and more pixels. The development of the ray-tracing algorithm may match pictures better to the mind. I want to direct your attention to the more fundamental construction of suitable data structures for handling geometry. The question is one of isolating significant structures. Richard Gregory (1987), in his important manual for computer people, *The Mind*, mentions the empirical discoveries of caricaturists in pointing to those features which are actually used by the brain in, for example, discriminating between similar faces. I remember similarly, when learning to recognise 300 different kinds of aeroplanes, how characteristic features are actively sought for and overemphasised. I think that Gregory's handbook is essential reading for all those dealing with computer graphics.

APL (A Programming Language) is a mathematical notation designed for the expression of the various processes needed in handling data structures, especially those in which arrays of numbers or symbols are central. It was first designed to express the needs of the user and only later implemented as a computer language; it was thus in advance of its time and has become progressively more appropriate as the computing power necessary for its operation has become available. It includes, for example, as a central feature the calculation of the left inverse of a matrix, so that least squares solutions to linear equations are found extremely rapidly. In APL this calculation is written in a few characters, whereas the corresponding traditional Fortran program is many lines long. In a later version, APL2, some further refinements such as complex number algebra and the automatic extraction of eigenvalues and vectors have been added. A good example of demonstrations in physics implemented in APL has been given by Chaitin (1985). Chaitin shows that the daunting expressions for curvature in four dimensions can be handled most expeditiously.

APL has now become cheaply available for small microcomputers. I have it implemented on a Sinclair QL (using words instead of the APL symbols) and on a Commodore Amiga (using standard APL symbols). I am trying, with much pain, to develop graphics on the latter.

It is now most desirable to follow this trend and to design a symbolic system, later to be translated into computer terms, which will deal with the special requirements of the physics of structures in three-dimensional space. The production of a suitable language for computer graphics has not yet been adequately achieved, but this approach is first to evolve an algebra for geometry and later to deal with the problem of representing it on a graphics screen.

I must interpolate a comment to the effect that I have tried to learn APL using both the original symbols and an expanded alphabetic version where words are used (MicroAPL, Ltd., 1986). I find that I greatly prefer the word version because I do not have to find the symbols on the keyboard but can use the motor memory for the positions of the alphabetic letters and also have the mnemonic reinforcement of saying the names of the operations as I type them. (This view is contrary to the opinions of APL purists!)

The applications of such a notation are clearly numerous and central in the study of crystal structures, molecules, glasses, textures, hydrodynamics, crystallisation, wave propagation and so forth.

We see a strong parallel with the introduction of vector notation, which greatly improved the expression of physical problems. When computer calculations are done with vectors, they still have to be reduced to Cartesian coordinates. However, this process can be done purely internally and should be of no concern to the user. Weatherburn (1924, 1939), for example, demonstrated the improvement obtained from this notation introduced by Gibbs and Heaviside (both, we might note, outside the mainstream of mathematics). Devising a notation is not a trivial task but demands fundamental physical insight.

With the example of APL in mind, we wish to evolve a notation suitable for the concise expression of physical processes in space and later to examine how it might be implemented on computers, bearing in mind the steady trend towards parallelism. The essence of the problem is to design data structures which embody the geometrical properties of the actual structures (Faux and Pratt, 1979; Gasson, 1983).

How Does This Differ from Computer-Aided Design?

Perhaps in practice it does not differ, although the aims are exploratory rather than for the execution of something which is already clear in the mind. The principal difference might be in the concentration on the handling of molecules and biological structures (Barrett and Mackay, 1987). In these we do not have the hard edges of the simple spheres, cylinders and edges of conventional machinery. We represent mainly the electron density around atoms. In this case the discontinuities in density gradient are removed and it should thus be possible to build in operations involving the gradient of such densities which have physical significance.

Central Concepts of Spatial Structure

The use of large, multi-dimensional arrays is a central feature. APL allows this and experiments may be made using APL systems.

Scalar Fields

$N \times N \times N$ arrays.

Vector Fields

$3 \times N \times N \times N$ arrays (both of these may have real and imaginary components). Provision may be needed for handling singularities in vector fields. Rapid production of projections and sections of three-dimensional fields in arbitrary directions. Computer tomography.

Fast Fourier Transform (FFT)

It may be assumed that it may be required to produce the Fourier transform (in either orthogonal or spherical coordinates) of many spatial distributions. This assumes the automatic use of complex numbers.

Lines (in Space)

(These need immediate calculation of curvature and torsion and length.) Calculation of geodesics; integration along paths. Thanks, perhaps, to the evolutionary experience of our ancestors in dealing with trees, our appreciation of a mass of lines, passing in front of and behind each other, is good.

Surfaces

The present representation of surfaces is rather unsatisfactory. Structures of surfaces one behind the other are particularly difficult to see, to apprehend and to represent. Appreciation of an external surface can be helped by shading and highlighting, perhaps by the drawing of normals, like "fur."

Calculation of curvatures. Fitting of minimal and other surfaces to given boundary conditions (equivalent to finding geodesics). Calculation of intersections between lines and surfaces. See, for example, Duncan and Mair (1983) for an account of their particular system, Polyhedral NC, for machining arbitrary surfaces.

We may comment adversely on the art of sculpture, as practised perhaps by Henry Moore, in that in many cases only a single external surface is presented. There is, in contrast to a real skull or the membranes in a cell, no significant structure inside. Whereas painting in two dimensions is a highly developed art where the art matches the task, in sculpture, the creation of an interesting three-dimensional structure, nature is still far ahead of art.

Variation of Metric

Operations in spaces of different metric are essential for general relativity.

Projections

A variety of projections may be needed to express physical relationships appropriately (e.g., stereographic projection for angular relationships, Gaussian projection of normals to surfaces).

Differential Geometry Generally

Symmetry Operations

Automatic application of crystallographic and other symmetry operations is highly desirable and point and space groups of symmetry would be built in.

Topology

The handling of arrangements of points (perhaps atom centres) and the rapid calculation of neighborhoods. There are relationships, such as Euler's law, relating the conjunction of edges, faces and volumes.

Adjacency and Connectivity Matrices

We must keep in mind the possibility that eventually the physical properties of macromolecules will be handled by parallel processors with one complete microprocessor per atom and that object architecture and computer architecture will converge to similar spatial configurations.

Optimisation by Various Algorithms

Many geometrical problems can be optimised by, for example, application of the Metropolis simulated annealing algorithm, which should thus be available in simple form.

Approach

We would aim to take a number of typical problems, depending strongly on actual spatial arrangements, and see how the notation and processes of calculation could be improved if packaged processes were available. Some of these processes could themselves be written in terms of existing APL notation. Considerable experience has now been collected in preparing problems of macromolecular physics for computer graphics and for computation generally.

Implementation

The question of implementation of functions and processes in machine language is a very technical one which is clearly machine dependent and beyond our competence and control. We would wish to influence future machine architecture in an appropriate direction. Machine capabilities are expanding extremely rapidly and we wish to follow Iverson's example in trying to produce a notation independent of machine capabilities. (Iverson, 1962).

Implications for Robotics

In many ways the geometry of molecules is isomorphous with that of robot manipulators (Paul, 1981; Craig, 1986). However, molecules are relatively softer and distort substantially. A successful notation would thus also be important in this field. It might be mentioned that the generalised inverse of a matrix, a function still not supplied, even for APL2—it is equivalent to the singular value decomposition so strongly recommended by Press et al. (1986)–is most useful in preventing the pathological cases when the Jacobian is singular and the robot does not know which way to move. "Gimbal lock" is the simplest example of this class of occurrence.

Implications for Expert System

An effective notation is a pre-requisite for constructing an expert system which will deal with spatial problems, from negotiating a two-dimensional maze upwards.

In a classic account of how creativity actually works (*The Road to Xanadu*), Lowes (1927) described how over many years Coleridge collected appropriate subroutines and then was one day able to put the fragments together to make his famous poem, which thus was not really completely spontaneous dreaming but represented the success of his brain in organising the disparate images into a coherent whole.

In Xanadu did Kubla Khan
A stately pleasure dome decree:
Where Alph the sacred river, ran
Through caverns measureless to man
Down to a sunless sea.
. . .

This, of course, was a design executed in the literary mode. I would like to have available the facilities for doing something like this in the pictorial mode in a more scientific way than is done in the average arcade adventure game. How about XANADU as a project for computer-aided design and indeed as a name for a more flexible and powerful computer language for graphics? I would very much like to recruit help in a project with such an objective and propose that an interested group of people should look into it (again a visual metaphor).

Although, as I have said, I do not take to Henry Moore's work, I think that we must follow the attitude of the sculpture and try to depict, not just the external view, but the hidden internal relationships which are the true realism. This takes work and, literally, insight.

We do not see with the eye. We see with the mind. Moreover, we also look with the mind. We apprehend things with our prehensile intellect. Seeing is an active process and many mistakes and illusions are caused by trying to impose preconceived patterns on what we see. If you are presented with a concave human face, then you just cannot see it as concave. Your mind revolts and will not accept what you see. Visualisation is not just a matter of providing more and more pixels. It is a matter of providing congenial clues which employ to the greatest extent what we already know.

The eye is indeed the window of the mind, but we must now try to look through it in both directions, although God did not give us an output organ to match the visual input organ. I have been able to assemble the words for this text on an early word processor but, for lack of a correspondingly convenient visual prosthetic output organ, I have not been able to include the illustrations appropriate for this essay. If we have a suitable language for visualisation, then the process has two parts—a viewer who receives the message and, more important, a transmitter who has something visual to say. We do not even have a word for "to say in visual images"!

References

Barrett, A.N. and A.L. Mackay (1987) *Spatial Structure and the Microcomputer.* Macmillan, Basingstoke.

Chaitin, G. (1985) "A Computer Gallery of Mathematical Physics," *Proc. SEAS Anniversary Meeting*, vol. 1, pp. 611–620. SHARE European Association, The Netherlands.

Craig, J.J. (1986) *Introduction to Robotics.* Addison-Wesley, Reading, Mass.

Duncan, J.P. and S.G. Mair (1983) *Sculptured Surfaces in Engineering and Medicine.* Cambridge Univ. Press, London.

Faux, I.D. and M.J. Pratt (1979) *Computational Geometry for Design and Manufacture.* Ellis Horwood, Chichester.

Gasson, P.C. (1983) *Geometry of Spatial Forms.* Ellis Horwood, Chichester.

Gregory, R.L. (1987) *The Oxford Companion to the Mind.* Oxford Univ. Press, London.

Gruenbaum, B. and G.C. Shephard (1985) *Handbook of Applicable Mathematics,* vol. VB. W. Ledermann and S. Vajda, eds., p. 728. Wiley, New York.

Hoffman, D. (1987) "The Computer-Aided Discovery of New Embedded Minimal Surfaces", *Math. Intell.* 9(no. 3):8–21.

IBM Corporation (1984) "APL2 Programming: Language Reference," form SH20-9227-0.

Iverson, K.E. ca. (1962) *A Programming Language.* Wiley, New York.

Llull, Ramon (ca 1272) "AArbre Exemplifical," Majorca.

Lowes, J.L. (1927) *The Road to Xanadu.*

Mackay, A.L. (1985) "Non-Euclidean Crystallography," *Colloq. Math. Soc. Janos Bolyai,* No. 48, *Intuitive Geometry* (Siofok), p. 347–371.

MicroAPL Ltd. (1986) "APL.68000 for the Commodore Amiga."

Paul, R.P. (1981) *Robot Manipulators.* MIT Press, Cambridge, Mass.

Press, W.H., B.P. Flannery, S.A. Teukolsky and W.T. Vetterling (1986) *Numerical Recipes—The Art of Scientific Computing.* Cambridge Univ. Press, London.

Swift, J. (1726) *Gulliver's Travels,* p. 159. Nonesuch Edn.

Weatherburn, C.E. (1924) *Advanced Vector Analysis.* Bell, London.

Weatherburn, C.E. (1939) *Differential Geometry of Three Dimensions.* Cambridge Univ. Press, London.

Winfree, A.T. (1980) *The Geometry of Biological Time.* Springer, Berlin.

Realism and Computer-Integrated Manufacture

Paul Brown

Pretty soon you'll be able to go to a party and be the only person there.

—Andy Warhol

Introduction

The basic algorithms for representing synthetic scenes with high degrees of realism are now well developed and generally available. Very high-performance, low-cost computer systems are already on the market. It is now possible for end-users to produce sophisticated images that even two years ago could have been made only by a team of highly trained specialists with access to major computer power. In this paper I predict that one consequence of this revolution will be an expanded definition of the term computer-integrated manufacture (CIM). In particular, the graphic arts systems will become on-line workstations. This will allow pre-production processes like financing and post-production activities like promotion, marketing and training to become users of a single integrated database.

Two Approaches to Digital Imagemaking

Graphic arts workstations have developed with two distinctly different structures. The earlier systems utilise pure raster graphics. They consist of one or a number of digital framestores and provide functions that allow the operator to draw, paint and manipulate images by operating directly on the framestore contents. Pictures can be input from a variety of sources like video and laser scanners or can be created using the inbuilt drawing functions. In general, the data structures for these kinds of systems are very simple. The image is represented by a matrix of digital samples held in a framestore. Each sample holds the colour and illumination data for a single point, or pixel, on the output medium.

Because of this inherent simplicity, these systems are very easy to use. Operators can be trained quickly and need no knowledge of representation systems (like coordinate geometry) or of computers. They do, however, have a major limitation. Any requirement to enlarge the image requires interpolation of the pixels. Since there is no underlying data structure, this has to be done by crude pixel replication. A number of image enhancement techniques have been developed to improve quality but a certain degree of softening of the image results.

Research by Geoff Watters and Phil Willis (1987) at the University of Bath has demonstrated the creation of a framestore-independent database by storing command strings of user interations on the paint system. This database can subsequently be re-executed at different resolutions and so overcomes the limitations of traditional systems.

As a consequence of their resolution limits, systems based on the traditional paint approach tend to be dedicated to a particular application. Low-cost workstations provide standard broadcast video resolution and have been dubbed paint systems. Higher-cost systems are made for the print industry and use virtual framestores, which can often require over 40 Mbytes of disk space for a single image.

The second approach uses a vector database which is independent of the resolution of the video display system. Originally dubbed slide systems, these are more commonly called vector systems now their application base has expanded. These systems work by scan converting the polygonal database and resolving the priority of its elements at the resolution demanded by the output peripheral. For interactive work this will normally be a standard video resolution framestore. For eventual hard copy output the resolution might be 2000 to 4000 lines for low-cost slide recorders, 6000 to 8000 lines for better quality film recorders, or better than 16,000 lines for reprographic output scanners.

Many systems also correct for aliasing errors introduced by the fixed pixel sampling frequency using antialiasing techniques. These correctly sub-sample the area of the image covered by the pixel and produce an average colour.

Although a variety of techniques for scan conversion have been developed, the most common are based on a scanline-by-scanline approach first suggested by Watkins (1970). These handle variable-resolution output more efficiently. Antialiasing can be expensive. The A-buffer technique proposed by Carpenter (1984) uses fixed sub-pixel sampling and resolves priority by simple boolean operations. Since it can also support post-production compositing (Porter and Duff, 1984) it is commonly used in commercial systems.

Because of their additional complexity these workstations are not as easy to operate as a paint system. Employers will typically recruit designers with some experience of computer graphics or, since these are thin on the ground, expect a knowledge of basics like coordinate geometry.

Although workstations of this kind must determine the priority of graphics elements in order from the eye (for example, a typographic character stands in front of its drop shadow), they are essentially two-dimensional devices like paint systems.

The addition of a third dimension, the Z coordinate, and a perspective projection technique provides the means for the representation of three-dimensional objects. Many algorithms have been developed for solving the hidden surface priority of scenes and for rendering them in realistic ways. They fall into two classes: those that approximate perception and those that simulate perception.

In general, the former work by resolving priority by comparing the Z depth into the scene of the polygonal elements that compose the scene (Sutherland, Sproull, and Schumacker, 1974). Ray tracing, which solves the hidden surface problem and also provides methods for simulating specular reflection and refraction, was pioneered at MAGI Synthavision in the late 1960s (Mathematical Applications Group, 1968; Appel, 1968) and developed by Whitted (1980). More recent research has investigated techniques for using radiation interchange equations developed by architects in the nineteenth century for predicting illumination and acoustic effects in buildings. These radiosity techniques (Goral, Torrance, Greenberg, and Battaile, 1984) model diffuse reflection and produce images with subtle nuances of ambient light.

Kajiya's rendering equation (Kajiya, 1986) integrates the calculation of both specular and diffuse reflection. It renders images that compare favourably with the real world—if anything, they contain less noise. Unfortunately, any scene more complex than a couple of spheres will also render your local supercomputer speechless with awe.

A growing variety of mapping techniques can be used to enhance the realism of synthetic scenes. They include texture mapping to add colour detail, bump mapping to simulate rough surfaces, chrome mapping (watch out for the flying news logos), and reflection and transparency mapping. Discussion of these techniques is beyond the scope of this paper. The two most common methods in use are MipMaps (Williams, 1983) and summed area tables (Crow, 1984). Unpublished research from Cranston/Csuri has demonstrated how summed area tables can also be used to approximate depth of field and fog effects by altering the table sample convolution using Z depth data to index a focus and/or fog look-up table.

Commercial systems mainly use Z-priority rendering algorithms. A growing number integrate ray-tracing techniques for all or parts of the scene. I am not aware of any commercial implementations of radiosity techniques, although some top-end production companies, like the UK's Amazing Array (who use an Elexi Mini Supercomputer connected to a network of array processors), intend to be offering the technology soon.

Workstations that integrate 3-D modelling and rendering, like the commercially available animation systems, are generally more difficult to use than 2-D systems. It is usual to find that at least one of their operating staff has a programming background.

Commercial Graphic Arts Workstations

Traditional top-end commercial graphic arts systems like the Quantel Paintbox and print-oriented workstations tend to be expensive and single application. They are also well established in the marketplace. Indeed, the Paintbox has survived as the pre-eminent paint system for broadcast television for over five years—a remarkable achievement for a digital system. They consequently have high credibility, particularly for new purchasers.

Advances in very large scale integration (VLSI) technology have provided low-cost, high performance graphics and general-purpose processors. They have also made small-run custom VLSI production cost effective, and competitive performance products can now be produced more cheaply. Developers of new systems are now attacking the traditional marketplaces. They are attempting to attract credibility by offering their workstations as "open architecture" multiple application systems which support third-party software packages.

Several products currently on the market offer a broadcast video paint system, a variable-resolution 2-D vector system and 3-D modelling, rendering, and animation at video and film resolution. Post-production tools may include a compositor that can merge images from all these sources, a titling package and video-tape controller.

Of particular interest at the Computer Graphics '87 Exhibition held in London in October 1987 was the number of developers who were announcing links to both CAD systems and electronic publishing.

Digisolve, who manufacture a system called Video Imagemaker which fits the description in the previous paragraph, are an example. They have developed links which allow users of CAD systems with Intergraph or DFX file formats to port their data across for graphic arts processing. Dalim licence Video Imagemaker as a sub-system of their own high-performance presentation and print graphics workstation.

CAD data can now be coloured, retouched, rendered in three dimensions, composited with background photographs, reduced and enlarged, cut and pasted and stripped into the printed page. Headlines, graphics, other illustrations and half-tones and body text can be added—all on one system. Although I have no information regarding Digisolve's future plans, the next logical step would seem to be either to network directly to the CAD system or to port across the CAD software itself and open the system up as multi-user.

Cambridge Computer Graphics approached the problem from the other side. They originally produced a speed-up board for PC-CAD packages.

They then integrated their own graphic arts software package. Soon after that they implemented Postscript and licenced desk-top publishing packages like Ventura and Pagemaker. At CG 87, along with co-developers Centaurfax (a company with a background in print reprographic systems), they launched Artisan. It's a full-colour, half-tone page make up system. Just two of the workstation resources that the designer can have available are AutoCAD and RoboCAD.

"We Don't Need Any More Pretty Pictures. . ."

Back in 1985 at the EUROGRAPHICS UK Chapter Conference at Bath University a heated debate ensued between the computer graphicists and the engineering CAD/CAMmers. No prizes for guessing which side of the fence the delegate who made the comment above came from. In the past there has been a strong reaction from the engineering community against the high cost and computational overheads necessary to produce realistic images.

Attitudes are changing. At SIGGRAPH 87 the Panel on Computer Aided Industrial Design discussed the growing integration of CAD systems into the "design styling" area and its advantages and problems. In particular, the panel noted the importance of good looking design: "even military shoppers are known to insist on good looking hardware." Expensive automobiles are bought for their looks. Buyers want something to externalise their back to the earth politics, tell the public they're rich and powerful or exhibit their macho inadequacies.

One panelist was David Royer from the Ford Motor Company. He discussed the problems associated with using a proprietary animation package to produce realistic images of future cars. He pointed out that the rendering algorithms used (most likely Z-priority with reflection mapping) were all right for animation but gave misleading impressions of the actual geometry of the automobile surface.

"The specular reflection of the horizon on a car's surface is a key design element as important aesthetically as the car's profile. Its proportions, even its apparent size, can change when specular reflection is missing." said Royer (quoted in Coates, 1987). Whereas in many graphic arts applications users are satisfied with something that looks convincing, in the field of CIM rendering has to be correct to be useful.

Nevertheless, "CAD has brought about a degree of consolidation and coordination of the diverse personnel and organisation involved in product design and development that might not have been achieved otherwise. *This is due simply to the fact that everyone working on a project now refers to the same database*," claimed Bruce Claxton of Motorola Corp. (also in Coates, 1987) (italics added).

Approximation versus Simulation

Similar concerns contrasting the requirements of the entertainment industry and those of the scientific community were voiced by speakers at another SIGGRAPH 87 panel: Supercomputer Graphics. The message was simple—realism doesn't come cheap. Almost all of the work on show that satisfied the requirements of an adequate simulation of a true physical event had been produced in research environments using supercomputers.

Integration

There are now several systems on the market that provide an integrated pathway from initial design to final manufacture. Parts can be designed and visualised. Assembly can be simulated. The database can be used for pre-production testing, which may investigate material properties like the effects of stress, temperature and aerodynamics.

The database can be used to produce control data for the numerical control (NC) machines that will manufacture the parts. Some systems allow the design, simulation and eventual control of the robot assembly lines that will fabricate the complete product (Porter, 1987).

As Bruce Claxton pointed out, more people are now getting involved with this process. He and the other panelists were industrial stylists—people from an art and design background. In some design areas the relationship between design styling and the engineering design is tenuous. Many desktop micros are examples. The requirements are an ergonomic screen and keyboard position, technical provisions like vents to let the heat out and a small desktop "footprint." Take the back off many systems and you soon discover that there is little relation between form and function.

Many applications, which include consumer-oriented products like automobiles, demand a much closer relationship. Currently, designers produce several small-scale and then full-scale models that can be painted and finished. The visual appeal of highlights and the horizon reflection can then be seen "for real." This process is time and labour consuming although pioneers like Pierre Bézier (1974) have produced systems which can rough-cut scale models using NC technology. Clearly, the provision of physically correct full-colour simulations could significantly increase productivity, and it's not surprising that auto developers like Ford and General Motors (Dill, 1981) are at the forefront of research in the area.

CIM, Graphic Arts and Realism

The low-cost, very high performance computer systems are beginning to hit the marketplace. They include AT&T's Pixel Machine and the Real World Graphics system launched at CG 87 and, coincidentally, called

Reality. These and other systems offer two potentials. The first is real-time manipulation of solids for construction and scene composition using the computationally inexpensive Z-priority renderers. The second is stop-frame rendering of composed scenes using the more expensive but physically correct techniques. With due apologies to Real World Graphics (and to God), cost-effective reality has almost arrived!

The possibility of making physically correct images of products before they are produced, either in model form or as the final commodity, should have a major effect on industry. Designers and engineers will be able to justify their ideas to management by preparing full-colour corporate documents that integrate credible images: half-tone photographs, technical illustrations, working drawings, and production charts and diagrams. Management can then take that same data, reprocess it for output on high-quality reprographic equipment, tart it all up and prepare the prospectus for a share issue, or for the venture capital houses, in order to raise the money to underwrite the product development costs.

Market research will also use the database. They will be able to present their public with full-colour variations on the design brief in order to ascertain the most commercial version and develop the marketing strategies.

Once the product has gone into production, the design and engineering staff will use images to feed back into the design and development process. They will also be able to present images to keep management happy. Management can use the same images to maintain the confidence of their financial backers.

The marketing and sales people can now move in. The graphic arts studio can use the same database to start producing the packaging, brochures and advertisements for the press and, using computer animation techniques, film and television commercials. They will also be preparing the manuals and training support materials for sales teams, service engineers and end-users.

Because a single integrated database is being used, an important consideration is the reduced likelihood of error. And all this is happening before the manufacturing process has been completed. It's possible that future financiers will want to see all this material before making the decision to underwrite the development and manufacturing production process in the first place.

Pie in the Sky?

The current versions of graphic arts workstations have begun to integrate tools which point to the beginning of the kind of product described above. Some impressive systems are already on the market. The Klein Newsletter recently reported on a new corporate publishing package from Interleaf.

The package runs across a mixed network whose nodes can include Mac II, Sun, Apollo and IBM PC-RT workstations. Of particular interest is the claim that changes made on one node will automatically echo throughout the network.

If this evolution of desktop publishing is possible, then the use of graphic arts systems to bridge CIM and electronic publishing should be feasible. In particular, the recent involvement in this marketplace of major multinationals, who have capital and research facilities, should facilitate this development.

A major problem is standards. In a recent conversation with Rae Earnshaw, I expressed my views that standards didn't evolve from academic goodwill but rather from market exploitation. In the late 1960s a variety of competing standards existed for non-broadcast video systems. Indeed a tape recorded on one system might not play back on a similar model made by the same manufacturer. Consequently, there was a small market for these recorders and it was quickly saturated. The present video standards were introduced when cartels of manufacturers agreed to develop them in order to increase the market size. It is believed that over one-third of UK households now own a video-cassette system. The technology is widely in use in education and in the corporate area. Back in the early 1970s it's likely that the entire UK market for video systems was less than 5000 units.

Computer graphics is fast evolving from a cottage industry. The big nationals and multinationals have been convinced of its value and are investing. They are developing their own products and buying up the undercapitalised small fry. They offer the potential of a computer graphics technology that could be like VHS video or hi-fi: a modular approach where different sub-systems can be bought from different manufacturers, plugged together and be working immediately. If these companies think the potential market is big enough they will do it. Favourable signs include the growing number of domestic TV receivers that have integral framestores and allow simultaneous viewing of two or more channels. Some include digital video effects like posterisation and mosaic. One of the most recent includes frame-grab, keying and paint facilities.

These large companies that are beginning to dominate the business are the very ones that could benefit most from many of the advantages offered by the integration of graphic arts and CIM technology and it is their decisions that could, and in this author's opinion will, make it happen.

References

Appel, A. (1968) *Some Techniques for Shading Machine-Renderings of Solids*; SJCC 68. Thompson Books, Washington, D.C.

Bézier, P. (1974) "Mathematical and Practical Possibilities of Unisurf." In R.E. Barnhill and R.F. Riesenfeld, eds., *Computer Aided Geometric Design*. Academic Press, New York.

Carpenter, L. (1984) "The A-Buffer, an Antialiased Hidden Surface Method," *Computer Graphics* 18(3), July (Proc. SIGGRAPH 84).

Coates, D. (ed.) (1987) "Computer Aided Industrial Design: The New Frontiers," *Computer Graphics* 21(4), July (Proc. SIGGRAPH 87).

Crow, F.C. (1984) "Summed Area Tables for Texture Mapping," *Computer Graphics* 18(3), July (Proc. SIGGRAPH 84).

Dill, J.C. (1981) "An Application of Colour Graphics to the Display of Surface Curvature," *Computer Graphics* 15(3), July (Proc. SIGGRAPH 81).

Goral, C.M., K.E. Torrance, D.P. Greenberg and B. Battaile (1984) "Modelling the Interaction of Light Between Diffuse Surfaces," *Computer Graphics* 18(3), July (Proc. SIGGRAPH 84).

Kajiya, J.T. (1986) "The Rendering Equation," *Computer Graphics* 20(3), July (Proc. SIGGRAPH 86).

Mathematical Applications Group Inc. (MAGI) (1968) "3-D Simulated Graphics," *Datamation*, February.

Porter, S. (1987) "Animation on the Factory Floor," *Computer Graphics World*, November.

Porter, T. and T. Duff (1984) "Compositing Digital Images," *Computer Graphics* 18(3), July (Proc. SIGGRAPH 84).

Sutherland, I.E., R.F. Sproull and R.A. Scumacker (1974) "A Characterisation of Ten Hidden Surface Algorithms," *Computing Surveys* 6(1), March.

Watkins, G.S. (1970) "A Real Time Visible Surface Algorithm," Univ. of Utah Computer Science Department, UTEC-CSc-70-101, June.

Watters, G. and P. Willis (1987) "UltraPaint: A New Approach to a Painting System," *Computer Graphics Forum* 6(2) May.

Whitted, T. (1980) "An Improved Illumination Model for Shaded Display," *Commun. ACM* 23(6) June.

Williams, L. (1982) "Pyramidal Parametrics," *Computer Graphics* 17(3), July. (Proc. SIGGRAPH 83.)

The Visualisation of Structural Complexity: Some Thoughts on the 21st Anniversary of the Displays Group

George L. Mallen

Perspective

A 21st birthday party should be a joyful celebration of something achieved and the promise of much to come. Like the British Computer Society itself, the Displays Group has spanned a revolutionary period in technological development. At the macro level, society seems to have accepted the information revolution and has painfully absorbed the changes entailed in habits of work and thought. At the micro level, the Displays Group has seen and influenced the life cycles of at least three main display technologies: refresh, storage and raster. What can we learn from this experience and what do the next 21 years hold?

As it happens, my interest and involvement with computer graphics began roughly 21 years ago. In the mid-1960s I had just left the Royal Aicraft Establishment, having worked on digital simulations of air traffic control systems. I was fortunate enough to have been invited to work with Gordon Pask, one of the seminal figures in cybernetics and artificial intelligence, and to apply the digital simulation techniques I had learned at Farnborough in this new area. Pask had created a small independent research group to pursue a range of topics related to cognition, cybernetics and computing, and I was fired by some dimly understood notions about the relation between entropy and information and the role of computer modelling in the human scheme of things. Under Pask, I became convinced that the computer was not just another tool for mechanical computation but, through its simulation capability, was indeed a new medium which we could use to explore and explain the workings of systems as complex as minds and societies. Most of my professional concerns since then have been addressed to the problems of making the technology do this. I was convinced then and I am convinced still that computer graphics has a central role to play in helping us understand complex systems. The first 21 years of my professional life seem to have been just an apprenticeship in a volatile craft. Perhaps I'm a slow learner but these years broadly correspond with the history of the Displays Group and I suspect that this has been an apprenticeship for it too. The main labours and, I hope, excitements lie ahead.

In the rest of this essay I will review briefly the philosophical basis for the central importance of computing and computer graphics and try to indicate their future roles in relation to our understanding of complex systems.

Cognition, Structural Complexity and Computing

As walking, talking, cognate animals there are two main kinds of complexity we have to deal with. For the purposes of this paper I will call the first kind "mechanical complexity." This is the complexity we face when we know how the system should work; we just have to sort out why it doesn't. The whole panoply of modern science and engineering is geared to telling us how more and more systems work and so more and more of our problems should come into this category. Mechanical complexity is characterised by interacting cause-and-effect chains, and armed with procedures and professional training we are supposed to cope. We can launch satellites, we can install central heating systems, we drive motor cars, we manage large bureaucracies, we travel from A to B and so on.

The second kind of complexity is the kind we face when we haven't a clue as to how the offending system works but we have to respond somehow. Because I like physics and the magic of quantum theory I shall call this kind "quantum complexity." This is the complexity of emotion, of instinct, of creativity, where there are no established cause-effect chains and much judgement and praying. We jump but we don't really know where.

Now it seems to me that much of human intellectual endeavour is concerned with transforming quantum complexity into mechanical complexity. Copernicus, Kepler, Newton et al. replaced the theological mysteries of the heavens with celestial mechanics. More recently, in 1943, McCulloch and Pitts specified a "logical calculus of the ideas immanent in nervous activity," neuronal network theory, as a step towards the mechanics of mind. The poet said, "God said, Let Newton be and all was light." This illumination of the "den of the metaphysician" continues unabated at many levels, certainly at the cosmological, but also at the sub-atomic, at the mathematical and, with the encroachment of the "logical calculus" and artificial intelligence, at the behavioural. What are the dynamics of this transformation process, how is it fuelled, can it continue? These are some of the questions that arise and it is our nature to try to answer them. The result should be a better understanding of the dynamics of cognitive systems as a whole and thence some insight into their control.

Our great progress in the understanding of mechanical complexity is seen most clearly in physics and, above all, in the great conservation principles of energy, mass, momentum and parity. In looking for parallels between these and the notions of cognitive dynamics, we can speculate that the mind does something akin to work when it transforms quantum complexity into mechanical complexity. Thus quantum complexity could be like potential energy; when it is made available to minds they start working on it and turn it into mechanical complexity. The conversion process, as we might expect, would be inefficient. The grist in this particular mill is the scientific process of conjecture and refutation, generating some heat and sometimes a little illumination. This leads us to the intriguing possibility that the processes of human communication are analogous to losses in thermodynamic systems but perhaps taking us down the entropic hill rather than up.

There are many other interesting and probably contentious conjectures arising from this analogy between thermodynamics and cognitive dynamics. This is not the place to explore them, but at least one seems to me to be very pertinent to the concept of visualisation. That is, there seems to be a conservation principle at work, a conservation of perceived complexity. Once we have extracted some order, possibly a law, from quantum complexity, that law inevitably results in new deductions, and often in new technologies, which change the way we perceive the world. So, by and large, the amount of mystery we perceive seems to remain constant. We are just as much in awe of black holes as our forebears were of comets. Visualisation is the basis of that cognitive process which finds cohesion in a multiplicity of sense data and projects it back into the world. It helps preserve that stability, the conservation rule, which prevents us, on the one hand, from finding quantum complexity too difficult to deal with, for this would result in our opting out through frustration, and on the other hand from finding it too easy, for this would result in our opting out through boredom. As in thermodynamics, there is an awesome inevitability about cognitive dynamics but also great beauty and delicate balances.

Insofar as the computer enhances our visualising and modelling capabilities, it will profoundly affect the conservation of perceived complexity. Through its logical calculus we will accelerate our understanding of mind and related social processes. How will quantum complexity hit back, I wonder? Thus the computer now sits at the centre of the material, social and intellectual processes of modern civilisation. The Displays Group's future concerns should, I believe, be seen in this light.

Visualisation

We can paraphrase some 2 million years of hominid evolution as follows: erect posture, adaptation of neck and jaw muscles to balance the head, folding of the brain inside the cranium, development of manual dexterity and speech, creation of tools and images, then language, writing and computing. Language, imagery and tool making are intimately bound together in our development, and just as we have the capacity to speak and make things so we have the capacity to visualise. We remember faces and places and we dream in pictures. But visual memory is not just a random store of stills and short clips, like a video disc. It seems to be more active. Through studying reactions to optical illusions and ambiguous images, psychologists seem pretty certain that we impose meaning on what we see. To a great extent we see what our brains expect to see rather than what is actually out there. We build and use models of the world to make predictions and avoid trouble. It is my contention that the computer is developing into the social equivalent of the individual's physiological visualisation capabilities and that computer graphics are the key to articulating these capabilities at the social level. Growing columns of red and shrinking columns of blue on stock exchange visual display units recently sent shock waves through Western economies. The visual appearance of the screens had begun to substitute for the physical interactions and "mood" of the trading floors.

Today the visual vocabulary of computer graphics is very much in its infancy. I find it surprising that the display of quantitative information, sadly often referred to as business graphics, still rests predominantly on the invention of graphs, time series and bar charts. Even with the massive growth in data display, visual media and computer graphics, the evolution of this visual vocabulary is slow. Recent promising developments are:

The choropleth, the use of colour or shading to represent data about grographical regions on maps.
The metraglyph, an icon with circular body and attached spikes whose diameter, length and angles can represent data sets.
The Chernoff face, a special kind of metraglyph in which the parameters of the geometry of a recognisable object, like a face, represent the data.

Animated charts and diagrams representing physical processes now figure prominently in production and management techniques, and in these we find that some features commonly recur. Flows from sources to sinks and associated valves and decision points are a kind of staple representation and we should expect some common forms, an animation vocabulary, to emerge eventually.

Another area of great interest is multi-dimensional representation. Ten years ago techniques for data analysis and multi-dimensional scaling (MDS) were cumbersome and slow even on mainframe computers. Now powerful micros allow analysts to explore complex data sets interactively. This capacity to interact with, to explore and to find structure in multi-dimensional data is novel. It depends critically on display technology and is a key area for future development.

Conclusion

There are now very few areas in research, industry and commerce where computer graphics techniques do not catalyse and support decision making. This is very different from the situation 21 years ago. Nevertheless, as I have argued above, the emerging role for computing and computer graphics in our affairs is now so important that the need for a Displays Group to co-ordinate and promote the necessary interdisciplinary effort is greater than it has ever been. Keep at it.

Part 2 Art

Computer Graphics—Can Science Help Make Art?

Richard Wright

Introduction

While painters and sculptors rarely need to justify their choice of media, many people feel that computer algorithms are inappropriate for the tackling of artistic problems. Only the use of paintbox and similar software, which seeks to emulate traditional media, seems a promising outlet for the artist; how can computers contribute to a totally new medium for artists?

Such an artistic use of computers is often objected to on the grounds of an incompatibility between the motives of artists and scientists (Knowlton, 1986). Computers and computer algorithms were originally designed by scientists for scientific research. When graphic output was first achieved by a computer, any claims for its artistic status seemed to be due mainly to the coincidence that art and science both just happened to be producing nice-looking pictures, for whatever reasons. Any deeper connection would seem to imply that science was now addressing itself to artistic issues and ultimately that it could embody subjective meanings and values just as art does.

One could argue that although computer images might be created using mathematical techniques, their validity as science or as art is dependent only on the context in which they are seen. To take an obvious example, a graphic representation of, say, the average annual precipitation over a land mass would signify to a scientist a particular relationship between meteorological conditions on a portion of the globe. To an artist, on the other hand, it might appear as a swirling pattern of vivid colours, possibly suggestive of organic growth and vitality. This implies that after an object or image has been created it can be freely interpreted without necessarily having to know anything about the process that created it. At any rate, we have been taught that the artistic viewpoint is something vague and imprecise and that anything that cannot be subjected to measurement and analysis is inaccessible to scientific comment. The author believes, however, that this view of art and science is oversimplistic and misleading.

New Art, New Science

The distinction most often made is that science is objective and attempts to uncover the "truth" about reality—to insist that some things are true and others are false—whereas art is subjective and offers many different viewpoints and flights of fancy without any hope of resolving them. This distinction is partly dependent on the level of art and science being referred to. Theoretical science abounds with differing opinions and heated debates about various paradoxical concepts and the significance of different results. What people are usually referring to as objective are the applied sciences, which deal with relatively simple causal systems within well-defined theoretical frameworks. Likewise, when people talk about art they usually mean the fine arts of painting, sculpture and music and forget the applied arts of technical drawing and graphic illustration, in which the restrictions placed upon the artist can be quite uncompromising so as to ensure as "realistic" a description as possible.

Whether one judges science and art to be subjective or objective depends partly on the level of the activity in question and its corresponding conceptual framework. Obviously, a scientist must be able to think imaginatively in order to develop new ideas and explore alternatives, just as artists must be able to justify their work so that it does not become arbitrary or pointless. To make this discussion as far reaching as possible we shall concentrate our attention on the fine arts and theoretical sciences.

If we look back in time to the dawn of civilisation, we can see some suggestions that art and science share a common origin (Biederman, 1948). Anthropologists tell us that for the cave-painters art had particular mystical functions to perform—such as gaining mastery over hunted animals and ensuring the rains would come for a successful harvest (Gombrich, 1950). Talismen were used to ward off evil forces and amulets were kept by the priests and witch-doctors to restore the harmony of mind and body. Man felt that the elemental forces of nature were very close to him, that the spirit of nature pervaded every object providing an unseen unifying energy; this belief was known as animism. The artifacts he created, which functioned as both artworks and early scientific tools, might help him control them and understand them, just as later science was to do in a more systematic way.

After the initial creative impetus of the Renaissance, Western art and science settled into a mechanical view of nature based on the philosophy of atomism, that nature could be broken down into fundamental physical parts which could be analysed to find their individual properties (Koestler, 1978). The basic "stuff" of creation would then be re-combined and its initial conditions used to determine all future states. Art became mainly concerned with rendering separate physical objects in a fixed Euclidean space, an array of individual styles expressing essentially the same viewpoint. Science tried to reduce complex phenomena to straightforward causes and effects expressed as the basic equations of the universe. Because it was dealing with the simplest level of organisation in nature, the physical sciences were the most successful at this and began to take precedence over art as well as the higher sciences such as psychology and even biology for a time. So it was that by 1700 the French Academy under LeBrun announced that all problems in painting had been solved, and similarly by the end of the nineteenth century textbooks stated that science had uncovered most of the fundamental laws of the universe and that the rest would soon follow.

This guiding principle—that the world was composed of isolated parts that could be considered independently of each other—also defined the way man saw himself in relation to his environment. Because man now saw himself as separate from nature, in direct contrast to the oneness felt by early man, it was thought possible to view nature perfectly objectively, to cleanse any subjective meaning from our observations and to approach the "truth." Although apparently value-free, science does not have to address philosophical issues directly in order to actually embody a philosophical outlook. The very concept of being detached and value-free is itself a value which has led to a certain world view and has also manifested itself in works of art. In this century formalism and constructivism (and some computer art) have attempted to purge art of subjective meaning or self-expression by restricting themselves to "formal" relationships (Rickey, 1967). This usually involved concentrating on the two-dimensional properties of a picture plane—flat colours, smooth lines and geometric proportions. But a straight line is still a tremendous mental construction and an abstraction from nature, and this approach has resulted in some rather boring-looking pictures as well as highlighting the problem of subject matter in abstract art. When people talk of viewing an image in an artistic context they often limit that notion to a consideration of the visual aesthetics, the balance and harmonies of form and colour on a surface, but as far as artistic content is concerned this is only the tip of the iceberg. It is as important to avoid having abstract art become merely decorative as it is to avoid having science become a meaningless game played within a formal set of rules.

Around the turn of the century there was the start of a shift in the outlook of art and science when both began to question their philosophical foundations (Capra, 1982). Fundamental particles gave way to more fundamental particles which were so sensitive to outside influences that it was not possible to observe them detachedly without actually affecting them at the same time. Art, too, discovered new worlds of form not confined to representational space. Impressionism, which began as an attempt to use colour for a more "realistic" rendering of lighting conditions, became concerned with exploring colour effects for their own sake. As science encountered intangible organising forces at work in the heart of matter itself, there was a growing body of opinion that the physical world did not have a physical basis. As scientists began to look at the importance of process rather than structure, artists such as the action painter Jackson Pollock emphasised the role of paintings as visual records of the process of painting instead of objects in their own right (Tuchman, 1971). Computer art would take this one stage further by dispensing with the art object altogether and retaining only a procedure represented by intangible voltages in digital circuitry.

Progress in art and science is more than just a matter of closer and closer approximations to the "truth" (Gablik, 1976; Kuhn, 1962). Art and science are both functions of man's general mental and cognitive development; they are the major means by which he forms and communicates his changing conception of the world (Piaget, 1950). It is this current state of man's evolving perceptual abilities that determines his belief system and how he understands the world. The peculiarity of classical art and science was that they believed that their perceptions could be made independent of any external influences or mental limitations, objective, enduring and absolute. Hence the difficulty of regarding science in particular as embodying values at all, let alone in defining what they were.

By taking slices through history and examining the state of artistic and scientific thought at various periods we can see strong similarities in the general trends of both (Waddington, 1969). Art as well as science has always been used to explore and communicate the most important ideas and concepts of the time. It is these underlying beliefs of man at various periods that have determined his lifestyle and culture. Bricks and mortar do not build a civilisation; ideas do. Art is used to re-affirm these beliefs and give them further substance. Scientific method is also used to build up a system of knowledge of the world and expresses its views in as exact a language as possible, preferably mathematical. Art is also concerned with understanding the world but expresses its ideas in a language of direct sensory experience, for example visually, aurally, or some combination. With the development of computer graphics even this distinction is becoming eroded.

The Role of Computer Graphics

For some natural processes a general formula to describe the system's total behaviour is not known to exist and the system's properties are too complex to be deduced by studying its components in isolation. In these cases scientists more profitably adopt a method of investigation that relies on computer simulation (Wolfram, 1984). The scientific laws that define the relationships between variables are synthesised back into the phenomenon itself and often presented graphically, in the same way that art crystrallises concepts into pictures.

The evolution of some systems generated by simple rules can lead to extremely complex and chaotic patterns of behaviour which cannot be predicted from the data we have begun with. One example of this is in iteration theory, where given infinitesimally different starting conditions we often end up with wildly different outcomes (Pietgen and Richter, 1985) (Fig. 1).

Nature is now seen to be determined but not determinable.

If the initial starting conditions or fundamental parts of such a system cannot be defined in any accurate way, then reducing nature to a few basic components will not be a useful way to describe her, and we must concentrate on rules of interaction that constitute procedural systems. Similar ideas of turning our attention from the part of the "whole" are now becoming common in many branches of science such as organismic biology, morphogenesis and psychology (von Bertalanffy, 1971). In computer imagery the idea of building up an object by individually specifying facets or with geometric primitives is now being complemented by procedural systems that can generate intricate structures from very small databases (Smith, 1984). For example, a fractal object will remain defined under an infinite degree of scrutiny, emphasising the importance of process rather than structure (Mandelbrot, 1977) (Fig. 2).

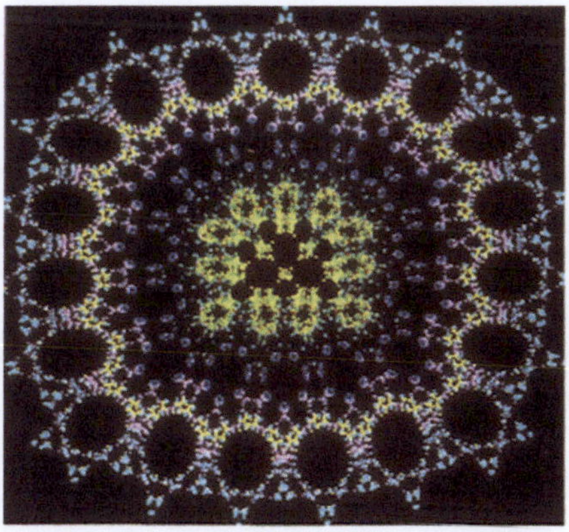

FIGURE 1

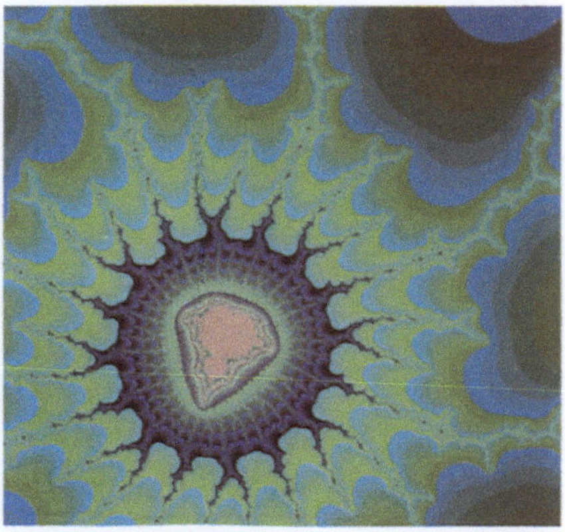

FIGURE 2

A mathematical object generated using an iterative function. Is this and the next figure's status as an art object merely due to its visual attractiveness, or can such images embody deeper symbolic meanings? (Reproduced by kind permission of Dr. Barry Martin. All rights reserved.)

A familiar example of the Mandelbrot set.

Since the recent advances in rendering algorithms, much computer graphics has concentrated on mimicking the superficial appearance of recognisable objects. Whilst these achievements are certainly good news for the disciplines of computer-aided engineering, graphic design and advertising, the sight of Platonic solids drifting through space is of limited interest in computer art shows. This obsession with the glittering eye-world of reality was last pursued most diligently by the Dutch genre painters of the seventeenth century (Fig. 3). Their work is now seen by many historians as a tool with which the rising Flemish merchant class of the time celebrated and advertised their new-found wealth and prosperity (Berger, 1972). Seen in this light, the glossy images of everyday artefacts in synthetic photography merely underline society's rather gloomy preoccupation with accumulating material posessions and are reminiscent of the materialism of classical science.

Mathematicians and computer scientists have met the challenge of modelling natural phenomena by developing new fields of geometry and procedural models. To use them exclusively to imitate mountains and landscapes for backdrops is to neglect their potential for demonstrating, for example, the evolution of living forms in nature (Kawaguchi, 1985) (Fig. 4). Computer graphics as art must be able to say something relevant about the world we live in; we cannot mindlessly churn out still-lifes and wallpaper patterns.

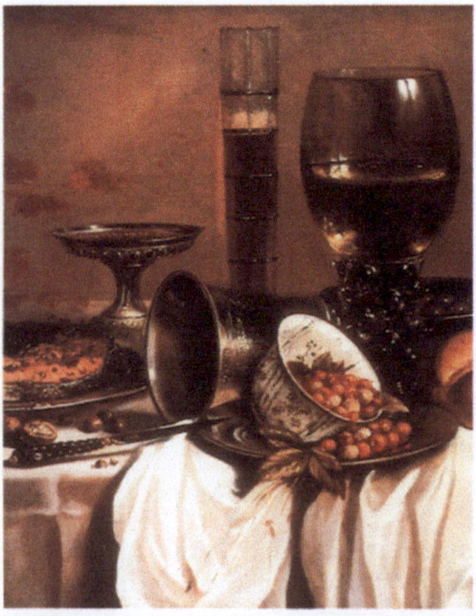

FIGURE 3. *Still-Life with Drinking Vessels*, Claez, Flemish, ca. 1700s.

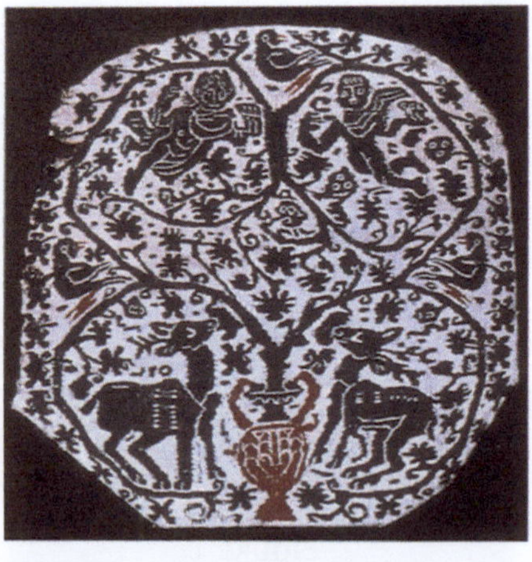

FIGURE 4. *Tree of Life*, Egyptian textiles, Graeco-Roman tapestry, ca. A.D. 4. An early space-filling curve put to symbolic use?

CELLS: An Example of an Algorithm as Art

The purpose of writing CELLS was to design an algorithm to show how a simple deterministic procedure can give rise to many different phenomena so as to suggest an underlying unity in nature. It works by taking a cell and replicating it across the plane according to a set of transformations. Once one structure is completed it can be combined by superimposing it on to another to create a kind of 'interference' pattern.

The basic vocabulary of the language is the primary colours. These will combine optically to produce most other colours and the addition of black provides a full tonal range. This helps to emphasise that the final appearance of the picture is dependent on the distribution of each colour and not the colour as such. The effect of changing the colours of an automaton is to bring out some characteristics of its structure and suppress others, otherwise retaining some similarity (Figs. 5 and 6).

A pattern is generated in such a way that it can produce a regular tessellation across the whole plane and allow a more articulated control over the figure and ground relationships. If the automata could only add on more cells we would tend only to get single trees emerging as in conventional growth models (Fig. 15). Here we can also get a more integrated all-over effect across the picture. Another artistic problem this algorithm attempts to tackle is how to relate a form to the limits and shape of the picture surface. In this system the size of the final image can be controlled by the number of operations in the generation of the automaton and will always be conveniently contained within a square format. There is no need to arbitrarily crop an image by the sides of the picture frame; the end of each operation will always provide a natural

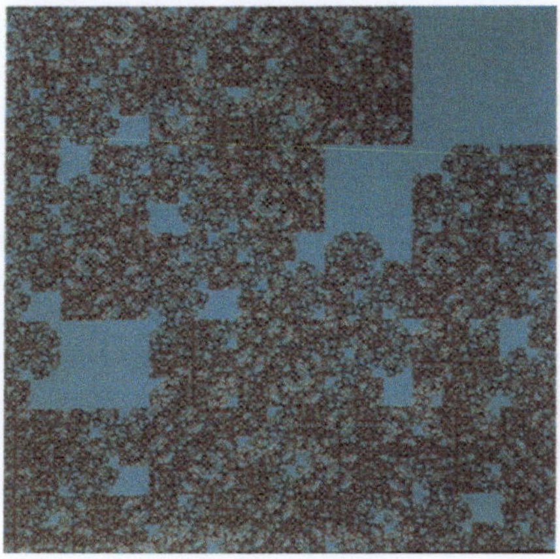

FIGURE 5

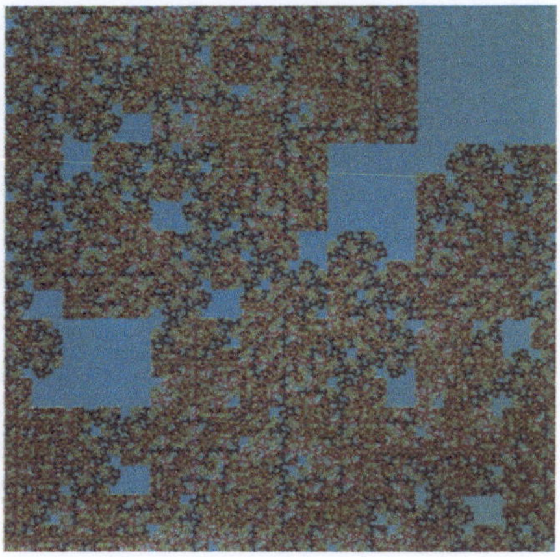

FIGURE 6

boundary and at the same time suggest the potentiality for further growth. In a wider context this is analogous to defining the transition between the individual and his environment.

When it comes to combining automata together the results range from very regular and symmetrical wallpaper patterns (Fig. 7) to amorphous fields of dots (Fig. 18). Some pictures appear similar to textile designs, carpets and Islamic art (Figs. 7, 8 and 10). Sometimes they look a bit South American, sometimes Oriental. Some pictures bear a resemblance to natural forms such as biological moulds, plants, crystals and mineral textures (Figs. 5, 17, 11 and 12). There are also examples of a version that produces data in three dimensions instead of two (Figs. 19–22). It is impossible to tell the result of generating any automaton in advance, but some general idea can often be gained by a study of the parameters chosen. This gives the algorithm that quality of determinism and unpredictability characteristic of a typical creative process or natural system without having to resort to random numbers.

The best way to present this work is to view a large number of different images so that their variety and similarities become clear. As this is in danger of becoming impractical, an ideal way would be to produce a piece of animation showing how each image can metamorphose into another, and this has also been accomplished. The CELLS algorithm itself is presented as the work of art–its concept, its use, the pictures that result and even this paper as well.

Conclusions

Traditional tools already allow a range of approaches wide enough to satisfy most artists. Moreover, many are interested in the very physicality of these media–assemblage, collage, installations and their use in demonstrating relationships between actual objects, images and symbols. A fine artist might therefore conclude that there is no reason to use a computer graphics system if it tends only to simulate conventional media and is usually much more limited when trying to compete on their terms. Computerised art-making must be able to offer something unique in terms of some inherent potential not possessed by other media. Computer software can fulfull this condition by showing in a systematic and convincing way the underlying properties of the natural world as well as the subtlety of man's relationship with it.

The author has tried to suggest a change in emphasis in the use of computers in the arts by concentrating on *why* artists produce art rather than *how* and showing that scientifically formulated concepts can form a valid subject matter for art. Just as photography became the culmination of artists' interest in depicting the surface appearance of the world, computer graphics can be thought of as an "abstract camera" revealing the hidden forces in nature from which it derives its many visible forms.

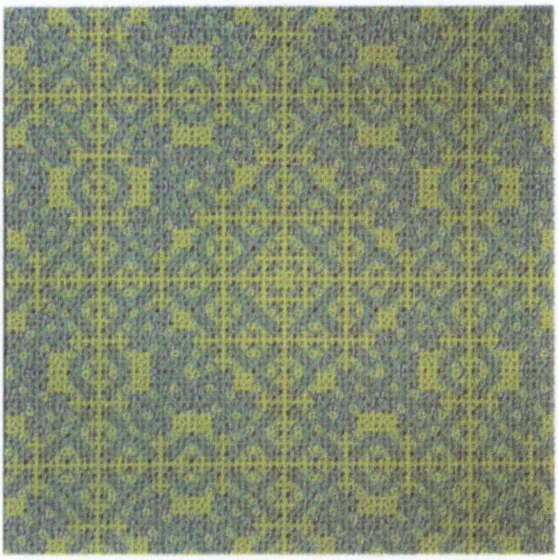

FIGURE 7

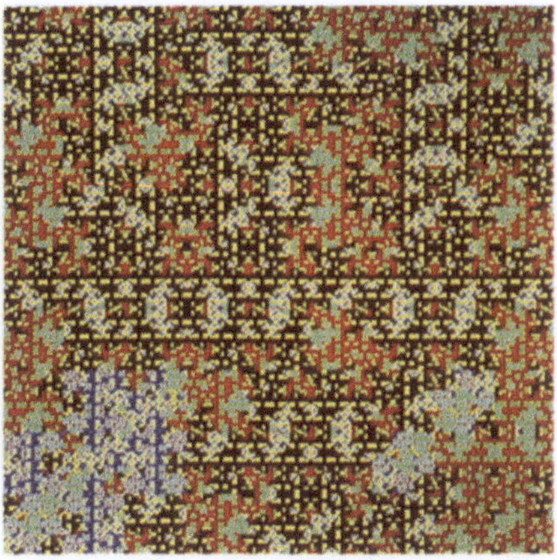

FIGURE 8

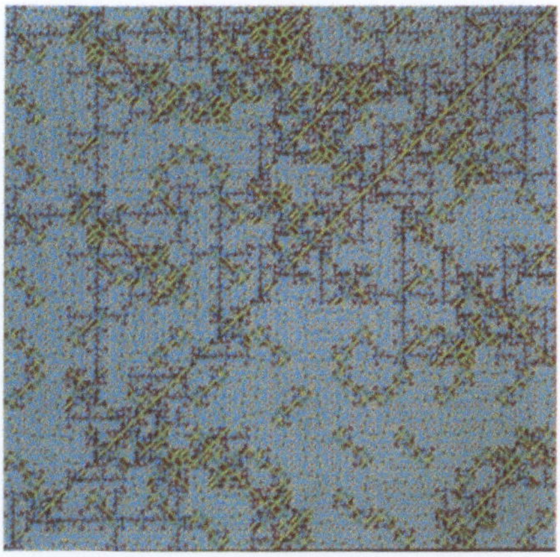

FIGURE 9

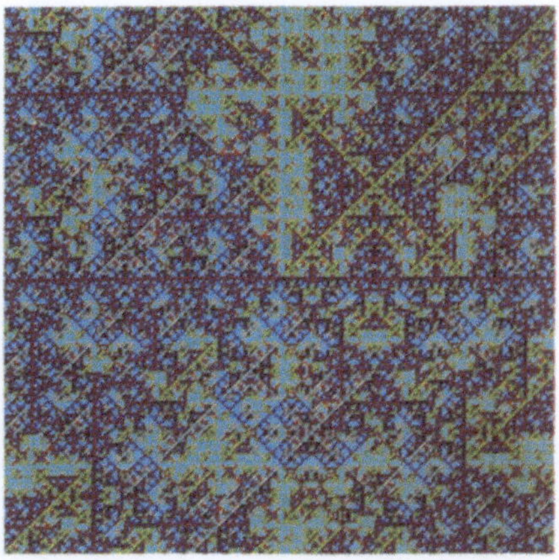

FIGURE 10

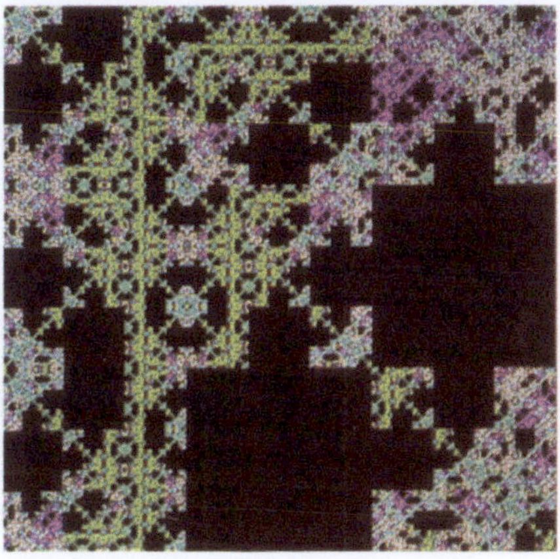

FIGURE 11

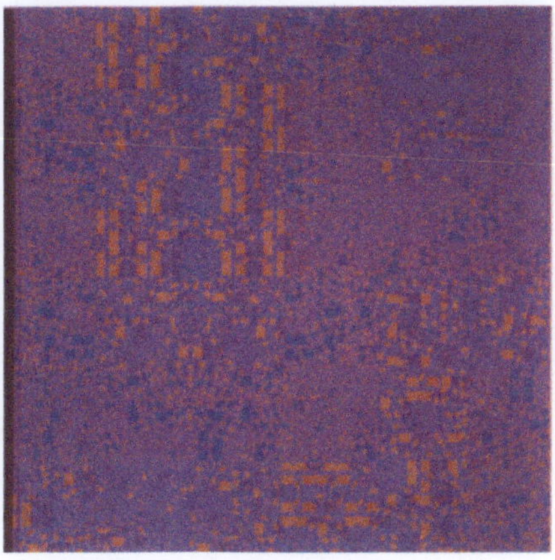

FIGURE 12

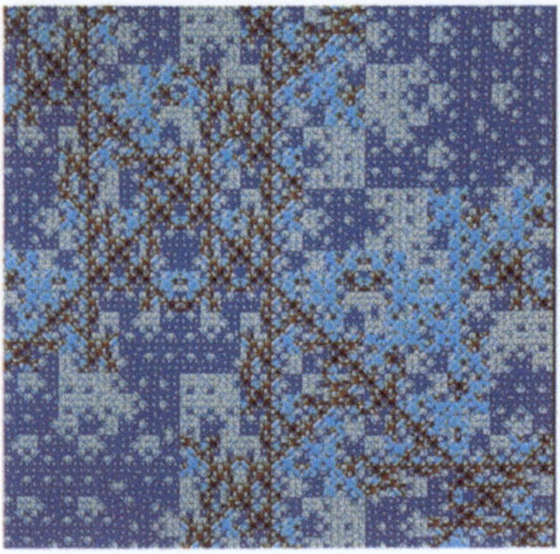

FIGURE 13

FIGURE 14

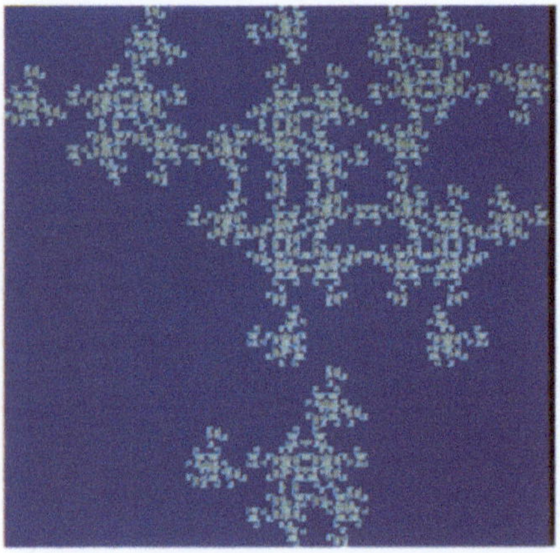

FIGURE 15

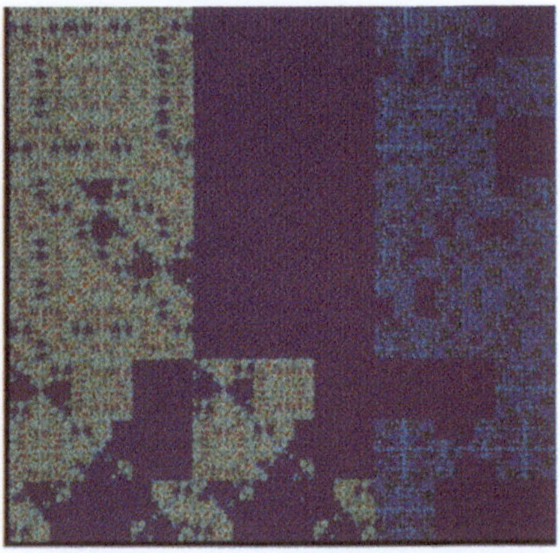

FIGURE 16

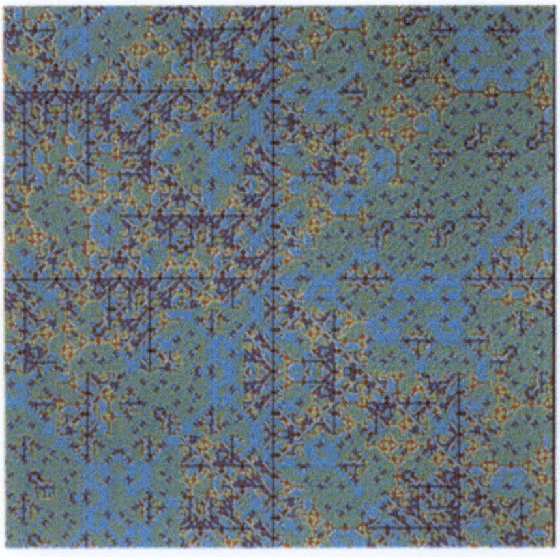

FIGURE 17

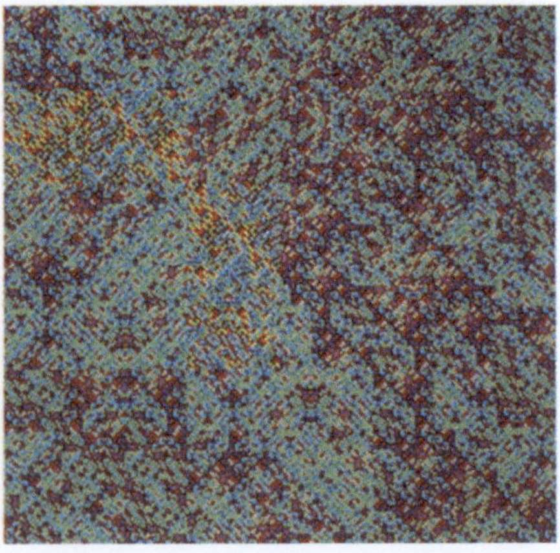

FIGURE 18

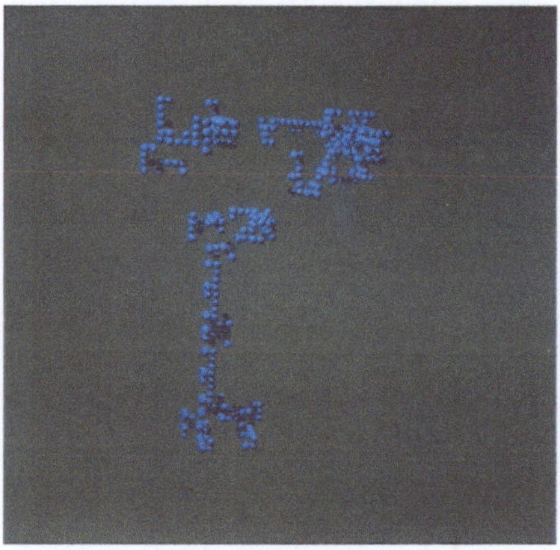

FIGURE 19

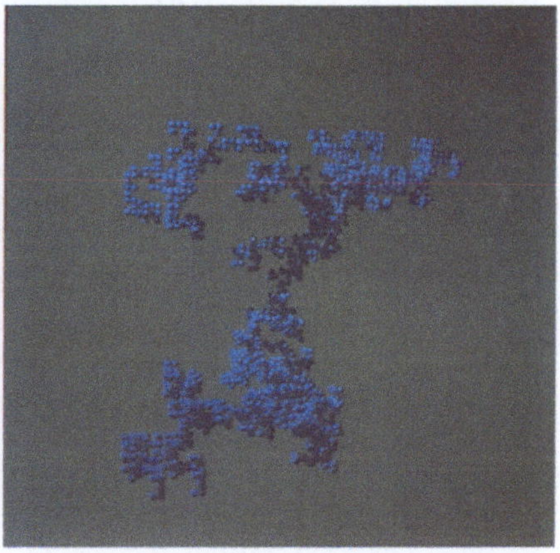

FIGURE 20

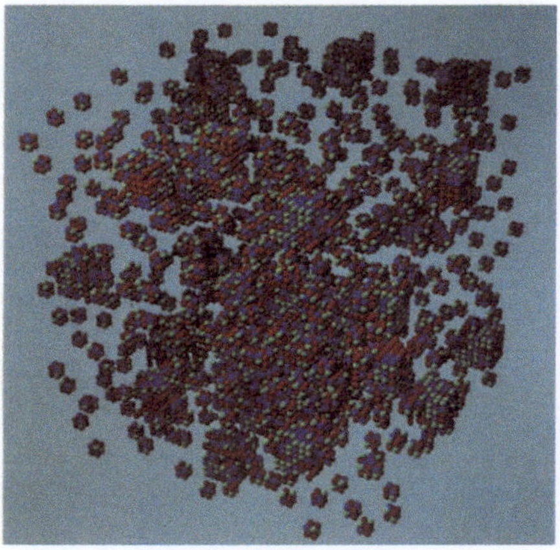

FIGURE 21

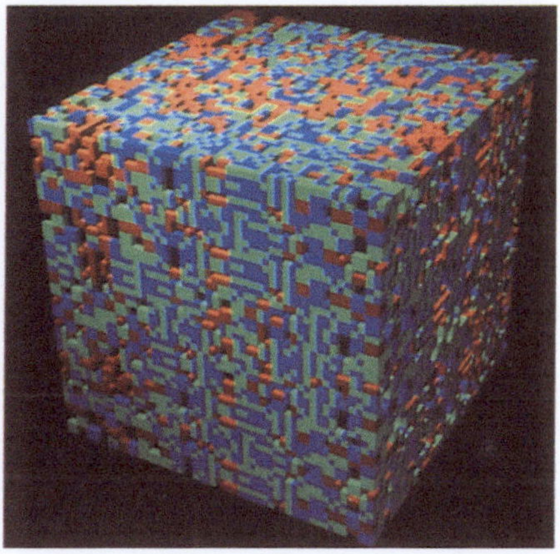

FIGURE 22

Computer graphics has the potential to express a level of human thought beyond that of either art or science and to reveal beauties both displayed and inherent in nature.

References

Berger, J. (1972) *Ways of Seeing*. BBC and Penguin Books, London.

Biederman, C. (1948) *Art as the Evolution of Visual Knowledge*. Red Wing, Minnesota.

Capra, F. (1982) *The Turning Point*. Fontana, London.

Gablik, S. (1976) *Progress in Art*. Thames & Hudson, London.

Gombrich, E.H. (1950) *The Story of Art*. Phaidon, London.

Kawaguchi, Y. (1985) "The Making of Growth. II: Morphogenesis," IEEE *Computer Graphics and Applications*, April.

Knowlton, K. (1986) "Why It Isn't Art Yet," Catalogue, ACM SIGGRAPH '86 Art Show, Dallas.
Koestler, A. (1978) *Janus: A Summing Up.* Hutchinson, London.
Kuhn, T. (1962) *The Structure of Scientific Revolutions.* Univ. of Chicago Press, Chicago.
Mandelbrot, B.B. (1977) *Form, Chance and Dimension.* Freeman, San Francisco.
Peitgen, H.O. and P.H. Richter (1985) "Frontiers of Chaos," Exhibition Catologue, University of Bremen, Bremen.
Piaget, J. (1950) *The Psychology of Intelligence.* Routledge & Kegan Paul, London.
Rickey, G. (1967) *Constructivism: Origins and Evolution.* George Braziller.
Smith, A.R. (1984) "Plants, Fractals and Formal Languages," *ACM SIGGRAPH '84 Proc.*, vol. 18, no. 3.
Tuchman, M. (1971) The New York School. Thames and Hudson, London.
von Bertalanffy, L. (1971) *General Systems Theory.* Penguin, London.
Waddington, C.H. (1969) *Behind Appearance.* Edinburgh Univ. Press.
Wolfram, S. (1984) "Computer Software in Science and Mathematics," *Scientific American*, September.

Towards an Integrated Computer Art System

Mike King

Computer Art Media

Broadly speaking, one can consider existing computer graphics systems for the computer artist as being one of four types:

1. paint systems,
2. drafting systems,
3. solid modelling systems, and
4. user-programmed systems.

These four types of system can be thought of as representing a range of new creative media for the visual artist. The decreasing cost of raster systems has brought a TV-resolution paint system down to a cost of about £5000, though a top-of-the-range system can cost around £100,000. Paint systems at the lower end of the price range are appearing in art colleges around the UK and are beginning to be within reach of the free-lance artist and designer. Vector-based systems, associated more with drafting packages, still offer the computer artist a powerful medium and many new avenues of exploration. Solid modelling systems have not been explored much in fine art, possibly with the exception of the Rodin system (Nahas and Huitric, 1982), but decreasing costs should again change this. User-programmed systems cover anything from 8-bit home micros to mainframes, and computer artists with programming abilities have been exploiting these for around 25 years.

I believe that there are three main reasons for using the computer in visual fine art:

1. increase in productivity,
2. exploration of new types of imagery, and
3. development of the computer as a more equal partner in the creative process.

The paint system certainly allows artists to be more productive, given that they want to produce images with TV (or sometimes higher) resolution and with the range of colours limited by the RGB phosphors in a cathode-ray tube. To a limited extent I believe that the paint system does also allow new types of imagery to be generated, though the artist is somewhat at the mercy of the range of options provided by the system. Radically new types of imagery are possible if the artist is willing and able to program the system. Possibilities of exploring the computer as a creative partner are opened up through more sophisticated programs, particularly if some approaches from artificial intelligence are adopted. Some of these possibilities have been described by Lansdown (1978, 1980) and Wilson (1983) but are not directly the subject of this paper.

Synthesis from Primitives and Basic Operations

Nearly all the manipulations within a computer art medium can be considered in terms of *synthesis from primitives*, where primitives are incorporated into groups and groups of primitives can be moved, deleted, copied and otherwise manipulated. Primitives have various types of attributes, which can be determined before or after incorporation.

In a paint system the primitives are the pixel and the free-hand curve, while the attributes of these primitives are primarily colours. The number of pixels is usually fixed and equal to the horizontal resolution times the vertical resolution.

In a drafting system the primitives are the drafting elements such as lines, rectangles, circles and ellipses, which may have attributes of colour, line width and line style. Attributes of groups of elements may also include orientation and scale. Figure 1 shows the primitives available with a simple drafting system called Macdraw (available for the Apple Macintosh).

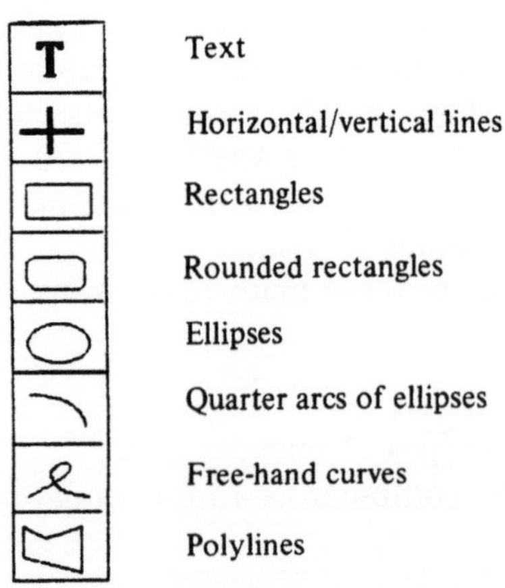

FIGURE 1. Primitives in Macdraw.

1. moving or changing the focus of attention,
2. incorporating a primitive,
3. altering an attribute of an item,
4. finding an incorporated item,
5. defining and labelling a grouping at a given level within a hierarchy,
6. ungrouping an existing grouping at a given level within a hierarchy,
7. removing an item,
8. moving an item,
9. copying an item.

FIGURE 2. Basic operations.

In solid modelling systems a wide variety of primitives may be supplied, though they usually fall under one of two categories: area primitives or volume primitives.

Whatever the medium, the set of operations required to give the artist full interactive control over it is fairly small. I call these the *basic operations* (see Fig. 2) and have selected them on the basis of case studies carried out on a variety of commercial systems. In user-programmed systems the categories (paint/drafting/solid modelling) become more blurred and the basic operations are less clearly defined.

Arbitrary and Algorithmic Synthesis from Primitives

In computer art I like to make a distinction between two approaches to synthesis from primitives: *arbitrary* and *algorithmic.* By arbitrary synthesis from primitives I mean any kind of user interaction that results in a sequence of manipulations on the medium that do not have a clear mathematical basis. An arbitrary sequence of the basic operations will not usually be arbitrary to the artist—they take the artist step-wise closer to the finished piece. However, the sequence of operations is quite arbitrary to the machine.

In algorithmic synthesis from primitives the medium is manipulated by operations repeated under some kind of algorithm—for example, the repeated incorporation of a motif to form a half-drop pattern. I aim to show that algorithmic synthesis from primitives is related to geometries of various types and is one of the powerful attractions of computer graphics media.

Interactive and Scripted Computer Media

Another distinction that I like to make in computer graphics is that between *interactive* and *scripted* computer media. An interactive medium is one where each manipulation has an immediate effect on the medium, and whose results are clearly visible. The operations in these media are usually carried out with the kind of hand-eye feedback associated with the traditional visual arts. Paint systems, drafting systems and some solid modelling systems are interactive media in this sense. Scripted media, on the other hand, involve the writing of a script or computer program to create the image, and in this case feedback is provided only after the execution of the program. The script or program is in effect a description for the computer of how to create the image. Development of imagery in scripted systems follows a cycle of write/execute/evaluate/rewrite.

In general, interactive systems are associated with arbitrary synthesis from primitives, while scripted systems are associated with algorithmic synthesis from primitives. The distinction between interactive and scripted systems can be a little blurred at times and may depend simply on whether an operation on a medium can be carried out fast enough to give immediate feedback to the artist.

The Computer Artist's Geometrical Toolkit

If an artist wishes to pursue types of imagery which do not involve much geometry, then the interactive systems like paint and drafting systems are ideal and offer increases in productivity and certain new types of imagery. However, to really exploit the computer as a medium, I believe that one needs to explore the areas covered by my concept of algorithmic synthesis from primitives. This can be done within interactive systems to some extent, but at present in-depth exploration of this area means a scripted system—or, more prosaically, writing programs.

When I first looked at the concept of algorithmic synthesis from primitives I gathered together a list of techniques or algorithms that computer artists and scientists have so far developed, and in looking at them I realised that in fact they represented different types of geometries. Robert Dixon, a computer artist who has worked for a time at the Royal College of Art, made this point (Dixon, 1983): "Geometry is the branch of mathematics or more precisely the root, that derives from spatial intuition, and insists upon visual expression of its theory." Scientists have been using computer graphics to give visual expression to mathematical theories for some time now, and, turning the situation around, the computer artists has rich feeding-grounds for the discovery of mathematics (or geometries) that give rise to interesting visual expression.

Islamic art is a good example of visual expression that relates very closely to certain types of geometry—the tesselations of the Euclidean plane. Since the time of Pythagoras, on whose geometries Islamic geometry is largely based, mathematics has developed tremendously, and with computer graphics the visual expression of these ideas has become commonplace. I see the development of computer art as being closely related to the use of these geometries, both old and new. Figure 3 lists the algorithms or geometries that I have identified in connection with computer art, under two rather arbitrary headings: classical and recursive geometries.

The distinction between classical and recursive geometries lies in the computing techniques behind them. In a recursive geometry the positioning of gometrical elements such as lines or motifs is the result of successively using the output of one calculation as the input to the next. The classical geometries, while often using some repetitive technique, do not base a given calculation on the previous one. This is a slight simplification, and in fact a recursive geometry can be created without using the programming technique called recursion. To illustrate the idea of a recursive geometry, consider the diagrams in Fig. 4, which show a line segment (initiator) being replaced by a shape consisting of eight line segments (generator). On each "recursion" or generation in the production of the image, each existing line segment (initiator) is replaced by the generator, scaled down to fit.

There is not space here to describe in detail all these geometries and algorithms or their uses to a computer artist, but I will discuss a few. Nets, bands and tessellations are very important in working with pattern and are well described in Macgregor and Watt (1984). Figure 5 shows a simple net of motifs (motifs placed on a regular grid), while Fig. 6 shows

CLASSICAL GEOMETRIES

- Euclidean geometry of parallel lines, triangles, rectangles and polygons
- conic sections: circle, ellipse, parabola and hyperbola
- nets, bands and tessellations
- non-recursive functions
- Lissajous figures, cardioids and cycloids
- parametric curves

RECURSIVE GEOMETRIES

- iterative functions (recurrence relations)
- random numbers
- recursive patterns
- fractals and graftals
- particle systems
- growth models
- linear and array grammars
- Markov chains

FIGURE 3. Classical and recursive geometries.

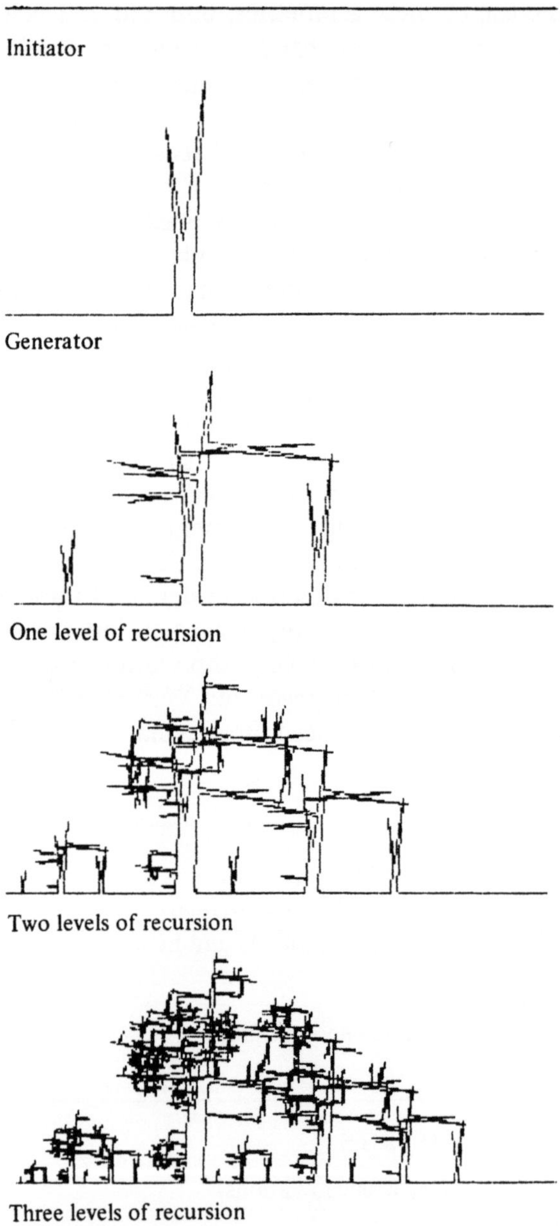

FIGURE 4. Recursive (fractal) trees.

tessellations produced from an interactive program called Tessellator (Addison-Wesley).

Non-recursive functions have been important for a long time in computer art. These functions are used to control the x and y position of

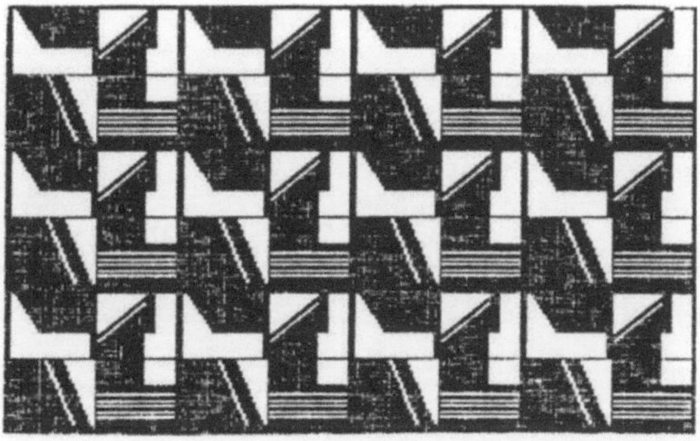

FIGURE 5. A net of motifs.

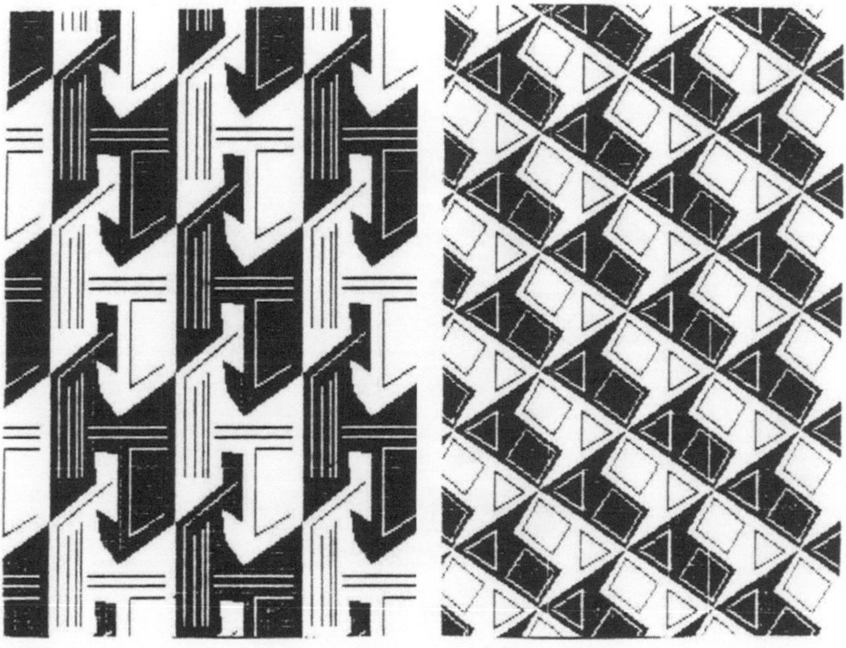

FIGURE 6. Simple tessellations.

some primitive (often just a dot or line) and the output is in effect a type of graph of the function. Franke (1971) shows many such images, including his own work, while Leavitt (1976) again shows the work of a variety of computer artists who have used this technique. Figure 7 shows output from a function designed by computer artist Joseph Jacobson (1982).

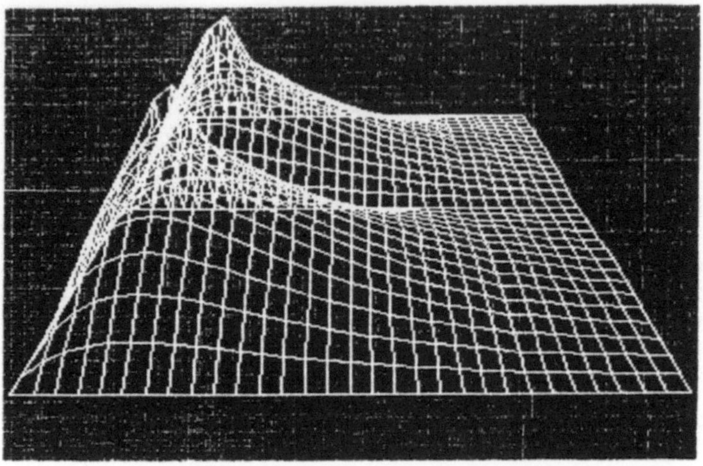

FIGURE 7. Output from a mathematical function.

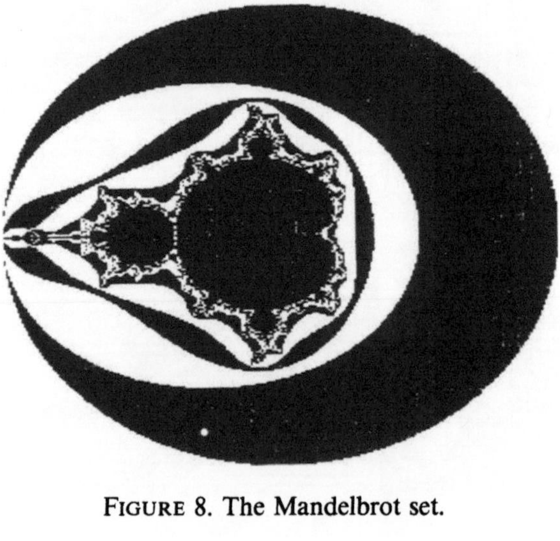

FIGURE 8. The Mandelbrot set.

Parametric curves, such as the B-spline, are of importance in computer-aided design for automotive and aerospace design and allow the description of curved lines and surfaces from a few control points. These can be very useful to the computer artist (in particular the computer sculptor) and have already been exploited in the Rodin system.

The recursive geometries offer the artist imageries and techniques quite unique to the computer, such as fractals and graftals. Figure 8 shows the Mandelbrot set, and Figure 9 shows a simple tree generated from a set

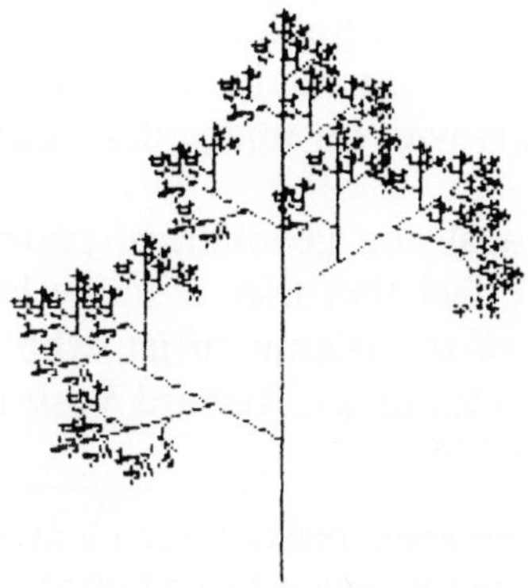

FIGURE 9. A graftal tree.

of rules known as a grammar and described by Alvy Ray Smith (1984) as a "graftal"—something like a fractal but not quite the same.

I see the collection of geometries and techniques listed above as making up a toolkit for the computer artist, a toolkit which is of course open-ended—new developments will continually add to it. The power of these techniques is that they can be combined in ways unique to a particular artist's way of thinking or way of exploring. Output from different techniques can be "matted" together, that is, just overlaid in different ways, or they can be combined in more fundamental ways, where output from one function, for example, may modulate the output from another.

Some of the elementary classical geometries are provided within paint and drafting systems, but as soon as the user attempts to create more complex geometrical structures it becomes very difficult. Even the simplest kind of pattern such as a half-drop often has to be created by copying the motif individually, which is absurd when the programming of such a geometry is a trivial exercise. In order to explore the more complex geometries, such as fractals, the artist is forced firstly to research the techniques and secondly to write programs from scratch to implement them. If the artist wishes to combine various geometries, then again they have usually to be programmed from scratch.

The Importance of Computer Geometries

The computer offers firstly free-hand or interactive methods of working, which allow relatively traditional approaches to image generation to be used, and secondly *programming* approaches. If the artist is going to use programming, then computer geometries, both classical and recursive, open up vast territories for exploration. It is easy to dismiss these techniques as pattern making of a sophisticated kind, but this does not do them justice. Firstly, the image generated from a mathematically or geometrically based program does not have to be the end product—it can be used as a starting point for interactive techniques as in a paint system. Figure 10 illustrates this with an image that started as the fractal trees of Fig. 4.

Secondly, mathematical and geometrical patterns have a profundity about them due to the fact that they describe laws of nature. This, of course, is the attitude of the Islamic artist, who sees the geometries in terms of cosmology and astrology. Richard Voss, in an article on fractals (Voss, 1985), quotes Galileo:

> Philosophy is written in this grand book—I mean universe—which stands continuously open to our gaze, but it cannot be understood unless one first learns to comprehend the language in which it is written. It is written in the language of mathematics, and its characters are triangles, circles and other geometrical figures, without which it is humanly impossible to understand a single word of it; without these, one is wandering about in a dark labyrinth.

Richard Voss and Benoit Mandelbrot (1982)—the discoverer of fractals—believe that fractal geometry is in fact more suitable for a description of the world than the traditional geometries. An artist will probably not directly agree with Galileo, but the fact remains that geometries of various kinds have been tremendously important in the development of fine art. For example, the golden mean as a geometrical entity has been at times elevated to the stature of religious symbolism. In our present culture, fractal geometry and the recursive geometries that I have outlined above are less likely to be regarded in a religious or mystical sense (though some might do so) but are more likely to be considered in relation to aesthetics. I believe that we can learn from the Islamic artists, and other religious

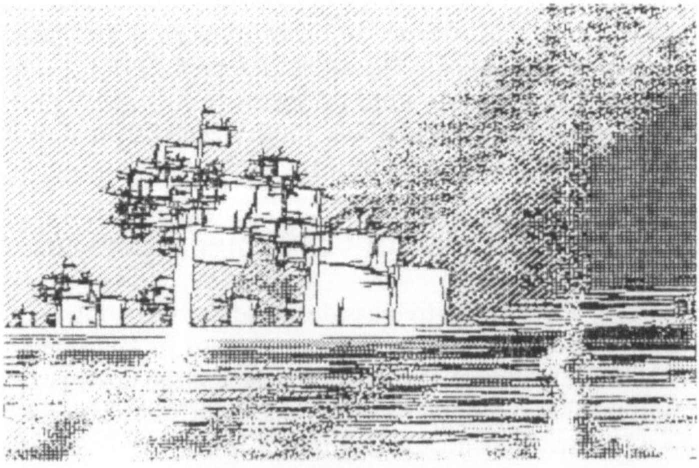

FIGURE 10. "Treescape 1."

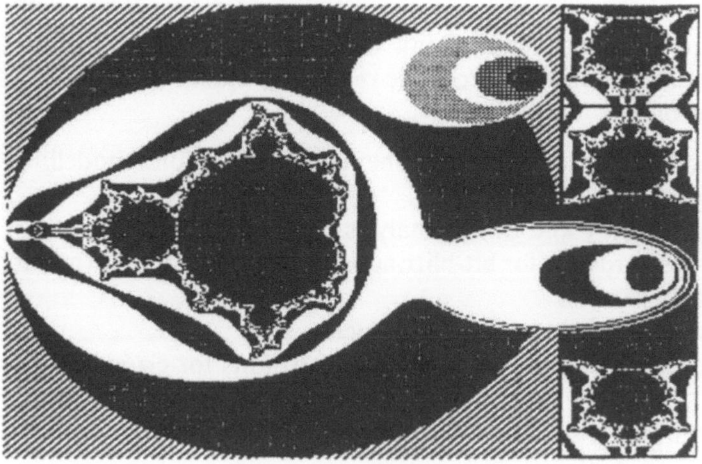

FIGURE 11. "Tongue in Mandelbrot's cheek."

artists of Christian, Hindu and Buddhist traditions, methods of using geometries in an aesthetic manner. In Islamic art, for example, much is made of the balance between the "crystalline" and the "biomorphic," that is, between the geometrical and the more whimsical or organic elements (Critchlow, 1976). This relates very well to the development of imagery where one uses computer geometries to generate an image which is then added to or further manipulated using arbitrary synthesis from primitives (as in a paint system). Figure 11 shows a Mandelbrot set which I have "modified."

Proposals for an Integrated Computer Art System

If one accepts that computer art needs both the interactive "arbitrary" approach and the algorithmic computer geometries, then what kind of system allows the artist to exploit and mix these methods? The answer, at present, is that no such system exists and that many existing systems work against this approach, either by being "closed" paint or drafting packages which cannot be extended with the various geometries or by being programming environments with no interactive components. A system that offered both approaches could be called an integrated computer art system, or ICAS for short. The system that comes closest to being an ICAS is the Juno system built by Greg Nelson (1985) as a prototype. This is an interactive drafting system with a scripted component where geometrical entities can be specified using a simple language of "constraints." The use of constraints represents an attempt to develop a more powerful programming language than the usual languages such as BASIC, Fortran and Pascal—I refer to this as "scripting at a higher level."

An ICAS should incorporate all the geometries so far discussed and allow interactive synthesis at many different levels (solid modelling, drafting and painting). Analysis, in the form of image processing, or other methods of taking data from the real world must be catered for. An ICAS should offer:

Interactive and scripted components, including solid modelling, drafting and painting.
Image-grabbing and image analysis.
Graphics hardware for bit-blitting and similar operations (moving chunks of picture).
A general programming environment.
Scripting at a higher level such as constraints for classical and recursive geometries.
Frame-buffer output and vector output to plotters.

In working with an integrated system one could just use the paint system facilities if desired, but a more usual route would be to start at a more *modelled* level of construction. One could, for example, script a geometrical algorithm which would allow many possible types of output and rendered image; this script would act as the most abstract description of a series of images. At a lower level one might take the output of the script (for example, a sequence of vectors) and manipulate these with drafting techniques. Finally, a single image could be created by taking the output from the drafting part of the system into the painting part, where the image can be manipulated on a pixel basis—for example, using flood-filling and the creation or addition of "biomorphic" elements, as in the Mandelbrot set example of Fig. 11.

Other routes would include three-dimensional modelling, the use of standard visual realism techniques and the integration of different elements within the geometrical toolkit. Yet another starting point could be with a frame-grabbed image and the manipulation of this data in various ways. Analysis of such an image could be the start of a Markov chain approach to generating imagery or even just the creation of texture for certain purposes. An interesting technique devised by Brian Reffin-Smith while at the Royal College of Art was to calculate the angle of a line segment based on the pixel value in a frame-grabbed image and output the results onto a plotter.

I have concentrated so far on the computer artist rather than the designer or graphic designer. I believe, however, that the untrammelled explorations of the computer artist will have an impact on the vocabulary, certainly of the graphic designer, who will make increasing use of the computer even for the most trivial and conventional of briefs, and also on the product designer and architect. If a revival of interest in ornament in architecture and design should take place, then the computer will be at its centre and should have a profound impact on its nature. Algorithmic synthesis from primitives and the elements of the geometrical toolkit could bring about a new interest in decoration and ornament, but with a contemporary style.

Conclusions

The computer offers interactive or free-hand techniques and also programmed approaches which allow the exploration of more sophisticated computer geometries. An integrated computer art system would incorporate features from the major interactive systems with a scripted or programmed component, allowing the artist to explore both traditional geometries and those which arise from recent research in mathematics, physics and biology. I believe that widespread use of such systems would make commonplace a new visual vocabulary, which would have an impact at the least on areas traditionally involved with pattern-making.

References

Critchlow, K. (1976) *Islamic Patterns.* Thames & Hudson.

Dixon, R. (1983) "Geometry Comes Up to Date", *New Scientist* 98(1356), May 5:302–305.

Franke, H. (1971) "*Computer Graphics—Computer Art*" Phaidon.

Jacobson, J. (1982) "Analytical Computer Art," *1982 IEEE Symposium on Small Computers in the Arts,* pp. 47–55.

Lansdown, J. (1978) "The Computer in Choreography," *IEEE Computer,* August, pp. 19–30.

Lansdown, J. (1980) "Is the Computer a Tool?: The Question in an Art Context." in B. Sundin, ed., *Is the Computer a Tool?* Almqvist & Wiksell, Stockholm.

Leavitt, R. (1976) *Artist and Computer.* Harmony Press.

Macgregor, J. and A. Watt (1984) *The Art of Microcomputer Graphics.* Addison-Wesley, Reading, Mass.

Mandelbrot, B.B. (1982) *Fractals: Form, Chance and Dimension.* Freeman, San Francisco.

Nahas, M. and H. Huitric (1982) "Computer Painting with Rodin," 1982 *IEEE Symposium on Small Computers in the Arts,* pp. 95–103.

Nelson, G. (1985) "Juno, a Constraint-based Graphics System," *Computer Graphics* 19(3):235–243.

Smith, A.L. (1984) "Plants, Fractals and Formal Languages," *SIGGRAPH* 84, pp. 1–10.

Voss, R.F. (1985) "Random Fractal Forgeries." In R. A. Earnshaw, ed., *Fundamental Algorithms for Computer Graphics,*" NATO ASI Series. Springer-Verlag, New York.

Wilson, S. (1983) "Artificial Intelligence in the Arts," *Leonardo* 16(1):15–20.

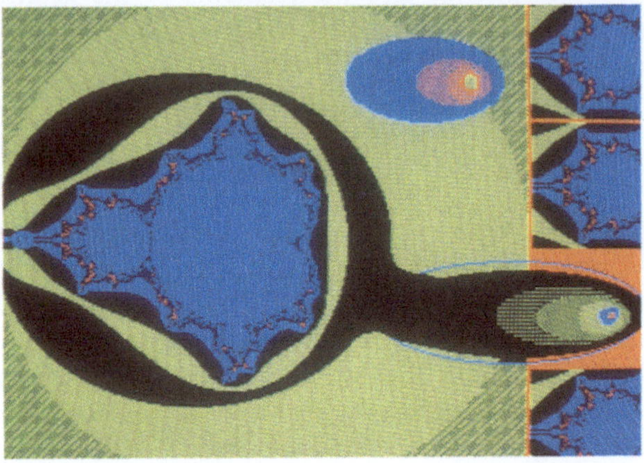

PLATE 1

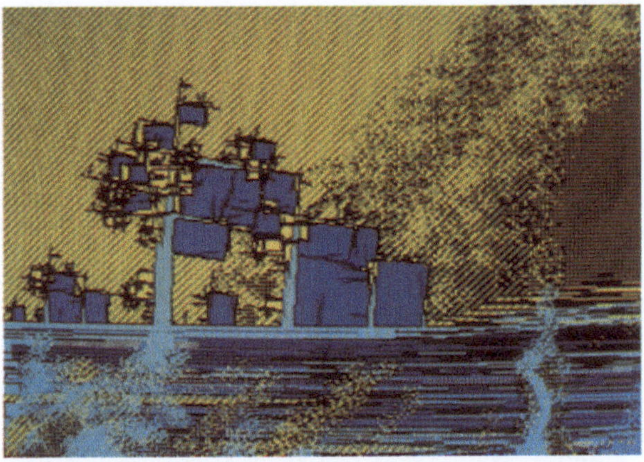

PLATE 2

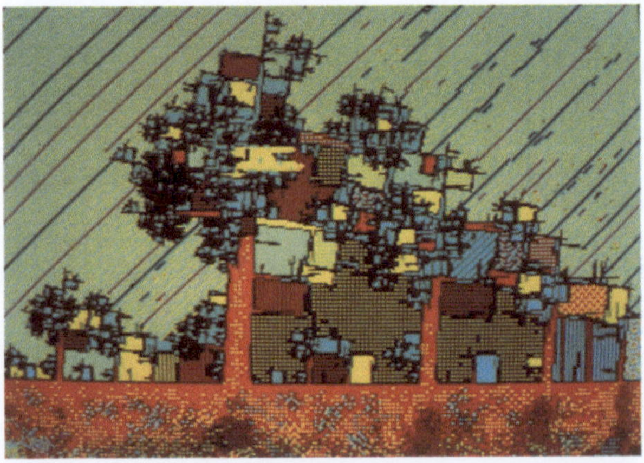

PLATE 3

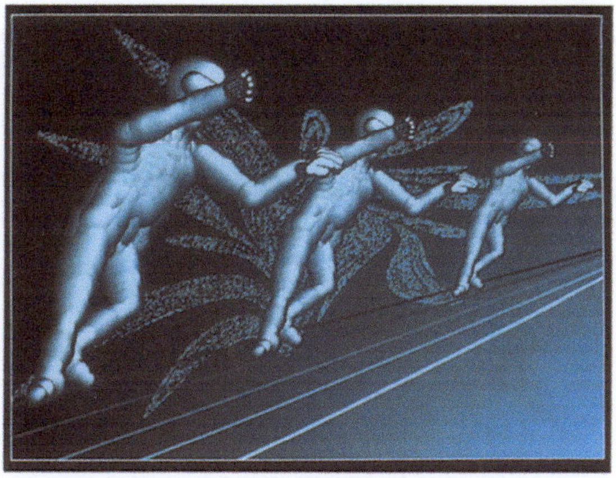

PLATE 4

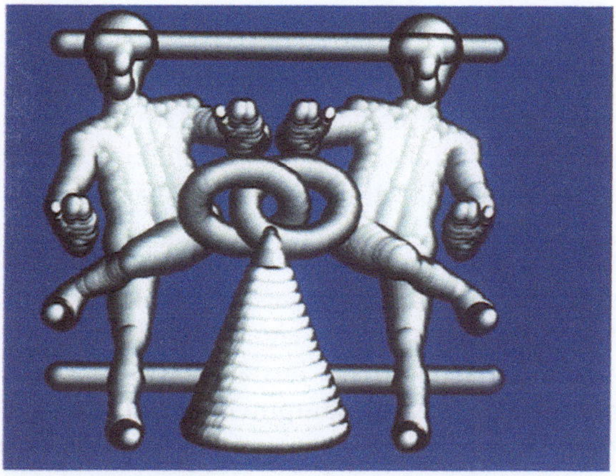

PLATE 5

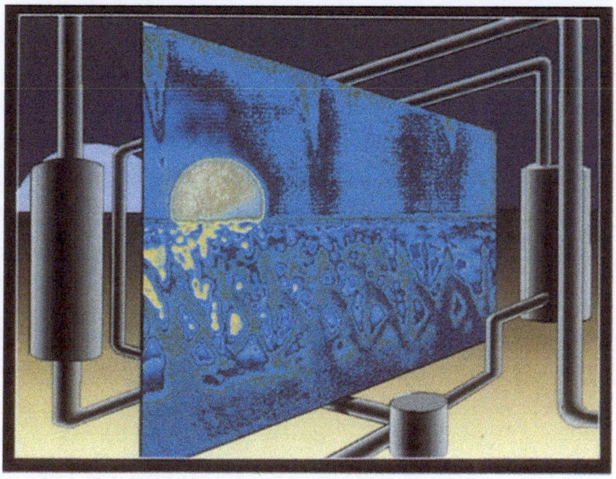

PLATE 6

Generative Techniques in Graphical Computer Art: Some Possibilities and Practices

John Lansdown

Introduction

When creating a work of graphical computer art, an artist has the choice of three basic methods of working:

1. Writing a program to assist in realising a particular art image;
2. Writing a program to implement a generative concept;
3. Using a paint system as the medium and making the picture in a way analogous to conventional drawing and painting.

This paper will not deal at all with the last of these methods and has little to say about the first but looks at the second in some detail.

It is important to understand the significant difference between methods 1 and 2. In the first, an artist has a particular image in mind and invents new or employs existing computer procedures to help externalise it. In the second, the artist invents or employs computer procedures—as it were in abstract—and explores their visual potential. Of course, in the first method, the artist does not always have a clear, fixed picture in mind: when working on its realisation the mental image alters as new ideas suggest themselves. Gradually what is pictured and what is being produced converge until the artist is satisfied with the result or the whole is rejected. This mode of working therefore resembles the conventional manual one. Artistic judgement is also applied in the second method, although it is the computer which "creates" the works. Artists using this approach often do so in order to produce a large amount of output from which they make a selection based on aesthetic considerations (see, for example, the interesting insights by the French computer artist Vera Molnar, 1981). The two methods are, though, profoundly different both in intention and in outcome.

The paper shows a number of figures. Except in the case of Figs. 13 and 14 by Manfred Mohr, these were not created as art works but as illustrations of the principles discussed. They should therefore be judged in this light and seen as pointers towards what might be achieved rather than art images in their own right.

Types of Generative Technique

We can broadly classify the techniques as follows:

1. *Functional:* where, using mathematics and logical constructs, we map one set of numbers into another and plot the result;
2. *Manipulative:* where a drawing is built up of individual elements which, in some sense, are assembled or arranged;
3. *Birth/death-like:* where the drawing is "grown" from cell-like elements whose presence or absence and position are determined by rules which depend entirely on local considerations and not on the drawing as a whole.

This classification is quite artificial and others could equally well be set up. This one, however, serves to bring out some of the main features of generative techniques. It must be stressed, though, that the techniques are not all equally popular in computer art: the third, indeed, is not often employed. It is included because it seems to have a considerable, if presently unrealised, potential.

Functional Techniques

Classical Functions

Perhaps the oldest form of generative technique in computer graphics is that of directly plotting two-dimensional mathematical functions—usually combinations of the circular functions, sine and cosine—with progressively changing values of parameters (Fig. 1). Indeed, long before computers existed, mechanical devices were frequently used to make drawings of a similar sort. One such drawing device was the popular Victorian amusement, the Harmonograph, first shown around 1879. The Harmonograph comprised a pendulum attached to a pen which moved in a elliptical orbit over a table which was free to rock under the influence of another pendulum. The composite motion produced drawings of sufficient complexity to intrigue, but combined with a satisfying element of regularity. Examples of the types of drawings produced (and something of the machines that make them) are shown in Cundy and Rollett (1961).

Even earlier, in 1815, the American mathematician Nathaniel Bowditch described the types of curves that could be drawn by a swinging pendulum. In 1857 the French mathematician Jules-Antoine Lissajous, studied these curves in great detail using a pendulum which dripped a line of fine sand as it swung. Curves defined by the formulae: $x = a \cdot \sin(mA$

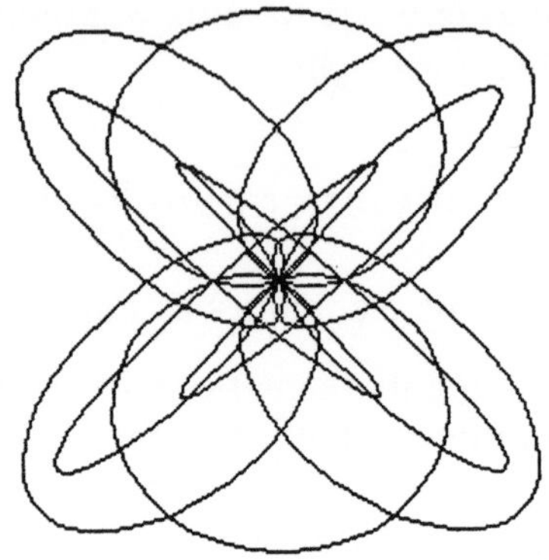

FIGURE 1. A Lissajous figure.

+ b), $y = c \cdot \sin(nA + d)$ with varying values of A,a,b,c and d are now known as Lissajous figures in his honour. Much more recently—in the 1960s—a children's educational toy, the Spirograph, comprising a set of circular plastic discs which could be rotated in relation to one another and used as templates for drawing, effectively took the place of the Harmonograph.

Because of its long history, we can call direct plotting of 2-D mathematical functions the "classical" technique. Its employment often gives rise to reasonably arresting images, especially when some imagination is applied to the choice of functions and values of parameters. But the fact that drawings of the Lissajous form can be so easily produced by non-computer means—as well as our over-familiarity with the type of imagery arising—has reduced their current popularity in computer art.

On the other hand, the plotting of three-dimensional functions (and those of higher dimension too) has been made easier by the use of computer graphics and no machine other than the computer exists to assist in this task. Mathematical volumetric forms of arbitrary complexity (as well as 3-D projections of hyper-volumetric forms; see, for instance, Brisson, 1978) can easily be put into perspective and viewed from any angle by use of standard computer graphics techniques (Fig. 2).

Most of the drawings of 2-D and 3-D functions tend to be linear plots of the sort very well illustrated in Dixon (1987) or Delahaye (1986). However, point plotting, as we shall see, is often of value—particularly when the functions themselves take only integer values.

Interpreted Functions

A variation on the classical technique is when the function—often a point function—used is not plotted directly but is, in some sense, "interpreted" and the result of the interpretation is plotted. The interpretation can be

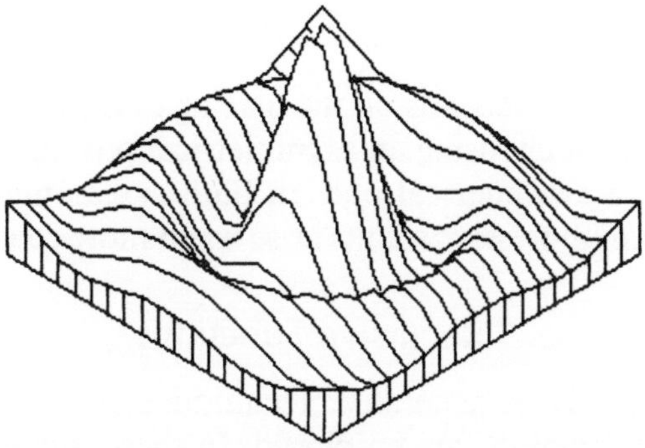

FIGURE 2. A two-dimensional mathematical form.

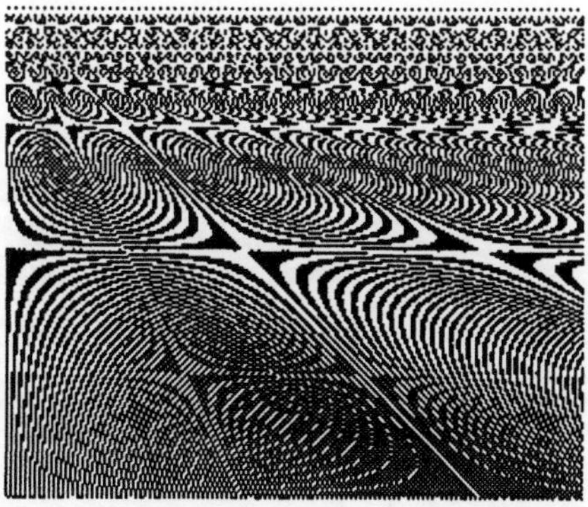

FIGURE 3. A Saunders character map.

as simple as a change of colour in a point plot, the colour depending on either the absolute position, the value of the function or a simple count of points plotted. These methods are really mappings of three-dimensional functions into two dimensions of geometrical space and one of colour space.

One type of interpreted function was originally described by Saunders (1972) and called a "character map." Here a function is defined over a rectangular grid of cells. The function is computed for each of the cells and an interpreted value is displayed at that cell point. Saunders showed that drawings having interesting characteristics could result by using an interpretation based on the value of the *n*th decimal place of a simple function. Figure 3, for instance, shows a plot of the third decimal place mod 2 of the simple function x/y.

Another interpreted function method is due to Connett (Dewdney, 1986), in which a grid of cells is set up and the integer distance calculated between each cell and a chosen reference cell. A particular cell is then represented on the drawing by a colour dependent on a function of this distance mod the number of colours available. The degree of symmetry of the resulting image depends on the placing of the reference cell. Figure 4 shows the effect of choosing an asymmetrical position for the reference cell and Fig. 5, a symmetrical one. In both cases only two colours are used. Much more impressive results arise when more colours are available.

Recursive Functions

A whole new family of generative techniques arises when two-dimensional recursive functions are employed. In these, successive values of x and y are calculated from previous values. Thus, these functions are of the generic form

$$x_{n+1} = f(x_n, y_n) \qquad y_{n+1} = g(x_n, y_n)$$

Gumowski and Mira (1974) proposed a pair of functions:

FIGURE 4. A Connett function with asymmetrical reference cell.

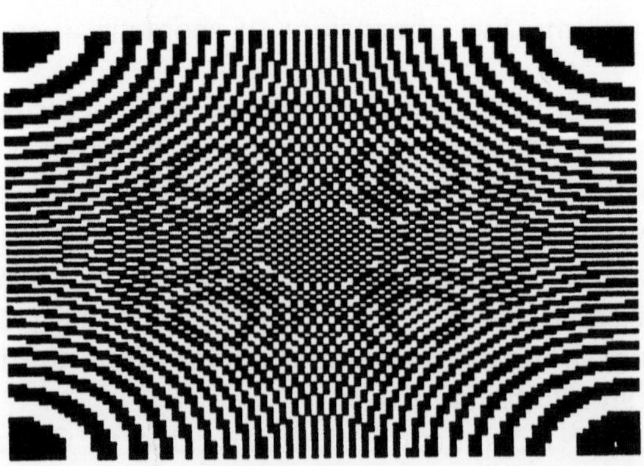

FIGURE 5. A Connett function with symmetrical reference cell.

$$x_{n+1} = h(y_n) + f(x_n), \qquad y_{n+1} = -x_n + f(x_{n+1})$$

where

$$f(x) = cx + 2x^2(1 - c)/(1 + x^2), h(y) = d(1 + a + by^2)y$$

In these formulae, x and y are calculated for large values of n (typically from 10,000 to 100,000 or more) and the results plotted as a succession of points. Vastly different images are seen by making slight changes to the parameters a, b, c and d (Fig. 6). Lansdown (1978) gives a simple BASIC program for exploring the formulae. Martin also uses two-dimensional recurrence relationships to produce the striking images that he illustrates elsewhere in this volume. Colour is added to his drawings by a process of interpretation.

Just as the classical functions producing Lissajous figures describe the action of some physical occurrence such as the path traced by a compound swinging pendulum, so the recursive functions which give rise to the types of pictures that Martin or Gumowski and Mira produce often describe the action of physical phenomena such as turbulence in water and air. A growing body of theory is developing to explain and amplify the physics and mathematics involved. This goes under the name of *chaos theory* (see, for example, Bai-Lin, 1984, or Peterson, 1987) and should be better known by those wanting to find new sources of generative techniques. Pickover (1987) shows the graphical potential of a particular branch of chaos theory—bifurcation. Figure 7 shows an elementary example of the forms that can arise from the use of bifurcation. Pickover (1986) gives a method for generating 2-D forms closely resembling biological specimens.

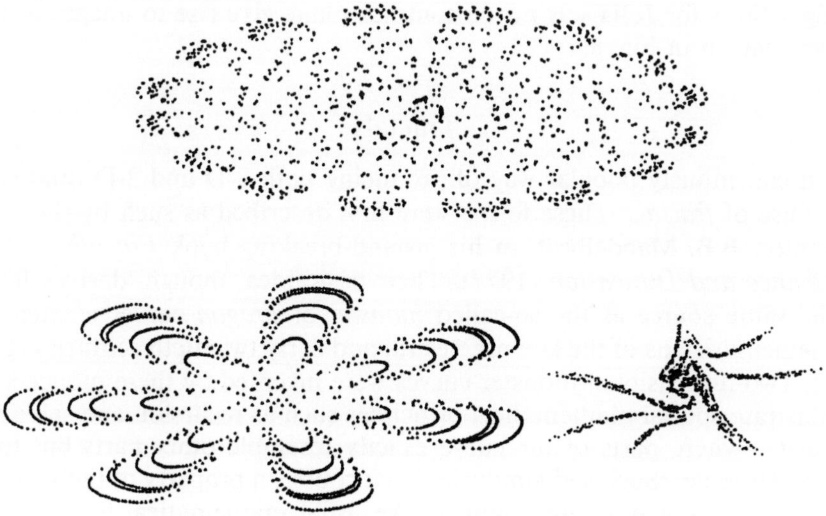

FIGURE 6. Three versions of a Gumowski function.

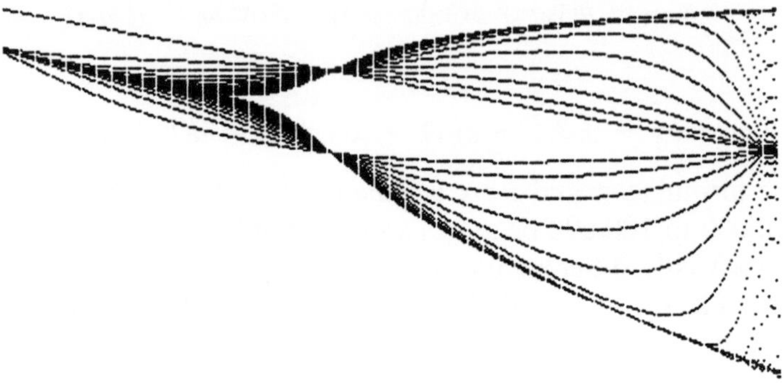

FIGURE 7. A bifurcated form (after Pickover, 1987).

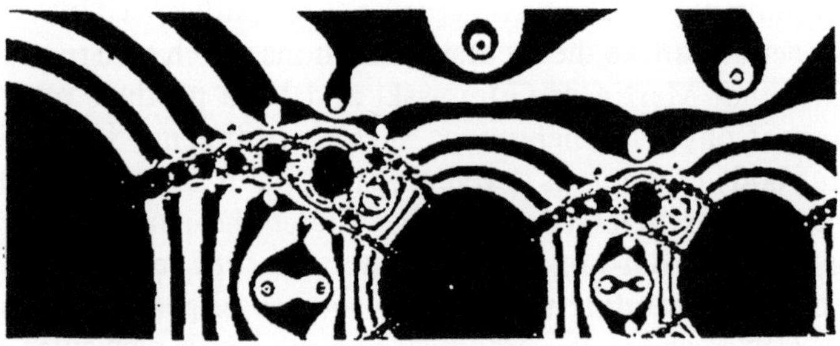

FIGURE 8. The Julia set (after Peitgen and Saupe, 1983).

These images arise from using functions defined over the complex plane as do those in Pickover (1988). See also Peitgen and Saupe (1983), whose algorithms for Julia sets in the complex plane give rise to images of the type shown in Fig. 8.

Fractals

An enormously popular way of producing both 2-D and 3-D images is by use of *fractals*. These forms were first described as such by their inventor, B.B. Mandelbrot, in his ground-breaking book *Fractals: Form, Chance and Dimension* (1977). Their basic idea, though, derives from the same source as the so-called *monster* or *dragon* curves created by mathematicians of the late nineteenth and early twentieth centuries (Fig. 9). Two-dimensional monster curves were invented by these pioneers to illustrate special mathematical principles such as recursion and self-similarity—where parts of the curve exactly resemble other parts but to a smaller scale. (Such self-similarity is, of course, a property of the straight line but is not normally found in the usual mathematical forms.) The work was done by these pioneering mathematicians in the belief that they

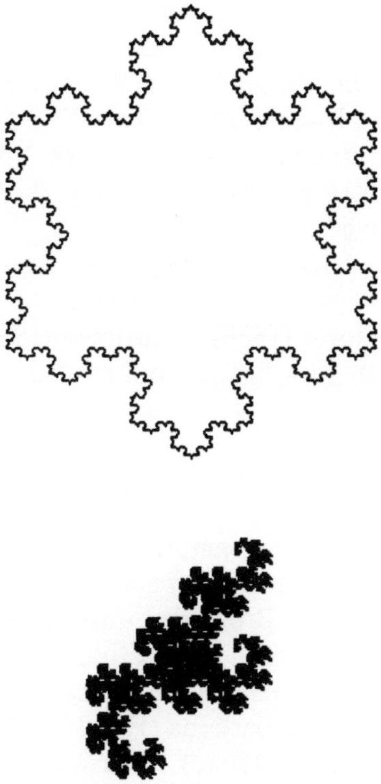

FIGURE 9. Two "dragon" or "monster" curves.

were creating shapes of an entirely artificial nature having nothing whatever to do with the real world—indeed which completely broke the rules of the real world, where Euclidean geometry held sway. Mandelbrot's major contribution was to show that, far from having no counterpart in the physical world, the principle of proportional self-similarity embodied in these shapes (and other things flowing from it, such as fractional dimensionality) was absolutely at the heart of the formation of all sorts of natural objects: trees, leaves, coastlines, mountains and much more. The "natural" geometry, therefore, was not Euclidean but fractal. Because of this insight, the use of fractals is now universal in making images of such objects and Mandelbrot's idea is used in most new algorithms for modelling natural forms—although sometimes in ways which do not strictly conform to his rigorous mathematical definition of fractals (see, for example, his rather ill-tempered letter: Mandelbrot, 1982a).

Mandelbrot's two books (1977, 1982), an article by Fournier, Fussell and Carpenter (1982), an excellent exposition by Voss (1985), and a beautiful book by Peitgen and Richter (1985) are the prime sources for the graphical work on fractals. The latter book deals extensively, too, with those fascinating 2-D fractals, the Mandelbrot set and the previously mentioned Julia set. These and other 2-D fractals—especially those in the complex plane described in the previous section—are also very well covered by Casey (1987), who includes useful program listings. Production systems and L-grammars (Smith, 1984; Prusinkiewicz, 1986) can also be used to generate fractals—and other forms. See, for example, Coyne and Gero (1985) and Koning and Eisenberg (1981) on production systems, techniques which are so powerful and comprehensive that they warrant a chapter to themselves.

Stepoway, Wells and Kane (1984) present a straightforward recursive method of programming 3-D fractal images of terrain. Their method is summarised in Lansdown (1988). Lansdown (1987a) gives a fairly comprehensive bibliography on fractals and related subjects.

Arrangements, Manipulations and Distortions

A major source of interest in generative computer art is in pictures built up from the *arrangement* and *manipulation* of images; see, for instance, the work of Brownrigg and Brownrigg introduced elsewhere in this volume. Arrangements can consist of repetitions of a relatively simple element or "module" usually over a grid—resulting either in one or other of the 17 plane tessellation patterns (Fig. 10) or in some non-repeating pattern (Fig. 11). Hargettai (1986) is an authoritative source on such patterns. Manipulations and distortions are often applied to these modules in an incremental way to produce a field of related images (Fig. 12). One of the motivating forces behind much of this work is the often

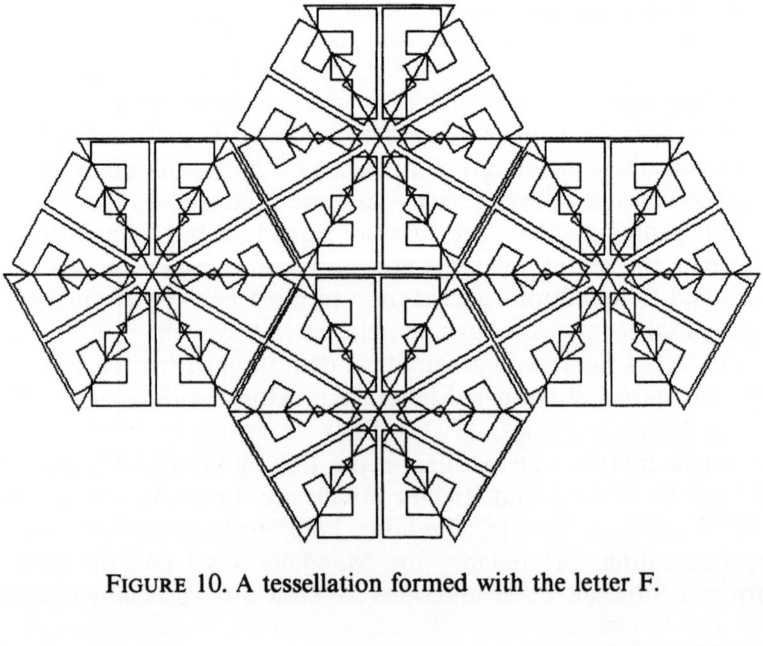

FIGURE 10. A tessellation formed with the letter F.

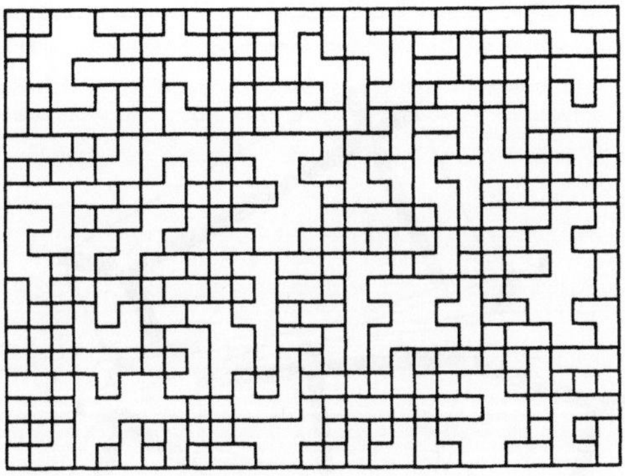

FIGURE 11. A non-repeating use of the letter F.

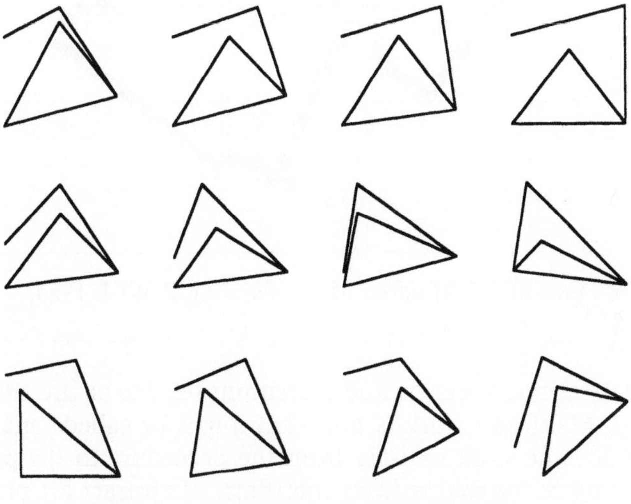

FIGURE 12. A field of related images.

surprising *emergent forms* that arise where versions of the module adjoin or overlap one another.

Although the exploration of modification and arrangement is pursued by many computer artists, undoubtedly one of its best exponents is Manfred Mohr (Gassen, 1987). Born in Germany in 1938, Mohr now lives in New York and, since 1969, has produced all his artwork by the application of systematic rules and with the assistance of computer plotting. Recently, his pre-occupation has been with making paintings from computer-generated perspective views of a cube which have been cut into sections and rotated independently of one another to form something like a collage (Fig. 13). Earlier works comprise the repetition of a number of small sign-like elements which read en masse as if they were calligraphy or, more accurately, a tablet of hieroglyphics (Fig. 14). Although com-

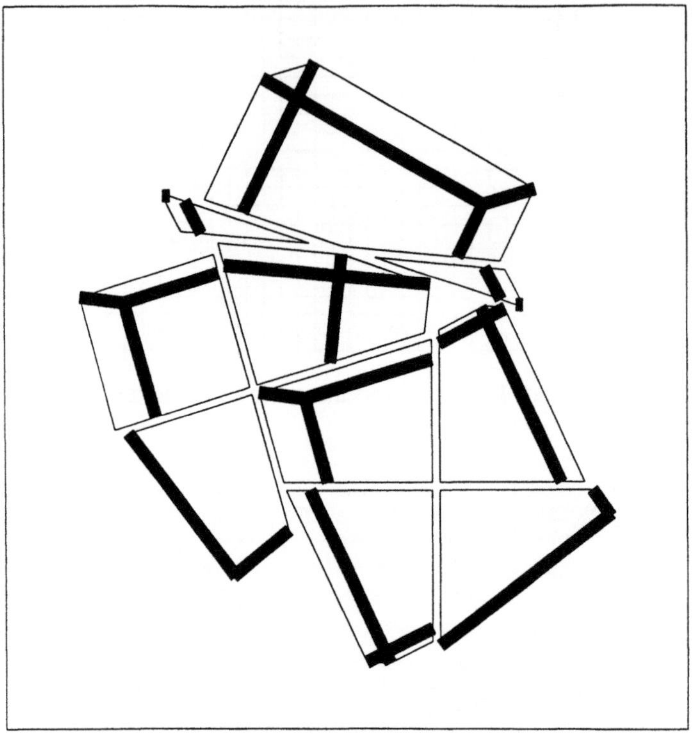

FIGURE 13. Manfred Mohr: Painting P-361-E 1984.

puters are used in its creation and algorithms have to be invented in order to proceed, Manfred's work is not what might be called "mathematical art." Nor does he work entirely from the procedure to the picture. His work is firmly in the mainstream traditions of abstract art pioneered by artists such as Mondrian, Malevich, Pasmore and Moholy-Nagy. But Mohr's work illustrates the power of algorithmic manipulation in a more cogent way than the work of any other artist.

A Language Analogy

There are various techniques by means of which the modules of an art work can be arranged and manipulated. Indeed, as I pointed out in Lansdown (1970), in some cases it can be advantageous to think of the modules as the *vocabulary* of a language and the rules of arrangement as a *grammar* which lays down the conditions under which elements in the vocabulary can combine with one another. This is to set up an analogy with natural language, where the modules are words and the grammar is the permitted syntax. What guides the choice of words to be used in a given statement in a natural language is the message one wishes to convey. The intended meaning selects the elements of the vocabulary to be used and the gram-

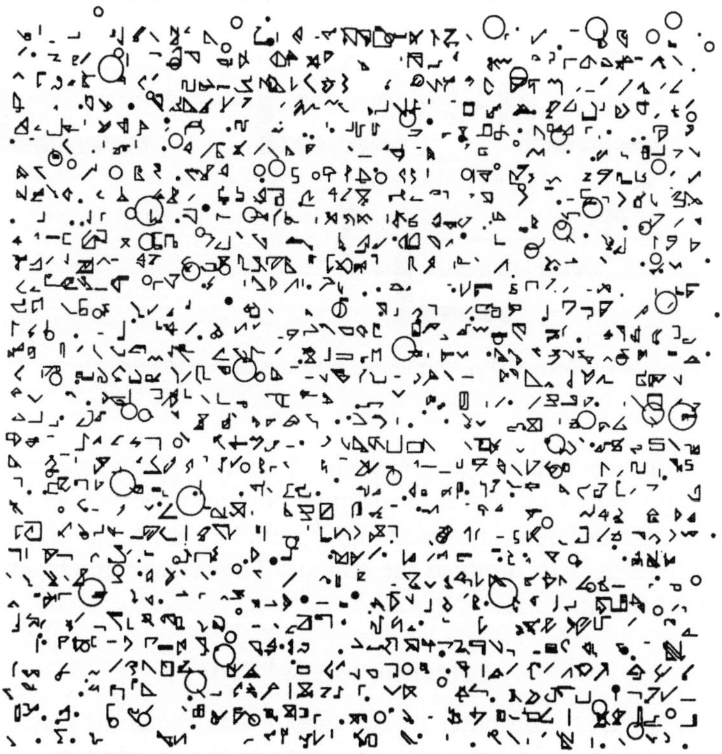

FIGURE 14. Manfred Mohr: Formal Language 1 1970.

mar ensures that these are arranged in an agreed way to allow the easy decoding of the encoded message by others.

Art works such as musical compositions, poems, paintings, dances and so on do not carry messages in the same clearcut way as everyday prose. Decoding them is usually not easy—nor is it meant to be. Ambiguity and multiple meanings are inherent in such things. These meanings derive as much from the way they set up resonances with their listeners' or viewers' own feelings and experiences as from any pre-existing message. Sometimes, indeed, the arrangement of elements in an art work is meant primarily to convey nothing more than information about the arrangement itself. In an art work, then—particularly and abstract one generated by computer—the *selector* is not "meaning" but some artifical device which simply chooses elements of vocabulary within the rules of the grammar. Meaning flows from these choices: it is not the starting point of them.

One other parameter arises in this language model of computer art (Fig. 15). This can be called the *presentation*. Just as in natural language, where the spoken and written forms often differ (in some languages, quite markedly), so too—but even more sharply—the manner in which an art work is to present itself to its viewers or listeners actually affects the

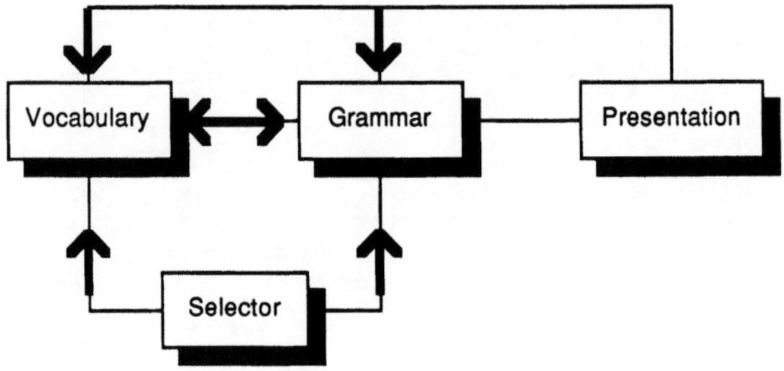

FIGURE 15. A "language" model of computer art.

make-up of vocabulary and grammar. A computer music composition, for instance, presented as a conventional score for musicians to play from, needs a quite different grammar and vocabulary from one in which the computer itself is to produce the sounds. The selector might also be of a different form.

Selecting the Selector

In the early days of computer art the selector was frequently just a random number generator. In graphical applications the vocabulary often consisted of nothing more than the plotter instructions MOVE and DRAW. The generator then produced a stream of numbers which controlled the progress of the line plot, usually by successive pairs of numbers acting as the coordinates for each movement of the pen. The grammar was restricted to rules preventing the lines going outside the confines of the paper.

However, the use of a random selector without the mediation of a sophisticated grammar tended to give rise to unsatisfactory drawings (see Fig. 16, for instance, where a random number technique is used with a grammar which starts chains of seven lines running from the centre of the drawing—the only restriction on the choice of coordinates being that they should fall within the drawing surface). It is easy to see why this approach will usually produce uninteresting results: the coordinates of each successive line are, by the nature of the generative method employed, almost completely independent of one another. Each line has, as it were, no *memory* of what has gone before. The presence of memory can be simulated either by making the grammar more restrictive or by changing the way the selector works. As an example of the first approach, we might make the grammar insist that each successive pair of coordinates take the line into the next nearest clockwise quadrant of the drawing. As an example of the second, we might use a *deterministic* selection algorithm where the chosen numbers are related in a way that we can more readily

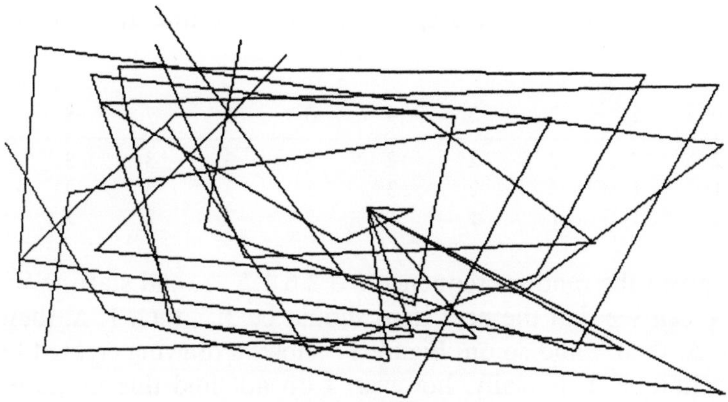

FIGURE 16. Random pattern.

recognise. (I am aware that the algorithmic random number generators incorporated in computer programs are, at heart, completely deterministic. They are designed, though, to simulate properly random behaviour such as the discharge pattern of neon tubes, the action of gas particles and so on—where each happening is effectively independent of the last. Random number algorithms are deterministic in working, then, but random in behaviour. By a deterministic selection algorithm, I mean one that is deterministic in its methodology and regular in its apparent behaviour.)

Markov chains, in a sense, embody memory (Kemeny, Snell and Thompson, 1960). By setting up a matrix of transition probabilities which take us from one element of the vocabulary to another, we can guide the selector towards a particular outcome whilst still retaining a certain amount of unpredictability. A simple technique for doing this is via the use of state transition tables. For example, given that a vocabulary comprises the three symbols Δ • ˆ, and that each symbol follows the other in the following manner:

Item1	Item2	Percentage of time
Δ	Δ	0
•	Δ	50
ˆ	Δ	50
Δ	•	20
•	•	20
ˆ	•	60
Δ	ˆ	40
•	ˆ	50
ˆ	ˆ	10

(this should be read as "• follows Δ 50% of the time" and so on), we can use a selector based on this specification, by setting up transition table thus:

	0	1	2	3	4	5	6	7	8	9
1	2	2	2	2	2	3	3	3	3	3
2	1	1	2	2	3	3	3	3	3	3
3	1	1	1	1	1	2	2	2	2	3

Then, given the random sequence 6 0 2 6 1 5 . . . and starting with item 2: •, we can see that the next item should be 3: ˆ, then 1: Δ, then •, then ˆ, then Δ, then ˆ, and so on. Figure 17 shows a drawing created by use of this technique. Personally, however, I do not find this mixture of randomness and order as satisfying as the totally deterministic (and more readily understood) drawing shown in Fig. 18.

Image Transformation

In the last chapter of his fascinating and seminal book *On Growth and Form*, Thomson (1917) illustrates the way in which the shapes of various animals can be related to one another by simple geometrical transfor-

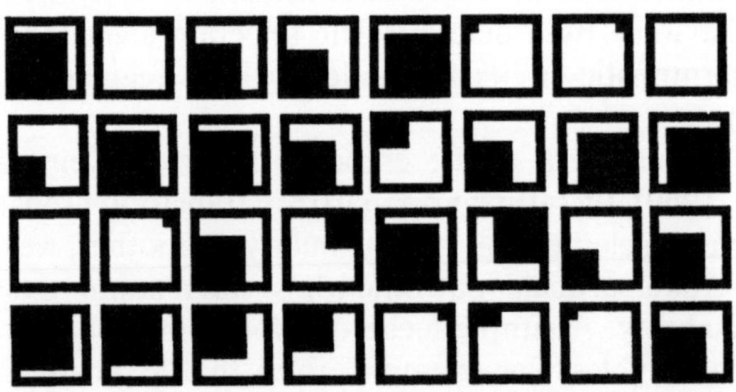

FIGURE 17. Mixture of randomness and determinism.

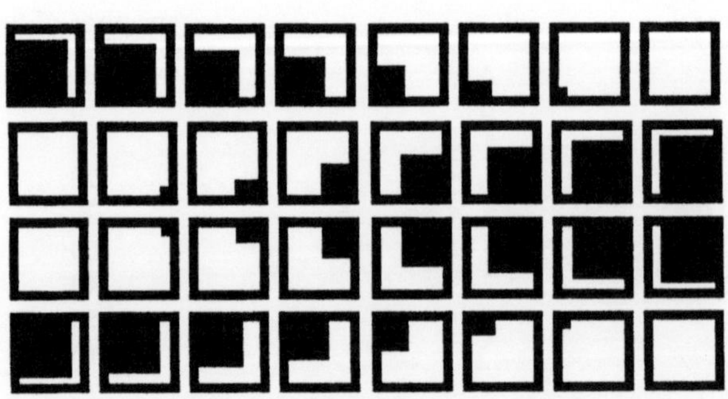

FIGURE 18. Deterministic pattern.

mations. Thus, for example, by plotting the outline of a skull of one species—say a rhinoceros—on a rectangular Cartesian grid, one can mathematically transform the grid so as to produce the skulls of other species—such as tapirs, horses or even rabbits. Similarly, the human skull can be changed to look like the skull of a chimpanzee or a baboon by what Thomson terms, "one harmonious and congruent transformation." Artists like Dürer and, perhaps, even Vitruvius were also aware of the power of grid transformations to make new images. In his *Treatise on Proportion*, Dürer showed examples of how different human heads and facial expressions could be derived from transformations of what, elsewhere in this volume, I call "a prototype."

Interesting images can be achieved by the use of Thomson's techniques and by a related method: "compositing" an existing image with a mathematical function. Here, we take the x-y coordinates of the start image and associate them with a function $f(x, y)$. Computer artists, notably Charles Csuri and Leslie Mezei, have worked with this process and it seems to be a fruitful source of artistic experimentation (Franke, 1971). Figure 19 shows the effect in action.

Simple *addition* of the original and the function is usually sufficient to produce effective results (Fig. 20), although a little-known process called "inversion" can also be interesting. In the process of inversion, we convert a point (x, y) in a Cartesian coordinate system to its polar coordinate equivalent (α, r) and then plot $(-\alpha, 1/r)$. Strange and unexpected images can result from this process (Fig. 21).

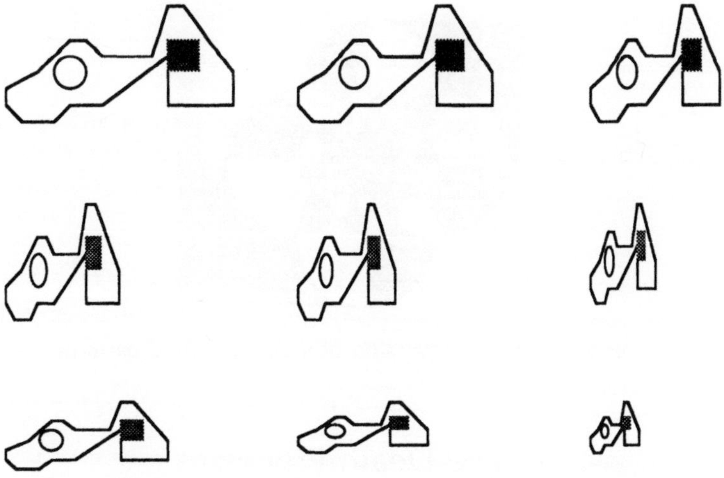

FIGURE 19. Image undergoing various transformations.

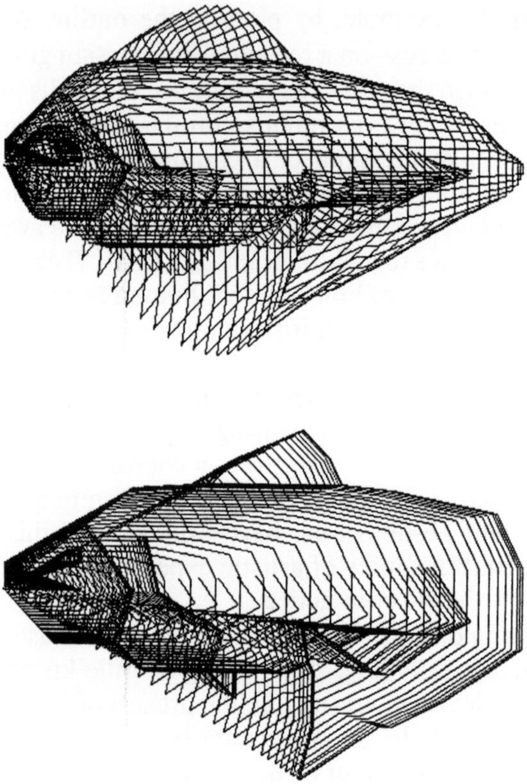

FIGURE 20. Compositing of picture and functions.

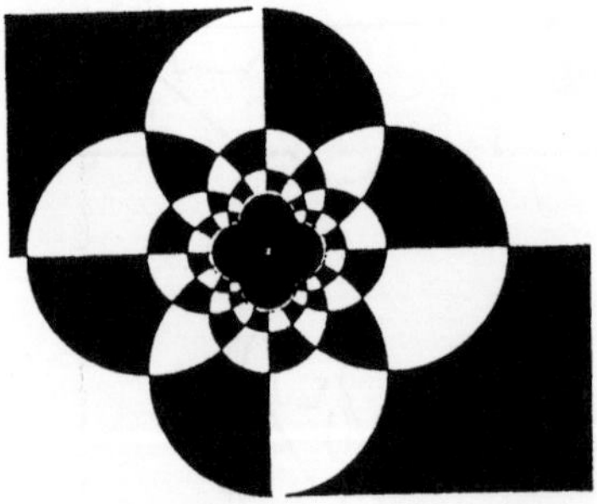

FIGURE 21. An inversion of a checkerboard pattern.

Life-Death Processes

Whenever artists make conventional pictures, their compositions are usually based on holistic considerations. In theory at least, every mark on the paper determines the subsequent position and attributes of all the others. It therefore seems unlikely that there would be any potential in picture-generating methods which depend on entirely local considerations, that is, where each new mark depends only on the attributes of the marks nearest to it. In a sense, the random pictures we looked at earlier—those without any, or with only limited, memory—were of this nature and they were generally unsatisfactory. There is a technique, however, that has considerable artistic promise but which creates its effects by the birth, life and death of "cells" whose progress depends only on the status of immediately neighbouring cells. The technique arises from a branch of mathematics and computing theory concerned with *cellular automata* (Toffoli and Margolus, 1987).

Cellular automata can exist in any number of space dimensions, although the most studied ones are only one-dimensional. Because they change over time, however, 1-D cellular automata are usually depicted in 2-D to indicate the time course of development of each generation. The progress of 2-D automata is usually shown in separate drawings or—if a particular generation has special visual appeal—in a single picture.

One-Dimensional Automata

In the one-dimensional case, the progress of an entity in given cell, $A(n)$, depends on the states of the entities in adjoining cells ($A(n - 1)$, $A(n + 1)$ (and, sometimes, on the states of those in slightly more remote locations). For example, what happens to an element in a given cell in its next generation could be determined by the rules: If the two adjoining cells are occupied then the element in the given cell dies before the next generation. If both adjoining cells are unoccupied, then the given cell continues in its present state (either occupied or unoccupied). If either adjoining cell is occupied, then an element is born in the given cell. Figure 22 shows the pattern that emerges from this rule set with each generation shown on a separate line. Images become more interesting and complex if any change from generation to generation is indicated by a change of colour. Drawings of greater complexity, like Fig. 23 arise when more complex rules are devised.

Two-Dimensional Automata

Perhaps the best known example of this form is that embodied in the computer game "life" (Gardner, 1971). This ingenious pastime was invented in the 1960s by the British mathematician, J.H. Conway, and its effects have been studied by a large number of people since then. As with one-dimensional automata, the 2-D versions can exhibit one of a set of modes of behaviour: (1) death of all elements, (2) evolution to a fixed finite size, (3) infinite growth, and (4) growth and contraction in a periodic

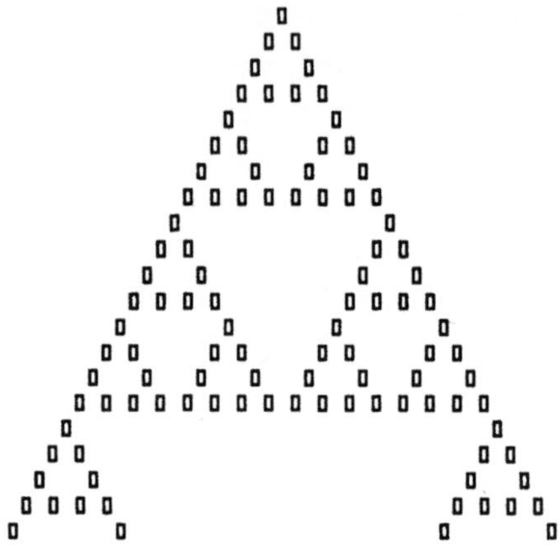

FIGURE 22. Simple cellular automaton.

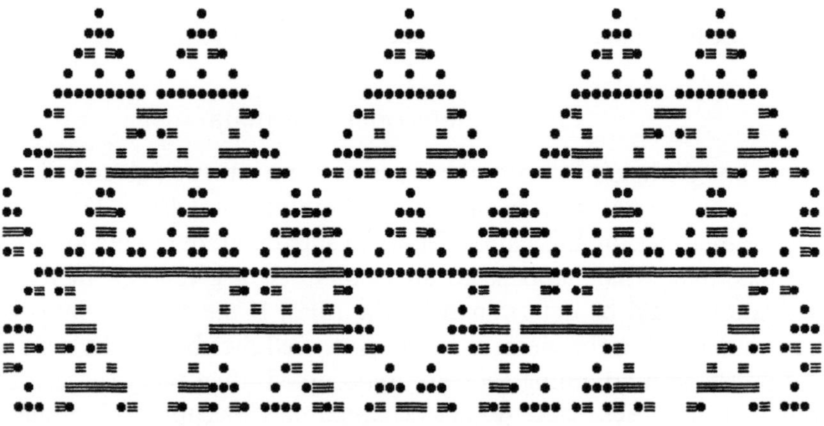

FIGURE 23. Multi-state cellular automaton.

way (see Wolfram, 1984, for examples of these behaviours in the 1-D case).

The full artistic potential of cellular automata has not yet been nearly fully explored by computer artists. Although cellular in appearance, drawings created with the methods of Saunders and Connett explained earlier under the heading of Interpreted Functions, cannot really be thought of as cellular automata. The best examples of the use of cellular automata proper are probably by the Dutch computer artist and mathematician Lambert Meertens, who created a set of pictures based on a cellular automaton acting on a randomly generated pattern of black and white squares. The automaton was applied to each square in turn to "grow" it towards greater order. The effect can be seen in Fig. 24 where the state of any cell depends on the state of the cells on its diagonal corners. The

FIGURE 24. (Left) A random pattern of black and white squares. (Right) The pattern after undergoing six generations of change.

rule applied is that the colour of any given cell should be the negative of the colour of the majority of those on its diagonal corners. The figure shows the original random pattern and the effect after applying the automaton for six generations.

Another method of using only local variations to grow a pattern towards some desired end has been shown in a biological context by Dawkins (1986). Here he has outlined a way of changing a random—and often symmetrical—pattern of lines (looking like an insect form) towards more recognisable shapes simply by randomly changing individual elements and then, from the resulting dozen or so representations that arise from these small changes, choosing the one that is closest to the target pattern. Iteration continues until the picture conforms to the desired pattern. Dawkins' work is aimed at supporting his belief that evolution can be shown to be entirely a product of small incremental changes (see also Dewdney, 1988). Artists who wish to explore the possibilities of an evolutionary path to producing "families" of forms would do well to examine this approach.

Concluding Remarks

Some questions arise: Can all these algorithmic generative possibilities give rise to a new aesthetic, to a computer art which differs fundamentally from conventional art? What, above all, is the point of such work? These are not easy questions to answer. In looking at—and listening to—a great many computer-generated works over the last 20-odd years, few major differences from conventional art seems to emerge. But there are some: they concern the product, the process and the motivation.

First, there is a special quality of drawings plotted in the very precise and regular way that computer output devices can often achieve. The output, untrammelled by the intuitive and subconscious modification that artists often add to manual drawing, invariably gains something simply by its mechanical perfection.

Second, unlike the conventional case, artists using the sort of techniques discussed here very often wish to reveal rather than disguise the generative principles and processes involved in the creation of their works: to, as it were, let the grammar–and even the selector–play their own visible parts in the created image. Generative works that do this are a little like poems of a formal nature where metre, rhyme and rhythm as well as the unusual juxtaposition of images all combine to provide us with the possibilities of extra "meaning." William Empson (1961) considers two lines of poetry:

Swiftly the years, beyond recall.
Solemn the stillness of this spring morning.

(These are from a Chinese poem: I will say nothing about the resemblance between these lines and those of computer poets.) He points out that

> [these] statements are made as if they were connected, and the reader is forced to consider their relations for himself. The reason why these facts should have been selected for a poem is left for him to invent; he will invent a variety of reasons and order them in his own mind. This, I think is the essential fact about the poetical use of language.

Poetry, then, is not a sort of eccentric prose in which everyday words and concepts are manipulated in order to conform to some arbitrary set of academic rules; the structure that arises out of the rules and out of the unfamiliar association of parts adds enormously to the poem's aesthetic and our understanding of it–so much so that, as in classical music, sometimes the structure itself is revealed to be the meaning. In computer art this revelation does not always arise from viewing just one work; a whole series of similar works has to be seen before an understanding of the principles of creation can be understood and an extra meaning derived from them.

One other point about process emerges too. People are outstanding at making art works whose creative force comes from emotion, experience and intuition. What they are not so good at–if this is something they wish to explore–is the unaided use of randomness on the one hand or the strict conformity to rules on the other. Schoenberg, for instance, intellectually defended his invention of the formal rules of the 12-tone system with great vigour but if, after applying the rules, he did not like what he heard, he would sometimes change his composition to suit! By deviating from his rule set, Schoenberg denied us the opportunity to appreciate their undiluted effects. On the other hand, we know that uncontrolled randomness is neither intellectually nor aesthetically pleasing and the pursuit of this line is likely to prove fruitless. However, we are only just beginning to realise the possibilities of rule-based techniques–at which the computer can excel.

Finally, there is motivation. In all art there is the idea of "otherness," of "making strange," of what the Russian Formalists of the 1920s called *ostranenie*. Both in the experiencing of art and in its creation there has always been the need to distance oneself from the work in order to understand more fully what it has to say. Renaissance artists would view their half-finished paintings upside down or through a mirror to help achieve this effect. Picasso, speaking about the otherness involved in the Cubist invention and use of collage, said, *"We sought to express reality with materials we did not know how to handle, and which we prized because we knew their help was not indispensible to us, that they were neither the best nor the most adequate"* (Golding, 1959, p. 103). In a sense, the use of computer programs to make pictures is the ultimate in ostranenie. Here an artist is distanced from his or her work in a unique way and the computer presents a special challenge to his or her mastery over resources.

It is in all these factors that we might see a new aesthetic arising.

References

Bai-Lin, H. (ed.) (1984) *Chaos*. World Scientific Publishing, Singapore.

Brisson, S.W. (ed.) (1978) *Hypergraphics*. Westview Press, Boulder, Colo.

Casey, S.D. (1987) "Formulating Fractals," *Computer Language* 4(4):27–40.

Coyne, R.D. and J.S. Gero (1985) "Design Knowledge and Sequential Plans," *Environment and Planning B* 12:401–418.

Cundy, H.M. and A.P. Rollett (1961) *Mathematical Models*, (2nd ed.). Oxford University Press, Oxford.

Dawkins, R. (1986) *The Blind Watchmaker*. Longmans, Harlow.

Delahaye, J.-P. (1986) *Geometric and Artistic Graphics*. Macmillan, Basingstoke.

Dewdney, A.K. (1986) "Computer Recreations," *Scientific American* 255(3):14–23.

Dewdney, A.K. (1988) "Computer Recreations," *Scientific American* 258(2):84–87.

Dixon, R. (1987) *Mathographics*. Basil Blackwell, Oxford.

Empson, W. (1961) *Seven Types of Ambiguity*. Penguin, Harmondsworth.

Fournier, A., D. Fussell and L. Carpenter (1982) "Computer Rendering of Stochastic Models," *Commun. ACM* 25 (6):371–384.

Franke, H. (1971) *Computer Graphics—Computer Art*. Phaidon, Oxford (2nd ed., 1985, Springer-Verlag, Berlin).

Gardner, M. (1971) "On Cellular Automata, Self-Reproduction, the Garden of Eden and the Game Life," *Scientific American* 224(2):112–117.

Gassen, R.W. (1987) "Fractured Symmetry." In *Catalogue of Manfred Mohr Exhibition*, Wilhelm-Hack-Museum, Ludwigshafen am Rhein.

Golding, J. (1959) *Cubism—A History and an Analysis*. Faber & Faber, London.

Gumowski, J. and C. Mira (1974) "Point Sequences Generated by Two-Dimensional Recurrences." In *Information Processing 74*. North-Holland, Amsterdam, pp. 851–855.

Hargettai, I. (ed.) (1986) *Symmetry: Unifying Human Understanding*. Pergamon, Oxford.

Kemeny, J.G., J.L. Snell and G.L. Thompson (1960) *Introduction to Finite Mathematics*. Prentice-Hall, London.

Koning, H. and J. Eisenberg (1981) "The Language of the Prairie: Frank Lloyd Wright's Prairie Houses," *Environment and Planning B*. 8:295–323.

Lansdown, J. (1970) "Computer Art for Theatrical Performance," *Proc. ACM International Computing Symposium*, Bonn.

Lansdown, J. (1978) "Gumowski," *Creative Computing*, June, pp. 88–89.

Lansdown, J. (1987) "The Creative Aspects of CAD: A Possible Approach," *Design Studies* 8 (2):76–81.

Lansdown, J. (1987a) *Selective Reading List on Fractals and Related Concepts*, Working Paper, System Simulation Ltd., London.

Lansdown, J. (1988) "Computer Graphics: A Tool for the Artist, Designer and Amateur," In M.M. de Ruiter (ed.), *Advances in Computer Graphics III*. Springer-Verlag, Berlin.

Mandelbrot, B.B. (1977) *Fractals: Form, Chance and Dimension*. Freeman, San Francisco.

Mandelbrot, B.B. (1982) *The Fractal Geometry of Nature*. Freeman, San Francisco (revised 1983).

Mandelbrot, B.B. (1982a) "Comment on Computer Rendering of Fractal Stochastic Models, *Commun. ACM* 25 (8):581–584.

Molnar, V. (1981) "The Role That Randomness Can Play in Visual Art, PAGE 47," The Bulletin of the Computer Arts Society, pp. 3–9.

Peitgen, H.-O. and D. Saupe (1983) "Julia—A Scheme for the Generation of Self-Similar Images," *Proc. CG83 Conference*. Online Publications, Pinner.

Peitgen, H.-O. and P.H. Richter (1985) *The Beauty of Fractals: Images of Complex Dynamical Systems*. Springer-Verlag, Berlin.

Peterson, I. (1987) "Toying with a Touch of Chaos," *Science News* (1929):277–278.

Pickover, C.A. (1986) "Biomorphs: Computer Display of Biological Forms Generated from Mathematical Feedback Loops," *Computer Graphics Forum* (5):313–316.

Pickover, C.A. (1987) "Graphics, Bifurcation, Order and Chaos," *Computer Graphics Forum* 6 (1):26–34.

Pickover, C.A. (1988) "Pattern Formation and Chaos in Networks," *Commun. ACM* 31(2):136–151.

Prusinkiewicz, P. (1986) "Graphical Applications of L-Systems." In M. Goldberg and R.J. Woodham (eds.), *Graphics Interface 86*. Canadian Information Processing Society, pp. 247–253.

Saunders, R. (1972) "A Description and Analysis of Character Maps," *Computer Journal* 15(3):160–169.

Smith, A.R. (1984) "Plants, Fractals and Formal Languages," *Computer Graphics* 18(3):1–10.

Stepoway, S.L., D.L. Wells and G.R. Kane (1984) "A Multiprocessor Architecture for the Generation of Self-Similar Images," *IEEE Trans. Computers* C-33(11):1041–1045.

Thomson, D.W. (1917) *On Growth and Form* (2nd ed., 1951). Cambridge Univ. Press, Cambridge.

Toffoli, T. and N. Margolus (1987) *Cellular Automata Machines*. MIT Press, Cambridge, Mass.

Voss, R.F. (1985) "Random Fractal Forgeries." In R.A. Earnshaw (ed.), *Fundamental Algorithms for Computer Graphics.* Springer-Verlag, Berlin, pp. 805–835.

Wolfram, S. (1984) "Cellular Automata as Models of Complexity," *Nature* 311(4):419–424.

Form Synth: The Rule-based Evolution of Complex Forms from Geometric Primitives

William Latham

Introduction

Artists through history have used many different methods to invent new forms, shapes and images. Picasso and Braque invented cubism and Jackson Pollock started action painting. These methods in art historical terms are called art styles. Often several artists will share a particular art style. For example, Malevich, Tatlin and Rodchenko all worked in a Russian constructivist style. This means they all used a similar method for inventing new shapes, forms and images. When an art style is taken up and used by a large number of artists there will be felt a marked influence in the culture they live in—for example, baroque art in Europe. As a result of this, original work by artists will widely influence the design of artefacts.

An art style can be defined as a framework of rules or beliefs within which the artist or artists will work using a particular technique such as painting or sculpture. When the most interesting permutations allowed within the framework of rules have been discovered, the framework is either extended or replaced entirely with a new set of rules. It is the extension and replacement of framework rules which enable new art styles to be born and for art to advance. The advent of modern art represented a complete overthrow and redefinition of the existing art rules. The rules or beliefs for a particular art style are not clearly defined and only form the boundaries within which the artist works, and only when artists near the boundaries of a given style is it truly apparent what the constraining rules are. Artists themselves will claim they work independent of such constraints, though this can easily be disproved by the overview of art history, which is able to locate most artists within different art styles (See Fig. 1).

As a result of this continuous exploration and discovery of new art styles it would appear that art has no long-term goal. Since each art style is different from the previous art style it would seem that art is undergoing an evolution based on changes in the current cultural environment, historical context and general aesthetic and that the development of a new

Cubism	Surrealism	Pop Art	Minimalism	Russian Constructivism
Picasso	De Chirico	Warhol	Donald Judd	Rodchenko
Braque	Magritte	Lichtenstein	Carl Andre	Tatlin
Juan Gris	Dali	Rauschenberg	Sol Lewitt	Malevich
	Yves Tanguy	Oldenburg	Tony Smith	Gabo
	Delvaux		Richard Serra	Pevsner

FIGURE 1

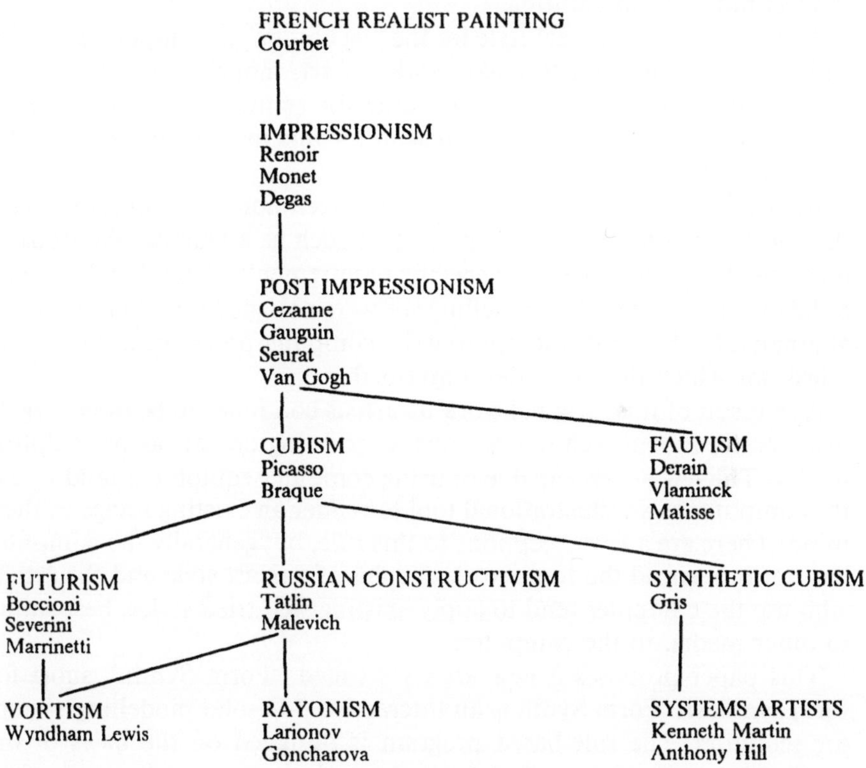

FIGURE 2

art style is based on altering or extending the rules which defined the previous dominant art style. (See Fig. 2.)

The artist's purpose is to invent new images, shapes and forms which in terms of human perception have artistic qualities; these qualities can be defined as being aesthetic or expressive. The quality of the forms the artist will produce will depend on:

1. The ability of the artist to make interesting creative decisions within the framework of rules of the art style.

2. The ability of the artist to change the rules and devise new rules as the interesting permutations of rules within an art style run out.

In this paper a clear distinction is made between "technique," the "artist" and the "art style." The technique is the physical use of materials. The artist is the supplier of idiosyncratic and subjective ideas. The art style is the framework of rules within which the artist works. Invariably there will be one technique which is best suited to the art style, in that this will allow the artist the greatest experimentation within the given framework of rules of the art style; for example, Impressionist artists used the technique of oil painting.

At present there is no art style for the "technique" of computer graphics which artists could use to make works of art, though this is strange in that the computer is the ideal machine for setting up a framework of rules within which to work. The reason for this may be the lack of clarification of the rules for an art style.

At present, artists who wish to use the technique of computing have the choice of either using a paint system such as a Quantel Paintbox, a machine designed to meet the specific requirements of graphic designers, or laboriously using solid modelling software designed for other purposes; alternatively, they may attempt to write computer programs of their own, a task for which they are often untrained.

As a result of this, original work by artists continues to be done largely using conventional techniques, such as painting on canvas or sculpting in clay. The few artists capable of using computer equipment tend to use the computer as an illustrational tool to render an existing image in their mind. There are a few exceptions to this rule, but generally the computer has not influenced the framework of rules of any art style and the artists who use the computer tend to apply existing well-tried styles, best suited to other media, to the computer.

This paper proposes a new art style called "Form Synth," short for form synthesis. Form Synth is an interactive 3-D solid modelling system for sculptors. The rule-based program is designed on the basis of the requirements of artists and relates to the evolutionary development of art and the 3-D modelling process used by sculptors.

Form Synth represents an entirely new approach to solid modelling. A complex form is "evolved" as opposed to being "constructed." This approach differs greatly from existing 3-D modelling systems, where complex forms in general are laboriously constructed using building blocks constructed from points, lines, solids or surfaces. Form Synth works like an evolutionary tree. Form Synth foreseeably has applications in the world of design; this is discussed later in the paper.

The program Form Synth when fully implemented will work by the multiple use of a set of inbuilt commands. These commands define operations which, when carried out on a geometric form will change its shape. As a result of successive operations being carried out on it, the geometric form becomes increasingly complex. The present prototype's set of geometric forms are cylinder, cube, cone and sphere and the set of operations are stretch, twist, scoop, slice, beak, add and subtract. In practical terms, the user chooses a geometric form and then chooses an operation to be carried out on it, the chosen operation changes the shape of the form, and the user assesses the new form and selects another transformation until he is satisfied with the complex form.

Works of Art and Designs

An evolutionary approach is more closely akin to the way the human design process works than is allowed by existing modelling systems. Existing modelling systems require considerable information on what is being designed to use the system; Form Synth allows gradual modification of 3-D design, starting with geometric primitives and finishing with a highly complex form. This method relates to the way a sculptor works. In the visual arts x-rays of old masters' paintings reveal considerable alteration and repainting and sometimes a complete change in composition and subject matter. The different states of Rembrandt's etchings show the gradual development of images. Picasso's sketchbooks likewise reveal the development of a simple sketch into a major painting. A film of Jackson Pollock shows the artist rapidly painting on a large piece of plate glass in his "dip stick" fashion. The painting is almost complete, the entire surface covered in thick paint, yet for some reason he deletes the entire image and starts again. Creative decision-making in fine art therefore is a very subtle, flexible and complex process.

The inability to design creatively using 3-D modelling software has been experienced in other design fields. This problem is highlighted by John Frazer in the October 1986 issue of *CAD International* in an article on CAD architecture systems (Pipes, 1986):

> The problem with most systems on the market is that they only help you to draw what has already been designed.

The actual process of drawing is a thinking process; if this process is replaced by a 3-D modelling system, then this thinking process is removed. An architect's hand-drawn sketches on paper will invariably show a gradual sophistication of the design, from simple sketch to detailed drawing. In sculpture the drawing process takes the form of making small maquettes in clay. The problem is that the user interface on 3-D modelling programs is not an adequate alternative to designing by hand drawing. Quoting John Frazer from the same article on CAD architecture:

> It is an insult to an architect who has spent seven years training to be shown an article on how to draw. That's computer obstructed design.

The process of designing, in fact, can become a struggle instead of a pleasure—for example, when using the Cubicomp system, as discussed later.

The sculptor Henry Moore explained in an article in 1960 his own personal process for drawing and inventing sculptures (Sylvester, 1978):

One doesn't know really how any ideas come. But you can induce them by starting in the far little studio with looking at a box of pebbles. Sometimes I may scribble some doodles, as I said in a note book; within my mind they may be a reclining figure, or perhaps a particular subject. Then with those pebbles, or sketches in the notebook, I sit down and something begins. Then perhaps at a certain stage the idea crystalises and then you know what to do, what to alter. You dislike what you've just made, and change it. At the end of a week you're sitting in that nice little easy chair with the bench in front, and there'll be probably some fifteen or so maquettes about 5 or 6 inches long, if it's a reclining figure, or that height if it's an upright. Then either I know that a few of those ideas I like, or that I don't like any of them. If some are ones I like, then I'll do a variation on that idea, or I'll change it if I am critical. Done in that way the thing evolves. In my mind always though, in making these ideas, is the eventual sculpture which may be ten or twelve times the size of the maquette that I hold in my hand.

The creative decision-making process can be explained in the following way. Which is more beautiful, a sphere or a cube? The question is not possible to solve objectively. The question can be solved subjectively by the answer, "I think the cube is more beautiful than the sphere." There is no logical reason for this answer; you the reader may think the sphere is more beautiful than the cube. What is important is that a decision is made. To make a work of art the artist will cumulatively make thousands of subjective judgements of this type. The decisions made will be based entirely on what the artist personally believes to be beautiful or ugly. The result is a highly sophisticated man-made object that we call a work of art.

Existing 3-D Modelling Programs

It would be worth briefly at this stage assessing how three existing 3-D modelling packages allow the user to invent complex forms. The Cubicomp and Easy 3-D software allow the user to use the operations Rotate and Jigsaw. The user may Rotate a 2-D shape into a 3-D form about a given axis or may cut out a 2-D shape, which is then extruded into a 3-D form. The user determines the angle of rotation and length of extrusion. These forms may then be combined in a boolean fashion; that is, with the operations union, intersect and subtract. The Geomod system allows boolean types of operations to be carried out on a set of geometric primitives. The Sculptor program by Mike King allows the user to construct complex forms from individual spheres or groups of spheres. Form Synth differs from these systems in one major aspect; the programs Cubicomp,

Geomod, Easy 3D and Sculptor involve the construction of complex forms as a result of *arbitrary synthesis from primitives.* The system Form Synth involves the *algorithmic* or rule-based synthesis of form. These terms make a useful distinction in this context and were devised by Mike King, who explains them further in King (1986).

The Difference Between Techniques and Operations

Sculptors have a number of practical techniques at their disposal to make 3-D forms, for example, welding, chiseling, adding small pieces of clay, wood carving, construction in plastics. These techniques are the same as would be used to build a house or repair a car. However, what is characteristic is that sculpture is not produced by aimless chiselling or randomly adding pieces of clay but by the artist purposefully using a technique to produce larger design effects. For example, Barbara Hepworth, in order to create a hollow in a form, would use hundreds of individual chisel blows. This hollow can be defined as a major transformation of the form as it radically changes the shape of the form, whereas a single chisel blow by itself on the form would change the design very little. Likewise, hundreds of aimlessly aimed blows on the surface of the form would change the form little. Barbara Hepworth purposefully used the hollow operation to make an interesting sculpture. She used the hollow operation in many of her sculptures. The hollow operation can therefore be defined as one of the rules she followed within the framework of rules for the art style. Figure 3 shows a simplified diagram of the most important operations used by a number of 20th century sculptors.

There is a clear distinction between technique and operation. The operation is what determines the design of the sculpture; the technique determines how the sculpture is physically made. Likewise, an architect does not design a building brick by brick but thinks and designs in terms of openings, enclosed spaces and surfaces. On a lower level these openings, enclosed spaces and surfaces can be defined as windows, courtyards, rooms, roofs and chimneys and on a lower level still as bricks, beams and tiles. The actual process of design uses abstract high-level thinking in general terms, but the architect has the bricks, beams and tiles in the back of his

Artists	Operations	Techniques
Giacometti	Stretch	Clay modelling
Henry Moore	Add lump	Clay modelling
Barbara Hepworth	Hollow	Stone and wood carving
Donald Judd	Add geometric form	Construction
Antony Caro	Stick complex form	Welding

FIGURE 3

Artists	Operations	Techniques
William Latham	Beak	Computer graphics
	Bulge	Hand drawing/xerox
	Scoop	
	Twist	
	Slice	
	Stretch	
	Add/subtract geometric form	
	Add/subtract complex form	

FIGURE 4

mind. The writings of Frank Lloyd Wright (1943) reveal this thinking process.

The problem with existing modelling systems is they allow the user to think only at the bricks, beams and tiles level, as revealed by the operations in Cubicomp and Easy 3D—"rotate" and "jigsaw"—terms familiar to the woodwork shop. These operations, by the categories being used in this paper, should come under the category "technique," as they are just a technique in order to physically make a 2-D into a 3-D form. The sculptor does not need to think in 2-D first and then think in 3-D, but thinks in 3-D all the time. The two operations are convenient in terms of computer programming but not to the artist.

The problem is then what selection of operations Form Synth should offer to the sculptor to make sculptures. The solution is to offer a number of operations already used by sculptors, for example, "stretch" and "add geometric form," and a large number of operations not already used by sculptors, for example, "beak," "bulge," "scoop," "twist." Exactly what these operations do to the form will be explained later in the paper. The reason for this selection is that if Form Synth is to be a new art style it must have a different framework of rules from the previous art style. Using this new framework of rules it therefore will be possible to make original sculptures, because the generative rules will be different. The exact selection of new operations was chosen by the author intuitively based on his own requirements as a sculptor (see Fig. 4).

Beginnings of Form Synth

The main concept behind Form Synth, however, did not grow out of any existing art style but from another area altogether, the rule-based construction of complex polyhedra from geometric primitives. The following illustrations show how the set of construction rules used to build regular complex polyhedra from geometric primitives (Cundy, 1960) can be replaced with a new set of arbitrarily chosen rules which can then be carried out on the geometric primitives to build irregular complex 3-D forms. This concept formed the basis of Form Synth in that it allowed a flexible invention of new 3-D forms but at the same time allowed the implementation of rule-based structure appropriate to the computer.

The following diagrams show how Form Synth developed from the rule-based construction of complex regular polyhedra (see Fig. 5). The rules "stellate," "truncate" and "add" are carried out on a set of five geometric primitives, namely tetrahedron, cube, octahedron, dodecahedron and icosahedron to build Archimedean polyhedra, Kepler-Pointsot polyhedra and compound forms (see Fig. 6). The rules "stellate," "truncate" and "add" are replaced with a new arbitrarily chosen set of rules, namely "beak," "bulge," "scoop," "slice," "stretch" and "add" (see Fig. 7). Four extra geometric primitives, cone, cylinder, sphere and torus, are added to increase the set of geometric primitives to nine. The new operation rules are then carried out on the geometric primitives (see Fig. 8). The

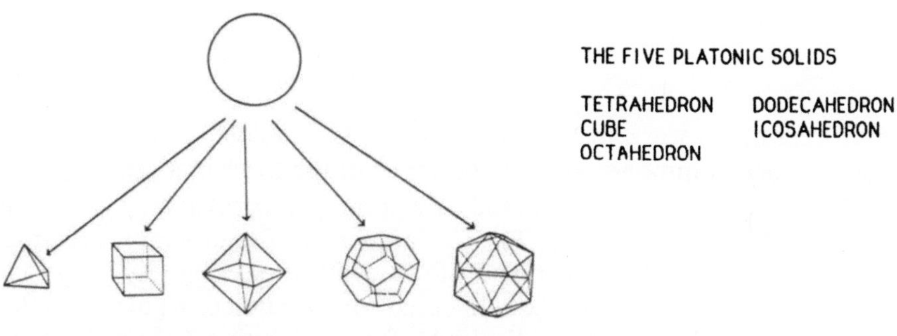

FIGURE 5

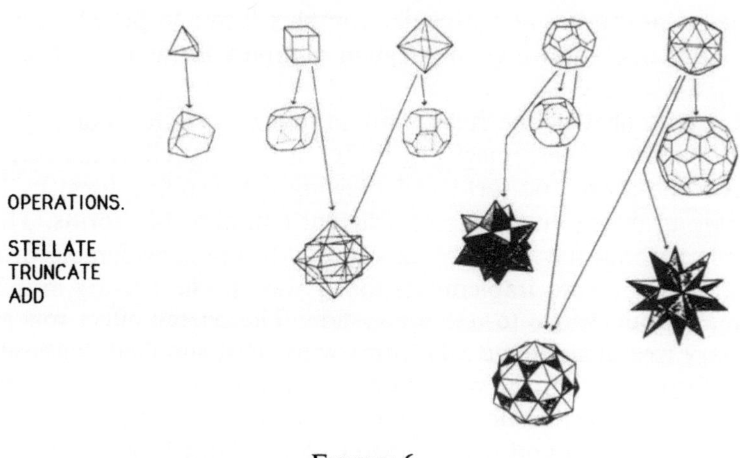

FIGURE 6

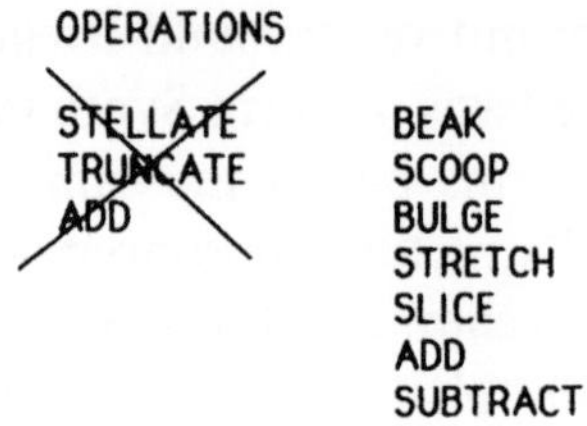

FIGURE 7

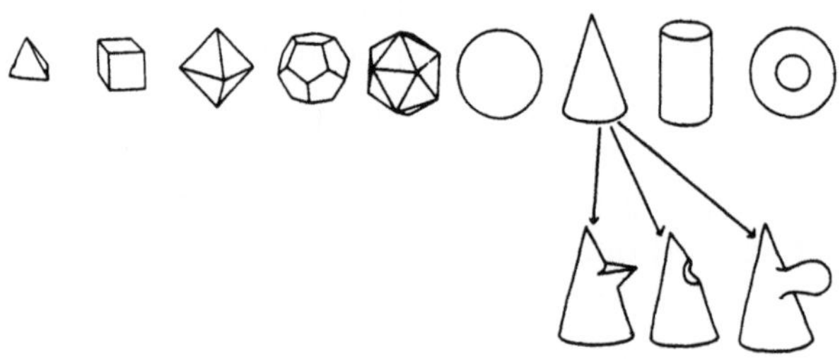

FIGURE 8

new operations work in a similar fashion to "stellate," "truncate" and "add." Each command changes the shape of the form in a different way. The artist chooses one command at a time to progressively change the shape of the form (see Fig. 9). The sequence of commands the artist chooses will determine the type of form evolved (see Fig. 10).

It is worth noting that in the rule-based construction of regular complex polyhedra the given mathematical rules for constructing 3-D regular complex polyhedra determine the complex form's evolution, but in Form Synth the form's evolution entirely depends on the intuitive choices of commands that the user makes. The artist uses the rules successively on geometric primitives and irregular complex forms to produce large "evolutionary tree" drawings of irregular complex forms (see Figs. 11 and 12).

By strictly obeying the rules, I found that by making choices from the set of operation rules, imagining in my mind what effect the rule would have on the geometric form and drawing the resulting form by hand I was able to evolve hundreds of different complex 3-D forms. This was possible without having to be involved with the considerable problems of graphics software implementation. I was in effect using myself as a graphic output device to test the system. The overall effect was an evolutionary tree of synthetic 3-D forms with artist-supplied "natural selection." Figures 11 and 12 were produced in this manner. This next stage was to select complex forms from the map and make them into 3-D sculptures in wood and plastic. (See Colour Plates 1 and 2 on p. 92.)

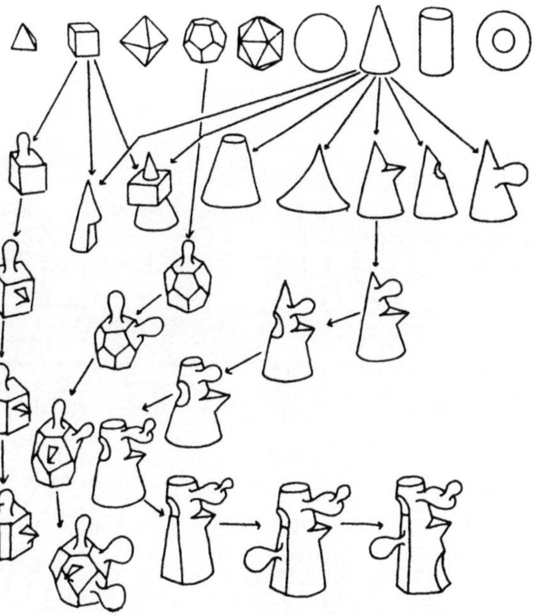

FIGURE 9

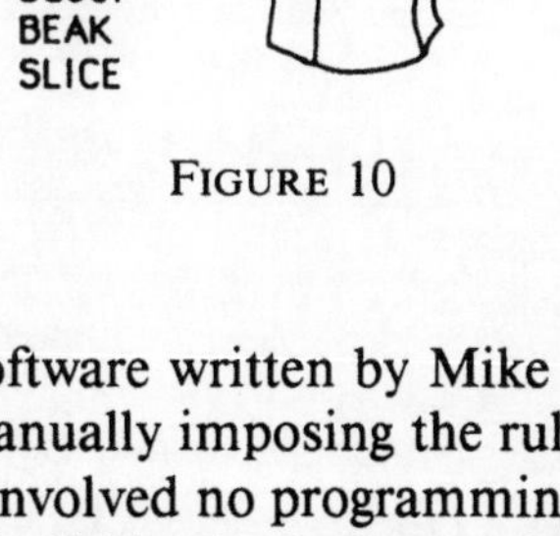

FIGURE 10

Using the Sculptor software written by Mike King, I was able to simulate Form Synth by manually imposing the rules of Form Synth on the Sculptor program; this involved no programming on my part. I first used the Sculptor system to build beaks, bulges, cones, spheres and cylinders out of hundreds of spheres. I then followed the rules of Form Synth in my head to determine where and how the beaks, bulges etc. were positioned on the cone, cylinder and sphere. The result is an evolutionary tree of complex forms. (See Colour Plates 3, 4, 5 and 6 on pp. 93–94.)

The artist moves down through the tree structure, employing his own form of natural selection based on which forms he chooses to continue to evolve and which he does not. This selection is based on his subjective selection of form and he feels no worries about leaving certain branches

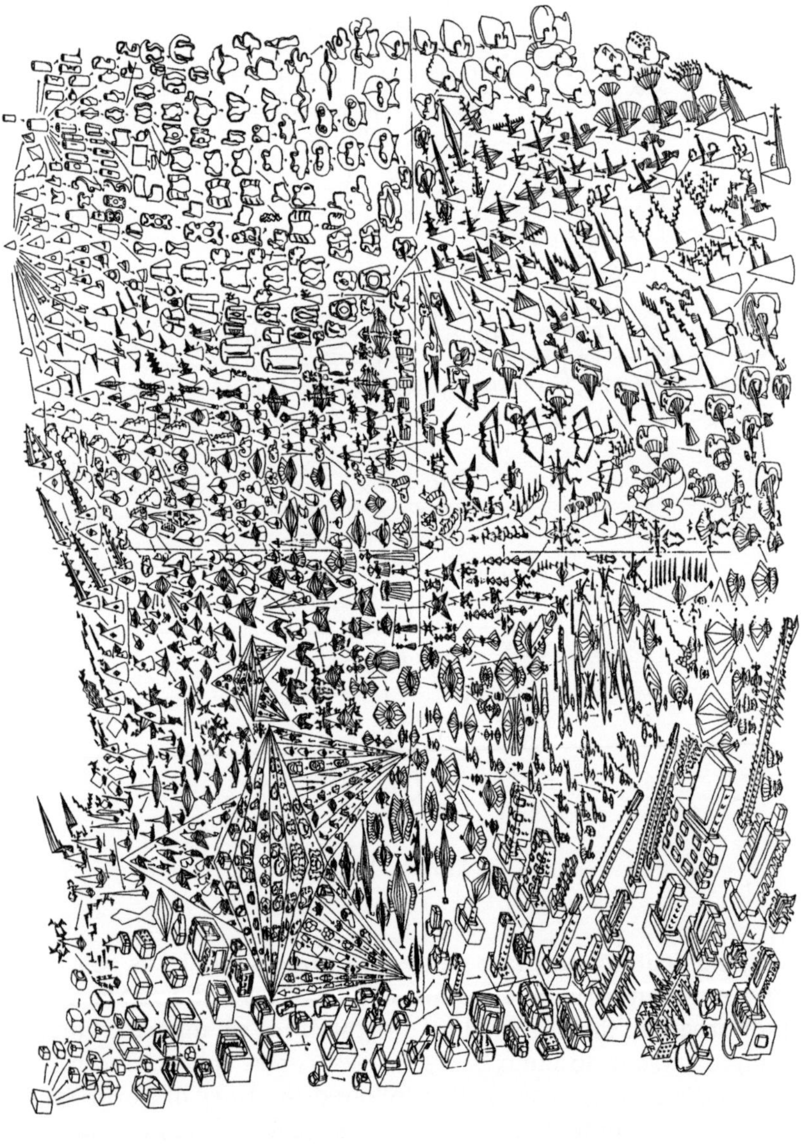

FIGURE 11

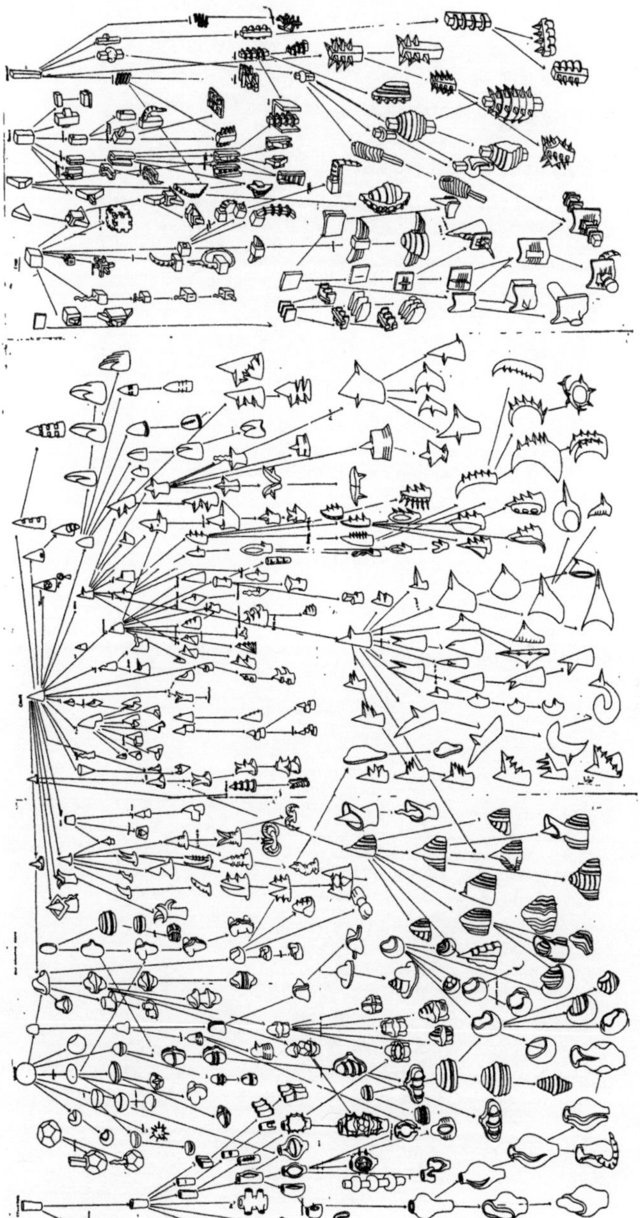

FIGURE 12

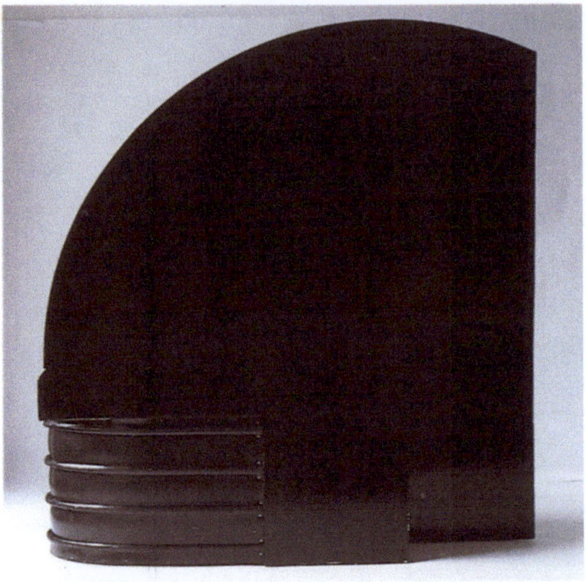

Plate 1

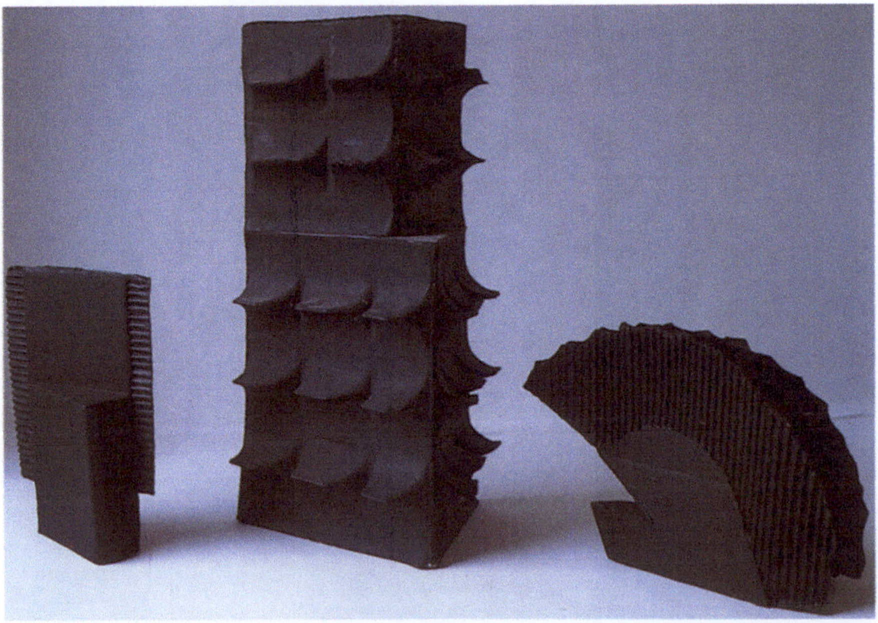

Plate 2

Plates 1 and 2. "Sculptures" by William Latham. Made of wood and plastic. Three-dimensional design for sculptures produced using Form Synth.

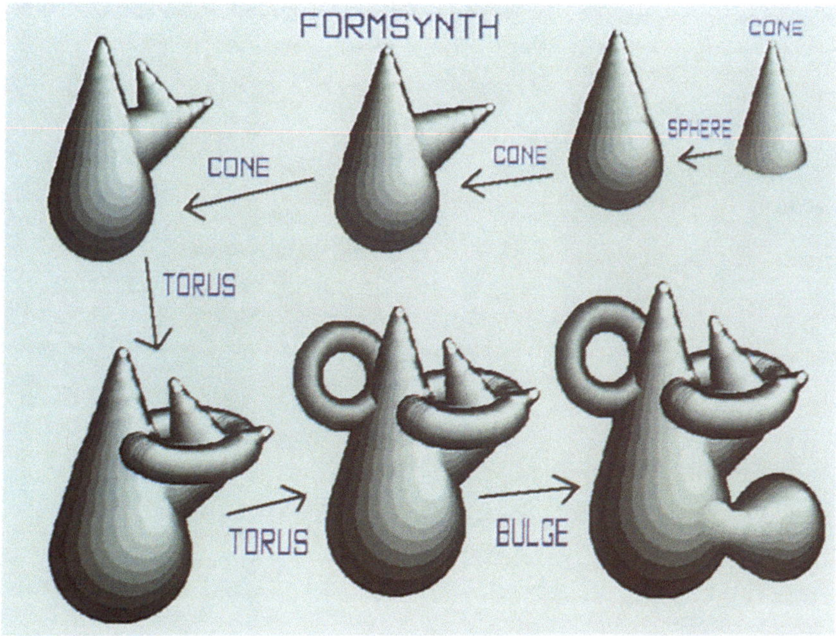

PLATE 3

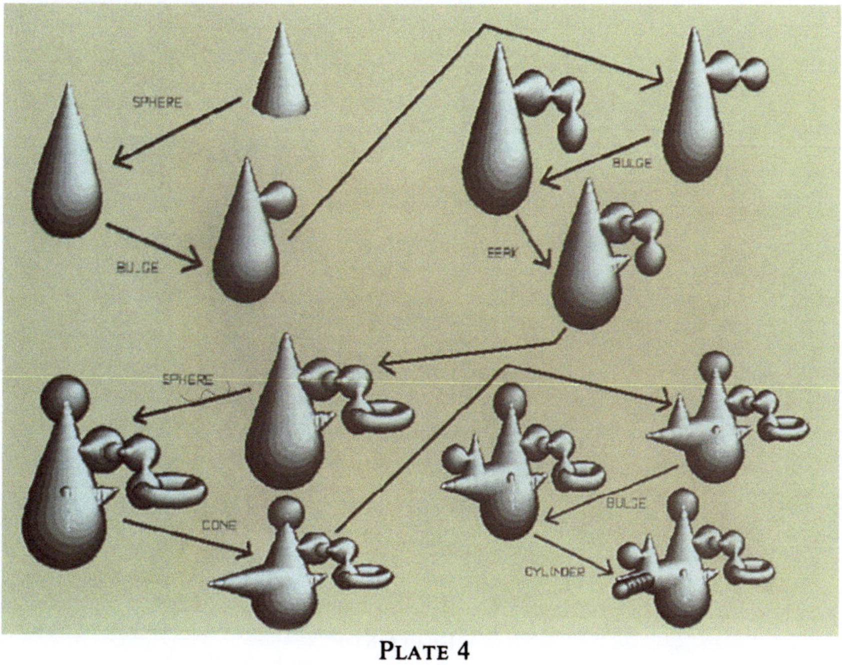

PLATE 4

PLATES 3 AND 4. Evolution of sculptures. Form Synth, simulated by manually imposing rules on the Sculptor program by Mike King.

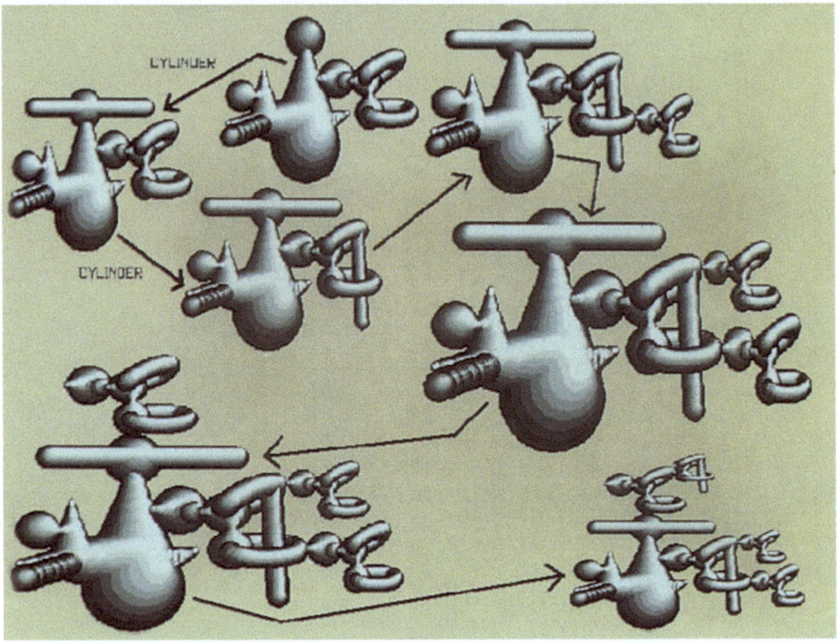

PLATE 5

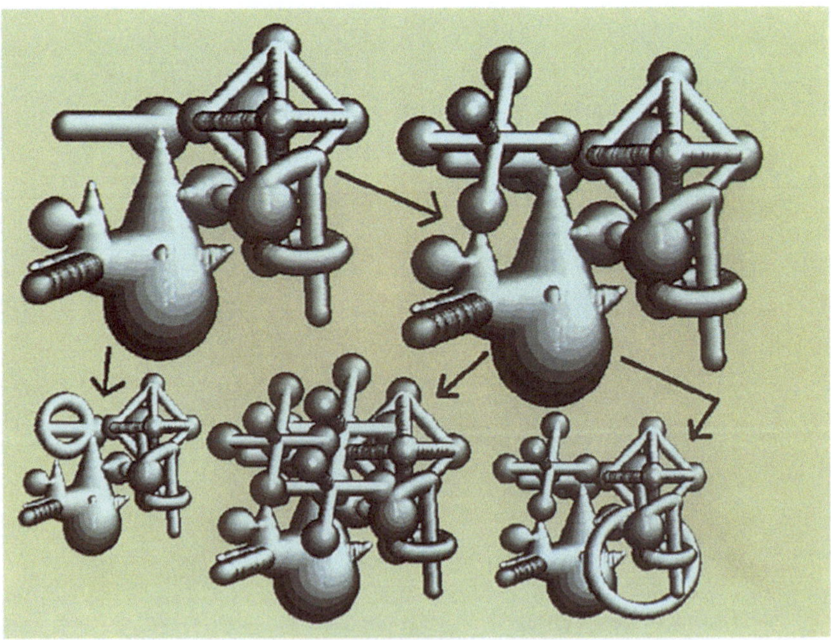

PLATE 6

PLATES 5 AND 6. Evolution of sculptures. Form Synth, simulated by manually imposing rules on the Sculptor program by Mike King.

of the tree unexplored. These form maps are in many ways similar to maps of the "Old World" with large tracts of unexplored territory. Likewise, the artist can use the map as a way of plotting a course to forms he finds interesting. (See Figs. 11 and 12.)

The system has two major advantages:

1. It allows a rule-based description of any evolved forms in that the particular form can be defined as a list of the rules chosen by the user to make it (see Fig. 10).
2. The possible number of different rule combinations is almost infinite; therefore the artist would never run out of new forms to discover and as a result would not feel creatively restricted.

An Evolutionary Tree of Synthetic Forms

The design of Form Synth as an evolutionary tree has further implications. The productivity of some artists is comparable in output to nature's productivity; for example, in the natural world there are 20,000 species of orchids. Orchids come in all shapes and sizes and have descriptive names such as Swan Orchid or Little Bull Orchid. In comparison, in the world of art there are thousands of different art works by Picasso and, like orchids they come in all shapes and sizes, Picasso's oeuvre contains many thousands of paintings, sculptures, drawings, prints and ceramics. All this work stems from one man, Picasso. One of the peculiarities of Form Synth is that it encourages the user to be creative on a comparable scale in that the artist is forced, as a result of obeying the rules of the art style, to keep selecting forms from an ever widening evolutionary tree of complex forms. This works in the following way: as the artist works down through the tree, a gradually increasing number of possible directions he could follow present themselves, that is, each time he makes a choice from the set of operations. As a result of this, the artist never runs out of ideas, as he is never short of tempting avenues to travel down. Without his realising it, the artist's creative output rises as he never runs out of new forms to discover. Form Synth could be seen as way of improving an artist's creativity.

What is beginning to emerge is that Form Synth acts as more than just an inert creative tool in that the artist is being conditioned in what he legally can and cannot do. The inherent rules in Form Synth set up limits within which the artist must work in the same way that the physical laws of climate, geology and chemistry control the limits of evolution in the natural world. However, this limitation strangely may well be to the artist's advantage in that by limiting the rules the artist may use, it makes it easier for the artist to arrive at interesting forms, as this reduces the number of dead-end leads he could follow. These restrictions are similar to the restrictions imposed by the framework of rules for an art style.

In response to this, it could be argued that the system over-constricts the artist in that there would be certain forms which the artist would never be able legally to invent or that the number of rules necessary to do it would be impractical. This is a fair argument, though it can be answered in three ways:

1. The number of various forms which the system is capable of evolving is almost infinite and it is likely that the artist would be able to find amongst this vast number forms of equal interest.
2. The intention of the system is to be a new art style; as already stated, this means a new method to invent new 3-D forms, not a draughting method to reconstruct previously invented forms.
3. In terms of existing art styles through history there has been a varying demand for certain types of forms; for example, Michelangelo had no demand for the totem pole-like forms used by Brancusi. Likewise, in architecture the ancient Greek architects did not make temples in the shape of Anglo-Saxon churches. Similarly, in the twentieth century artists will without realising it have no demand for certain types of forms.

It is important, however, that the system allows the user to invent a variety of forms.

Rules for Form Synth

General description: Form Synth works by the multiple use of inbuilt commands. These commands define physical operations which, when carried out on a geometric form, will change its shape. As a result of the successive use of these commands, the geometric form becomes increasingly complex.

Flow diagrams:

1. Form Synth broken down into three simple units (Fig. 13).
2. Form Synth expanded flow diagram (Fig. 14).

How the system works:

1. Start. The user starts the program with no clear idea about what forms he wishes to produce. This is in contrast to existing CAD systems, where the user has to have a fairly clear idea.
2. Choose form program. The artist proceeds to select a primitive to be evolved. The user may select either a geometric form or a complex form. The geometric primitives are sphere, cube, cone, torus and tetrahedron. A complex form is a form which has previously been evolved using Form Synth.
3. Location points on forms.
   a. Surface points. Each geometric primitive is mapped by a set number

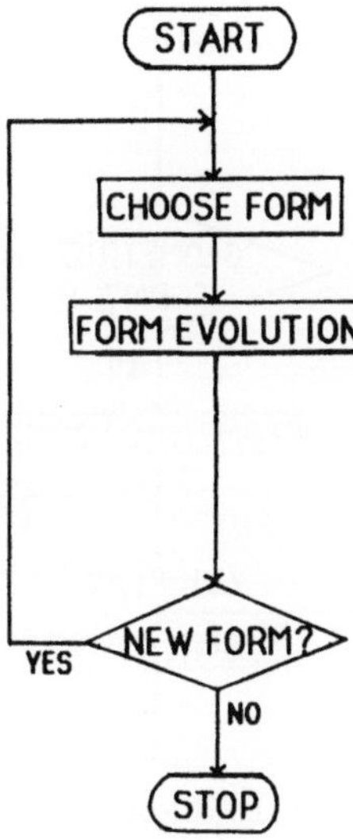

FIGURE 13

of surface points. (See cross symbols on geometric primitives in Fig. 15). The number of surface points varies depending on the complexity of the form; for example, the torus has 64 surface points (see Fig. 16). These surface points define legal points at which other forms can be stuck, inserted or removed or where the manipulation commands beak, bulge, scoop can be carried out (see Fig. 17). All other points on the form's surface are illegal. *Example*: By using operation commands and location points on forms it is possible to start to make rule-based complex forms (see Fig. 18).

b. Internal points. Each geometric primitive has a set number of internal points; see the dot circle symbols on geometric primitives in Figs. 15 and 16. These points are used to carry out the construct commands "insert," "union," "remove" and "negative." Internal points are also used to carry out stretch and slice commands. *Note:* The number of surface points and internal points of an evolving form will increase and decrease through time depending on what sequence of operations the form is being subjected to. The number of location and internal points will vary from form to form, but in general the more complex the form the larger the number of location points and internal points.

4. Evolution program. The user chooses between using a construct command or a manipulate command. The operation commands are grouped in two categories: Construct to do boolean operations such as add cube and manipulate for manipulation operations such as twist, beak.

a. Construct commands. The user first selects a complex form or a geometric form (which is going to be added to or subtracted from the

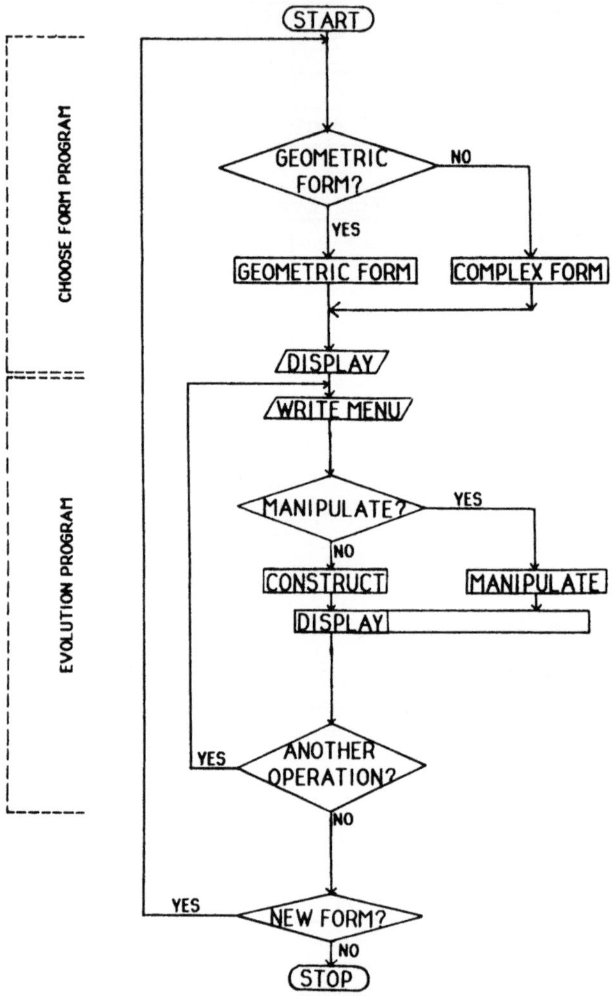

FIGURE 14

current form being evolved). Having chosen the form, the user decides whether to add it or subtract it. *Add:* The add command is subdivided into three operation commands; these are stick, union and insert (see Figs. 19 and 20). The stick command enables the user to stick the chosen form to the surface of the current form by choosing a surface point on each of the forms. The union command allows the adding of two forms together at one of their internal points in each form. The insert command allows the chosen form to be inserted into the surface of the current form so that the chosen form's internal point coincides with a surface point on the current form. *Subtract*: The subtract command is subdivided into two operation commands; these are negative and remove (see Fig. 21). The negative command allows the subtraction

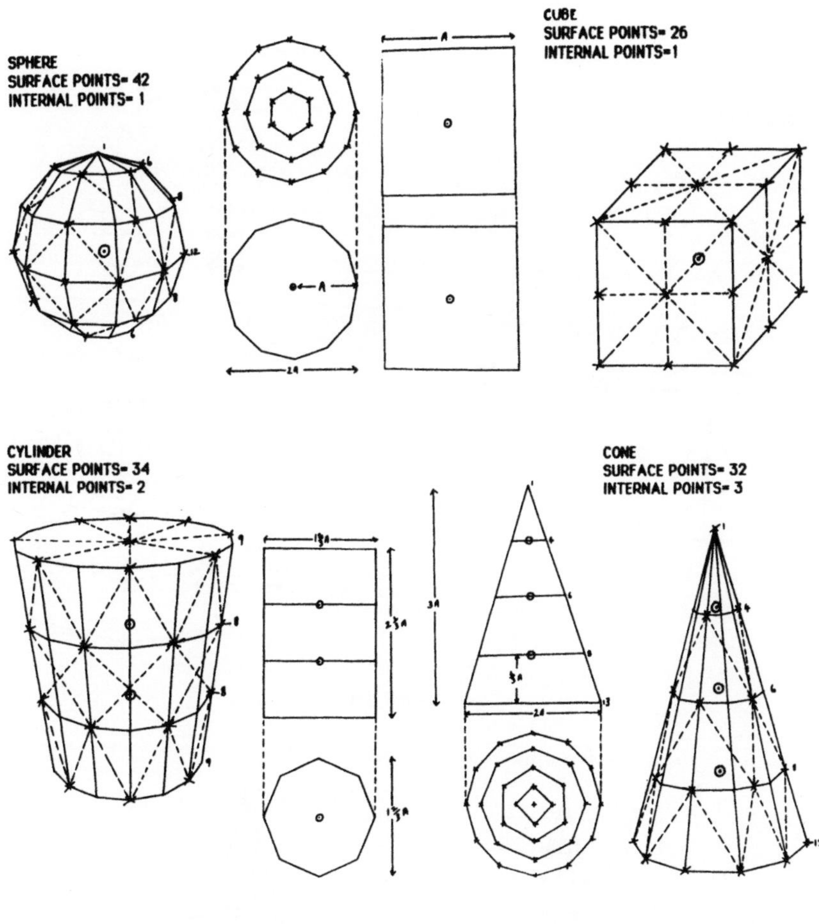

FIGURE 15

of the chosen form from the current form at one of their internal points. The remove command allows the subtraction of the chosen form from the surface of the current form so that one of the chosen form's internal points coincides with a surface point on the current form.

b. Manipulate commands: beak, slice, scoop, stretch and bulge (see Fig. 22). The commands beak, scoop and bulge require a user-chosen surface point on the evolving form (see Fig. 18). The slice and stretch commands each require a user-chosen internal point (see Fig. 23). The stretch command assumes three predetermined axes through the form, the *x, y, z* axes, along one of which the user may decide to stretch the form. The slice command assumes three predetermined axes centered on the internal point the user has chosen, *x, y, z*; the user may then decide along which axes he wishes to cut the form. The system is now ready for computer graphics implementation.

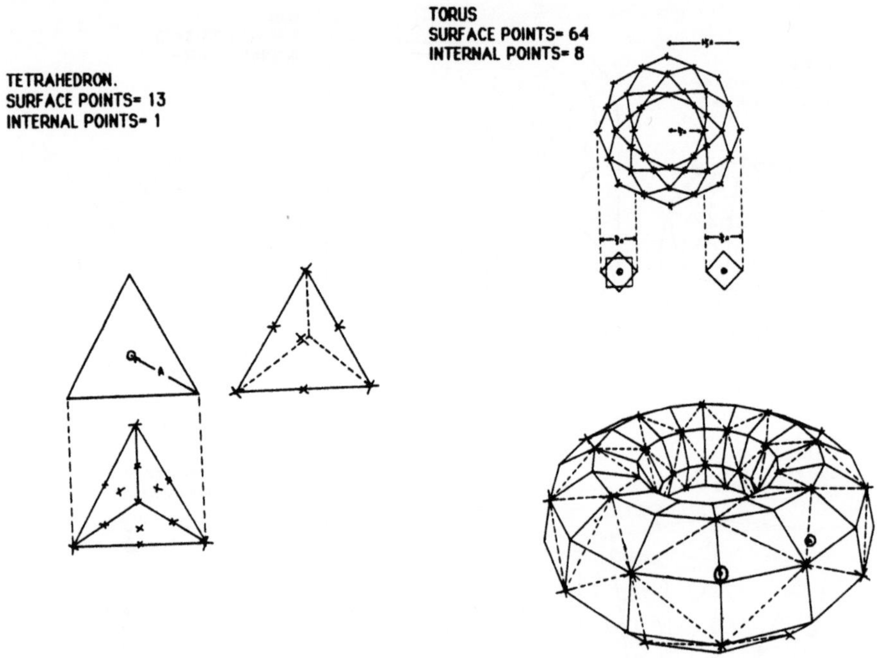

FIGURE 16

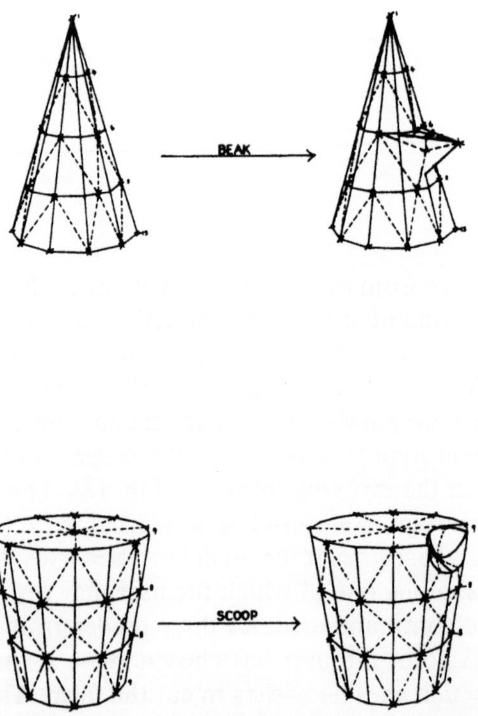

FIGURE 17

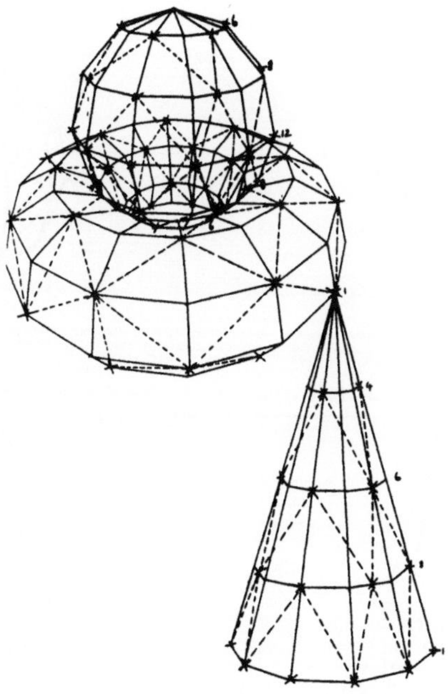

FIGURE 18

Foreseeable Developments

Even at this early stage it is possible to foresee the system's long-term implications in terms of the computer.

Taxonomy of Forms

Form Synth is an ideal test-bed for problems in taxonomical classification. In the conventional classification of natural forms, many factors have to be taken into account: "phenetic," e.g., number of arms and legs, and "cladistic," i.e., based on common lines of descent. The arguments are complicated and a given specimen will rarely fit into any category of classification easily. There is no rule-of-thumb method for locating specimens accurately. Form Synth's rule-generated forms are ideal guinea-pigs for testing rules of classification. The imaginary animals of Sokal (1966) are of direct relevance to this concept. Recent research by Richard Dawkins (1986) into biological adaption, genes and cumulative selection is also of interest to this field.

An area of further interest is the shape grammars discussed by Stiny (1980). Shape grammars can be used to describe the way geometric forms can be joined. Research work has involved the classification of architectural styles in terms of shape grammars, for example, Palladian architecture and styles of Chinese lattice work.

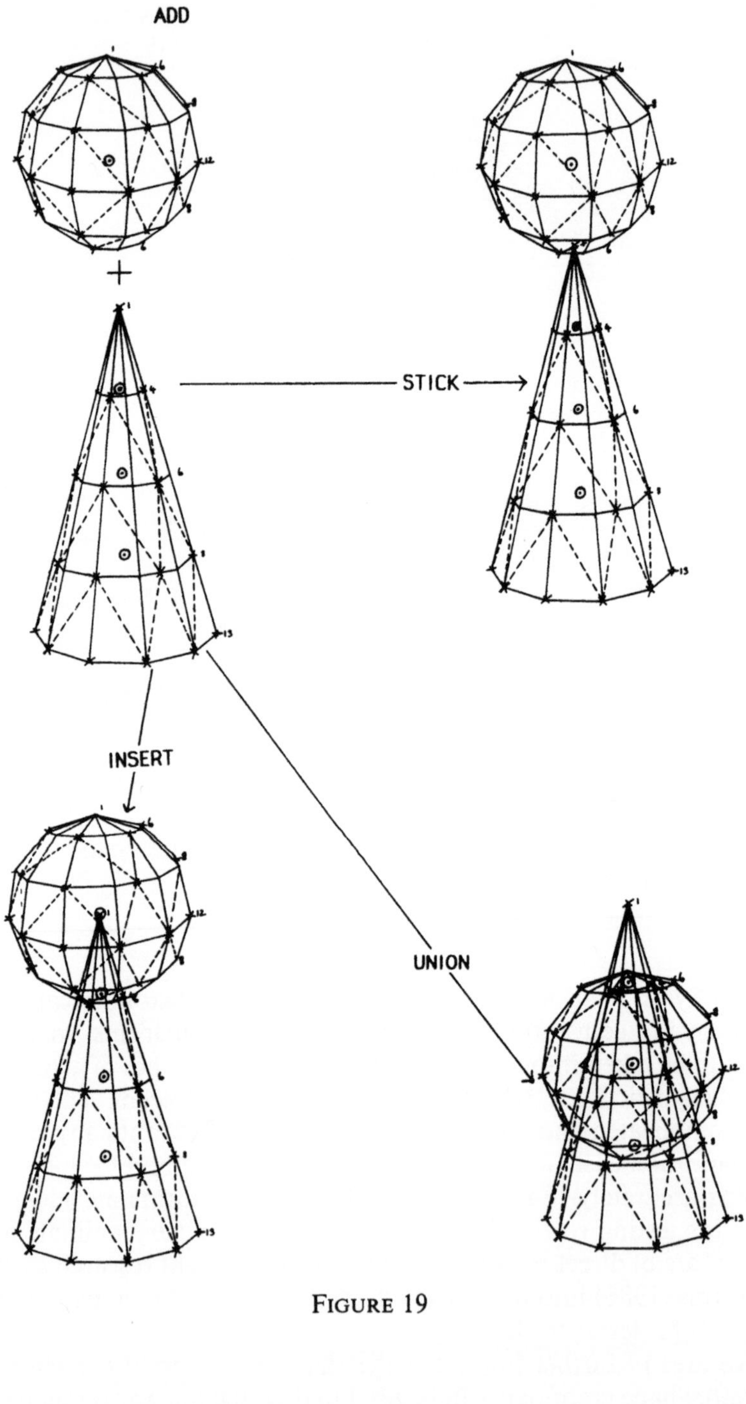

FIGURE 19

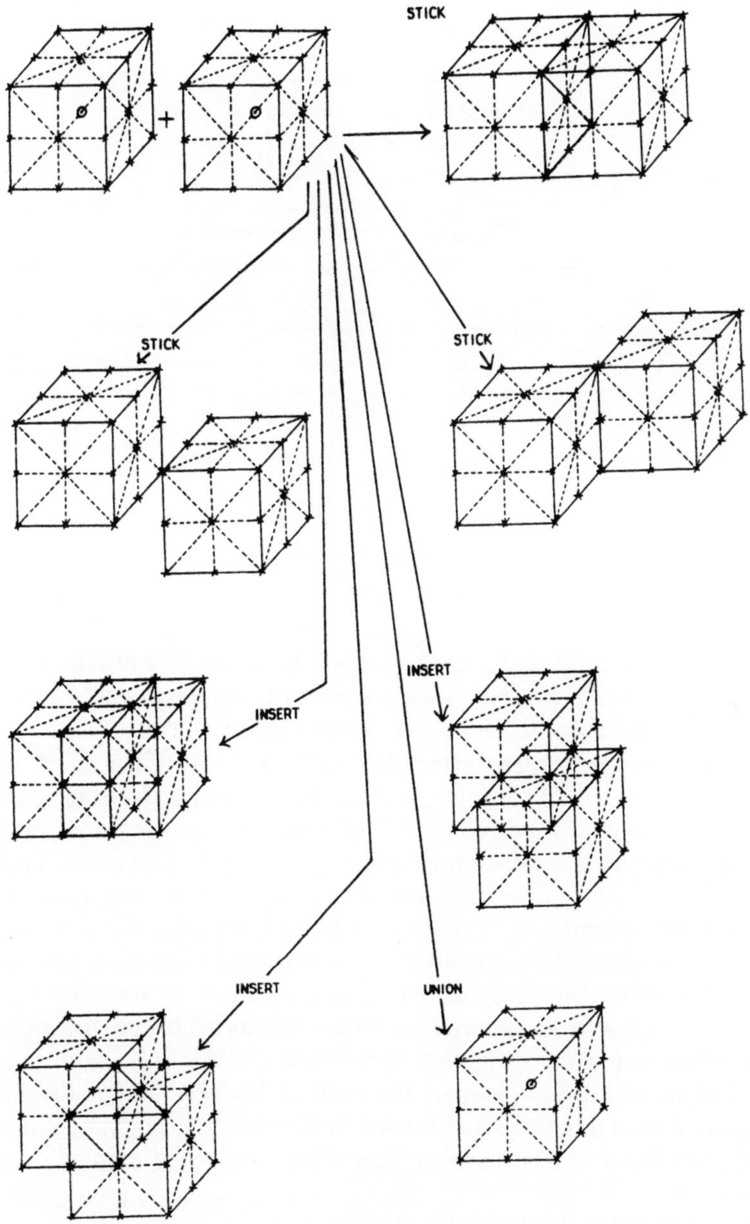

FIGURE 20

Applications of Form Synth in Design

Does Form Synth have applications in product design? The answer is yes; on a simple level the system could be used by a product designer for brainstorming in 3-D. These ideas are more than just speculation; as proved by the results of hand-drawn rule testing, the system can be used

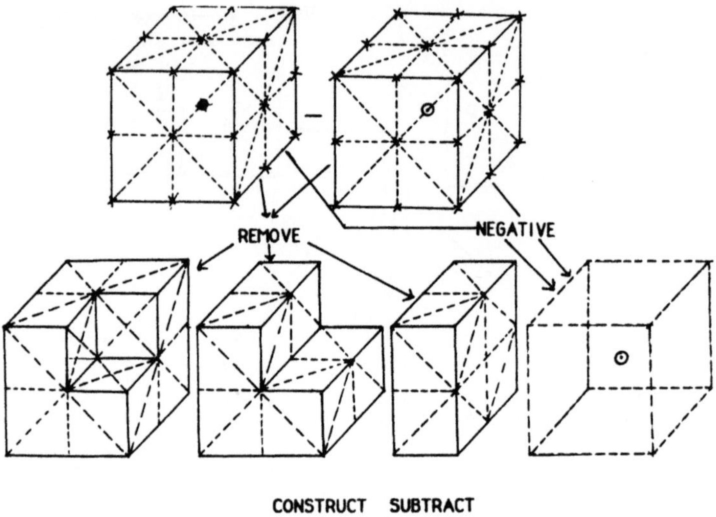

FIGURE 21

to invent a very large and varied number of forms. The argument is that the system which at present is used to invent sculptures could be altered by changing the rules to be used to invent design forms.

To make sculptures, the artist does not have to fulfill a brief; he can produce whatever 3-D form he chooses. In the world of design, generally the designer works directly from a brief to solve a functional problem, and there may be several solutions to the problem but he has to find only one of them. The typical brief will give a reasonably clear idea of what type of form is required. A designer who designs sofas has a fairly good idea of what type of design form he is expected to invent: sofa-shaped forms. Therefore the designer has severe restrictions on what types of forms he is allowed to experiment with—he has a limited vocabulary of form; for example, car designers spend their careers only inventing "car-like" forms. However, through the eyes of history, design forms have metamorphosed or changed over time; in the example given by Lansdown (1986), the horse-drawn carriage has metamorphosed into the car. Although this transformation has taken a hundred years, the design form has changed radically. Victorian design changed into art nouveau; using present design methods design forms evolve but can take hundreds of years. In Form Synth this type of evolution of a form is fast and could occur on the computer screen rather than in the real world. The user has the added option of being able to go back in time to evolve an earlier version of a form. I am not suggesting that the system could be used for designing cars but simply stating that the system can be used to evolve forms, as opposed to the "one-off" approach offered by other methods. This evolutionary approach appears to relate to the overview of what

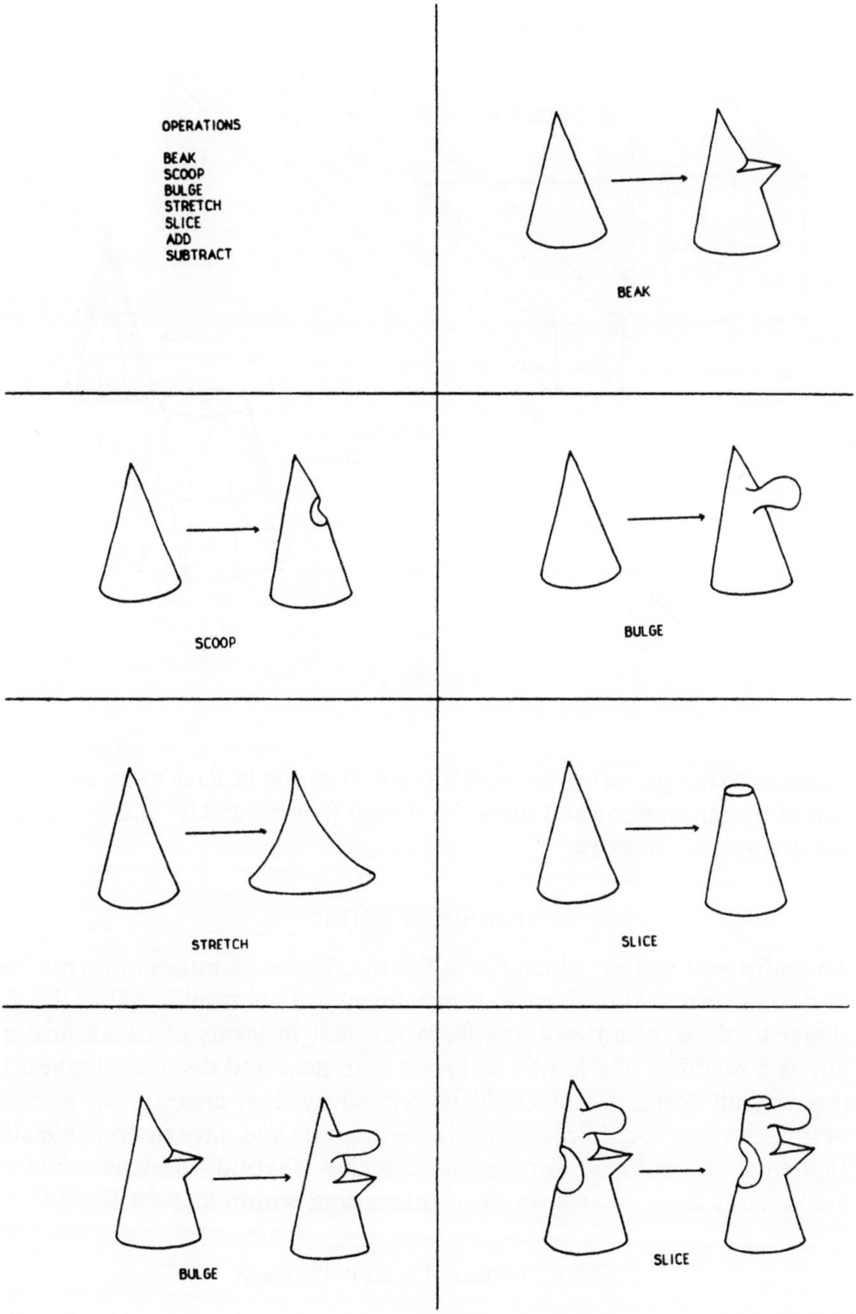
OPERATIONS
BEAK
SCOOP
BULGE
STRETCH
SLICE
ADD
SUBTRACT
BEAK
SCOOP
BULGE
STRETCH
SLICE
BULGE
SLICE

FIGURE 22

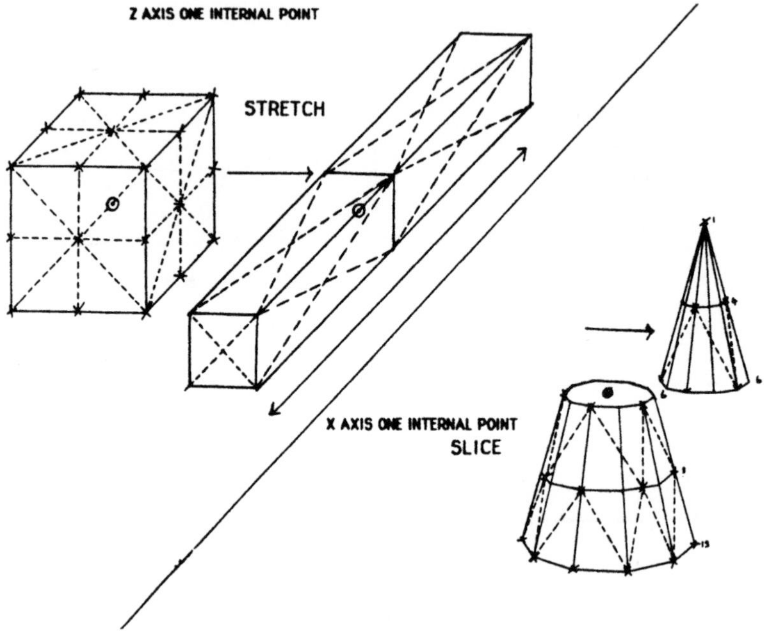

FIGURE 23

happens to design forms through history. It would be easy to try out more varied design options and arrive at design forms quickly, and as a result designs would improve.

Family of Forms

An additional feature which Form Synth offers is "families of forms" or, in design terms, "families of design forms." This would enable the designer to think of an evolving form not just in terms of its life-history but as a member of a family of forms with near and distant relatives. In this way all design forms could be related by their ancestry; as a result of this, designs could become more compatible and have interchangeable elements. It would be foreseeable also that "hybrid" designs could be deliberately evolved as a result of inbreeding within a given family.

The Human Design Process

A major facility which the system allows and which was mentioned earlier is the option of being able to analyse the cognitive process used by the artist/designer whilst designing, as revealed by the form lists (see Fig. 10). The facility will allow positive analysis of a successful sculpture invented using the system, and this could lead to greater understanding of what it is that makes one form good and another bad. Form Synth allows analysis and reconstruction of the choices made by the artist over a period of time, unlike other art styles, where the viewer has only an impenetrable finished painting or sculpture to look at. Form Synth reveals the artist's mind during the process of designing. This will allow the user not only to repeat the steps exactly to recreate a good art form but also to make alterations to it and develop the sculpture further at a later date.

Artificially Intelligent Artist?

There are two different methods for evolving complex forms:

1. Artist-made rule selections.
2. Algorithmic rule selection by computer program.

Millions of different types of forms could be evolved using these different rule selection methods. At present the system relies on the divine inspiration of the artist to get any art forms out of it. It was Picasso's divine inspiration which enabled him to make so many good art works. The amount of divine inspiration an artist will have will vary from artist to artist. In Form Synth the divine inspiration is input into the computer by the artist constantly making good rule selections. The idea of divine inspiration and computing is dealt with in Lansdown (1984). So what does the artist have which enables him to invent interesting forms by simply choosing rules? On the surface, the sequence of choices the artist makes appears random, and yet the forms do not appear random; the artist therefore must be employing a highly complex rule selection procedure at the operation selection stage. If this is the case, it would seem foreseeable that a program could be written to enable the computer to algorithmically choose rules for itself and have no need of the artist. This is a complex idea, but essentially what it means is that program will attempt to simulate the rule selection procedure used by the artist. Form Synth allows a common ground where rule selections can be made by the computer program or by the artist. The program implementing algorithmic selection could foreseeably be of two types:

1. The program could imitate an existing artist's method by using a set of defined operation rule sequences already used by the artist on certain forms in the hope that this sequence would work when applied to different forms.
2. The program could imitate the larger patterns of cumulative rule selections used by the artist and insert different rules into the patterns.

This raises an interesting question: will the algorithmic rule selection procedure be better than the artist at inventing complex forms? Up to this point it has been assumed that the artist will evolve the more interesting forms. I believe we may find that a very simple algorithmic rule selection program may evolve more interesting forms than the human.

Then can the computer gain divine inspiration? The answer is probably not. The artist's mind appears too idiosyncratic to be copied by such a primitive program, but what is interesting is that even if these methods fail, the forms that would be evolved using these rule selection procedures would be of great interest as they enable another part of the tree to be explored. These forms could define a new set of forms like 3-D fractals, cars or children's toys.

Acknowledgments. Early work on this project started in the Printmaking Department at the Royal College of Art. Recent discussion with Keith Critchlow has been of great benefit. I am grateful to Paul Brown at Middlesex Polytechnic and Gillian Crampton-Smith at St. Martins School of Art for access to computer graphics equipment. Cubicomp images were produced at Southwark College, London. Thanks to Mike King for advice and use of Sculptor software. I am especially grateful to John Lansdown for constant support and guidance.

References

Cundy, M. (1960) *Mathematical Models.* Clarendon Press, Oxford.

Dawkins, R. (1986) *The Blind Watchmaker.* Longman Scientific and Technical.

King, M. (1986) "Towards an Integrated Computer Art System," *Proc. Conference "The State of the Art in Computer Art and Animation,"* The British Computer Society Displays Group, Royal College of Art, London.

Lansdown, J. (1984) "Computing in the Creative Professions," System Simulation and Department of Design Research, Royal College of Art.

Lansdown, J. (1986) "Computer Graphics in Design," System Simulation Ltd. UK for International Summer Institute "State of the Art in Computer Graphics," Techniques and Applications.

Pipes, A. (1986) "The Big Build Up," *CAD International.* 5(10), October.

Sokal, R.R. (1966) "Numerical Taxonomy," *Scientific American,* December, pp. 106–117.

Stiny, G. (1980) "Kindergaten Grammars: Designing with Froebel's Building Gifts," Centre for Configurational Studies, The Open University, Milton Keynes, UK, *Environment and Planning B* 7:409–462.

Sylvester, D. (1978) "Henry Moore at the Serpentine," Arts Council of Great Britain.

Wright, F.L. (1943) *An Autobiography.* New York.

Graphic Potential of Recursive Functions

Barry Martin

Iteration as a Source of Patterns

I first became interested in the curious graphical structures that can be generated when iteration is applied to relatively simple mathematical forms after reading a paper by Hénon (1983). The "mapping" introduced in his paper is now the best known and most intensively studied non-linear, two-dimensional transformation of the plane into itself. Its particular fascination lies in the fact that it is as simple as possible, involving no more than a single quadratic term, yet it is believed to possess a *strange attractor*—an exotic infinite point set into which successive iterates are drawn. (To my knowledge it has not yet been proved conclusively that a strange attractor is really present, although a vast quantity of experimental evidence supports the contention.)

The features associated with these very complicated behaviours can also appear in one-dimensional maps of a line interval into itself. The study of these one-dimensional maps by Metropolis, Stein and Stein (1973) and by Feigenbaum (1983) has led to some striking theoretical results of a universal nature. They have discovered properties which apply to a wide class of maps irrespective of the exact nature of the particular mathematical functions employed. Their work looks destined to have a profound influence on a number of branches of science, but for applications to art, design and computer graphics the two- and higher-dimensional mappings are clearly of greater interest.

Iteration in One Dimension

To introduce the notions of iteration and chaos which lie behind the creation of these patterns, we will discuss the behaviour of a particular one—dimensional mapping of the unit interval to itself. This will help us, by analogy, to understand in an intuitive fashion some of the complicated behaviour observed in two and higher dimensions. My discussion of this one-dimensional situation is taken entirely from papers in the book edited by Cvitrovic (1984).

Consider the trivial quadratic equation

$$4\beta x^2 - (4\beta - 1)x = 0$$

in which β is a parameter confined to the range $0 < \beta < 1$. This equation has roots $x_0 = 0$ and $x_1 = 1 - 1/(4\beta)$.

Suppose now we were to try and discover these roots not by an explicit formula but by first guessing a value, $x^{(0)}$ say, and then refining it by the introduction of an iterative scheme. To do this we first rewrite the equation as $x = 4\beta x(1 - x)$ and then convert this form to an iterative scheme by introducing superscripts to label the successive iterates:

$$x^{(n+1)} = 4\beta x^{(n)} (1 - x^{(n)}).$$

This can be regarded as a mapping of the point with coordinate $x^{(n)}$ to the point with coordinate $x^{(n+1)}$. It is important to note that whenever $x^{(n)}$ is in the interval (0, 1) $x^{(n+1)}$ is also in this interval. Thus if $x^{(0)}$ is in (0, 1) then so are all subsequent iterates.

The two roots are called *fixed points* of the mapping. This scheme behaves very differently for different ranges of β. We shall look in some detail at each of these ranges by constructing a graphical representation. For convenience we will denote the function $4\beta x(1 - x)$ by $f(x)$.

The "staircase" in Fig. 1 shows the course of a particular iteration starting with $x^{(0)}$ slightly greater than 0.5. Convergence to the root $x =$

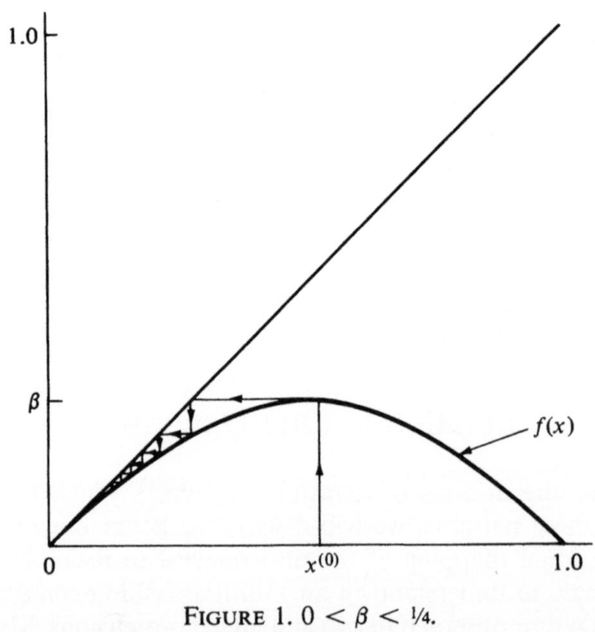

FIGURE 1. $0 < \beta < 1/4$.

0 is clearly demonstrated. This convergence to the root at the origin is independent of the initial guess (a few sketches with different starting values in the interval (0, 1) will soon convince the reader of this). The underlying reason for this behaviour is to be found in the gradient (value of the derivative) of $f(x)$ at $x = 0$. So long as the value of this gradient lies between -1 and $+1$ the root at $x = 0$ constitutes a "stable" fixed point. *This is always so for* $0 < \beta < 1/4$.

Now consider the range $1/4 < \beta < 3/4$. For any starting value the iterates are found to converge to the root at $x_1 = 1 - 1/(4\beta)$ (Fig. 2). This happens because the root at $x = 0$ has become an "unstable" fixed point. The gradient at x_0 is now greater than one, while the gradient at $x_1 = 1 - 1/(4\beta)$ is given by $2 - 4\beta$, which in the stated β range always lies between -1 and $+1$ and therefore gives rise to a stable fixed point.

Interesting things begin to happen as β passes through $3/4$. We observe that the gradients at both fixed points have absolute value greater than one. That is, both become unstable and so cannot "attract" the iterates. However, we also know that the iterates must remain in the interval (0, 1). So where can they go? The fascinating resolution of this puzzle depends on the behaviour of the iterated (fourth degree) function $f(f(x)) = f^{(2)}$. As x_1 "dies"— that is, becomes unstable — so *two* new stable fixed points of the mapping $x = f^{(2)}(x)$ are born. Let these two values be denoted by x_2 and x_3. Note that they are *not* fixed points of $x = f(x)$. (See Figs. 3 and 4.)

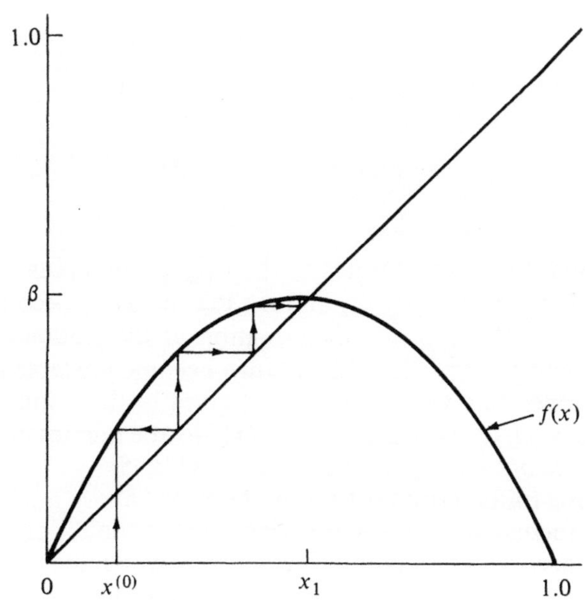

FIGURE 2. $1/4 < \beta < 3/4$.

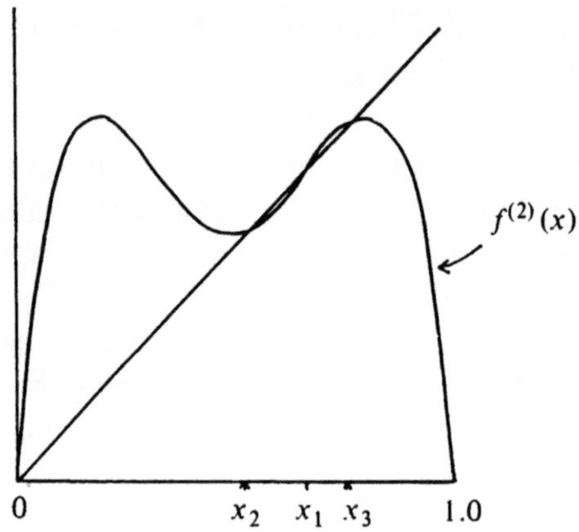

FIGURE 3. The fixed points of $f^{(2)}$.

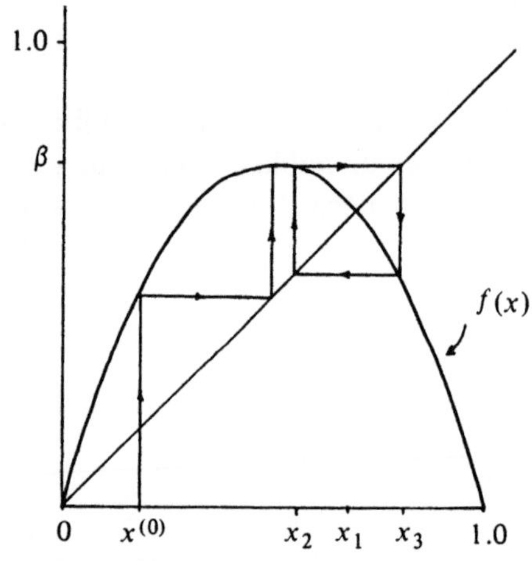

FIGURE 4. $3/4 < \beta < 0.86$.

Once settled down, the iterates in the original mapping are now seen to alternate between the pair x_2 and x_3; that is, as x_1 becomes unstable a *cycle of period two* appears. Examination of the gradients of $x = f^{(2)}(x)$ at these points shows that they in turn become unstable at $\beta = 0.86$. When β assumes this value $x = f^{(4)}(x)$ gives birth to four stable fixed points as the two fixed points of $x = f^{(2)}(x)$ die; the iterates now 'converge' towards a *cycle of period four*, x_4, x_5, x_6, x_7 (Fig. 5).

The splitting (bifurcating) behaviour described above now continues as β is further increased. The cycle period goes on doubling until at $\beta = 0.91\ldots$ an "accumulation point" is reached at which the period becomes infinite. The iterates are now *aperiodic*, a state now commonly called

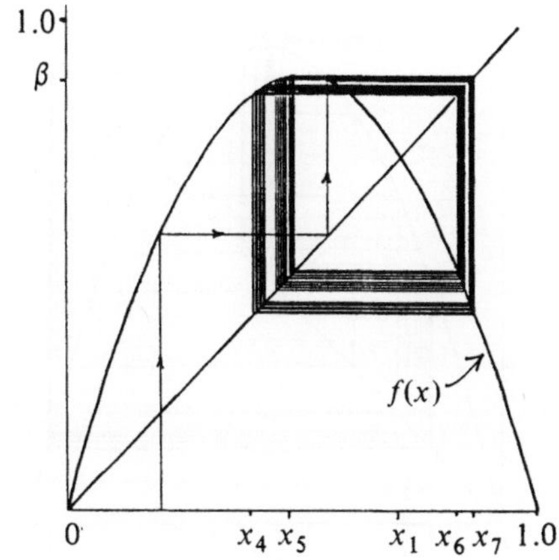

FIGURE 5. Period four.

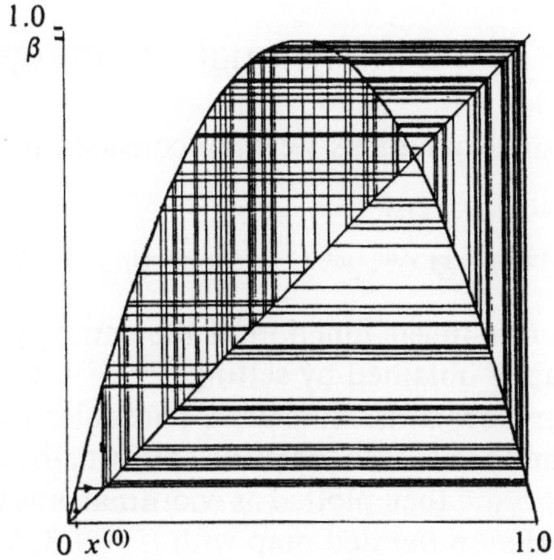

FIGURE 6. Chaos.

chaotic. The iterates will continue forever assuming values between 0 and 1 but can never return to one previously visited (this is analogous to the distribution of digits in the decimal expansion of an irrational number such as π or e). What we have described is called *the period doubling route to chaos* (see Fig. 6). It is not the only mechanism.

As β is further increased up to $\beta = 1$ chaos may alternately cease and reappear a number of times. Thus at $\beta = 0.96$ we observe a cycle of period three (Fig. 7), but on further increasing β chaos again takes over. A fundamental result of the mathematical theory is that the presence of a 3-cycle implies the existence of all other periods and of chaos.

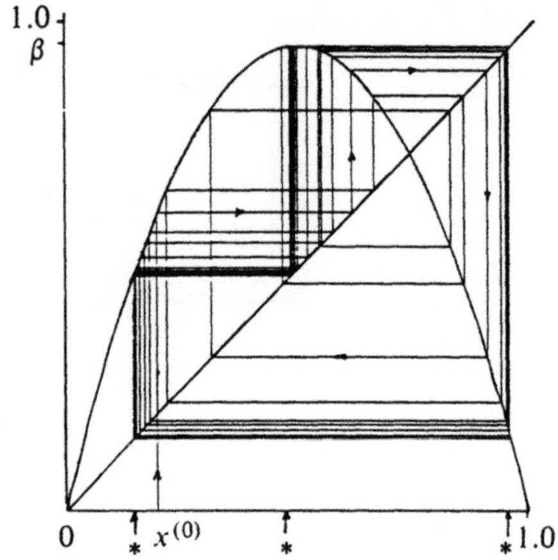

FIGURE 7. Period three.

Two-Dimensional Mappings

The two-dimensional mappings we shall consider are of the form

$$x^{(n+1)} = f(x^{(n)}, y^{(n)})$$
$$y^{(n+1)} = g(x^{(n)}, y^{(n)}), \qquad n = 0, 1, 1, 2, \ldots$$

where $f(x, y)$ is a non-linear function of the pair x, y.

The Hénon map is obtained by setting $f = 1 + y - ax^2$ and $g = bx$, where a and b are constants. To start a particular run we must choose values of a and b and then "seed the plane" by initialising the pair $(x^{(0)}, y^{(0)})$. Successive x, y pairs are then plotted as coordinates as they are calculated.

The form of a Hénon iterated map with $a = 1.3$, $b = 0.4$ is shown in Fig. 10. Note the structure: this "line splitting" persists no matter how high the magnification. The case with $a = 1.4$, $b = 0.3$ was studied extensively by Hénon (1976) and is believed to give rise to a strange attractor. The continual line splitting produces a structure known as a Cantor set. A full mathematical understanding of this mapping is difficult and has not yet been achieved.

My own empirical explorations in this field have been concerned with perturbing the Hénon mapping and noting how the introduction of new terms and mathematical functions affects the pictures produced. However, this has led me far afield and I am now looking at very different pairs of equations. This process of suck it and see—90% serendipity and 10% science—has proved quite efficacious and I think you will agree has led to some quite interesting pictures. Detailed descriptions of some of these new maps follow but for the moment let me make some general observations.

The patterns tend to develop in intermittent bursts of activity. Successive points may remain in the same region of the plane, perhaps a fuzzy annular zone, or a discrete set of "circles" for many iterations and then suddenly "colonise" a fresh region or return to fill out territory visited some thousands or millions of steps earlier. The one-dimensional analogy helps us to see how this can happen. Consider the situation in which a function, analogous to $f(x)$ above, comes very close to the 45° straight line. That is, it is almost tangent to it over a considerable distance but eventually veers away without actually touching the line. Iterates computed according to $x^{(n+1)} = f(x^{(n)})$ would be misled into "believing" they were approaching a fixed point; however, after a long approach they would pass the point of closest proximity and slowly begin to separate (Fig. 8). The iterates would then go off in search of another fixed point or cycle of points in some other region.

Short runs can scatter points over the screen and lead to the impression that successive iterates are appearing at random, but extended computation clearly demonstrates that this is not the case. Equations such as these have in the past been used by statisticians as random number generators. We are thus brought face to face with the problem of distinguishing between that which is genuinely random and that which is deterministic but very, very complicated.

For some parameter ranges the result after a few iterations can be an isolated point; that is, the process converges to a fixed point which is a solution of the *simultaneous equations*

$$x = f(x, y), \qquad y = g(x, y).$$

For other parameter ranges the iterates ultimately settle into a pattern in which a *finite set* of N points are continually visited in turn (a periodic attractor with a cycle of period N; see for example Fig. 14).

However, as illustrated in the one-dimensional case, it is also possible, and apparently not uncommon, for the sequence of iterates to go on

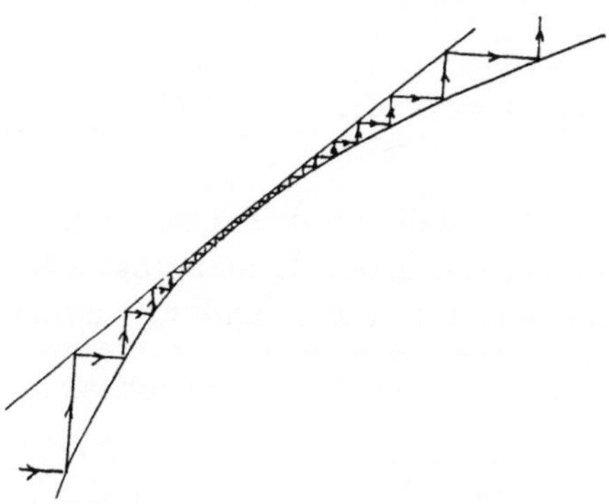

FIGURE 8. A close approach.

forever without repetition and thus without converging to a *finite* periodic attractor. These sequences may diverge to infinity or be contained within a finite region of the plane. This latter behaviour produces many of the most intricate and interesting forms.

The generation of a point set in the so-called chaotic regime is extremely sensitive to the precise values of the initial conditions and to the precision of the computer. Different machines can give widely different results for what is ostensibly the same data! Thus when results are published the machine used as well as the data must be reported.

Scientific Origins

The motivation for the study of these areas has come largely from applied mathematics, in particular from dynamics. Many studies have been in the field of nonlinear differential equations although, as John Lansdown points out elsewhere in this volume, Gumowski and Mira (1980, 1974) were studying iterated mappings in their own right and had computed some forms very similar to those which I am describing here in the early 1970s.

"Chaos" as a respectable subject of scientific interest is now emerging in many areas, the following of which illustrate this observation:

Subject	Example
Fluid flow	Turbulence
Demography	Population dynamics
Biology, medicine	Heart cell dynamics, neurological disorders
Optics	Lasers
Chemistry	Belousov-Zhabotinsky reaction
Electronics	Josephson function
Nuclear physics	Stability in particle accelerators

For further information on these and other applications to science see Chandra (1984).

Differential Equations and Poincaré Maps

Dynamical systems are usually modelled by differential equations and it is instructive to understand how 2-D mappings arise in their study. For concreteness we consider the case of Duffing's equation

$$\ddot{x} + k\dot{x} + x^3 = A\sin(t),$$

which occurs in the theory of damped forced vibrations. We cannot solve these equations analytically, but numerical methods, such as the Runge-Kutta scheme, are quite effective and we may easily generate solutions for differing values of k (the damping constant) and A (the amplitude of the forcing oscillation) and initial conditions on $\dot{x}(t)$ and $x(t)$.

The solution may be conveniently visualised as a curve in a three-dimensional space with orthogonal coordinates x, $\dot{x}$ and t. The plane $(x, \dot{x})$ is called the phase plane. By projecting the solution curve onto the phase plane we can, at a glance, discern a great deal about its qualitative behaviour. These projected curves are called trajectories. If after a transient the solution settles to a constant value we will see the trajectories "spiral" in to a single point, while if the solution becomes periodic we will see the trajectory approach a closed loop called a *limit cycle*. (If the period is a multiple of that of the forcing function this loop will intersect itself before closing.)

Chaotic solutions can also arise. When they do so the trajectory will twist and turn within a bounded region of the phase plane but never repeat a previous track—although it may come arbitrarily close to one (Fig. 9).

By plotting points only when t is a multiple of the period of the forcing term (in the above case every 2π) we get a "stroboscopic" picture of the motion known as a Poincaré map. Such a map shows the relation between successive positions $(x^{(n)}, y^{(n)}$, and $(x^{(n+1)}, y^{(n+1)})$ at intervals of 2π in t.

As we have seen, if a solution becomes periodic the trajectory converges to a limit cycle. If the period is 2π the Poincaré map will show convergence to a single point, a limit cycle of period 4π will ultimately consist of just

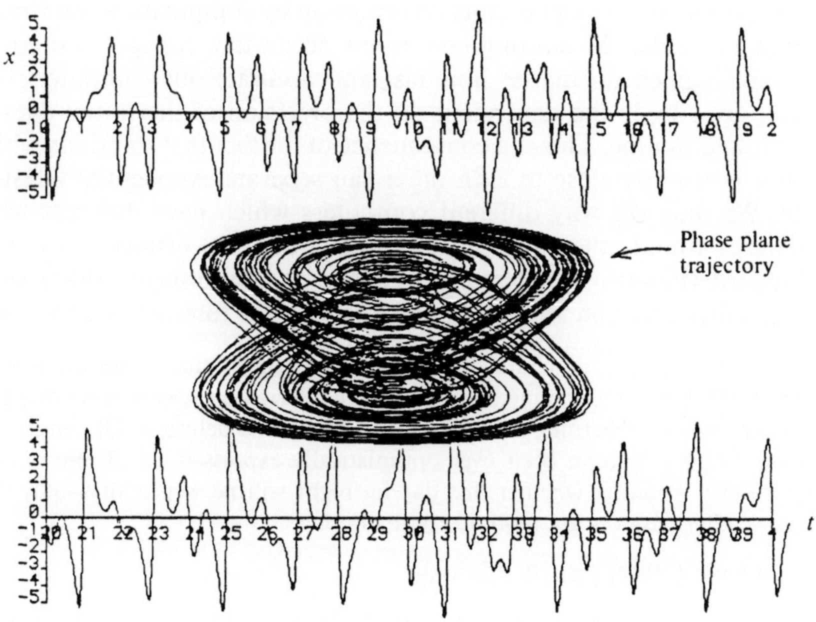

FIGURE 9. Chaotic solution of Duffings' equation.

two points and so on. Thus a periodic solution will give rise to a finite pattern of points on the Poincaré map. When a solution becomes chaotic a fractal pattern emerges composed of infinitely many non-repeating points (Fig. 30). Many pictures like this were given by Ueda (1980). (A transient will be seen as a scattered pattern preceding the structured pattern of the statistically steady long-term evolution.) It is evident that successive points in the Poincaré map must be determined by a *difference equation*, which in theory can be derived from the differential equation but which in practice is far too difficult to obtain analytically for any but a small set of relatively uninteresting cases. The Hénon map was proposed as a *model* for the Poincaré map of a differential equation since it possesses many apposite properties.

One of the surprising findings of modern research on differential equations is that a number of equations which were for a long time thought to be worked out have been found to possess previously unsuspected chaotic regimes. The lesson to be learned, as with the work on the Mandelbrot and Julia sets (Peitgen and Richter, 1986), is that apparently simple rules repeatedly applied can lead to extreme complexity and if results look like random rubbish they should not be automatically thrown away!

Another facet of this behaviour that has profound implications is that in chaotic modes the exact form of a solution becomes extremely sensitive to the initial conditions—so sensitive in fact that even if we are in full possession of the underlying laws governing a non-linear system that is no guarantee that we can predict its evolution by computation; we simply cannot prescribe the starting conditions accurately enough. Moreover, this will happen no matter how fast and accurate our computers: the details are simply too dependent on the precision of the initial data to be followed in time. This is a consequence of the fact that solutions which set out arbitrarily close to each other can separate exponentially fast in time. We thus see why different computers which have different word lengths or round differently can give totally different results.

Pippard (Emeritus Professor of Physics at Cambridge) (1985) summarises this situation with an allusion to weather forecasting as follows:

> It has been the habitual claim of physicists that they could make predictions whose verification underpinned the laws and conferred on science a validity that no other branch of learning could aspire to. Was this a delusion? Of course not, but the claim may have been over optimistically expressed. . . . There is little hope of ever knowing whether this day fortnight will be wet or dry—only that some weather patterns are more likely than others.

Cvitrovic (1984) puts it this way:

> The often repeated statement, that given the initial conditions we know what a deterministic system will do far into the future is false. Poincaré (1892) knew it

was false, and we know it is false, in the following sense: given infinitesimally different starting points, we often end up with wildly different outcomes. Even with the simplest conceivable equations of motion, almost any non-linear system will exhibit chaotic behaviour. A familiar example is turbulence.

As suggested above, at least one great mathematician had foreseen these developments. In 1892 Henri Poincaré had discovered behaviour (homoclinic tangles) in differential equations which he thought might be too complicated ever to be fully understood. G. D. Birkhoff (1932) had discovered a 'remarkable' thick curve (now known as Birkhoff's Bagel) but he could never have seen what it really looked like! However, we have the advantage of high-speed computers and high-resolution graphics enabling us to approximate, simulate and visualise these extraordinary configurations even when we cannot understand them.

Some Curious and Beautiful Maps

Let us now consider a few particular cases which lead to interesting shapes. However, I would stress that a huge range of "elementary" functions containing a parameter or two can be fine-tuned to produce extraordinary forms, and the delights of simply trying out ideas in empirical fashion are endless.

(I) Consider how the *real* iterated mapping

$$\begin{aligned} x^{(n+1)} &= y^{(n)} - \sin(x^{(n)}) \\ y^{(n+1)} &= A - x^{(n)} \\ x^{(0)} &= 0, \qquad y^{(0)} = 0 \end{aligned}$$

can behave when A is close to π.

With $A = \pi$ we simply get a repetition of the four points $(0, 0)$, $(0, \pi)$, (π, π), $(\pi, 0)$, corresponding to a cycle of period four. This fact determines the four-fold near anti-symmetry which persists when A is close to π. However, by perturbing the initial conditions and examining outcomes it seems that this point set constitutes a *repellor* of period four(?); that is, it is unstable and any departure from the set will not be reversible. Nevertheless, the iterates are reluctant to move far away until a bridgehead is established from which they can colonise the rest of the plane until a few hundred iterates have been generated.

With A approximately in the intervals $\pi < A < \pi + 0.07$ and $\pi > A > \pi - 0.07$, and with $x^{(0)} = 0$ and $y^{(0)} = 0$, the iterates form a "thick curve" which partially "tiles" the plane with "axehead"-shaped units. Minute changes in A within these intervals result in distinct evolutions (Fig. 11). Outside this range of A values the iterates seem to be confined to a *single* axehead or to *four* disjoint axeheads (Fig. 12). This is so at least up to half a million iterations.

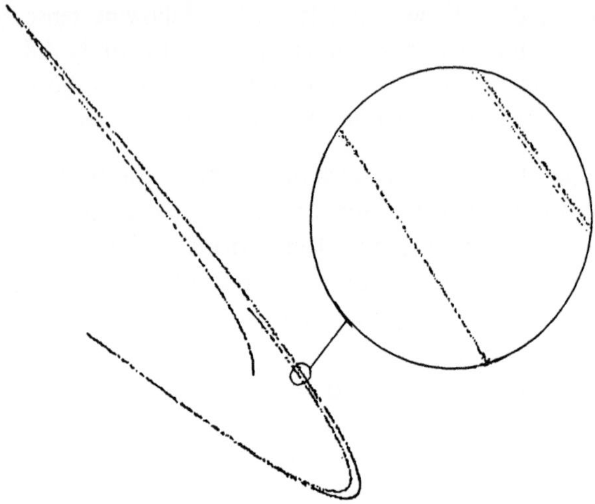

FIGURE 10. $a = 1.2$, $b = 0.3$.

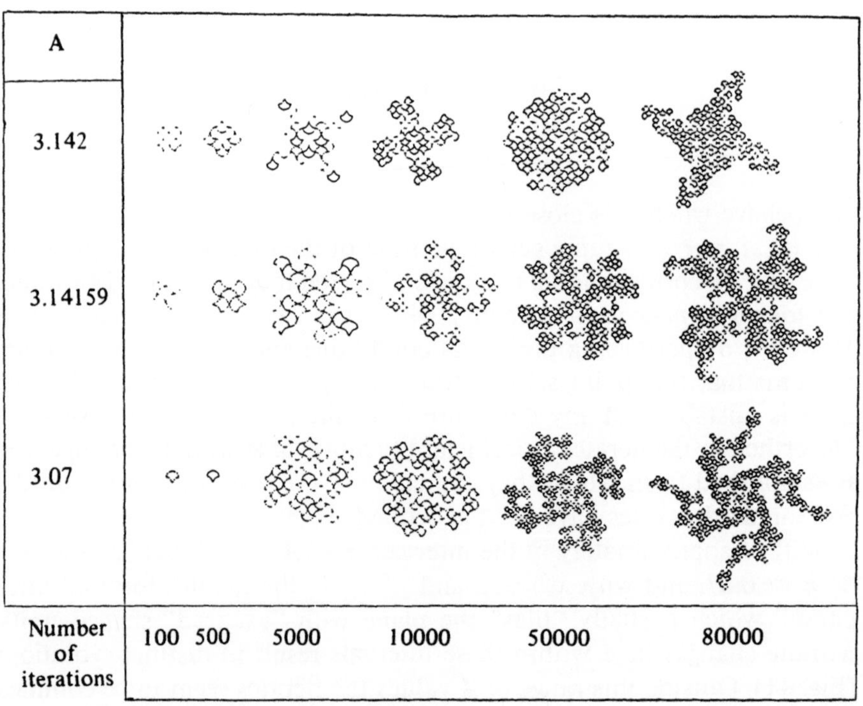

FIGURE 11

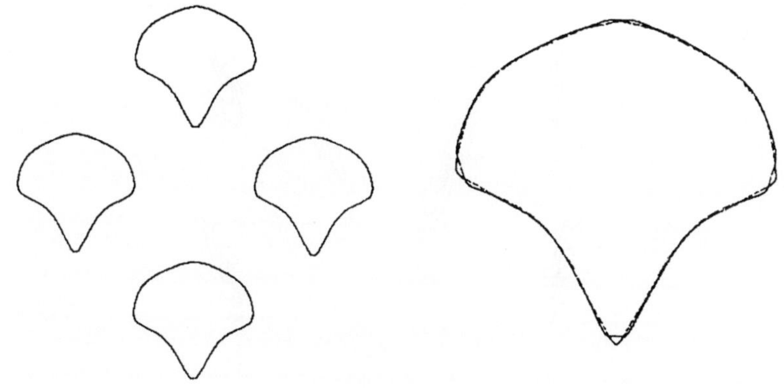

FIGURE 12

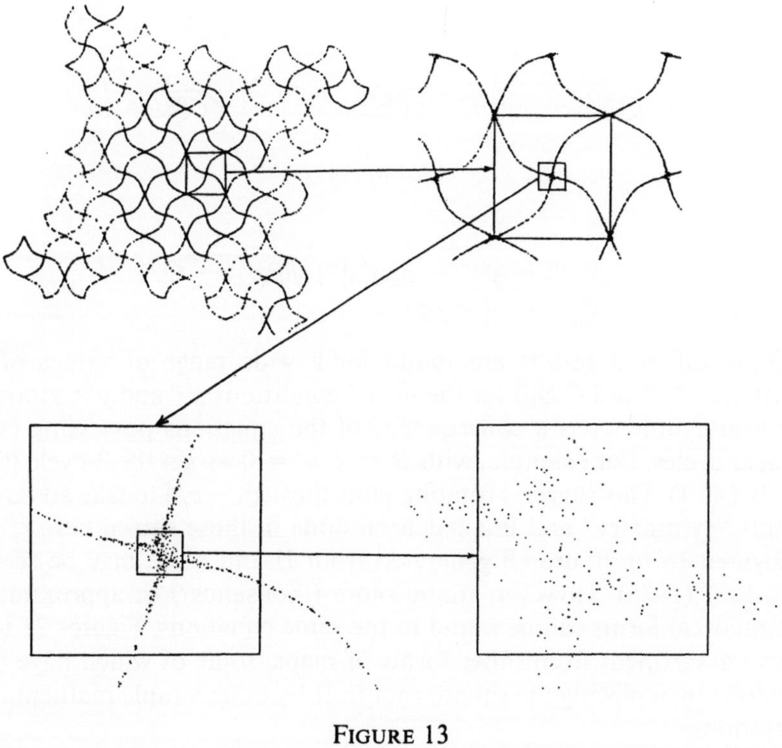

FIGURE 13

Close examination of these thick curves reveals a complicated scattering of points. Thus Fig. 13 points up the highly irregular fine structure near a "junction." Thus within the thick curves the distribution appears to be chaotic.

(II) A mapping which illustrates just how extraordinary the patterns can be is

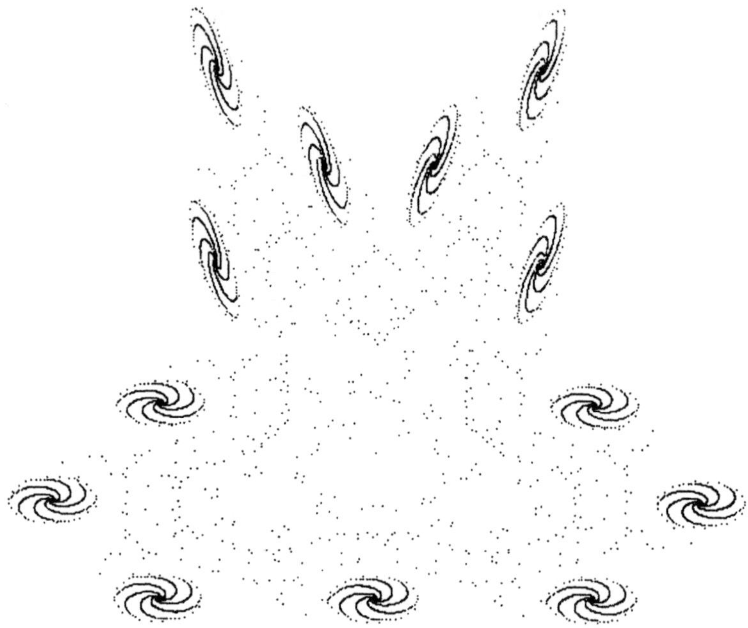

FIGURE 14

$$x^{(n+1)} = y^{(n)} - \text{sign}(x^{(n)})\sqrt{|Bx^{(n)} - C|}$$
$$y^{(n+1)} = A - x^{(n)}.$$

Quite different results are found for a wide range of values of the constants A, B and C and for the initial conditions $x^{(0)}$ and $y^{(0)}$. However, the near-symmetry is a consequence of the equations possessing cycles or near cycles. For example, with $B = A$, $C = 0$ we get the 3-cycle $(0, 0)$, $(0, A)$, (A, A). This suggests rotating plots through $-\pi/4$ to take advantage of this "symmetry" and this has been done in those shown here.

Figures 15 to 20 are all generated from II and more may be seen in Dewdney (1986). However, many more (thousands?) of approximately symmetrical forms can be found in the same equations. Figures 21 to 29 are an assortment from other forms of maps, some of which have been obtained by replacing the square root in II by other simple mathematical operations.

The plots shown each took between 5 minutes and 1 hour to grow on a VAX 11/750 and required between a few thousand and half a million iterations (of course, the same equations can give distinctly different forms when stopped after different numbers of iterations because a great deal of superposition of pixels occurs). Colours can be introduced at preset numbers of iterations and this has been done to produce slides. The slides were made by photographing a Tektronix 4107 screen (640×480 pixels). Colour introduction was originally used in an attempt to monitor the

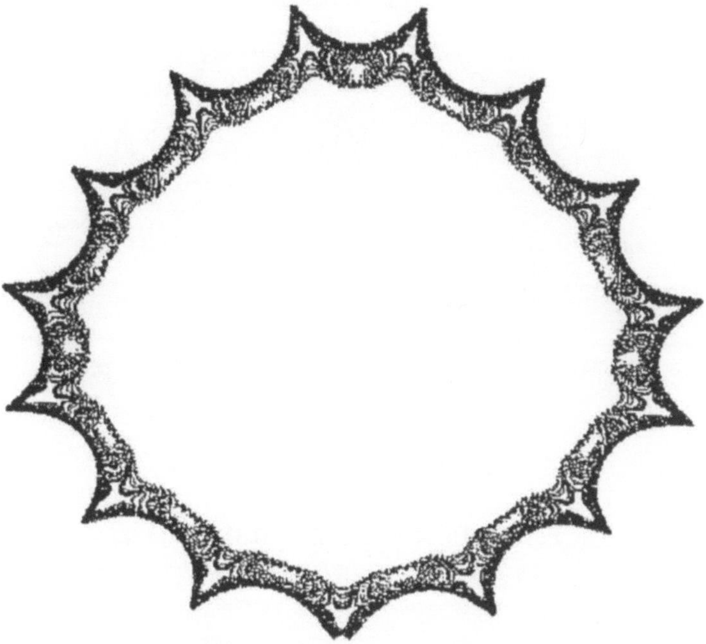

FIGURE 15. $A = 3.5$, $B = 0.125$, $C = 0$.

course of a calculation but can be controlled to produce subtle effects and attractive pictures.

Comment

When I began looking at these assorted shapes I had hopes of being able to find some mode of classification which related equation and form but I now think this highly unlikely apart from gross symmetries as indicated above. The sensitive dependence of detail on the parameters makes the task very difficult and probably impossible.

The production of new "chance" designs proves to be so easy that I can foresee the day when these techniques could be used commercially. A customer invited to sit at a terminal could produce original designs simply by inputting and varying a handful of numbers and, given the technology which is already on the horizon, printing it on paper, fabric, etc. directly they are satisfied with their "creation." On erasure of the parameters it would be quite impossible to recover the code that produced a particular design.

Devaney (1986), Schuster (1984), Fischer and Smith (1985), Thompson and Stewart (1986), and Holden (1986) are all useful sources on the theory of chaos.

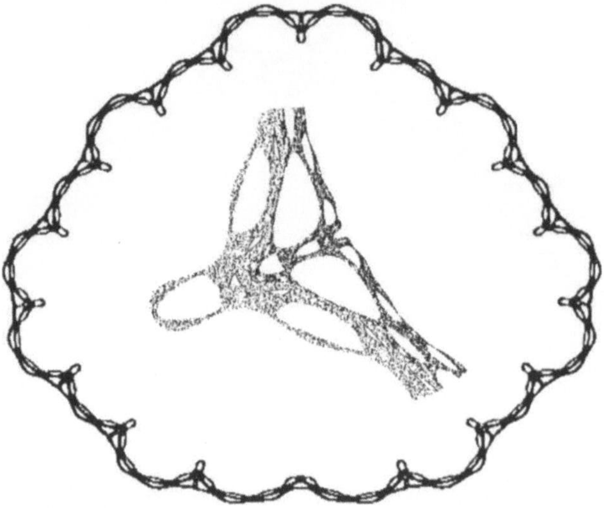

FIGURE 16. $A = 3.5$, $B = 0.318$, $C = 0$.

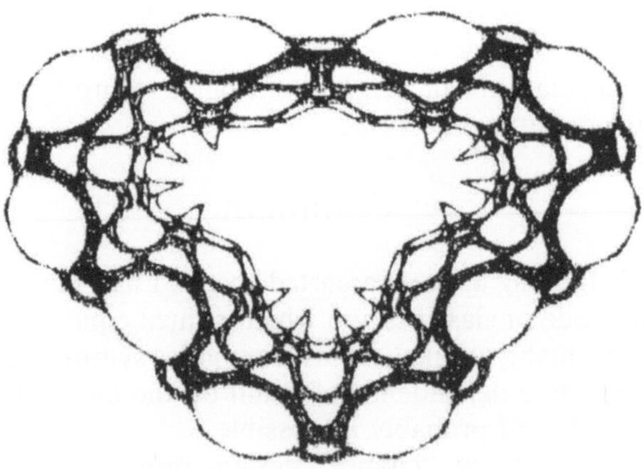

FIGURE 17. $A = 3.5$, $B = 1.2$, $C = 0$.

Acknowledgments. I must express my thanks to John Lansdown for suggesting the title, Barry Brookes for taking so much trouble in the production of slides, Nick Williams for programming the Duffing equation, Mark Harrington for his video presentation work and Dennis Sharp, erstwhile computer officer, for his patient help in sorting out computer problems.

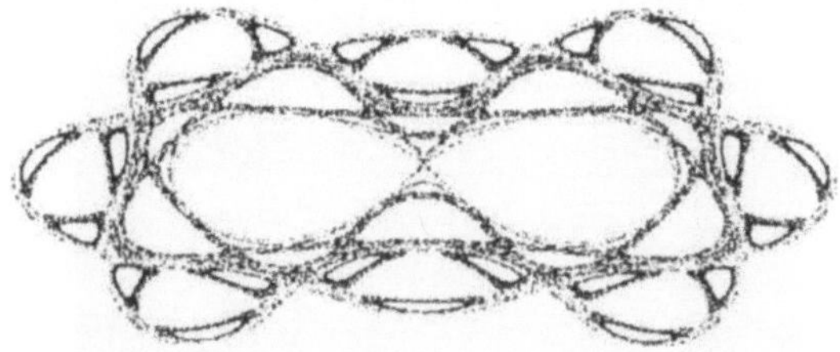

FIGURE 18. $A = 3.5$, $B = 50$, $C = 0$.

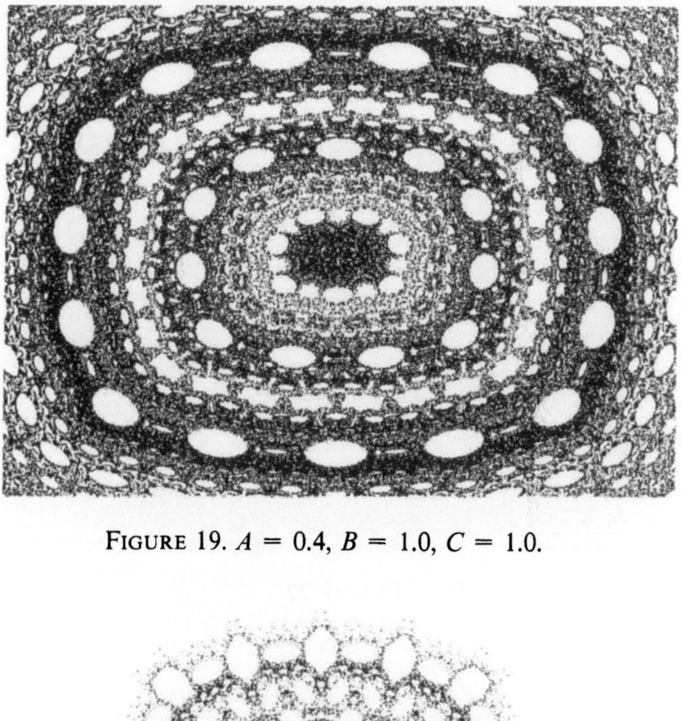

FIGURE 19. $A = 0.4$, $B = 1.0$, $C = 1.0$.

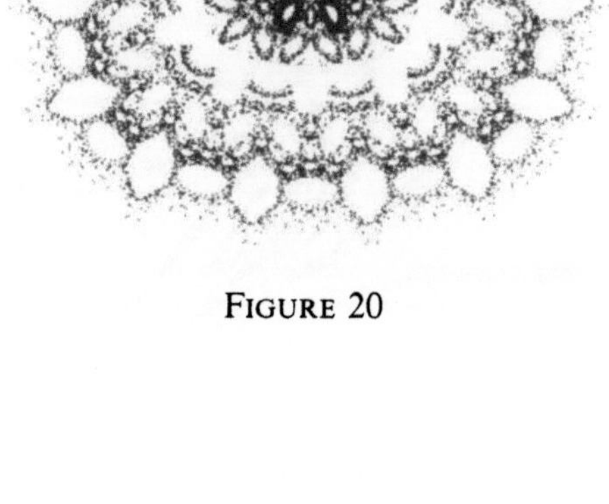

FIGURE 20

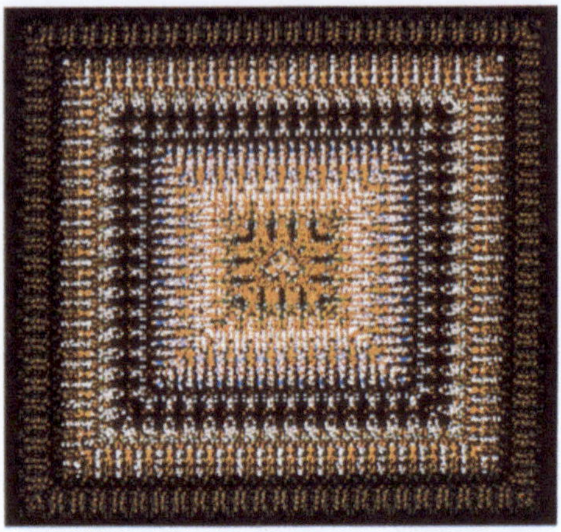

FIGURE 21

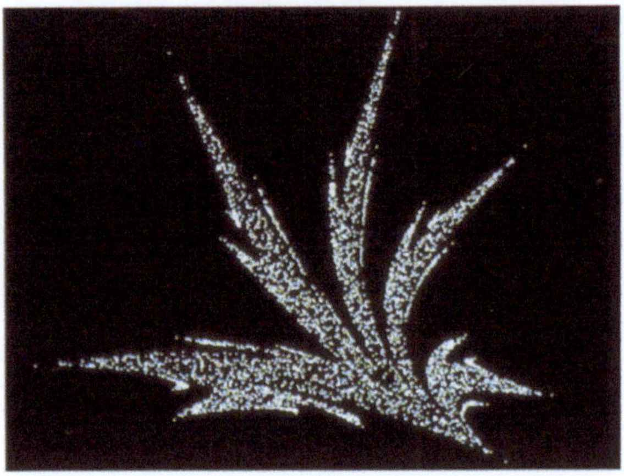

FIGURE 22

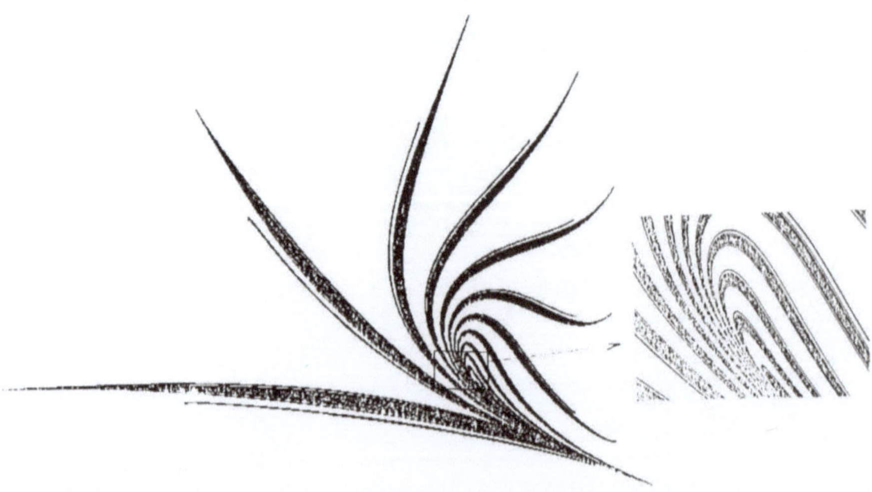

FIGURE 23

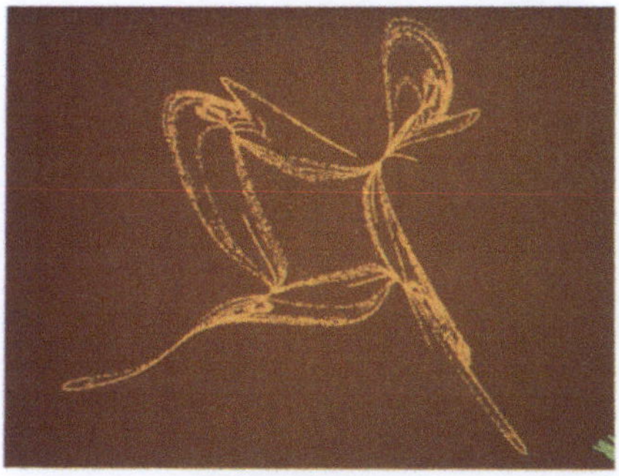

FIGURE 24

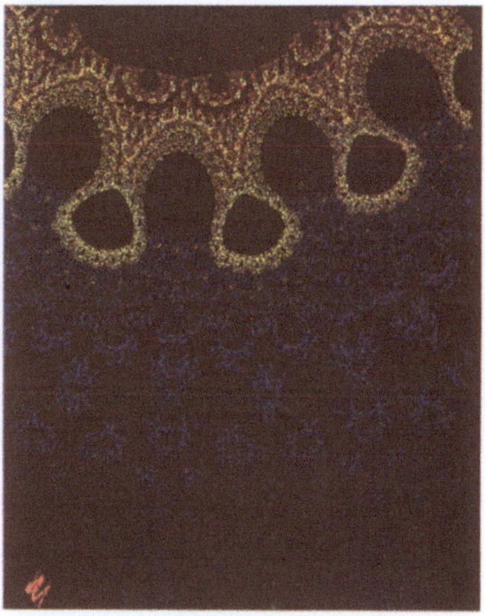

FIGURE 25

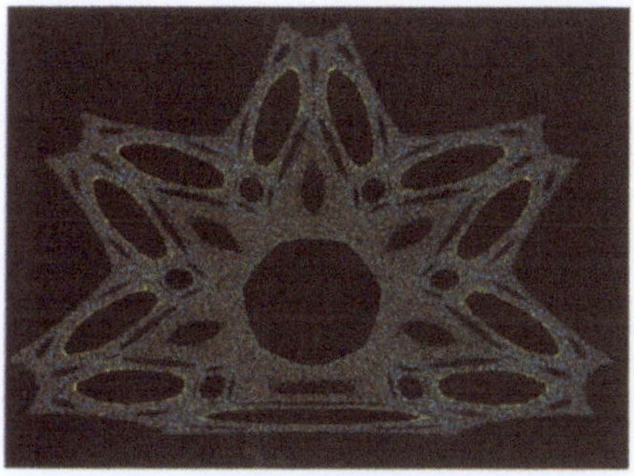

FIGURE 26

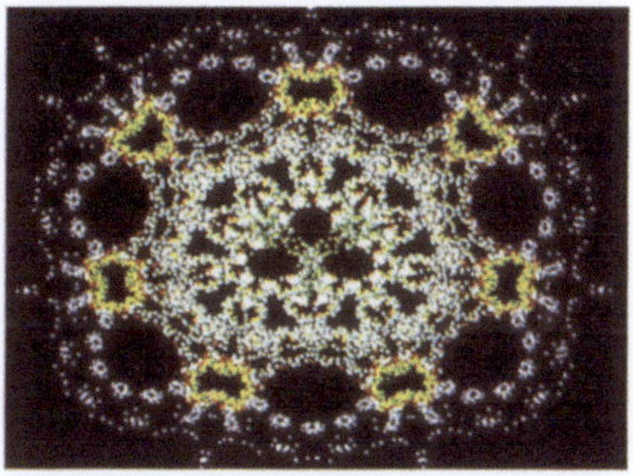

FIGURE 27

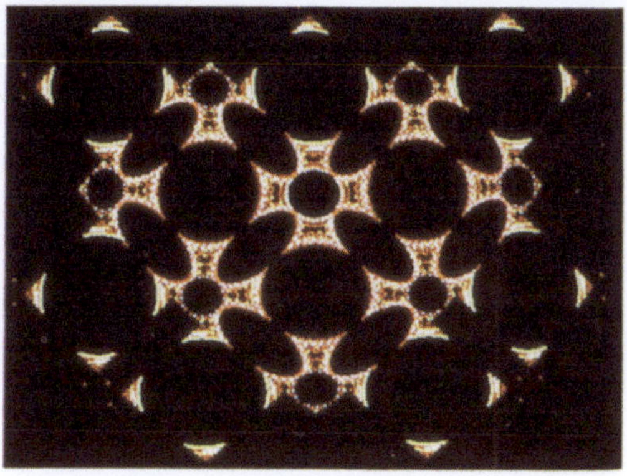

FIGURE 28

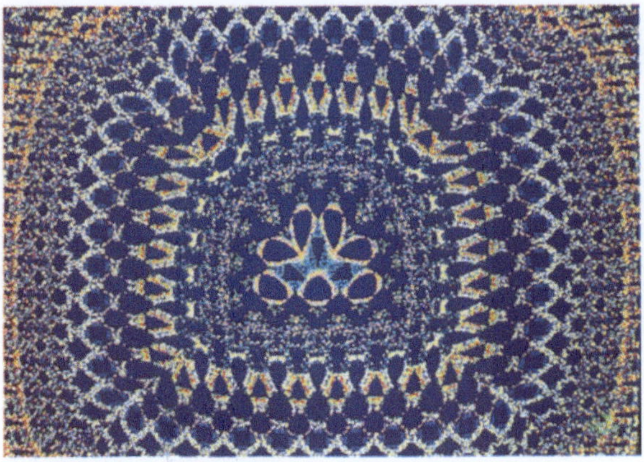

FIGURE 29

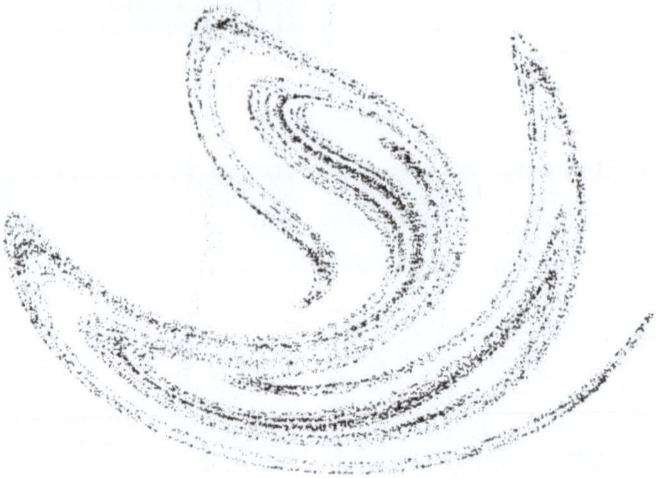

FIGURE 30

References

Birkhoff, G.D. (1932). "Sur quelques courbes fermées remarquables," *Bull. Soc. Math.* 60:1–26; *Collected Mathematical Papers*, vol. 2, pp. 418–443.

Chandra, J. (1984) *Chaos in Non-Linear Systems.* Society for Industrial and Applied Mathematics (SIAM), Philadelphia.

Cvitrovic, P. (1984) *Universality in Chaos.* Adam Hilger.

Devaney, R.L. (1986), *An Introduction to Chaotic Dynamical Systems.* Benjamin/Cummings, Menlo Park, Calif.

Dewdney, A.K. (1986) "Computer Recreations," *Scientific American,* September.

Feigenbaum, M.J. (1983) "Universal Behavior in Non-Linear Systems," *Physica* 7D:16–39.

Fischer, P. and W.R. Smith (1985) *Chaos, Fractals and Dynamics.* Marcel Dekker, New York.

Gumowski, J. and C. Mira (1974) "Point Sequences Generated by Two-Dimensional Recurrences." In *Information Processing 74.* North-Holland, Amsterdam, pp. 851–855.

Gumowski, J. and C. Mira (1980) *Recurrences and Discrete Dynamic Systems,* Lecture Notes in Mathematics. Springer-Verlag, New York.

Hénon, M. (1976) "A Two-dimensional Mapping with a Strange Attractor," *Commun. Math. Phys.* 50:69–77.

Holden, A.V. (ed.) (1986) *Chaos.* Manchester Univ. Press.

Metropolis, N., M.L. Stein, and P.R. Stein (1973). "On Finite Limit Sets for Transformations on the Unit Interval," *J. Combinatorial Theory* A15:25–44.

Peitgen, H.-O. and P.H. Richter (1986) *The Beauty of Fractals.* Springer-Verlag, New York.

Pippard, A.B. (1985) *Response and Stability* Cambridge Univ. Press, London.

Schuster, H.G. (1984) *Deterministic Chaos, an Introduction.* Physik-Verlag.

Thompson, J.M.T. and H.B. Stewart (1986), *Nonlinear Dynamics and Chaos.* Wiley, New York.

Ueda, Y. (1980) "Steady Motions Exhibited by Duffing's Equation: A Picture Book of Regular and Chaotic Motions." In *New Approaches to Non-Linear Problems in Dynamics,* P.J. Holmes, ed. SIAM, Philadelphia.

Tessellation and Image Generation by Electronic Kaleidoscope and Colour Table Modification of Video Input

David R.K. Brownrigg and Christine I. Brownrigg

Introduction

We outline here preliminary results of a collaboration on image processing between an artist specializing in photography, C.I. Brownrigg, and a computer scientist specializing in image processing and computer graphics, D.R.K. Brownrigg. A graphics processor coupled to a video camera and driven by a microcomputer was used to produce kaleidoscopes and images bordered with repeated subimages. These were displayed on a monitor with a number of colour table modifications. Screen photographs in black and white and in colour provided the basis for tesselations using repeated prints.

The layout of the equipment used in shown in Fig. 1. The IO Research PlutoII graphics processor used has a large number of firmware com-

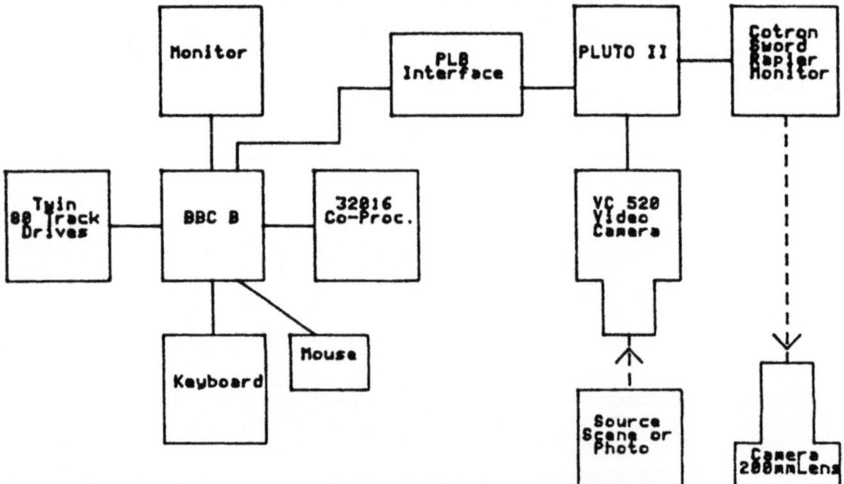

FIGURE 1. Schematic diagram of working setup.

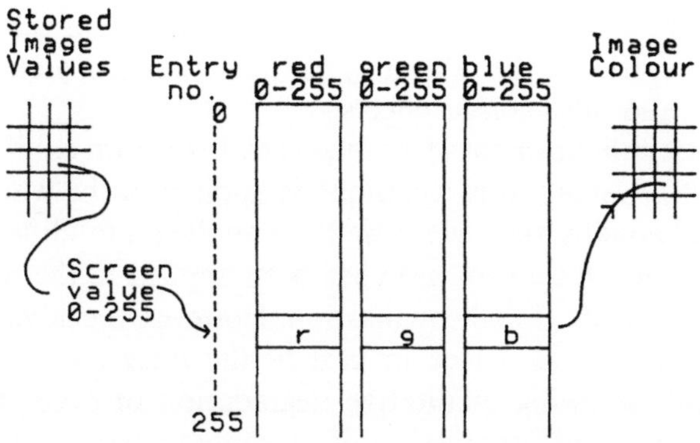

FIGURE 2. The relationship between stored image pixel value and displayed colour on the monitor is defined by an RGB colour table of 256 entries. Each entry consists of red, green and blue values which are in the range 0 to 255, defining the corresponding brightness for the monitor RGB colour guns.

mands in ROM, ranging from subimage copying to Gouraud shading. It includes 1 Mbyte of memory, providing symbol space as well as allowing two images of 768 × 576 pixels of 8 bits to be held simultaneously. The 8 bits per pixel allow 256 simultaneous colours from a palette of over 16 million. This is achieved by each pixel value being an index to a table where an entry consists of red, green and blue values, each with a value between 0 and 255 (see Fig. 2). Video input is via a chip that operates in real time, allowing accurate grabbing with preview. The current setup grabs in black and white using the first 128 pixel values.

The microcomputer used is a BBC model B with a 1-Mbyte 32016 coprocessor. The use of the coprocessor is still in the development stage. It will greatly enhance the speed of generalised subimage copying and allow more general image manipulation. Software is written in BBC Basic and utilises a machine code library of Pluto commands by PLB Ltd. Command and data transfer between the BBC and Pluto is via a PLB interface.

Results output is achieved by photographing a Cotron Sword Rapier monitor screen with a 35-mm camera using a 200-mm lens to reduce screen curvature distortion.

Basic Techniques

The working image is of 768 × 576 pixels. This may be modified in a number of ways, which may be combined in a user-selected manner.

Firstly, the colour table may be changed. On input from video each pixel is given a value i in the range 0 to 127 according to brightness. The corresponding colour table entry has values of $2i$ for each of red, green and blue, giving a grey level (thus (0, 0, 0) is black and (255, 255, 255) is white). The entries in the table may be freely changed, yielding contrast enhancement and false colour effects.

One contrast enhancement technique is by histogram equilisation (e.g., see Hall, 1979). Usually this technique is applied to the whole image to provide global equalisation. Here we have applied a modified version in which equalisation for a subimage has been applied to the whole image. This does not provide global equalisation. However, the advantage is that a local feature, such as a face in part of the image, may be correctly equalised while allowing qualitative degradation of other parts of the image, which may aid suppression of unwanted detail. In fact, the degradation is quantitative as information is usually lost through the reduction in the number of distinct grey levels.

This process is a particular case of a black-and-white transform, from a level r to a level s, of the form

$$s = T(r) \quad \text{(where } T \text{ is monotonic increasing)}$$

illustrated in Fig. 3. This shows contrast enhancement on a mid-tone region, with the gradient $dT(r)/dr > 1$ in the mid-region. Correspondingly, the high and low values of r transform to lowered contrast regions as the gradient is less than one.

Figure 4 schematically shows the effect of equalisation on a region with high and low tones predominating over mid-tones. In this case, all mid-tones would be rendered uniform grey. Selective use of these methods corresponds to variations in exposure length and paper hardness in photography, but may be made more general and controllable. Also, a mon-

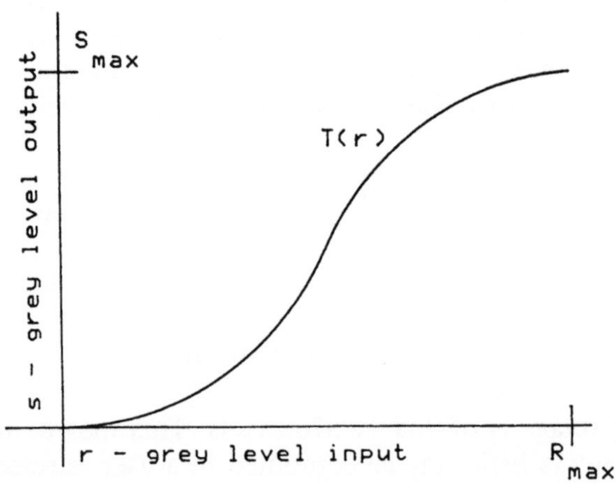

FIGURE 3. Monotonic grey level transformation giving mid-region contrast enhancement.

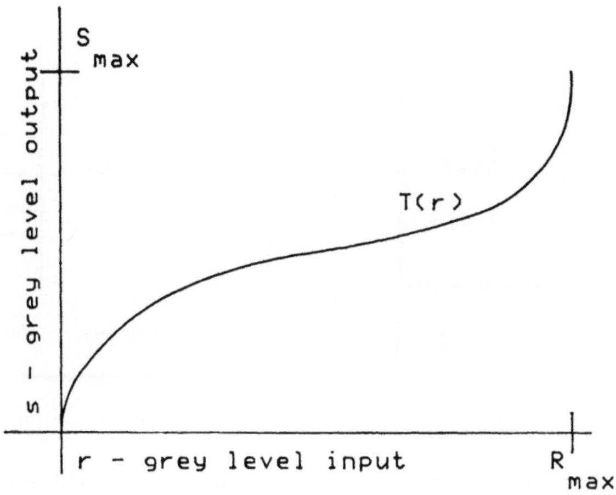

FIGURE 4. Monotonic grey level transformation giving mid-region contrast reduction.

otonic decreasing *T* function yields an effect analogous to a photographic negative.

We have also used non-monotonic grey level transformations to achieve contouring and solarisation effects, as illustrated below. Some of these effects have no direct photographic analogue as several distinct brightness levels may be rendered the same while intermediate levels range over other brightnesses.

Colour may be introduced by setting different values of red, green and blue for a given colour table entry. As each entry in the 256-index colour table can have one of over 16 million values, there are more than 10 to the power 1849 distinct colour tables. Trying these out by enumeration is infeasible and so a number of algorithms for generating appropriate and visually pleasing colour tables have been devised.

Apart from colour table changes, the input image may be modified by replacing some part of it by another. One method is to select a subimage as a central theme and border it with repeated copies of a subimage. This border may be single or multiple and the repeated subimage may be alternately flipped left-right sideways or up-down vertically, as illustrated in Fig. 5.

Another modification is to create an electronic kaleidoscope. In this case, a sub-image is selected and repeated by reflection in a border and rotation repetition about a chosen point. Figure 6 shows how a right-angled isosceles triangle and an equilateral triangle may be processed.

Symmetry in these kaleidoscopes allows the image to be shuffled to create a new kaleidoscope. For instance, Fig. 7 shows how, for the form

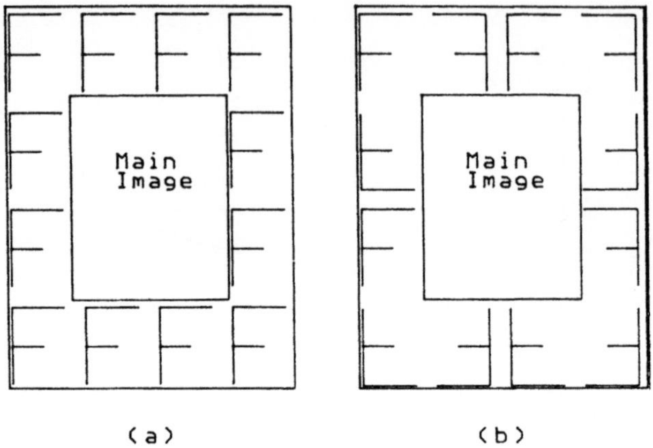

FIGURE 5. Image bordered with (a) repeated subimage and (b) repeated subimage with mirror flip.

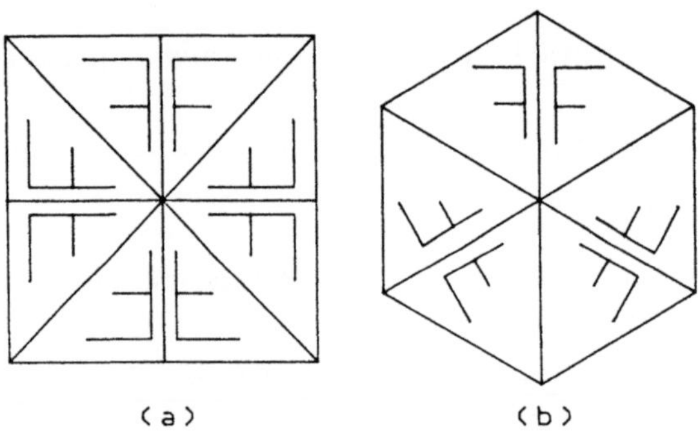

FIGURE 6. Kaleidoscope folding for (a) right-angled isosceles triangle subimage and (b) equilateral triangle subimage.

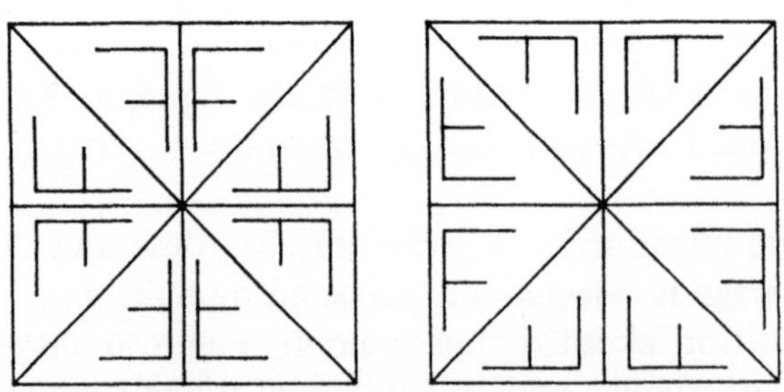

FIGURE 7. Result of shuffling the kaleidoscope form of Fig. 6a, using the symmetry properties of the basic triangle subimage.

in Fig. 6a, the corners can be placed in the centre and the centre moved to the corners.

Such images provide the units that are photographed from the monitor screen. The limitation in screen resolution restricts prints to about 10 by 8 inches if subjective sharpness is to be retained. However, large images may be generated in a number of ways. One way is to make multiple prints of an image and make a plane tessellation. The symmetry properties of the kaleidoscope guarantee smooth blending of the "tiles" of the tesselation, subject to correct squaring of the recording camera to the display monitor.

Results

The work presented here is limited to black and white. Plates Ia and Ib are two versions of a kaleidoscope of an onion and a carrot. The difference between the two is that they are mutual negatives. The colour table modifications have resulted in an image for which there is not a one-to-one correspondence between brightness levels used and those in the original scene.

Plate II is of an old fire engine. Some of the outer region of the original image has been replaced by a repeated sub-image, alternately flipped electronically. The colour table transform is approximately realistic with features that produce an effect similar to solarisation.

Plate III is an example of constructing a larger image from a repeated screen image. In this case the screen image is itself a kaleidoscope of a face made by folding and repetition. Four copies make the main centre part of the final picture. The screen image was then shuffled, as described in the last section in relation to Fig. 7. Two copies of the resulting screen were made and each divided in two to give four triangular image elements. These were added to the four-tile tessellation to provide a close but intentionally incomplete blending.

Plate IV is an example of using multiple copies of two different kaleidoscope images. The source material was a rubber glove and a lilac flower, with colour table modifications of a form that simulate contouring.

Future Work

Colour work on video input has already made some progress. However, with black-and-white video input, the result is false colour. Work is currently being done on true colour input using repeated grabs, with filters, to different sets of pixel planes.

The equilateral triangle tessellation, illustrated in Fig. 6b, is computationally expensive on a square pixel grid as pixels are no longer simply copied by rows or columns but must be processed individually. With a

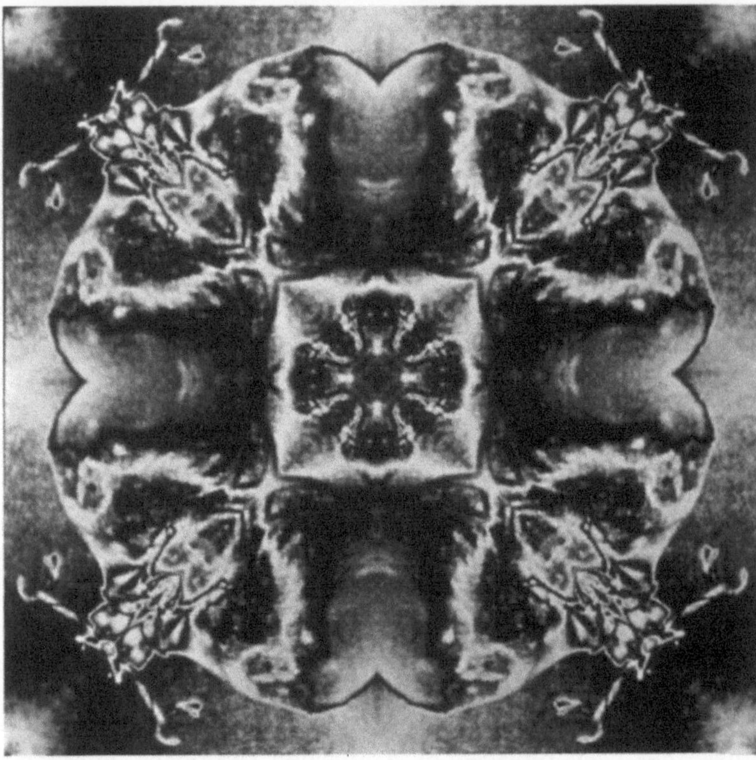

A

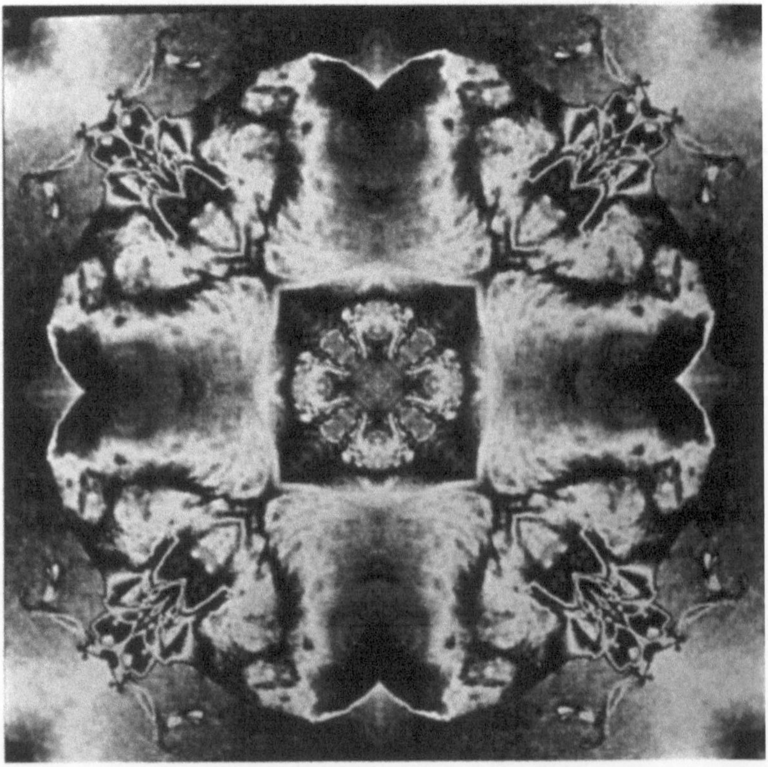

B

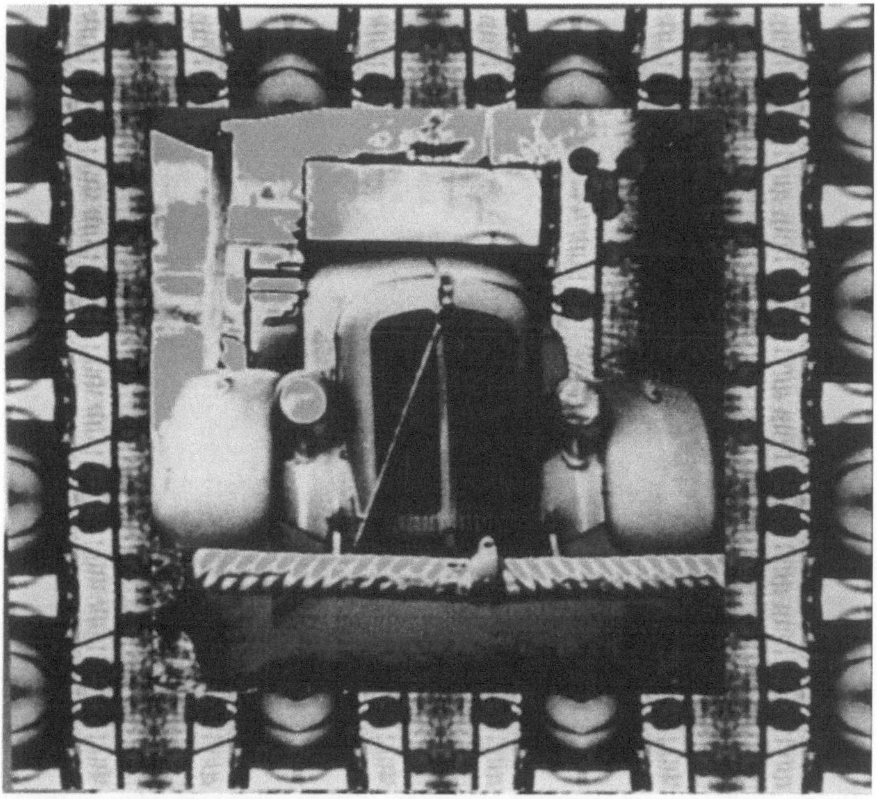

PLATE II. Solarisation effect on a picture of a fire engine in Tennessee. The bordering is created from a detail of the steering wheel.

BBC model B alone this requires an interface use for each pixel. Even utilising symmetry properties, kaleidoscope production takes over 3 hours. This means that interactive experimentation to optimise a composition is impossible. The 32016 processor will reduce the timing to a matter of minutes as large blocks of image can be transferred and stored in RAM with a single command. Advantage can then be taken of the higher processing speed available, as the system will no longer be interface bound.

PLATES IA AND IB. Computer-generated images can lead to attractive abstractions, as does this kaleidoscope of an onion and a carrot, where the simplification of the shading on the vegetables gives the appearance of faces or insects caught in a bubble. The plates are mutual negatives.

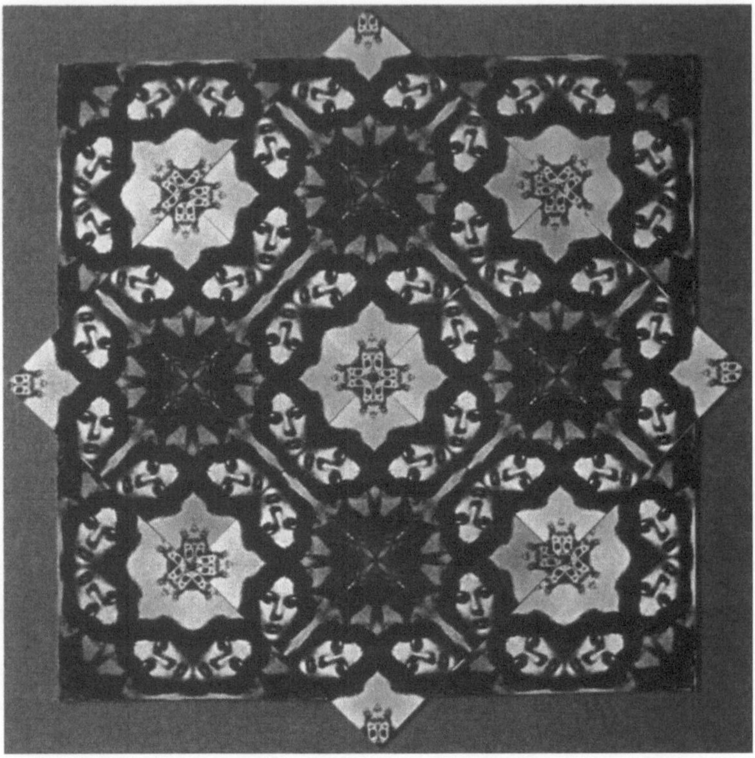

PLATE III. Computer-generated photographic print assembled. Diverse images can be brought together to form interesting and new designs.

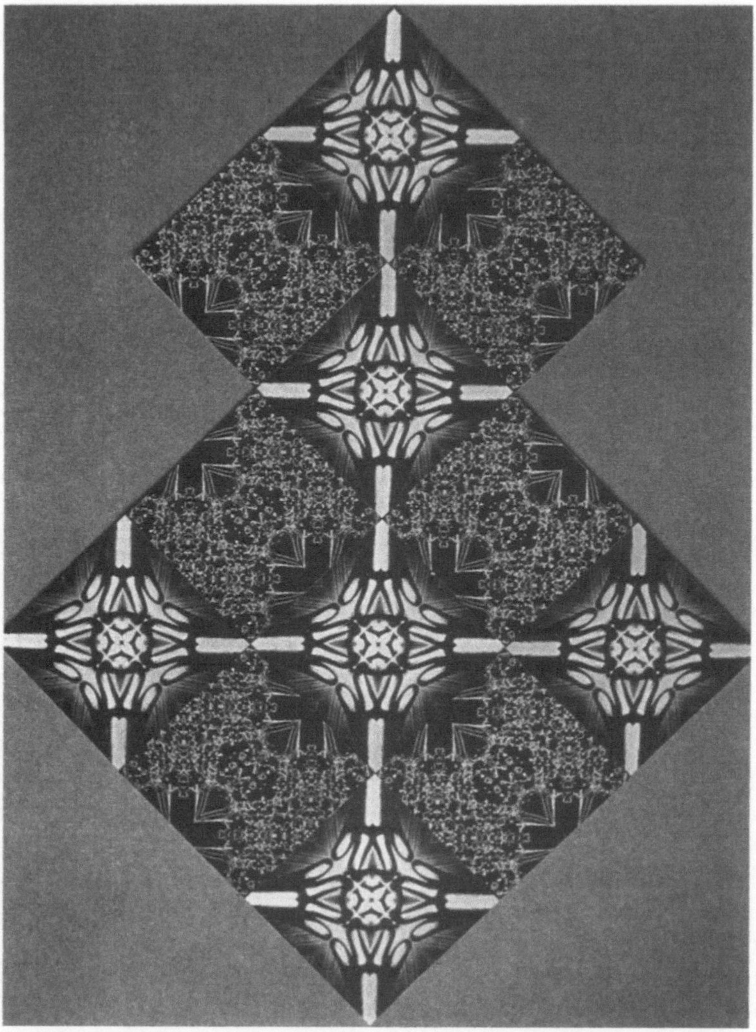

PLATE IV. Computer-generated photographic print assembled. Diverse images can be brought together to form interesting and new designs.

Acknowledgments. The equipment used is part of a graphics facility in the Department of Mathematical Sciences, University of London Goldsmiths' College. The authors thank the head of department for allowing them to access the equipment freely and for engendering a constructive atmosphere that has aided this work.

Reference

Hall, E.L. (1979) *Computer Image Processing and Recognition*, p. 166 et seq. Academic Press, New York.

Oct-Tree Encoding and Fractal Rendering of Polyhedra

Ian O. Angell and Cathy Sobhanpanah

History

Interest in polyhedral objects is as old as history. Pyramids were known before the ancient Egyptians and prisms were a fundamental part of the earliest architecture. The five polyhedra with regular planar faces and vertices were known to the early Greek philosophers, although information about their discovery is lost in the mists of time; the name *Platonic* solids became attached to them, probably because of the prestige of Plato (ca. 400 B.C.). Much mystical significance was attached to the Platonic solids by the (pre-Plato) Pythagoreans (sixth century B.C.), and some of the mysticism is still in evidence today. The semi-regular solids were named after Archimedes, the Syracuse mathematician (circa 250 B.C.), whose investigations on these polyhedra have unfortunately been lost. The duals (or reciprocals) of these 13 *Archimedean* polyhedra were not codified until 1865, by Catalan. The enumeration of the uniform convex polyhedra (including prisms and antiprisms) was not completed until the work of Kepler (1864).

There was a revival of interest in polyhedra at the end of the seventeenth century, spurred on by the then expansion of the science of crystallography. However, fascination with polyhedra goes well beyond the shapes that nature makes possible, with such unnatural figures as non-convex stellated polyhedra. The chief reason for studying regular polyhedra today is still the same as it was in the time of the Pythagoreans, namely that their symmetrical shapes appeal to the human aesthetic sense. This appeal is universal and obviously strikes a fundamental chord with us all; witness the prolific use of polyhedral shapes in televised advertising. There is something uncanny about the symmetrical properties of these solids that is both satisfying and reassuring to the human eye.

This has meant that there has always been a very good supply of systematic mathematical texts on the topic. Some of the earliest mathematical investigations of polyhedra were expounded by Theaetetus of Athens, and Euclid's Elements were written for the express purpose of constructing the regular solids. Some of the best modern analyses of the subject can be found in the books of Coxeter (1963) and Toth (1964). These mathematical investigations of polyhedra tend to be described in deep algebraic terminology, making it difficult for the layman to understand much of the underlying theory. Fortunately, many of the important concepts can be discovered by observation and experimentation using diagrams and models (Cundy and Rollett, 1961; Wells, 1970). Of course, these modelling techniques can now be extended into the realm of computers.

Introduction

With the advent of computers, in particular microcomputers, enthusiasm for constructing polyhedra has been rediscovered by a whole new generation. Coloured diagrams and line drawings of polyhedra, defined by keyboard input of vertices and facets, can be drawn with ease (Angell, 1985). More sophisticated methods enable a polyhedron to be generated using its underlying algebraic properties to construct a data structure model of the solid. This model can be used not only for graphical display but also for simulating real-world manipulations, such as slicing pieces from the polyhedron. Many techniques have been developed for the representation of three-dimensional polyhedral objects, where the definition of the scene is achieved by approximating to the surfaces using a polygonal mesh (e.g., Sobhanpanah and Angell, 1986). Here every object in the scene is defined as a list of facets; each facet is an ordered list of line segments, and each line segment is a pair of vertices. There is no need to limit the approach to three dimensions. The conceptual freedom given by computers make it possible to construct multidimensional polytopes (Coxeter, 1963).

Although any three-dimensional object can be represented as a set of polygonal surfaces, either precisely or by approximation, manipulation and display of such objects can require immense computing power, which thus restricts both the complexity of the scene and the type of manipulation that can be achieved. This is particularly true in a personal computer environment. So in this paper, instead of this traditional facet/line/vertex approach, we consider the solid modelling technique known as an oct-tree encoding algorithm (Meagher, 1982; Angell and Griffith, 1987), which although less efficient for simple displays, has enormous potential for complex manipulations of polyhedra.

The oct-tree method permits the definition of a scene as a combination of primitive objects; each primitive object is represented analytically, and not in terms of vertices and facets. These primitives are used in a robust definition notation to describe complex scenes. The scene is defined as the union, intersection and complement of various primitives, which can be written down as a postfix-notation representation of a binary tree. To compute the display file we use a hierarchical data structure (oct-tree) so that any object of arbitrary complexity can be drawn to the precision of the graphics display screen. This approach allows a very simple definition of polyhedra as a combination of half-space primitives. This ease of definition is to some extent paid for with an increase in processing overheads, although not necessarily in program complexity. One immediate gain is the possibility of using fractal techniques for the rendering of surfaces. This can be incorporated easily into the oct-tree at any stage of the spatial decomposition. Thus the rendering of the objects is performed as an integral part of the oct-tree encoding at minimal extra cost. Fractal surfaces are composed of stochastically defined polygonal surfaces. They have been used extensively in texture generation, for example, Mandelbrot's fractal mountains (Mandelbrot, 1982), because of the ease in which geometric methods using probabilistic functions can produce highly realistic scenes, which can be infinitely sub-divided so that any arbitrary level of detail may be obtained.

We use the qualities of fractal geometry to provide a mechanism for producing realistic surface rendering of the polyhedra without major additional computational requirements within the oct-tree encoding method. By varying the parameters controlling the fractal surface generation we can produce a wide range of rendering effects from marbling to rust. The fractal surface constructed during the oct-tree computations is used as a parameter controlling the colour attributes of a particular point on the surface of the polyhedra; it could also be used to denote displacement of the normal at points on the polyhedral surface in order to simulate texturing.

Modelling Polyhedra

Polyhedral objects may be defined as the union and intersection of various half-spaces. These half-spaces can be defined by a quadruple $\{A, B, C, D\}$, which represents the boundary of the half-space, the three-dimensional Euclidean plane

$$Ax + By + Cz + D = 0$$

with normal vector (A, B, C) pointing out of the half-space. We can imagine each boundary plane consisting of a material with given absolute red/green/blue (RGB) reflective coefficients and gloss and shine parameters (Angell and Griffith, 1987).

Any convex polyhedron can be described by the volume of intersection of a set of half-spaces, the so-called convex hull. Thus a cube of side two units, centred on the co-ordinate origin, may be defined by six half-spaces $\{1, 0, 0, -1\}$, $\{-1, 0, 0, -1\}$, $\{0, 1, 0, -1\}$, $\{0, -1, 0, -1\}$, $\{0, 0, 1, -1\}$

and {0, 0, −1, −1} respectively. If these are labeled 1, 2, 3, 4, 5 and 6, then the object can be described as a binary "description tree" which can be written in a postfix notation thus

$$1\ 2 \cap 3\ 4 \cap \cap 5\ 6 \cap \cap \quad (\cap \text{ denotes intersection}).$$

The complement of a given half-space $\{A, B, C, D\}$ is found by negating all the entries, thus

$$\{-A, -B, -C, -D\};$$

we can also represent this by placing a minus sign in front of the identifying number, thus the complement of object 1 is object −1. A non-convex polyhedron can be constructed by the union, intersection and complement of a number of different convex polyhedra. Thus a second cube, also of side two units, centred at (1, 1, 1) and defined by six half-spaces {1, 0, 0, −2}, {−1, 0, 0, 0}, {0, 1, 0, −2}, {0, −1, 0, 0}, {0, 0, 1, −2} and {0, 0, −1, 0} respectively, labelled 7, 8, 9, 10, 11 and 12, can be described by

$$7\ 8 \cap 9\ 10 \cap \cap 11\ 12 \cap \cap$$

and the combination of the two cubes into a non-convex polyhedron is described by the union ($\cup$) of the two cubes above:

$$1\ 2 \cap 3\ 4 \cap \cap 5\ 6 \cap \cap 7\ 8 \cap 9\ 10 \cap \cap 11\ 12 \cap \cap \cup.$$

Another non-convex polyhedron may be formed by taking away from the first cube that part which is common to both, thus:

$$1\ 2 \cap 3\ 4 \cap \cap 5\ 6 \cap \cap -7\ -8 \cup -9\ -10 \cup \cup -11\ -12 \cup \cup \cap.$$

See Fig. 1.

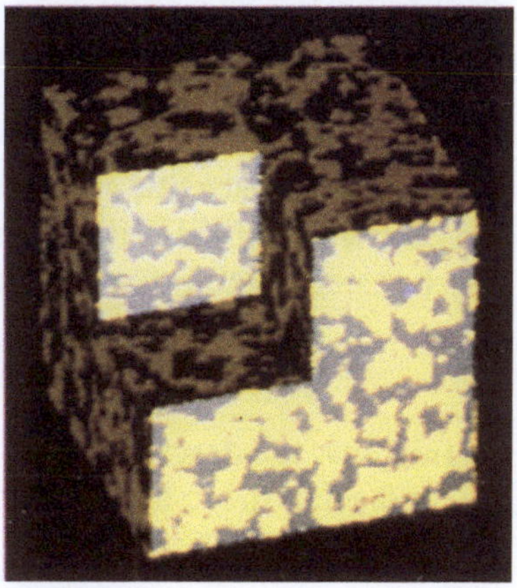

FIGURE 1

Oct-Tree Encoding of a Polyhedral Scene

The fundamental requirement of oct-tree encoding of polyhedra is the ability to compare a cube with each of the half-spaces in the scene and to find out whether the cube is inside (TRUE), outside (FALSE) or crosses the boundary plane (NEITHER).

It is initially assumed that the viewport screen is a square of 2^{SN} by 2^{SN} (square) pixels. We can imagine each square pixel extruded into a cube (or voxel). The whole viewport screen can then be considered as extruded into a cube composed of 2^{SN} by 2^{SN} by 2^{SN} voxels (the root cube). This cube can be identified with a large cube surrounding the polyhedral scene. The oct-tree method finds which voxels within this cube intersect the facets on the polyhedron and draws the equivalent pixel on the screen.

The method recursively breaks down each cubic block of 2^n by 2^n by 2^n voxels (a parent cube) into eight blocks (the children) each of 2^{n-1} by 2^{n-1} by 2^{n-1} voxels, starting with the root cube and ultimately reaching voxel level (2^0 by 2^0 by 2^0). Note that the name oct-tree refers to this breaking of cubic blocks into eight; it has nothing to do with the description tree, which is necessarily binary. There will be large blocks of voxels that do not intersect any half-space surface in the scene and these blocks can be safely ignored rather than recursively divided into eight. Similarly, certain large blocks of voxels will intersect some of the half-spaces but not others. Sub-blocks produced by subdivision will not intersect half-spaces that are not intersected by the original block. These situations are all catered for by the oct-tree method.

The method is to allocate a postfix description of a part of the scene relevant to the parent of a given block of pixels. Initially the description tree of the complete scene is allocated to the root cube. For each parent cube we have to find which of the half-spaces from its description tree is relevant to each of the eight children and hence calculate the binary description sub-tree for each child. If the boundary plane of a half-space does not intersect a child cube, then no occurrence of that half-space must occur in the description tree identified with the child. We calculate this tree by "reducing" the description tree of the parent. If we identify union, intersection and complement with the boolean operators OR, AND and NOT, and replace the numerical entries in the tree with their TRUE/FALSE values (NEITHER values remain as numbers in the tree), we can use boolean algebra for reduction, noting for numerical entry n:

$$n \text{ AND TRUE} = n; \qquad n \text{ OR TRUE} = \text{TRUE};$$
$$n \text{ AND FALSE} = \text{FALSE}; \qquad n \text{ OR FALSE} = \text{n}.$$

In this way, the description subtree identified with each child will contain all, and only, those half-spaces that contain facets which cut the edges of the child cube.

If, during such a reduction, the description tree for a child becomes empty (that is, it reduces to just TRUE or FALSE), then the child cube is either inside or outside the polyhedra and no part of a surface in the polyhedral scene will intersect this child cube, and hence no pixels equivalent to the child voxels will be coloured at this stage. If, however, the process continues until the individual voxel level is reached, then this voxel can be identified with both a pixel on the graphics screen and a point on a unique facet, and by implication the normal to this facet. Given the point in space, the normal, a light source (or even multiple light sources) and the material parameters of the facet, it is possible to calculate a shade of colour for that pixel which gives the effect of smooth shading and specular reflection over that facet as a whole.

If we add a further requirement that the oct-tree subdivision is ordered from front to back and insist that once a square of pixels has been coloured in, no cube of voxels behind that square should be coloured further, then we have an efficient hidden-surface elimination algorithm.

Rendering with Fractals

Thus far the colour of facets on the polyhedra is predetermined. Each facet has a fixed absolute colour, which is adjusted on plotting with regard to ambient light and diffuse and specular reflection. In order to create unusual rendering of surfaces, such as a marbling effect, alternative methods have to be developed. Fractal techniques (Mandelbrot, 1982), in particular triangulation fractal methods, have been used with great success in rendering general shapes. In this article we look at an alternative approach, a pointwise discrete fractal process which is apparently similar to the method of Woodwark and Bowyer (1986).

This method creates a cubic block of differing colours and simulates the 'sculpturing' of the required object from this block. The "root" cube is composed of a 2^{SN} by 2^{SN} by 2^{SN} block of voxels, identical to that manipulated by the oct-tree algorithm. The generation of a colour for each voxel is achieved simultaneously with the oct-tree process in the following way. The root cube is divided into $(2^{SN}/2^M)^3$ cubes each of size 2^M by 2^M by 2^M, and each of the corners of these cubes, $(2^{SN}/2^M + 1)^3$ in number, is allocated a number in the range zero to one.

At a given point in the oct-tree process, say when dealing with a 2^n by 2^n by 2^n parent cubic block of voxels ($n \leq M$), each corner of the cube is allocated a number in the range zero to one. When the block is divided by the process into eight children each of size 2^{n-1} by 2^{n-1} by 2^{n-1} voxels, then numbers must be calculated for the corners of each of the new cubes, 27 in total of which 8 are identical to the corners of the parent. Each of the remaining 19 corner numbers will be evaluated as a function of its position relative to, and the values of, the original eight corner numbers of the parent cube, together with some pseudo-random variation. This variation must be proportional to the size of the cube under consideration and can be introduced as the multiple of three values: a random number between minus one and one, a scaling factor (s say) and the size of the cube relative to the original block. The final number is adjusted to keep it in the zero-to-one range. We thus have a "self-similar" process that ultimately leads down to cubes at the voxel level during the oct-tree encoding of a given scene, and each of these cubes can be allocated a number between zero and one. For any given object in a scene, this number can be mapped into a logical colour value, which in turn is incorporated into a picture using the usual smooth shading and specular reflection techniques.

Results

So the parameters for rendering consist of:

1. A set of materials (RGB colour, shine and gloss).
2. A mapping of sub-ranges from zero to one onto a material.
3. An integer $M \leq SN$ denoting the initial division of the root cube into $(2^{SN}/2^M)^3$ sub-cubes each of size 2^M by 2^M by 2^M voxels.
4. An initial set of $(2^{SN}/2^M + 1)^3$ numbers in the range zero to one placed at the corners of these sub-cubes. These numbers may be input if a particular distribution is required, although for most applications it is effective to define them with a uniformly distributed set of pseudo-random numbers.
5. The scaling factor s, which is loosely related to Mandelbrot's fractal dimension and is a measure of maximum variation allowed from an interpolated mean value.

If the s value is set to zero (see Fig. 2 and 6), then the resulting rendering will be computed by a direct linear interpolation between the original $(2^{SN}/2^M + 1)^3$ numbers (and hence colours). Such a surface rendering will consist of areas of fixed colours, whose boundaries are delineated by smooth curves. A large value for s (the order of the size of the subranges in the material mapping) will result in an all but random distribution in colours. A zero value of M means that every voxel is predefined, and if the predefined values are uniformly distributed, then this too implies that each voxel is coloured randomly; a value $M = SN$ implies a very limited number (8) of discrete initial positions, which in turn restricts the effectiveness of the method. Values of $M = 4$ or 5 produce the best results. For four materials uniformly distributed in the range zero to one, a value for s around 0.03 gives an acceptable marbling effect.

Figures 2, 3, 4, and 5 show examples of a cube rendered using $M = 4$ and $s = 0.0$, 0.025, 0.05, 0.075 and 0.1, respectively. Figures 6, 7 and 8

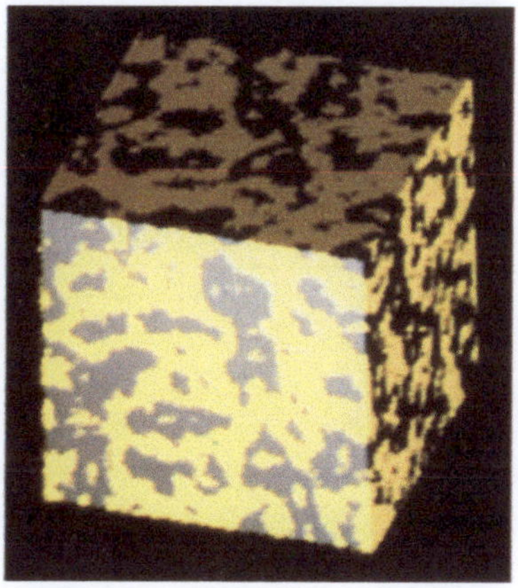

FIGURE 2

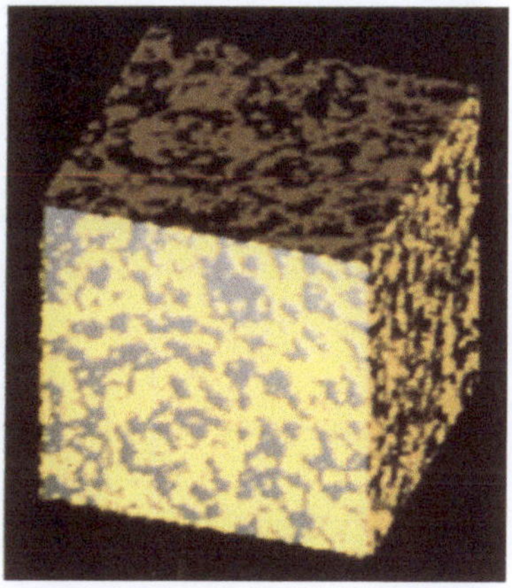

FIGURE 3

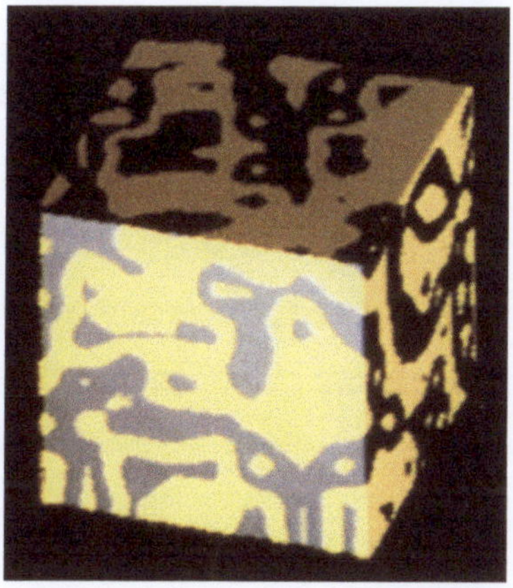

FIGURE 4

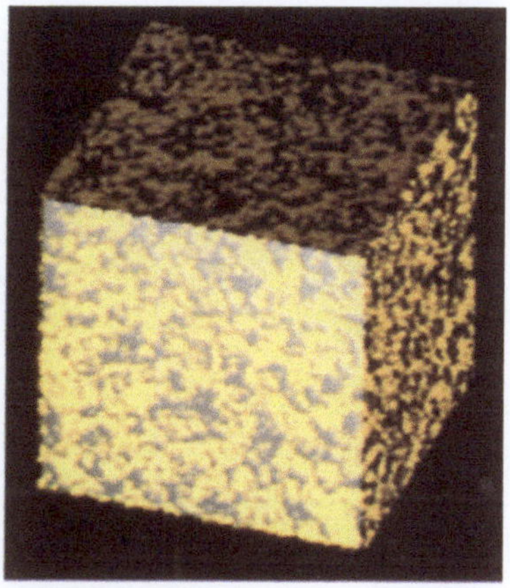

FIGURE 5

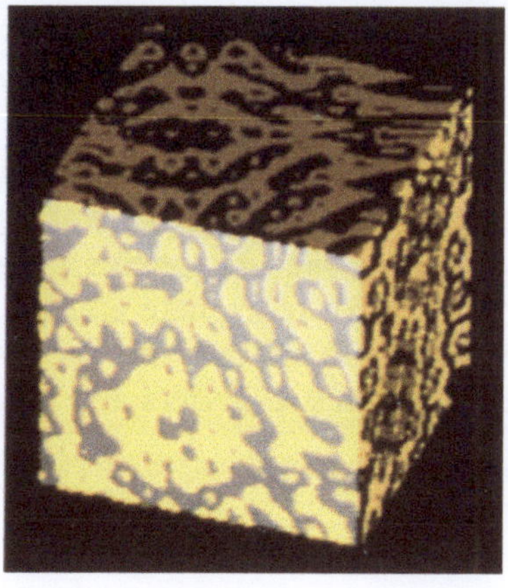

FIGURE 6

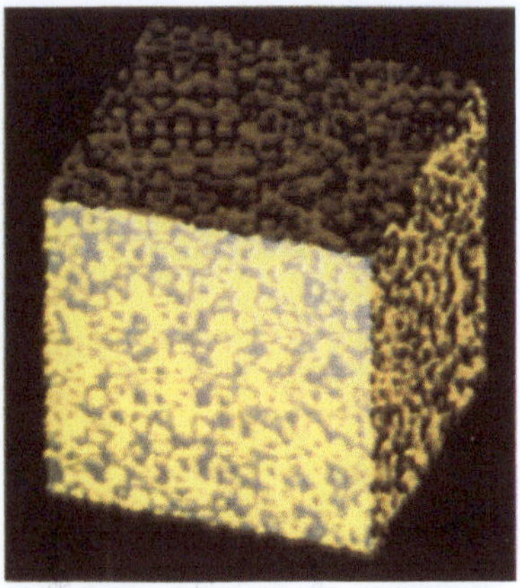

FIGURE 7

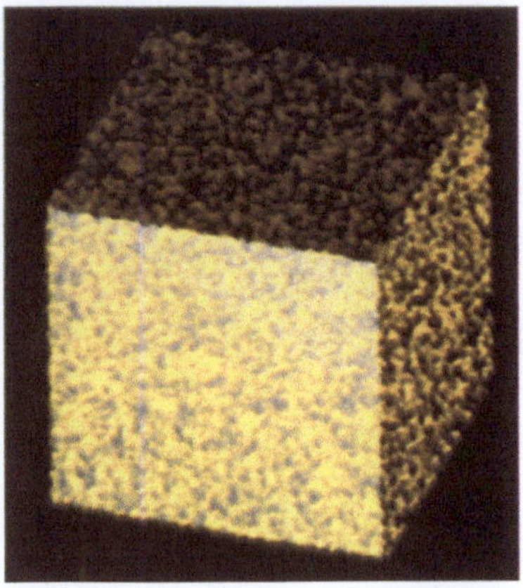

FIGURE 8

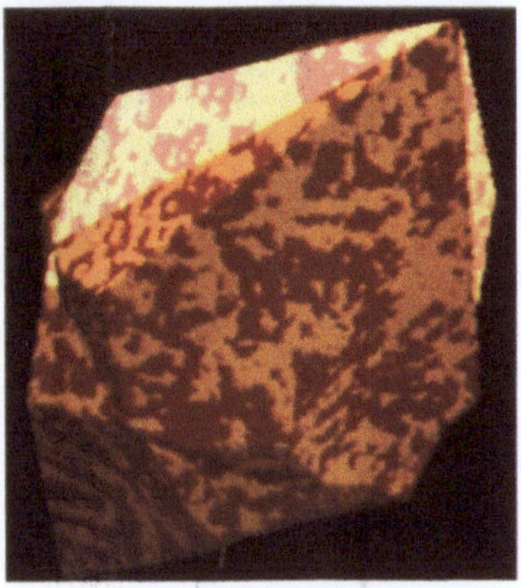

FIGURE 9

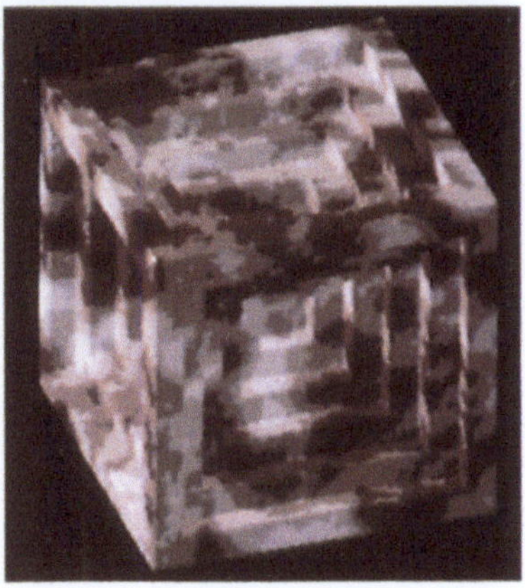

FIGURE 10

are for $M = 2$ and $s = 0.0$, 0.5 and 0.1, respectively. Figures 9 and 10 show colouring of some unusual polyhedra.

Of course there is no need to restrict the rendering and oct-tree method to combinations of half-spaces. The process works just as well with other primitive geometrical shapes, such as spheres, cylinders, tori, cones, and helices. Figure 11 shows a textured sphere and Fig. 12 three tori; Fig. 13 has these tori cut away from a sphere, and Fig. 14 shows a 'logo' combination of half-spaces, spheres, cylinders and tori.

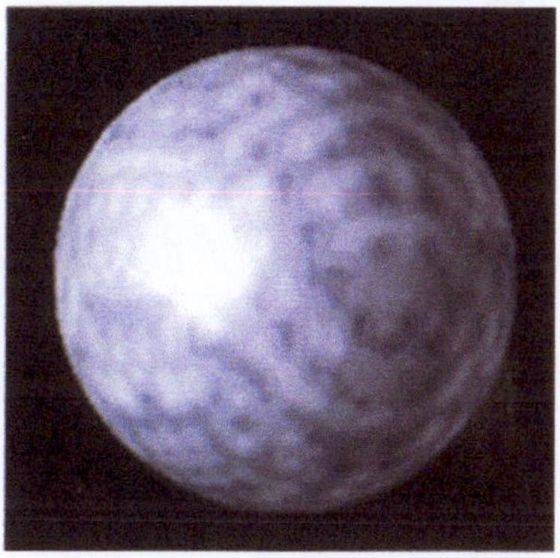

FIGURE 11

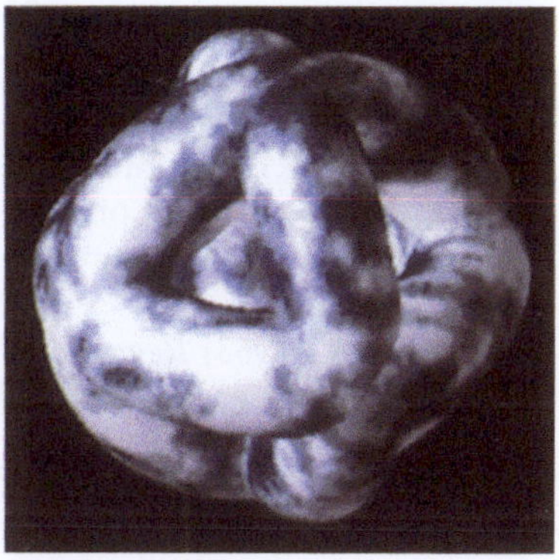

FIGURE 12

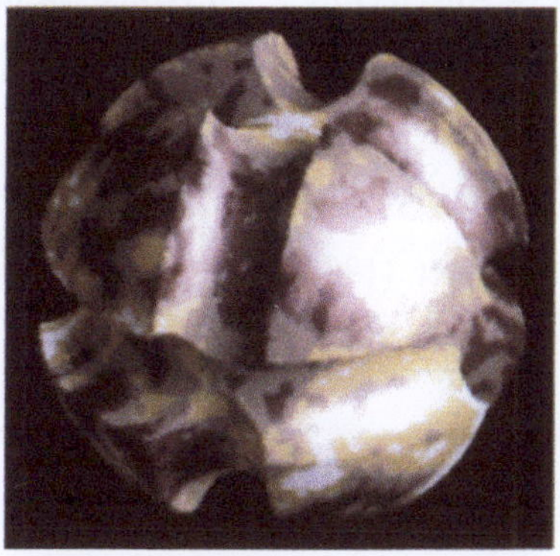

FIGURE 13

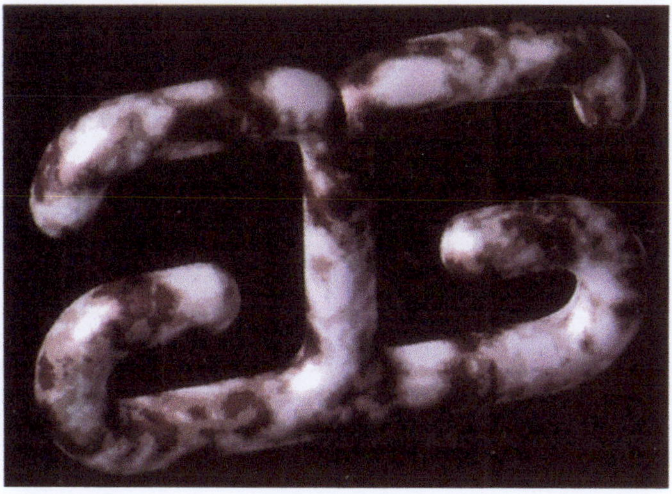

FIGURE 14

References

Angell, I.O. (1985) *Advanced Graphics with the IBM Personal Computer.* Macmillan, London.

Angell, I.O. and G.H. Griffith (1987) *High Resolution Computer Graphics Using Fortran 77.* Macmillan, London.

Catalan, E.C. (1865) "Mémoire sur la théorie des polyedres," *J. Ecole Polytechnique* 41:1–71.

Coxeter, H.M.S. (1963) *Regular Polytopes*, 2nd ed. Macmillan, New York.

Cundy, A.M. and A.P. Rollett (1961) *Mathematical Models*, 2nd ed. Clarendon, Oxford.

Kepler, J. (1864) *Harmonice Mundi, Opera Omnia*, Vol. 5. Frankfurt.

Mandelbrot, B.B. (1982) *The Fractal Geometry of Nature.* Freeman, San Francisco.

Meagher, D. (1982) "Geometric Modelling Using Octree Encoding," *Computing Graphics and Image Processing* 19:129–147.

Sobhanpanah, C. and I.O. Angell (1986) "Polygonal Mesh and Quad-Tree Display Algorithms for Non-Convex Crystal Structures." *Computing and Graphics*, Pergamon, Elmsford, N.Y.

Toth, F. (1964) *Regular Figures.* Macmillan, New York.

Wells, A.F. (1970) *Models in Structural Inorganic Chemistry.* Oxford Univ. Pres, New York.

Woodwark, J. and A. Bowyer (1986) "Better and Faster Pictures from Solid Models," *Computer-Aided Engineering J.*, February 198:17–24.

Part 3 Design

Computer Assistance to the Design Process

Philip Steadman

Introduction

In this paper I am going to try to draw a lightning sketch of the structure of the design process; to indicate where past and present computer aids fit within that structure; and then to offer some personal and rather fragmentary ideas as to where computer-aided design, and in particular its use of graphics, might go in the future.

Many authors have tried to describe the typical structure of the design process, and to set out the various activities which designers undertake in some formal scheme or flowchart. Some of the earliest to do this were the proponents of the "design methods movement" of the mid-1960s, including Christopher Jones (1970), the first professor of my own department, Bruce Archer (1965) at the Royal College of Art, and many others (March, 1976; Pahl and Beitz, 1984). These authors disagreed about terminology and produced a bewildering range of diagrams, differing greatly in form and complexity.

Of course there are good reasons why "the" design process should vary in reality between different design professions and industries. The basic nature of the geometry of the artefacts may differ—2-D, 3-D, rectilinear or with curved surfaces, assembled from few or many parts, and so on; the nature of the manufacturing process varies, and this in turn affects the design process; in some fields, as in much engineering design, the technical specification for an artefact is very tight, whereas in other areas such as architecture perhaps or graphic design, designers have much greater freedom of action.

The Basic Features of Design

Nevertheless it is still possible and useful I think for the present purpose to pick out some basic features common to most accounts of the design process and to identify some activities which are common to the designer's job in many industries (Fig. 1). The first activity is that of *specification.* Here the designer's task is set out; criteria for the performance of the artefact are laid down, either by the client or on the basis of market research; and information is collected from a great variety of sources about the potential market, manufacturing constraints, legal requirements and standards, and so on.

The second activity is that of *synthesis,* or generation of alternative designs. This is the very heart of the design process, where the designer's creativity and inventive powers are brought into play. Of course a great deal of designing is of an incremental or evolutionary character, making small changes to existing designs. But in other cases a completely new artefact is created by the permutation and recombination of components or elements in some quite novel configuration.

The third activity is that of *analysis* or evaluation, where alternative candidate designs, or parts of designs, synthesised in the previous phase, are subjected to tests and evaluated against the specification. These tests might be theoretical ones, made in the designer's imagination, or by means of calculations. Or they might be real practical tests on physical models or prototypes. Clearly the kinds of performance criteria against which designs might be evaluated could be of an almost infinite variety. But among the most common types of analysis or testing would be analysis of structural performance, analysis of thermal performance, kinematic analysis of mechanisms, testing of the logic and electrical behaviour of circuits, and perhaps most important for today's topic, the analysis of visual appearance of a product or building, including its *aesthetic* evaluation.

A diagram of this kind simplifies matters in many ways, but most of all by making this sharp conceptual separation between synthesis and analysis, between generation and evaluation. In practice the two kinds of activity are not so distinct. Nor do they necessarily follow each other in this orderly sequence. Rather, the designer generates some alternative possibilities, probably for certain selected features or elements of the design; subjects these to analysis and as a result rejects some of the alternatives; makes modifications to others, tests them again; and so on.

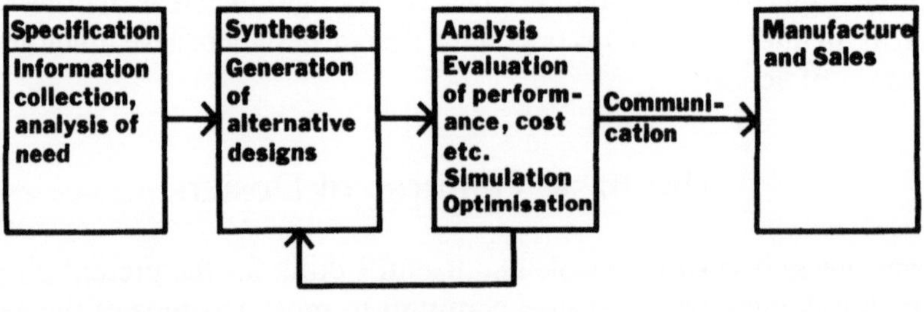

FIGURE 1

Most writers on design have agreed about this essentially *cyclical* or *iterative* nature of the design process. For example Herbert Simon in his *Sciences of the Artificial* speaks of designing as involving "first the generation of alternatives and then the testing of those alternatives against a whole array of requirements and constraints. There need not be merely a single generate-test cycle, but there can be a whole nested series of such cycles" (Simon, 1969). Part of the art of design, in Simon's view, consists in suitably constraining the generators such that they are guaranteed to produce alternatives which meet at least some of the stated requirements—that is to say, some of the tests are in effect *built in* to the generators. As the designer moves repeatedly round these generate-test cycles, so the design is developed from a vague, general concept, through progressively better-developed versions as the details are worked out, until the whole scheme is finalised.

I will come back to the question of these generate-test cycles. Meanwhile the last activity in the design process is *communication* of the finished design to the manufacturing or construction process. This will normally—at least in the traditional relationship of design to manufacture—be via working drawings of course, as well as schedules and other forms of written instruction.

With the help of this *very* schematic picture of the design and manufacturing process as a whole, we can begin to see where various past, present and possible future applications of computers fit in. Historically the first area of application, and today the most widespread in industry, is *computer drafting*—that is, automation of the production of working drawings (Fig. 2). Indeed it seems that for many British managers, computer drafting *is* computer-aided design, despite the fact that computer drafting leaves the central activities of design, the activities of synthesis and analysis, essentially unchanged. Computer drafting comes into play only when the design is all but finalised.

That said, it *is* certainly possible for designers to use drafting systems during the more creative phases of design, and especially so where the artefact in question is itself a two-dimensional work of graphic art. But

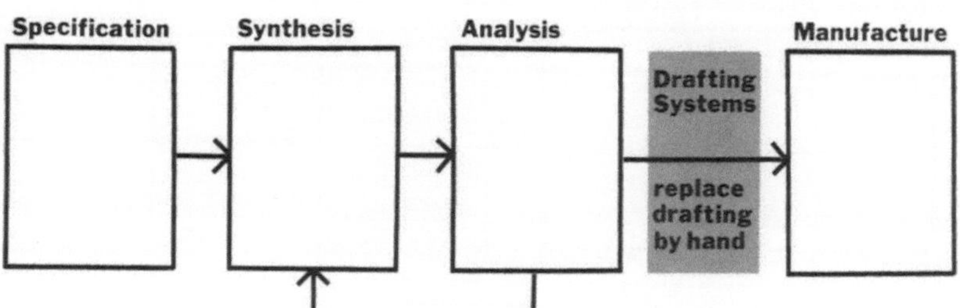

FIGURE 2

where drafting systems *are* so used, then designers will begin to demand different kinds of function, different kinds of capabilities, from those provided by most existing drafting packages. This is another point I will come back to.

The next step in CAD has been the development of a great variety of separate programs or packages for carrying out *analyses* of performance (Fig. 3). Some such programs allow the behaviour of designed objects to be *simulated*, for the purposes of evaluation. Where the constraints on design can be formally stated, and some performance objective can be quantified, then it may be possible to use mathematical methods to *optimise* the design with respect to that single objective. I will not try to enumerate the variety of these kinds of analysis package, but will simply make one general point. Such programs have again been intended mainly for use in the later stages of the development of a design, rather than in the early conceptual phase—since they tend to require detailed input data on shape, dimensions, materials and so on, in order to yield precise quantitative analytical results.

In the early days of computer-aided engineering and architectural design, these kinds of separate programs for analysis had one great disadvantage; they required that large quantities of data be taken by hand off paper drawings and entered to a different program for each type of analysis. This was as true for visual analysis through computer-generated perspective drawings as it was for say structural or thermal analyses. The problem is wholly avoided by taking the next logical step: to *model* the three-dimensional form and other properties of the design in the computer and to integrate this model directly with the automated analyses (Fig. 4).

The further advantage is that working drawings may now be produced automatically from the model itself; or else, in certain selected areas of manufacturing, the design can be transmitted electronically to the production process, and paper drawings can be dispensed with altogether (Fig. 5). At present this is a practical possibility in the machining of metal components, moulds and dies by numerically controlled (NC) tools; in

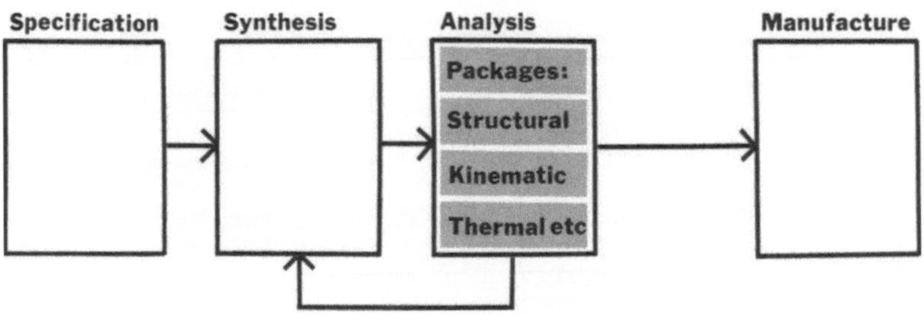

FIGURE 3

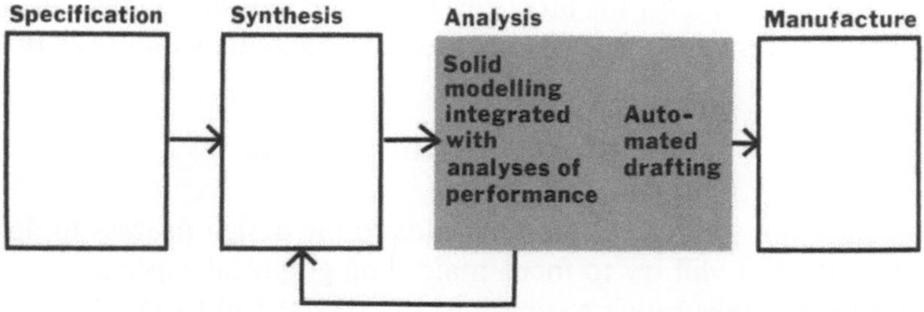

FIGURE 4

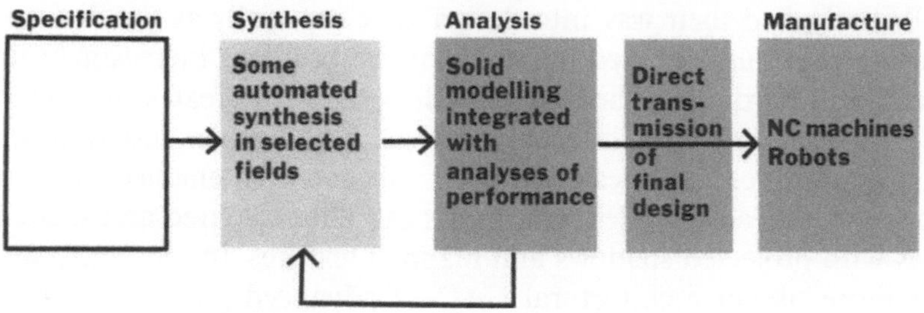

FIGURE 5

the preparation of photographic masks for fabricating printed circuits and microchips; and in the direct production of printing plates in the newspaper and publishing industries. Some links are being made between CAD and the programming of robots for assembly operations. But we are still a long way from the complete automation of the assembly process for complex products with many components. And in some fields, for instance in the building industry, it is difficult to see much significant automation of assembly operations in the foreseeable future. Here at least, paper drawings will continue to play their traditional role.

Integrated CADCAM systems incorporating solid modellers and linked analysis packages represent the most advanced and comprehensive types of commercially available computer aids to design in the mid-1980s. As I have emphasised, however, it is still necessary to bring to such systems a substantially well-developed design scheme or schemes, *before* these can be modelled and evaluated. Computer aids have barely begun to touch the earlier, conceptual or sketch stages of the design process. And in particular, computer aids have not in general been brought to bear on the activity of *synthesis*, or the generation of alternatives in design. There are some exceptions to this rule: in kinematic synthesis, in the automated layout of components and tracks in printed circuit boards and microchips, and (with rather uncertain commercial success) in automated floor layout in architecture. But for the most part computer aids to synthesis in design are subjects for research, and especially problematic subjects at that.

Future Developments

How then can we expect computer aids to the design process to develop in the future? I will try to focus mainly on graphical aspects.

It does not take much gazing into the crystal ball to see that one important direction of development is going to be towards higher-quality, ever more realistic colour images in CAD systems. The super-realistic graphics that we are seeing now in film animation or flight simulators will surely find their way into design aids, especially as the display processing previously carried out by software becomes increasingly implemented in hardware. The interest will perhaps be greatest in such areas as industrial design, architecture, landscape and urban design, where visual appearance is critical—but there are potential engineering applications too. Already, modelling systems can offer coloured and shaded images with projected shadows and mapped textures. In the future we may see more use in architectural CAD of advanced graphics to simulate effects of transparency, artificial and natural lighting, and atmospheric phenomena such as haze or mist—all of them factors which can crucially affect the real visual experience of buildings, but which are extraordinarily difficult to convey in conventional drawings. Another possibility is of course animation, to allow the surrogate experience of actually moving around or through some proposed building or urban scheme. Animation will no doubt be important too in engineering design, in kinematics and the analysis of motion.

There are no great conceptual difficulties in seeing what direction these developments in graphical realism might take, although there are great technical challenges. But what effects will they have on the design process, I wonder? One possible result is that some forms of *analysis* which were previously carried out through calculation and by the designer inspecting numerical output might be carried out *visually*. I am thinking for example of the analysis of levels of natural or artificial light in architectural interiors, or the analysis of glare from windows. With highly realistic ray-traced images, these things could be checked by a simple inspection of the pictures. Of course essentially the *same* calculations are still being made, but they have become embodied in the graphics and hidden from the user. Something of the same thing is already true for the design of curved surfaces using surface modellers and the analysis of potential spatial clashes between moving parts in mechanisms.

As pictures of designed objects become more realistic, and as the analysis or simulation of performance becomes less opaque and more readily comprehensible to the non-specialist, so designers are able to present *to their clients* a more complete and immediate impression of their proposals than they could through conventional drawings. The clients will see more clearly "what they are getting," and so, in principle at least, the clients can participate more actively in the design process itself. This implication of CAD, that it might open up design to a greater involvement of client bodies or of the general public, is one which a number of authors have commented on.

There is another possible consequence of the introduction of highly realistic graphics into such fields as engineering and architectural design—if not for graphic design itself. It is arguable that the conventions of representation traditionally employed in design have themselves exerted subtle effects on the nature of the artefacts produced, although the precise nature of those effects is very difficult to trace. It has sometimes been suggested for example—although in my view the point is debatable—that the *rectangularity* of most modern buildings is due to the fact of their being designed with T-square and set-square. The conventions of engineering and architectural drawing have developed of course out of the technology of the drawing-board and pencil, and have meant that three-dimensional objects are conceived in terms of projections onto 2-D planes and that surfaces and volumes are depicted and conceived in terms of their edge lines. It is not always easy to remember how very artificial these conventions are. There is a gap between code and message, between signifier and signified—not so great perhaps as the separation say between musical notation and music itself, but a wide gap nonetheless.

The introduction of solid and surface modellers, incorporating colours, shading and lighting effects, turns designers back into sculptors. As has been frequently remarked, the user of a solid modeller "sculpts in electronic space." The architectural designer employing such a system can work directly with planes and volumes. The mechanical engineer uses boolean operators as though they were machine tools, to add metal or to pare it away. Will this have consequences for the nature of the artefacts themselves? Will the design process in these fields become more like the design process in say pottery or painting, where there is no encoded representation separate from the artefact itself, and the artist manipulates and responds to the material directly? Will it be possible to design objects which were almost literally inconceivable through the medium of conventional paper drawings?

I will leave all these rhetorical questions hanging in the air and go on to the second kind of future development in CAD which I want to explore briefly; and that is the possible encroachment of computer aids onto the more creative and synthetic activities of design. I have argued that computer aids in use today largely serve the latter end of the design process, when the general scheme has been worked out, and what remains is the design of the details and the communication of information to the manufacturing process. But we are now seeing attempts to move computer aids "backwards," in terms of my earlier diagram, towards the earlier conceptual and generative stages of designing. For those of us who have lived with the development of CAD from its very beginnings in the early 1960s, and through the "design methods" debates of those same years, there is indeed a curious sense of déjà vu in seeing many of the topics which were discussed and worked on then, reappearing in the literature of artificial intelligence and expert systems applications in CAD today: general theories of the design process, generative procedures for automated synthesis in design and so on.

Computer Aids to Conceptual Design

There are many intrinsic difficulties in the way of providing computer aids to the early phases of the design process (which perhaps accounts for the relative failure and lack of commercial application of those early efforts of the middle 1960s and early 1970s). The first is that, as in all other domains of creative thought, the designer works with ill-formed, tentative, ambiguous and vague ideas; this ambiguity and imprecision are carried over into the representations which the designer uses, the sketches and doodles, and these are qualities which it is notoriously difficult to embody in computer programs.

The second difficulty is that the designer moves rapidly in his mind between different hierarchical levels, between consideration of the details and consideration of the whole, and between different aspects of performance and different evaluative criteria. He goes mentally through many nested cycles of "generate and test" in Simon's terms.

The third difficulty is that all this requires the designer to bring to bear large bodies of knowledge and experience—both technical knowledge from his specialised professional training and common-sense knowledge from his everyday experience of the world. This knowledge we can say is of two broad kinds (although the two are almost indistinguishably intertwined). The first is knowledge of *possibilities* for candidate designs or parts of designs which may be relevant to the problem in hand. However these are described—"preconceptions," "premodels," "protomodels" are some of the terms which have been used—it is clear that the designer must bring some such hypothetical ideas to the design task with which he is faced, for the process of subsequent development, evaluation and refinement ever to get started. The second kind of knowledge is that which is brought to bear in *evaluation*: again, both specialised engineering science-type knowledge, and general common-sensical knowledge of the environments in which artefacts are used and of the functions they must perform. All these considerations lead us inevitably into the fields of artificial intelligence and knowledge-based systems.

If computer aids *are* to be introduced into this central core of the design process, then this will necessarily involve the attempt to somehow formalise and represent these very large bodies of knowledge in the machine (Fig. 6). Computer aids for analysis and evaluation would have to be fully integrated *across* the design process, so that data could be passed readily and rapidly from one to the other. And computer aids would have to be integrated *longitudinally*, so that designs represented in the first place in highly schematic, simplified and abstract form might be progressively developed, elaborated and transformed into fully finished schemes. There has been some progress in the first of these tasks; but to my knowledge only Charles Eastman and colleagues at Carnegie-Mellon have even attempted to address the second (Eastman, 1985).

In practice we can expect the encroachment of AI techniques on computer-aided design to be gradual and incremental. Indeed that is what is happening now in many disparate areas of CAD research. One such area is the development of "intelligent interfaces" to complex evaluation packages, such as those for finite element analysis, intended to help the non-specialist user to formulate the right kinds of questions and to interpret the significance of the analytical results. A second possibility is that much of the rather low-level technical information which designers use and which is presently codified in manuals, standards, reference books and manufacturers' catalogues could be packaged up into "expert system" software and so made more accessible and convenient to use.

A third area is detail design, where the basic configuration of some device or mechanism has been decided by the designer, and the computer's job is then to assign values to dimensional parameters and to make decisions about materials and physical properties. One very interesting system of this kind, illustrated for the design of air cylinders, has recently been published by Brown and Chandrasekaran (1986). This sys-

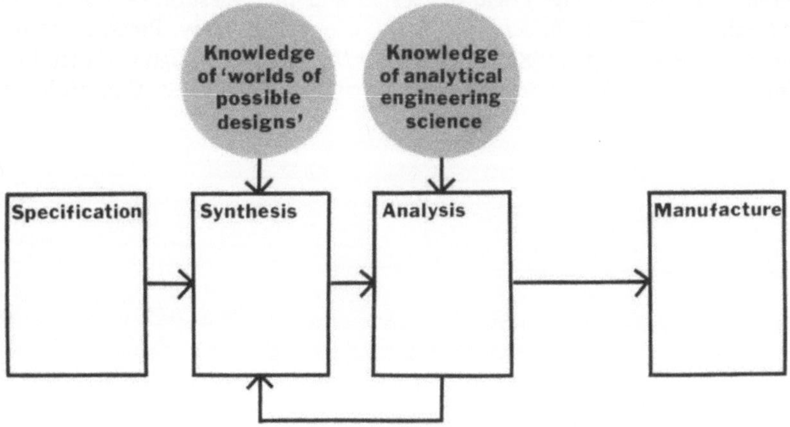

FIGURE 6

tem embodies a hierarchical structure of nested generate-and-test cycles of the kind which Herbert Simon discussed.

Finally in this high-speed survey of AI applications, and perhaps of greatest interest today, is the possibility of incorporating greater intelligence into computer graphics systems. In a conventional drafting system, for example, the computer has no "understanding" of the significance of the lines which make up an image. It may have no understanding even of simple geometrical relationships between lines—for example that four lines, entered separately, come together to form a square—let alone any understanding of the "semantics" of the image, for example that the square is to represent a window or the cross section of a beam. My colleague William Fawcett covers elsewhere in this volume his and other workers' attempts to incorporate (as yet relatively low-level) reasoning abilities into graphics systems, for some architectural applications.

Some people would question the ultimate feasibility and even the desirability of trying to emulate in the computer the highly creative faculties of the mind which are brought to bear in designing. I take a pragmatic view on these controversies. Experience will tell whether the kinds of ideas now being explored in research will prove really useful to the practising designer. I do not expect rapid progress, however, towards the wholesale automation of the central activities of design.

References

Archer, L.B. (1965) *Systematic Method for Designers.* The Design Council, London.

Brown, D.C., and B. Chandrasekaran (1986) "Knowledge and Control for a Mechanical Design Expert System," *Computer*, July, pp. 92–100.

Eastman, C.M. (1985) "Abstractions: A Conceptual Approach for Structuring Interaction with Integrated CAD Systems," *Comput. Graphics* 9(2):97–105.

Jones, J.C. (1970) *Design Methods: Seeds of Human Futures.* Wiley Interscience, New York.

March, L.J. (1976) "The Logic of Design and the Question of Value." In L.J. March (ed.), *The Architecture of Form.* Cambridge Univ. Press, London.

Pahl, G., and W. Beitz (1984) *Engineering Design.* The Design Council, London.

Simon, H.A. (1969) *The Sciences of the Artificial.* MIT Press, Cambridge, Mass.

A Theory of Computer-Aided Design: A Possible Approach

John Lansdown

Introduction

It is a truism to say that there is nothing so practical as a good theory. A relevant theory underpins and supports practice, giving it the sort of foundation that is lacking in more ad hoc working. It has a unifying effect to guide practitioners through the long dark nights of misunderstanding and doubt. Above all, a good theory suggests practical techniques and developments that might not otherwise have been devised. Computer-aided design (CAD) is an essentially practical subject in which theoretical discussion has largely been ignored and, to an extent, this has meant that the subject is strong on technique but weak on rationale. In this paper I tentatively suggest a theory which might have some application: that it is possible to see all designing (not just CAD) in terms of a particular model which I call *prototype modification* and that, in doing this, a new way of approaching CAD might result.

At the heart of the theory is the axiom that designing is a process of transforming an initial tentative description of an artefact into a more or less complete one. If this is so then it is possible to plot the degree of completeness of a hypothetical case against time (Lansdown, 1985). When we do this, certain discontinuities appear in the graph (Fig. 1). These occur at points where the existing set of motivating ideas seem to cease to have sufficient promise. At these points new ideas occur which initially set us back but then allow the transformation process to continue either until completion or until these concepts, too, are replaced by new ones. A characteristic of this situation is that in a sense, the discontinuities are sudden and depend perhaps more on the arrival of new ideas than on the realisation that the existing ones are inadequate. Indeed, the new ideas seem actually to block the development of the old and prevent further consideration of them. If this model is valid, one would postulate that the graphs of more "creative" designers would contain more discontinuities than those of others.

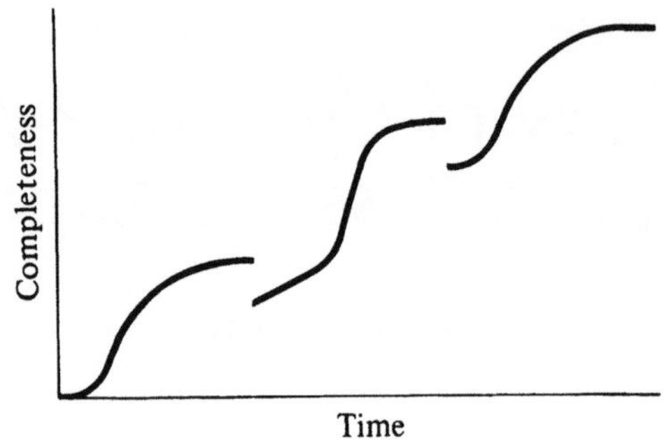

FIGURE 1

There is an important form of designing, however, that is not characterised by discontinuity. This is what has been called "robust design." In contrast to a "lean design," a robust design *is one that brings together several new divergent lines of development to form a new "composite" design, which is internally adjusted to form a new "consolidated" design, which is then further developed as a variety of "stretched" design* (Gardiner, 1986). In this case, innovation arises from incremental modification of existing, tried and true concepts rather than entirely new approaches. Here, the transformation from initial to final description is continuous: we are, as it were, fine-tuning a set of already working ideas rather than inventing something new—although the results might not resemble anything previously envisaged. This form of designing is common and, some would argue, more useful than highly innovative working.

I have suggested elsewhere that a straightforward algorithmic or procedural approach to designing would work only where the transformations are continuous—although I have always maintained that different types of CAD could assist in even the most creative of activities (Lansdown, 1970, 1985). In particular, the use of what can be called "parametric variation"—where one sets up a model of some aspect of the artefact being designed and systematically varies its parameters to change performance characteristics—is restricted to the continuous phases. This is because it is impossible to know, a priori, how many or what types of parameters will fully characterise the completed design—a point comprehensively made by Hofstadter (1985).

The Unified Nature of Designing

There is a tendency to view the two forms of designing—robust and lean—as entirely separate. It is more useful, though, to assume that they are degrees of the same. A model for doing this is provided (at least in part) by catastrophe theory (Thom and Zeeman, 1975). Catastrophe theory was originally propounded by René Thom in 1972 and concerns itself with situations where gradually changing forces produce sudden effects (Thom, 1972, 1975). To see the relevance of this in our case we can assume that the graph of progress through time is simply an incomplete two-dimensional view of a figure which, in fact, is a folded three-dimensional surface (Fig. 2). All possible designs lie on this surface and although I would not like to suggest that designing is equivalent to searching the surface, it represents, in terms of Mitchell (1986), the "state-space of design alternatives." The dimensions of the three-dimensional graph are "completeness," time, and what might be thought of as "inventiveness"—with the progress-trajectories of the most inventive, least robust, designs being furthest away from the time axis. Without loss of generality, we can look at a part of the diagram containing just one fold. This shows what Thom calls an *elementary catastrophe*—one of only seven having less than five dimensions. In particular, it is a *cusp catastrophe*, so-called because of the shape of its two-dimensional projection onto the horizontal plane (Fig. 3).

The model illustrates a number of important features to help us understand designing. For example, we see from it that there are at least two possible paths to arriving at any particular conclusion: one via a robust trajectory where continuous transformation is possible (trajectory 1), the other via a lean and inventive trajectory where continuous transformation is not possible—where a new idea has to be thought up for progress towards completeness to be made (trajectories 2 and 3). That there is at least one continuous trajectory to any point helps us explain why, via configurational studies, we can make production systems and shape grammars which reproduce the designs of Palladio, Frank Lloyd Wright and others (Stiny and Mitchell, 1976; Stiny, 1979; Gips and Stiny, 1980; Hanson and Radford, 1986). The model also illustrates the blocking effect of new ideas: it is easier to proceed forward than to jump back up to the old level.

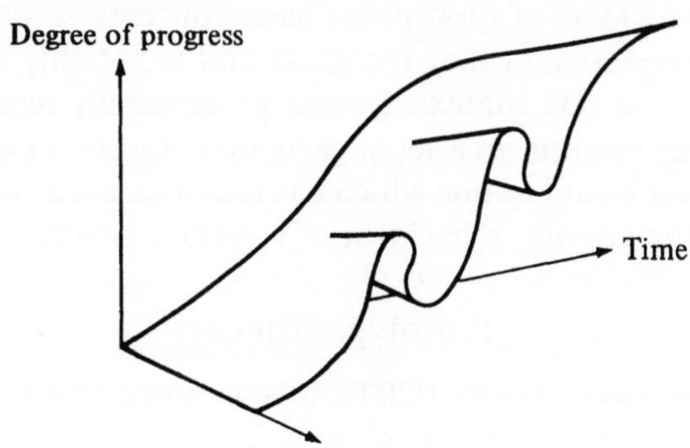

FIGURE 2

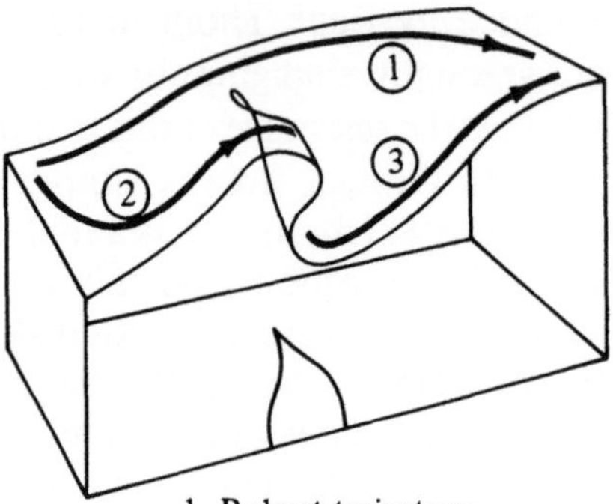

1 Robust trajectory
2, 3 Innovative trajectory

FIGURE 3

But, perhaps more than anything else, the cusp catastrophe metaphor suggests that, at any point in the development of a project, it is possible to switch from lean to robust designing and still make progress. Indeed, if this view is correct, we can think of designing entirely as a process of what we might term, "prototype modification." This has profound implications for CAD.

Prototype Modification

One of the few things we know about creativity is that creative people know a great deal about the subject in which they are being innovative. Tyros rarely generate worthwhile ideas (Lansdown, 1983). We can conclude from this and from observation of the work and working methods of creative people—their notebooks being an especially fruitful source—that even the most inventive designers do not arrive at new concepts as it were, out of a vacuum. Exactly how new ideas occur to inventive people is not clear but an explanation which is at least as plausible as any other is that they have a store of appropriate basic concepts—prototypes—whose potential for development they recognise and are readily able to exploit. By "prototype," in this context, I mean an especially representative but possible abstract example of a set of particular objects. Thus, for instance, a prototype chair would be one which has four legs, a seat which is roughly 43 cm above the ground, a backrest of a certain height and so on.

Prototype Theory

In cognitive prototype theory (CPT), it is assumed that a concept can be represented as a quadruple $\langle A, d, p, c \rangle$. A is the particular conceptual domain under consideration; d is a distance metric; p, the prototype, is a member of A and somehow typifies the domain: for chairs, say, the ordinary kitchen chair is more likely to fit this category than a 1960s beanbag chair or a 1980s typists' kneeling chair. The parameter *c* is a function with values in the range [0,1]—wherein the closer the object is to the prototype the smaller is the value of *c*. The exact interpretation of *c* is still a matter of debate in CPT—as instances, Osherson and Smith (1981, 1982) take a critical view of a fuzzy set interpretation of *c*, and Jones (1982) gives an ingeniously different interpretation. Neither of these interpretations exactly captures our intuitive understanding of closeness to a prototype, but that problem does not concern us here.

In order to use the representation to explain designing by prototype modification, we can add to it a further parameter, *m*. This factor indicates the extent to which modifications have been made to the individual features of the prototype in order to realise the particular concept. Here, too, we can use a metric in the range [0,1] with the characteristic that the smaller the number, the greater the extent of modifications. Were all modifications equally substantive, a convenient measure of *m* could perhaps be the reciprocal of the actual number of modifications (or, more usefully, the reciprocal of some inverse power of that number, such as the square root or cube root). But modifications are not all equal: some only affect detail; others are much more fundamental. For this reason more complex measures are needed. These, and their relation to different types of modification, are discussed in Lansdown (1986).

In our representation, the concept *chair* is equivalent to the quintuple:

$$\langle \text{CHAIRS}, d(chair), p(chair), c(chair), m(chair) \rangle$$

where

CHAIRS is the set of all possible chairs;

d(chair) is a real number metric measuring the "distance" between pairs of chairs such that smaller numbers represent closer similarity between pairs;

p(chair) is the prototype—an abstraction that typifies the domain and represents the designer's starting concept: this is unlikely to be exactly the same prototype as would be used in CPT;

c(chair) is a function assigning numbers in the range [0, 1] in such a way that closeness to the prototype indicates greater "chairness" and that this is expressed by smaller numbers;

m(chair) is a function assigning numbers in the range [0, 1] in such a way that the smaller numbers indicate the greater extent of modification of the prototype's features, a value near 0 indicating a very large number of modifications.

We can postulate that an "imaginative" or "innovative" design for a chair would give a value of *c(chair)* close to 1: for efficiency, we want this to be achieved with as few modifications as possible—giving rise to values for *m(chair)* also close to 1. Furthermore, it is my contention that the best prototypes are those which have the highest number of latent, potentially modifiable features. Although it could be used for sitting on, a cube would not therefore be a good candidate for a prototype chair. And yet, surprisingly, there are many three-dimensional CAD systems which only provide things such as cubes, cylinders and spheres as their prototypes (or, as they are called in that case, primitives). Designers are expected to build up their objects by merging these primitives together through a process of addition and subtraction. These systems are known as "solid modellers." They can be, and are being, used by designers, but what is needed are systems with a higher level of prototype.

Design Prototype Systems

For some time now I have been working on the elements of a CAD system to suggest possible prototypes and enable their easy modification. The earliest version of this approach goes back to 1973 and was used to assist in the design of unmodelled facades of buildings set in streets (that is, sandwiched between other buildings). On entering the system the designer was presented with a screen drawing of a prototype facade. The prototype could either be a pre-existing one or be distilled by a process of "averaging" with previously accepted designs. By means of a variety of built-in transformations and other manipulations, the user could quickly modify the prototype and interactively bring it closer to the desired end. As with conventional designing, feedback from modified image to mind suggested further modifications to the image and thus a cyclical, trial-and-error procedure emerged. The presentation and modification were entirely two-dimensional.

Whilst the system had the important characteristic that the extent, number and order of the modifications were completely in the hands of its users, it was otherwise not very flexible because it supported only a relatively limited repertoire of possible changes. However, within this repertoire, no restrictions were placed on the extent of application. Thus it was possible to do things that would be impossible in real life: windows could overlap one another or even be made bigger than the building itself, storeys could be set to impractical heights and so on. The system therefore had no "intelligence" and relied on its users to ensure that only feasible proposals were incorporated—which, in this particular case, they could do quite easily.

The great advantage of the system, though, was the speed at which it made it possible to go from a vague concept to a finished presentation—probably assisted by the fact that the designer did not have to start from a blank sheet. (Certainly my later observations of artists using paint systems confirms that they work more rapidly and with greater effect if they start with a frame-grabbed picture, even if this is totally disregarded in

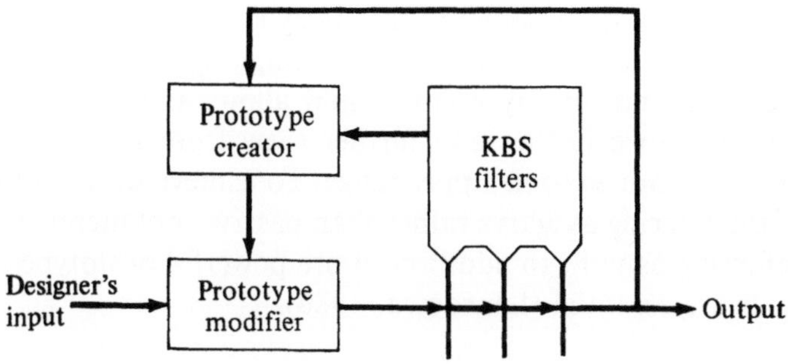

FIGURE 4

the final image.) Moreover, the lack of practical constraint was often useful in suggesting to the designer possible lines of new development, although these sometimes had to be pursued without further help from the system. A CAD system of this type was feasible because of its two-dimensional nature and the essentially limited number of elements expected to be incorporated in facade treatment. (Note that only repetitive elements were allowed and that these were restricted to the then current design idiom of the architectural practice in which it was used; for example, the system did not employ classical or post-modern features.)

To prevent impractical options being explored, later versions of this system (and some related ones) included constraints on possible prototype modifications; for instance, limits were set on sizes of windows, heights and numbers of storeys were restricted to lie within particular ranges and so on. However, these constraints were unconditional in the sense that they were not interrelated and it was still possible to choose, say, window heights independently of storey heights. In more recent versions, conditional constraints using knowledge-based methods were introduced. In these knowledge-based systems (KBS), the choice of any one option limited the choice of all the others more or less in the same way that it does in real life. The introduction of greater conditionality and "intelligence" has the effect of making these systems more practical whilst limiting their usefulness as idea-suggesting tools: the conditions act as filters (Fig. 4), sieving-out the more extreme and lean possibilities in favour of the more robust but, possibly, workaday.

Implications for CAD

From all this development it has become clear that a CAD system useful both in lean and robust designing needs to allow prototype modification with filtering which can be progressively applied as ideas develop. The filtering must be conditional and knowledge-based and, for robust designing, would be applied from the outset to limit infeasible or overly innovative lines of development (effectively keeping the value of m in its upper range and c close to zero). In lean designing, the filtering need only be on demand and, in any event, would allow (and perhaps, even, encourage) c to move further and further away from zero whilst still endeavouring to limit m to its upper range. To achieve these ends, we must think of the filtering as active rather than passive: not merely attenuating but reinforcing as well. In addition, more powerful prototype-modifying techniques are essential (Lansdown, 1986).

Some Problems

Knowledge-based filters, like all other KBS, depend on knowledge being explicitly representable; we cannot instruct a computer to do things that we do not know explicitly how to do ourselves. But it is not at all clear how much of designers' knowledge can be made explicit in this sense; certainly the tools of knowledge elicitation and acquisition need sharpening before substantial progress can be made in bringing implicit or tacit knowledge to the fore. Magee discusses some of the problems of capturing design knowledge in his Master's thesis (Magee, 1986).

Furthermore, there are problems in using straightforward KBS in design that are being revealed as more experience is gained in their development and use, although for example, Coyne (1986), with his work on rule ordering, has shown that one of the difficulties that originally looked as if it might be troublesome in the planning use of KBS can be overcome in a relatively simple way. There are, however, other problems which, in the general case, do not seem quite so tractable. Not least of these arises from the inadequacy of conventional KBS logics in dealing with incomplete or contradictory worlds: things which are the very stuff of designing (Lansdown and Roast, 1987). Systems using prototype modification and selective filtering have the potential to bypass some of these problems. In particular, it is far easier automatically to ensure that a physically consistent and feasible object is being dealt with if one is available from the outset and if only legal transformations are carried out on it.

The exact nature of the representations used also needs further study and development. Those unfamiliar with the various types of knowledge representations in common use are directed to the literature where they will see that most KBS use rule-based productions as their means of representation (see, for example, Mylopoulos and Levesque, 1984; Gevarter, 1984). But, whilst production systems are powerful and easy to understand, they are limited in their design usefulness. This is mainly because they fail to capture adequately the interconnectedness of design knowledge, which seems to be "chunked" into much larger elements than normal productions can handle. Semantic networks are better adapted to representing interconnectedness but, in practical cases, soon become unwieldy. Frames and frame-related representations appear to be potentially the most valuable—something that was thought to be the case when I wrote my 1982 report (Lansdown, 1982). More recent experiments both of my own and others have confirmed my feelings about these—see, for example, Fikes and Kehler (1985), Maeda et al. (1980), Huxor (1985) as well as Niwa, Sasaki and Ihara (1984).

Conclusion

In this paper I have tried to outline a theory of CAD that explains both lean and robust designing and brings them into the same orbit. The approach is through the technique of prototype modification and, within this paradigm, designing becomes a process of choosing appropriate prototypes and applying powerful transformations to them either solely under designer control or with active assistance of a KBS. In setting up systems to allow such working, new ways of creating and representing the prototypes have to be devised. In addition, new transformation techniques must be thought up. I do not describe these techniques here and direct the reader elsewhere for a discussion of the details (Lansdown, 1986). What can be said is that basically the transformations fall under two categories: augmenting and diminishing.

For a long while, the main value of CAD to designers has been increases in productivity. To date, these increases have been most marked in the production documentation and detailing stages of designing. Although more experimentation and development need to be done, it seems that systems based on prototype modification could bring similar benefits to the creative stages of designing. It has been shown (Brady, 1986) that designer-support systems that can respond quickly to the demands of users actually increase their creative productivity. Prototype-modification systems using frame-like representations promise to do just that.

References

Brady, J.T. (1986) "A Theory of Productivity in the Creative Process," *IEEE Computer Graphics and Applications* 6(5):25–34.

Coyne, R. (1988) *The Logic of Design*. Pitman, London.

Fikes, R. and T. Kehler (1985) "The Role of Frame-Based Representation in Reasoning," *Commun. ACM* 28(9)904–920.

Gardiner, J.P. (1986) "Robust and Lean Designs with State of the Art Automotive and Aircraft Examples. In Freeman C., *Design, Innovation and Long Cycles in Economic Development*. Frances Pinter, London, 1986.

Gevarter, W.D. (1984) *Artificial Intelligence, Expert Systems, Computer Vision and Natural Language Processing*. Noyes Publications, Park Ridge, N.J.

Gips, J. and G. Stiny (1980) "Production Systems and Grammars: A Uniform Characterisation," *Environment and Planning B* (7):399–408.

Hanson, N.R.L. and A.D. Radford (1986) "On Modelling the Work of the Architect Glenn Murcutt," *Design Computing* 1(3):189–203.

Hofstadter, D.R. (1985) "Meta-Font, Metamathematics and Metaphysics," *Visible Language* XVI 4:309–338.
Huxor, A. (1985) "An Analysis of Theories Relevant to Knowledge-Based CAD Systems" unpublished MA Thesis, Department of Design Research , Royal College of Art, London.
Jones, G.V. (1982) "Stacks Not Fuzzy Sets: An Ordinal Basis for Prototype Theory of Concepts, *Cognition* 12(3):291–297.
Lansdown, J. (1970) "Computer Art for Theatrical Performance," *Proc. ACM International Computer Symposium*, Bonn.
Lansdown, J. (1982) "Expert Systems: Their Impact on the Construction Industry," RIBA Conference Fund, London.
Lansdown, J. (1983) "Computing in the Creative Professions," Working Paper, System Simulation Ltd., London.
Lansdown, J. (1985) "Requirements for Knowledge Based Systems in Design," Working Paper, System Simulation Ltd., London.
Lansdown, J. (1986) "Notes on Prototype Modification as a Design Method," System Simulation Ltd., London.
Lansdown, J. and C. Roast (1987) "The Possibilities and Problems of Knowledge-Based Systems for Design," *Environment and Planning B* 14:255–266.
Maeda, Y., A. Takeshige, T. Kogushi, T. Tomiyama and H. Yoshikawa (1980) "Frame Operating System for CAD," *Proc. Man-Machine Communications in CAD*, pp. 11–14, IFIP, Tokyo.
Magee, H.K. (1986) "A Survey of Knowledge Elicitation Techniques for Use in CAD," unpublished MA Thesis, Department of Design Research, Royal College of Art, London.
Mitchell, W.J. (1986) "Colour Transformations in Computer-Aided Design," *Design Computing* 1(1):20–28.
Mylopoulos, J. and H.J. Levesque (1984) "An Overview of Knowledge Representation." In *On Conceptual Modelling*, M.L. Brodie, J. Mylopoulos and J.W. Schmidt (eds.). Springer-Verlag, New York.
Niwa, K., K. Sasaki and H. Ihara (1984) "An Experimental Comparison of Knowledge Representation Schemes," *AI Magazine*, Summer, pp. 29–36.
Osherson, D.N. and E.E. Smith (1981) "On the Adequacy of Prototype as a Theory of Concepts," *Cognition* 9(1):35–58.
Osherson, D.N. and E.E. Smith (1982) "Gradeness and Conceptual Combination," *Cognition* 12(3):299–318.
Stiny, G. (1979) "A Generative Approach to Composition and Style in Architecture," *Proc. Parc79 Conference*, AMK, Berlin.
Stiny, G. and W.J. Mitchell (1978) "The Palladian Grammar," *Environment and Planning B* (5):5–18.
Thom, R. (1972) *Stabilitê Structurelle et Morphogenese.* Benjamin, New York.
Thom, R. (1975) *Structural Stability and Morphogenesis*, D.H. Fowler, transl. Benjamin, New York.
Thom, R. and E.C. Zeeman (1975) "Catastrophe Theory: Its Present State and Future Perspectives," Springer Lecture Notes in Mathematics no. 468. Springer-Verlag, New York.

Linking Graphics and Inference

William Fawcett

Introduction

This paper is concerned with applications of computer-based graphics systems to design tasks, not with the characteristics of graphic systems themselves. Further, we are less concerned with the application of computer graphics in constructing detailed models of design objects than with the inference operations that determine what the design object should actually be. In current CAD systems this kind of inference is still expected to reside in the designer's head.

The title, "linking graphics and inference," raises three questions:

What is inference in relation to graphics?
How are graphics and inference linked?
What is graphic inference used for?

What Is Inference in Relation to Graphics?

Inference

Take a simple model of a design environment which uses computer graphics (Fig. 1). There is a computer, of course, and it is running a graphics system. The graphics system can hold graphic objects, and it knows something about geometrical operations. And then there is a boundary, beyond which is the application—some design task or activity. Across the boundary the application can cause geometrical transformations to be applied to graphic objects, including descriptions of objects (i.e., drafting); and the application can ask about the geometrical properties of graphic objects.

In this simple model, I define inference to be something that goes on within the application. It is what determines how the application:

Decides what graphic instructions to give.
Interprets graphic objects.

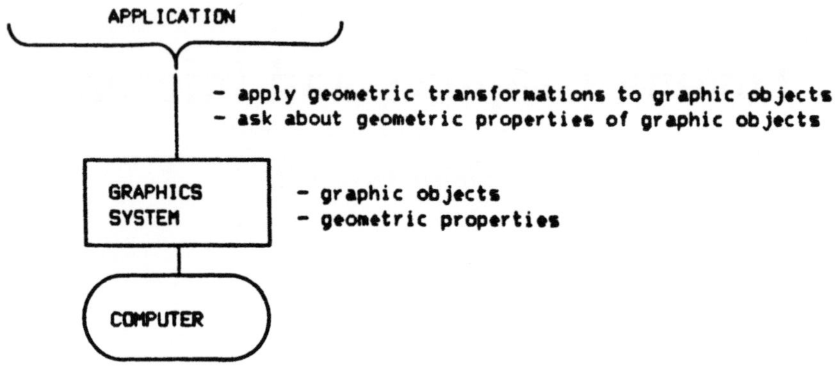

FIGURE 1. Diagram of a computer graphics environment; the application may be a designer or another computer program.

The application may be a human user—the designer—or increasingly it may be another computer program. I shall generally assume that it is a computer program.

Graphic Reasoning

Inference is always motivated by a design application, but graphic reasoning is something more generalised. Graphic reasoning occurs whenever the current state of a graphic system is called, and some operations are performed, as a result of which the graphic system is changed. When a user views a graphic display and inputs simple drafting commands which change the display, he is reasoning but the graphics system is not. User commands can be bundled up as macros, even parameterised macros which query the user for data (Fig. 2), but still the graphics system is not necessarily reasoning—just altering graphic objects in response to user commands.

But a CAD system does have functions that meet the definition of reasoning, such as the snap-to-object behaviour or filleting the intersection of two lines to a specified radius (Fig. 3). When executing such commands the graphics system has to examine the current state of the graphic objects it contains, and depending on what it finds it modifies the graphic objects. It can, for example, identify error situations—the system will give an error message if asked to fillet lines which are parallel.

These relatively low-level graphic reasoning capabilities are built into the graphics system; more graphic reasoning may be built into graphics systems in the future. But it is impossible to conceive of a graphics or CAD environment that will cover the diversity of reasoning tasks that occur in different worlds of design. The impossibility is implicit when describing a graphics system as "general purpose," that is, suitable for all sorts of applications on all sorts of tasks. Reasoning within general-

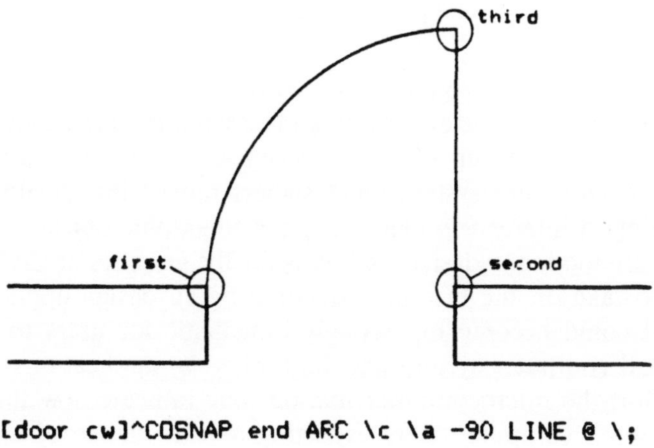

FIGURE 2. An AutoCAD command macro which requires user input (indication of three points) but involves no graphic reasoning; it drafts an arc and a line to represent a clockwise door swing on an architectural plan.

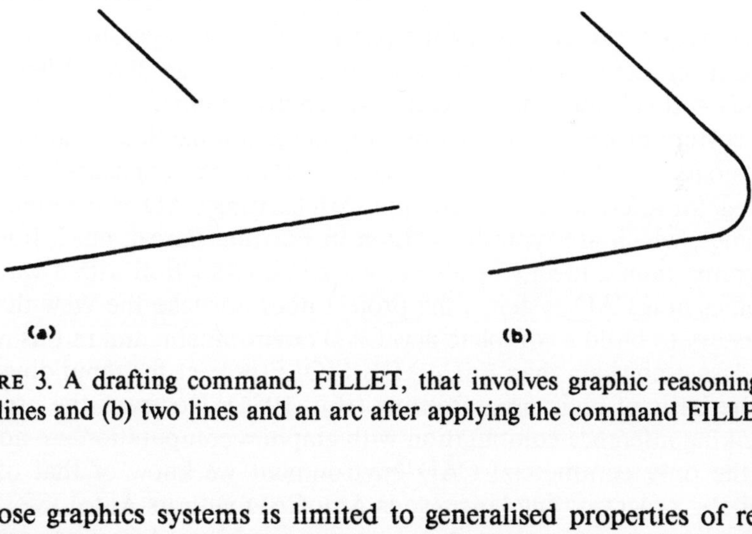

FIGURE 3. A drafting command, FILLET, that involves graphic reasoning. (a) Two lines and (b) two lines and an arc after applying the command FILLET.

purpose graphics systems is limited to generalised properties of representations–the lines on the screen–not meaningful objects in the design world.

Representations and Designs

The properties of representations–the lines on the screen–and the properties of designs are not independent. A representation is used because it presents an isomorphism of the design problem; by manipulating the isomorphism we learn about the design. The mapping of a design problem onto a graphic isomorphism varies from case to case, and this mapping characterises inference in the context of graphics for designers.

In a general-purpose CAD system the mapping of the design problem onto a graphic representation is entirely up to the user. In a CAD system tailored to a specific design domain the mapping is to a greater or lesser extent absorbed into the system; this makes assumptions about what the user wants to do, which is a risky business as users are rather unpredictable. A computer system for designers must allow flexibility in the programing of inference schemes applied to graphic objects.

There are too many design problems for the graphics or CAD software houses to take on the task of programming all design applications inhouse. It could become increasingly unrealistic for users to buy a sophisticated computer system and be limited to applications offered by the vendor; the microcomputer market may indicate how things could develop, with computer users expecting a wide choice of applications software.

Linking Graphics and Inference

There are other reasons for treating graphics and inference as distinct problems and dealing with them separately. Graphics operations are highly calculation-intensive, whereas inference is not. They have different demands and call for different computer environments.

A current project at the Centre for Configurational Studies at the Open University (OU) proposes the use of declarative languages, especially Prolog, for inference in conjunction with existing CAD environments for graphics, which are typically written in Fortran, Pascal, or C. Inference programs should ideally be able to work in conjunction with a variety of graphics and CAD systems; the project does not take the view that it is necessary to build a complete new CAD environment, and in this respect it is less ambitious than EdCAAD's MOLE project for rebuilding CAD on the basis of logic programming (Bijl, 1986). However, the problems of linking inference computation with graphics computation are not trivial; the only commercial CAD environment we know of that offers a symbolic programming language is AutoCAD with its AutoLISP. If system independence between inference and graphics is taken into account, then the AutoCAD/AutoLISP combination is not ideal.

In the project we have made two different working models of inference/graphics systems. In both cases the graphics component is not a developed CAD system; we have made do with low-level graphics systems, having basic graphics functionality broadly equivalent to GKS. The first model uses the Tektronix Plot-10 graphics system on the VAX at the Centre for Configurational Studies. The VAX also runs C-Prolog, and the connection between C-Prolog and Plot-10, which is a Fortran library, is achieved by writing and reading files. When an application program written in C-Prolog requires graphic output or input it writes a text file; a Fortran program that is permanently running intercepts the text file and calls Plot-10 subroutines. Similarly the Fortran program writes text files that are read by the C-Prolog application program. It is not an ideal arrangement.

The second linkage is between Digital Research's GSX system, a graphics extension to the MS-DOS operating system, and the Prolog implementation by Logic Programming Associates. There is a version of their Prolog Professional which can generate GSX calls. GSX is not an application program but an extension to the operating system, so the problem of communicating between high-level languages does not arise. This implementation is on an Apricot microcomputer.

Communication between programs for inference and graphics written in different high-level languages will probably be most efficient in a Unix environment, and this will be explored as the OU research continues.

Since the model implementations use low-level graphics environments rather than true CAD systems, they lack the user interface and high-level commands that are part of a CAD system. The first application programs written in Prolog, therefore, were for a minimal user interface and set of high-level commands, called VC (virtual CAD system) and MGL (minimum graphic language) respectively. VC sends input and output to the graphics system in the form of MGL commands. MGL is system independent, so in principle any application program with graphic input and output using the MGL syntax is portable between any graphics system with an MGL driver (Fig. 4), including the Plot-10 and GSX implementations. The drivers are written in Prolog. Portability is more difficult for the VC interface than for a typical applications program, as the interface is to some extent specific to the behaviour and configuration of the host computer and graphics system.

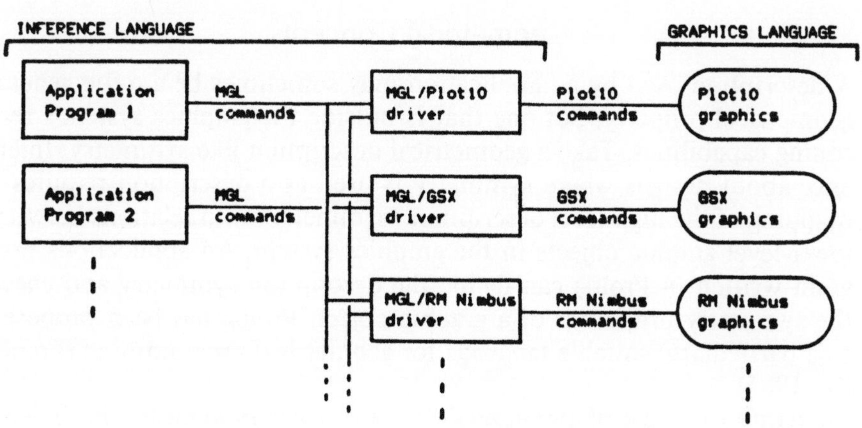

FIGURE 4. Inference programs using a standard command syntax (MGL) for output and input are portable to different graphics systems via suitable drivers.

These specimen systems provide the dual computer base that we have argued for, with distinct programming environments for graphics and inference. They allow us to proceed with the study of inference computing in design.

What Is Inference For?

Descriptions

Our ideas about design applications are strongly oriented towards the knowledge engineering/knowledge-based systems/expert systems paradigm. These ideas seem particularly relevant in design disciplines that have not proved amenable to numerical analysis and optimisation techniques, for example architectural design. Applications to design tasks will be selected to test these ideas.

But initially let us look more generally at inference on graphic objects. We noted that a graphics system may have some power of reasoning about low-level and generalised properties of graphic objects. Inference in a significant design application is concerned with high-level and often task-specific properties of design objects—these could be called descriptions of designs. In general, descriptions refer to relations between objects or attributes of objects.

It is the task of an inference scheme to map high-level descriptions of designs into relations between low-level graphic objects. The mapping ought to be transparent to the design world, which deals only with meaningful descriptions.

We will illustrate design descriptions and inference with three examples: high-level geometrical concepts, shape grammars and domain-specific representations.

Geometrical Concepts

A description used by an application may sometimes be a quite general geometrical property, but one that is outside the graphics system's reasoning capabilities. Take a geometrical description like symmetry. Inference about designs where symmetry is used as a description requires a mapping of the high-level description "symmetry" into relations between lower-level graphic objects in the graphics system. An applications program written in Prolog can define the description symmetry and check the symmetry properties of a graphic object. Prolog has been proposed as a particularly suitable language for geometrical programming (Franklin, 1985).

An important use of high-level descriptions occurs when graphic objects are modified, and the description has to be maintained. Suppose we wish to describe the fact that two points in a design object are coincident; they might be connected parts of a dynamic mechanism or adjacent components in a static assembly. We can represent the description "coincident" in a Prolog program and invoke the description when manipulating a graphic object. Thus

((coincident _firstelement _secondelement)
(element _firstelement line _xy1 _xy2)
(element _secondelement line _xy1 _xy3))

describes the coincidence of endpoints of two lines (using the Imperial College Prolog syntax). If a graphic object contains two elements

((element 1 line (1 1) (6 6)))
((element 2 line (1 1) (10 3)))

we can use the description coincident to ascertain that they have a coincident endpoint. If a graphic object contains two elements

((element 3 line (6 8) (21 7)))
((element 4 line _xy (18 2)))

we can use the description to determine that the variable _xy takes the value (6 8).

The description can be maintained when graphic objects are transformed (Fig. 5). Suppose we state that the description coincident applies to two elements

((coincident 5 6))

and we apply a transformation to the element

((element 5 line (4 18) (8 23)))

which changes it to

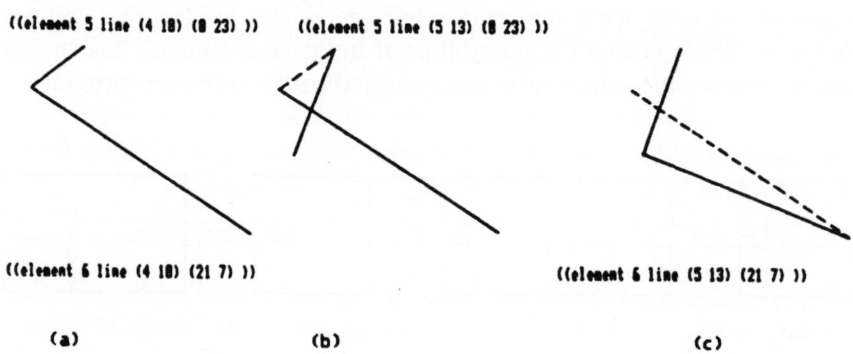

FIGURE 5. The geometrical description of "coincidence" applied to the endpoints of two lines. (a) Two lines; (b) the endpoint of one is moved; (c) the endpoint of the other moves to maintain the description.

((element 5 line (5 13) (8 23)))

Then the element

((element 6 line (4 18) (19 11)))

can be automatically transformed to

((element 6 line (5 13) (19 11)))

in order to maintain the description of coincidence.

The benefit of using a declarative language like Prolog for programming descriptions can be noted. A program using BASIC, a procedural language, to define and maintain coincidence as defined above is much longer and requires the explicit programming of recursion.

Shape Grammars

Spatial relations can be embedded in the formalism of shape grammars (Stiny, 1980). The use of a shape grammar involves a cycle of three operations:

1. Pattern matching shape rules against a current shape.
2. Deciding which rule to apply.
3. Transforming the current shape in accordance with the rule.

A human user can use simple shape grammars in a computer graphics environment without any computer inference, by performing the first and second operations in his head and sending drafting commands bundled up as macros to the graphics system for the third (Fawcett, 1986). The addition of inference allows far more effective implementations of shape grammars (Fig. 6). An inference program can take over the first operation, pattern matching on the current shape, and can perform the third operation, rule applications, for more sophisticated rules that require graphic reasoning rather than the simple execution of graphic commands.

These inference tasks enhance shape grammars as a design tool even when the second operation, rule selection, is still guided by a human designer. There is also the possibility of building automatic design generators where rule selection is incorporated in the inference program.

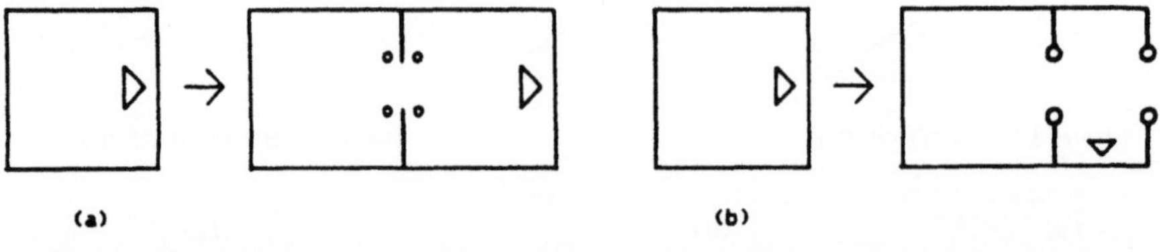

(a) (b)

FIGURE 6. Shape rules. (a) A shape rule that can be applied and re-applied without graphic reasoning, as it preserves scale and rotation, and (b) a shape rule that requires graphic reasoning to identify scale and rotation.

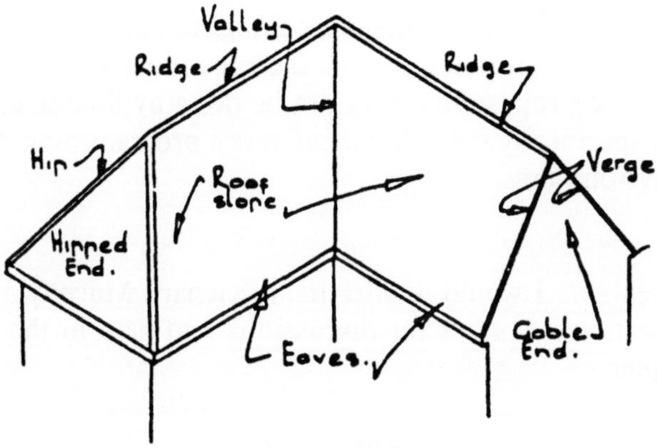

FIGURE 7. Established descriptions in the representation and design of pitched roofs.

Domain-Specific Descriptions

Design skills are often rooted in established descriptions–linguistic as well as graphic (Earl, 1986) (Fig. 7). It is possible to recreate these descriptions using an inference language linked to a graphics system.

The use of computer aids within the design process will be easier if established descriptions can be maintained, allowing the user to communicate with the CAD system in terms of the established descriptions. The role of inference is not to replace the designer, but to allow more effective communication with a graphic isomorphism of the design problem.

This is relevant only for designers who are already familiar with the established descriptions of a particular design domain. If designers were retrained, or fully automated design systems were created that did not need to interact with designers, then the established descriptions could perhaps be dispensed with altogether. However, if the desired products of a particular design task are themselves actually moulded by the established descriptions, then these descriptions still have to be active within an inference scheme.

The programming of domain-specific descriptions is getting close to the knowledge-based systems/expert systems model of problem solving. The inference language is a vehicle for applying these ideas in CAD.

Conclusion

The main proposition of this paper is that graphics for designers involves more than wonderful displays–though of course better graphics will always be enthusiastically greeted. We suggest that a key step is to introduce computer aids into design decision-making, to supplement the existing advanced state of computer aids in the modelling and visualisation of designs. And we propose that this can be done by linking computer environments specifically suitable for inference programming, to computer graphics environments.

Acknowledgment. I would like to thank Richard Murphy at the Centre for Configurational Studies for discussions and help in the preparation of this chapter.

References

Bijl, A. (1986) "Logic Modelling in Computer-aided Design," *Planning & Design* 13:233–241.

Franklin, W.R. (1985) "Computational Geometry and Prolog." In R.A. Earnshaw, ed., *Fundamental Algorithms for Computer Graphics*, pp. 737–749. Springer, Heidelberg.

Stiny, G. (1980) "Introduction to Shape and Shape Grammars," *Environment & Planning B* 7:343–351.

Fawcett, W.H. (1986) "An Elementary Rule Interpreter for Architectural Design." In *CAD86: Knowledge Engineering and Computer Modelling in CAD*, pp. 259–269. Butterworths, London.

Earl, C.F. (1986) "Creating Design Worlds," *Planning & Design* 13:177–188.

Superquadric-based Symbolic Graphics for Design

Avon Huxor and Iain Elliot

Introduction

In this paper we present a specification of a computer-aided design system aimed at the initial design stages. The proposed system is based upon superquadrics and employs the inferencing power of Prolog, which we believe would allow simple image description and manipulation. Two small test programs which implement the ideas support the claim that such an approach offers cognitive acceptability and computational feasibility.

Visual and Conceptual Design

Many activities come under the domain of design but have different characteristics, for example, very large scale integration (VLSI) design and product design. To make the problem more tractable we have therefore decided to concentrate on one aspect of design. More specifically, we are interested in the area of 3-D design with a significant visual component, such as architecture, industrial design and television graphics.

We have further chosen to concentrate on the development of a tool to aid in the early design stages. A considerable amount of work has already been carried out within conventional computer-aided design to support the designer in a number of tasks. However, these tasks are normally those that *follow* the initial design. Typically, existing commercial systems deal with such tasks as draughting, finite element method (FEM) analysis and numerical control (NC) data generation but *not* with initial design.

There are, however, a number of other reasons why we believe that initial conceptual design is an area worth investigating:

Empirical studies indicate that a considerable amount of the designer's time and effort goes into this conceptual stage.

Mistakes made at this stage are considerably more difficult and expensive to correct than mistakes made at later stages in the design process.

Requirements

It is possible to determine a number of initial requirements that the intended system should meet, at a strategic level. We believe the system should *aid* rather than replace the designer, be cognitively acceptable and be computationally feasible.

We take the view of Woods (1986) that the system should not make or recommend solutions but should aid the user in the design process. Thus we are not building a conventional expert system, but we hope to employ the inferential capabilities of Prolog as a tool to externalize the designer's intuitions. For example, when a table is called from the component library, its legs should, by default, stand on the floor.

Also, using such a system, the industrial designer should clearly be able to express that he wishes (for example) all angles in an object to have a certain value. The system should then ensure that as he constructs an object this constraint is met. The designer could then modify or erase the constraint easily to observe the effects.

We have therefore based the system on Prolog. However, a user interface would have to be provided in any production system.

Cognitive Ease

If we are to support the conceptual design phase, we must investigate the representations and reasoning that occur in design. The intention is to provide a "cognitive match" between the designer and the system. Our approach has therefore been to look at representations that people employ, as opposed to the traditional "engineering," Platonic solids approach.

There is some clear evidence to suggest that designers make extensive use of their visual capabilities. The appearance of a designed object is an important factor in the evaluation of a design, hence many design professions call heavily on visual imagery. Cohen (1977) notes that:

> In the visual and decorative arts, in architecture and town planning, sketches are tried out in the mind's eye before they emerge on the drawing board.

Tentative empirical evidence of the true importance of visual imagery to the design professions can be found in the recent work of Farah (1984). She investigated the neurological basis of mental imagery by analysing the patterns of deficits in mental imagery in patients who had reported loss of imagery following brain damage. A literature survey provided only 37 cases, rare compared with reported losses of other cognitive capabilities. She concluded that patients are less likely to complain about the loss of imagery than of many other cognitive abilities, as most people manage without it. However, it was noteworthy that one group seemed particularly troubled. Of the 17 cases where the patient's occupation or hobby was recorded, 8 patients worked in architecture, building, carpentry, painting or set design.

Thus, it seems reasonable to conclude that many of the design professions call on their imagery abilities a great deal. The loss of the ability seriously affected their work, which is why they brought it to the notice of their doctors.

There is also evidence to connect imagery to vision, both vision and imagery seeming to share the same mechanism (Kosslyn, 1981). Therefore we should be able to look at research in both vision and imagery as a source for an appropriate representation scheme.

To conclude, we believe the representation used should match as far as possible the visual mechanisms known to occur in humans.

Prototype and Deformation

The notion of prototype plus modification/deformation is employed in the frame-based knowledge representation method (Minsky, 1975). It assumes that we have a set of prototypes for objects and events in the world, which provide us with defaults. Instances are identified as being modifications of such prototypes. Frame-based systems have already been used for a wide variety of knowledge-based system applications.

Rosch (1973) shows that people also represent categories as "focal examples" and that instances are represented as differences from these prototypes. She further shows that these natural prototypes apply to visual categories and, at least for her work in two-dimensional forms, cross cultural boundaries and are thus general.

This strongly suggests that the system's object representation should be amenable to the prototype and deformation style of manipulation.

Computational Feasibility

One of our aims is to achieve results using existing hardware; the representation chosen must therefore not be excessively demanding on machine resources.

Also, it would be beneficial for the longer term if the same representation could be used throughout a potential future computer-integrated manufacturing (CIM) system. One immediate consequence of this demand is that the representation be capable of being used by a robotic assembly unit, through a vision or other sensor systems.

Summary of Requirements

The general set of criteria can therefore be summarized as:

Appropriateness to the design activity: how well the system specifically aids the designer.

Cognitive ease: how well the system reflects human "object" representation.
Computational ease: the object representation must be computationally feasible and be employable within an image recognition system.

Potential Solutions

From the above discussion it is clear that the work done on image recognition offers a good starting point.

Marr (1978, 1982) argued that shapes with a natural canonical axis are most appropriate for object recognition. His analysis led him to choose cylinders as the basis of his shape representation. This technique has been used extensively in commercial vision systems. This approach, however, suffers as it is extremely abstract and cannot reasonably describe many objects. Marr's solution is to transfer from cylinders to generalized cylinders by using a sweeping function. However, adding this sweeping function then makes the resulting representation neither compact or cognitively intuitive.

An alternative (based on work by Barr, 1981) has been developed by Pentland (1986a). Pentland's main notion is that the primitive for a representation system should be a "lump of clay." He argues that this corresponds to the notion of "part of an object." These "parts" have been implemented in his system as *superquadrics* which are used to generate a family of base forms such as cubes and spheres. These are then employed as prototypes which may be deformed using a number of deformation functions (such as scale, bend, twist, taper) to generate new forms. All the forms can then be combined using boolean operators to define more complex forms and objects.

This representation meets Marr's requirement of providing a canonical axis and our requirement of suitability for prototype and deformation reasoning. Furthermore, this approach was designed by Pentland to try and capture some of the possible formative history of the object, that is, how a given shape could have been constructed by joining lumps of clay. This is a particularly good approach in aiding conceptual design, as designers often employ the technique of moulding clay to arrive at a rough design. Some empirical investigation of this approach has been undertaken by Pentland (1986b). The conclusions he reaches support the thesis that such representations facilitate the initial sketching stage of design.

The same argument was put forward by Hollerbach (1975), who claimed that the representation he employed (generalized cylinders proposed by Binford and later developed by Marr) inferred something about how the objects (vases in his examples) were made.

The representation described by Marr would also be suitable for conceptual design, as Hollerbach demonstrated, but it suffers from problems when attempting to model more complex objects. Pentland's proposal has shown itself to be more suitable for modelling complex objects such as humans, inanimate objects, rock and trees.

Test Implementations

As the next step two small experimental programs were written. The first is an interactive graphics tool, which allows the user, by direct manipulation, to construct a complex object from simple primitives. The second links the object depiction and manipulation module to Prolog. The Prolog user specifies the object in Prolog, and this Prolog description is then interpreted to generate a picture of the object.

The goals of building the systems were (1) to informally evaluate Pentland's approach in terms of the criteria mentioned above and (2) to investigate the problems of interfacing this type of graphical representation to Prolog.

Interactive System

Initially four different prototypical objects, as suggested by Barr and Pentland, were programmed in the system:

1. A sphere.
2. A vase.
3. A "double vase."
4. A toroid.

Of these, the sphere was found to be the most useful and intuitive in informal user trials to create a wide variety of graphic objects and, in addition, corresponds more closely to the notion of a "lump of clay." The sphere was therefore taken as the base primitive for the subsequent Prolog system.

Five different deformations were also implemented (Fig. 1):

1. Scaling along any axis.
2. Squaring vertically or horizontally.
3. Bending along the x or y axis* towards either of the other axes.
4. Twisting along any axis.
5. Tapering along any axis.

The deformations used were all based on those discussed by Barr (1981, 1984) and on the results of a small informal experiment with modelling clay performed at the European Computer-Industry Research Centre (ECRC). The experiment indicated that the above deformations corresponded to those required to construct an object.

---

*The bending cannot be done along the z axis due to implementation limitations.

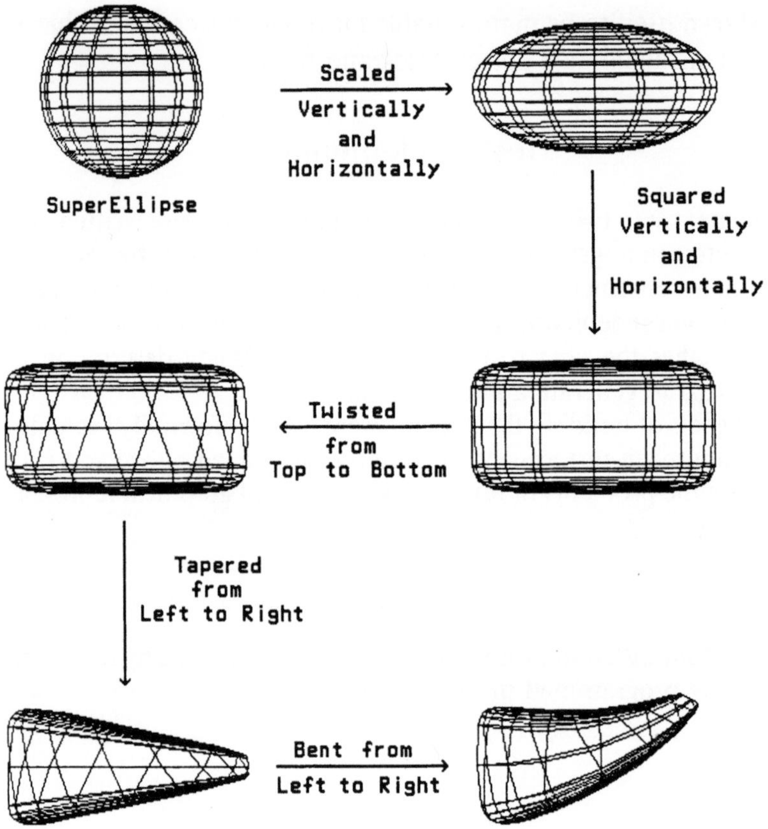

FIGURE 1. Examples of deformations used.

Prolog System

The object creation and deformation routines were taken from the interactive system and added to MuProlog (Naish, 1983), with real number and graphic extensions added by ECRC. The system consists of three levels (Fig. 2):

1. A interpreter written in Prolog which takes a symbolic description of the object and gives a numeric description.
2. A C interpreter which takes the Prolog numeric description and transforms it into a C structure.
3. The object pipeline, which takes the C structure description and generates a picture.

Only the symbolic Prolog level is discussed here, since this is the level at which a programmer would generally work in the construction of a design system.

An example program to generate (or recognize) a table is shown in Fig. 3. (The current system cannot easily describe spatial relationships,

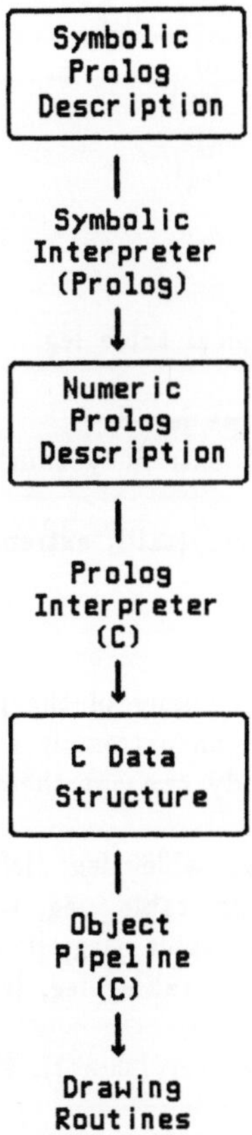

FIGURE 2. System architecture.

the top of the table "happens" to lie on top of the legs in this example.) An example of the output from this program is shown in Fig. 4.

The symbolic description in Fig. 3 is loosely based on Clark's (1973) analysis of English spatial adjectives and Denofsky's (1976) analysis of the far/near adjectives. There is, however, still some ambiguity (for instance, a table top would normally be described as thin, not as very, very short).

Despite the problems with spatial relationships, the advantages of this description over a conventional GKS-like description should be obvious. Even in comparison to other declarative Prolog picture description languages, such as those of Pereira (1983) or Helm and Marriot (1986) (which both use lines and points as primitives), this description appears more intuitive.

```
/*
 * Tell the system what parts make up a table.
 */
part(table, left_front_table_leg).
part(table, right_front_table_leg).
part(table, left_back_table_leg).
part(table, right_back_table_leg).
part(table, table_top).

/*
 * Give a description of a typical table leg.
 *
 * The way to read this routine is
 * A table_leg is a very tall, extremely thin and narrow cylinder.
 */
instance(table_leg, cylinder, [very(tall), extremely(thin), extremely(narrow)]).

/*
 * Now the parts of the table.
 * The legs are just translated copies of the prototypical leg
 * described above, the top is an extremely flat cube which
 * has rounded edges so nobody can cut themselves on it.
 */
instance(left_front_table_leg, table_leg, [left, forward]).
instance(right_front_table_leg, table_leg, [right, forward]).
instance(left_back_table_leg, table_leg, [left, backward]).
instance(right_back_table_leg, table_leg, [right, backward]).

instance(table_top, cube, [very(very(short)), slightly(rounded), very(high)]).
```

FIGURE 3. Example program.

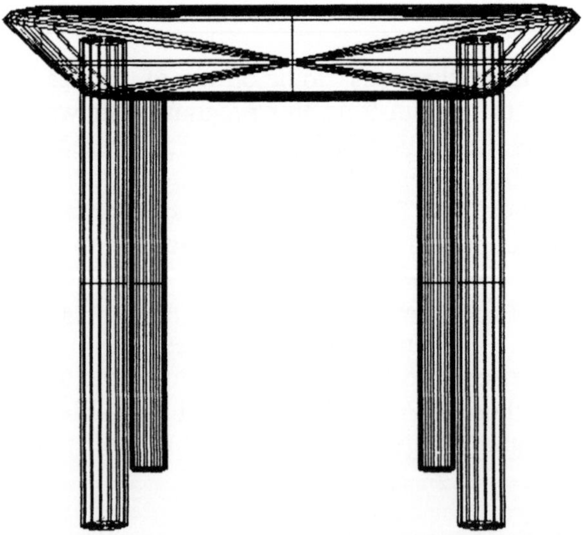

FIGURE 4. "Table" picture generated by symbolic Prolog program.

Conclusions

Even with the extremely simple programs written so far, it has been possible to draw a number of conclusions and, to some extent, it can be shown that this approach satisfies the requirements of cognitive ease and computational feasibility.

Cognitive Ease

A couple of examples of the use of the two systems may be illustrative. Although we are, of course, very familiar with the systems, it took less than 1 minute to generate a recognisable image of a telephone using the interactive system and it took less than 10 minutes to program the "table" using the Prolog system. And the program worked correctly first time. Figure 5 shows the use of the interactive system.

Subjectively, at least, the design process feels satisfactory. The salient points of the telephone were quickly and easily described in an intuitive manner.

There are a number of reasons to conclude that this means of representation is appropriate to the conceptual design task:

Roughly the same actions would be carried out to physically build a model of a telephone. This suggests that the system has quite a close match to primitives and processes used by designers.

When designing objects it was possible to test and discard ideas quickly. The extreme ease with which this could be accomplished reinforces the argument that such a system is appropriate to the early, tentative stage of design.

These points both seem to support Pentland's belief that his representation captures something of an object's formative history.

Computational Feasibility

The systems were coded without consideration to speed optimisation. Despite this, both the interactive and the interpreted Prolog systems were fast enough for interactive usage. This was due to the simple and powerful nature of the superquadric representation.

Although it may not be obvious at first glance, the Prolog program describing the table is reversible. By "reversible" we mean that the description may be used to generate an image of a table or to recognise an image given the lower-level description. Furthermore, both Pentland (1986a) and Solina and Bajcsy (1987) have shown that "parts" may be recognised within a digitized image and converted into a superquadric representation. With a suitable image processing front end, a superquadric-based system within Prolog could be used for image recognition.

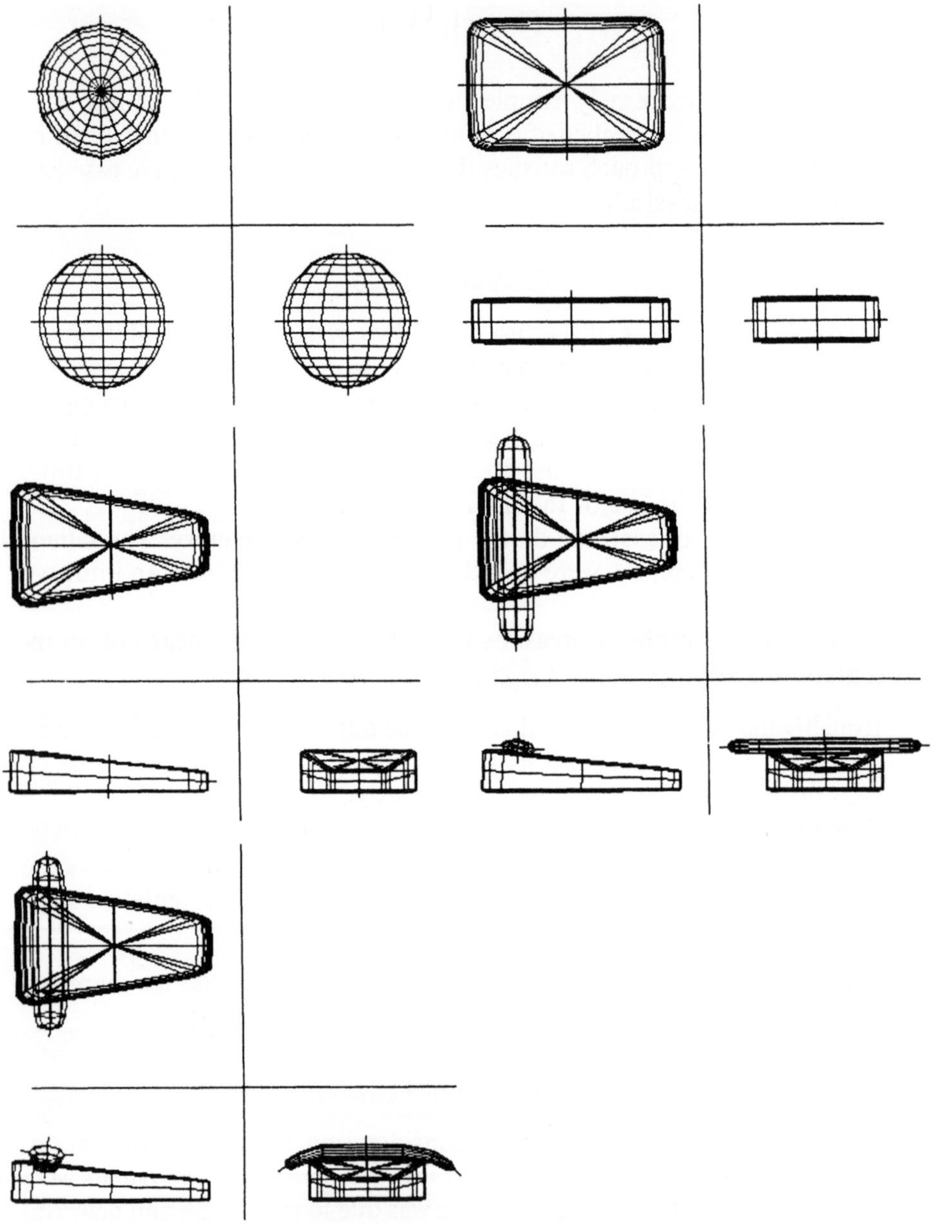

FIGURE 5. Telephone designed with interactive system.

Future Directions

The ideas proposed above are still at an early stage of development. A great deal of work must be done to solve a number of problems, particularly those of spatial reasoning and spatial positioning, before a usable system can be achieved. Another issue is that of alerting the user that an attempt to "undo" a specific modification of the object could cause a drastic, unexpected change in the object being drawn, due to the noncommutativity of many transformations. However, we hope that we have put forward sufficient arguments to encourage others to investigate the possibility of building a full design tool.

References

Barr, A.H. (1981) "Superquadrics and Angle-Preserving Transformations," *Computer Graphics and Applications* 1(1):11–23.

Barr, A.H. (1984) "Global and Local Deformations of Solid Primitives," pp. 21–30. ACM *SIGGRAPH*, Minneapolis, July.

Clark, H.H. (1973) "Space, Time, Semantics and the Child." In T.E. Moore, ed., *Cognitive Development and the Acquisition of Language*. Academic Press, London.

Cohen, G.(1977) *The Psychology of Cognition*. Academic Press, London.

Denofsky, M.E. (1976) "How Near Is Near," Memo 344, Artificial Intelligence, Lab., Massachusetts Institute of Technology, February.

Farah, M.J. (1984) "The Neurological Basis of Mental Imagery: A Componential Analysis," *Cognition* 18:245–272.

Helm, R.A. and K. Marriot (1986) "Declarative Graphics," pp. 513–526. International Conference on Logic Programming, London, July.

Hollerbach, J.M. (1975) "Hierarchical Space Description of Objects by Selection and Modification of Prototypes," Technical Report AI-TR-346, Artificial Intelligence Lab., Massachusetts Institute of Technology, November.

Kosslyn, S.M. (1981) "Research on Mental Imagery: Some Goals and Directions," *Cognition* 10:173–179.

Marr, D. (1978) "Representing Visual Information—A Computational Approach." In A.R. Hanson and E.M. Riseman, eds., *Computer Vision Systems*. Academic Press, London.

Marr, D. (1982) *Vision* Freeman, San Francisco.

Minsky, M. (1975) "A Framework for Representing Knowledge." In P.H. Winston, ed., *The Psychology of Computer Vision*. McGraw-Hill, New York.

Naish, L. (1983) "MU-PROLOG 3.0 Reference Manual," Technical Report, Department of Computer Science, Univ. of Melbourne, July.

Pentland, A.P. (1986a) "Perceptual Organization and the Representation of Natural Form," *Artificial Intelligence*, 28:293–331.

Pentland, A.P. (1986b) "Towards an Ideal 3-D CAD System," Unpublished paper.

Pereira, F.C.N. (1983) "Can Drawing be Liberated from the Von Neumann Style?" Technical Report 282, Artificial Intelligence Center, SRI International, March.

Rosch, E.H. (1973) "On the Internal Structure of Perceptual and Semantic Categories." In T.E. Moore, ed., *Cognitive Development and the Acquisition of Language.* Academic Press, New York.

Solina, F. and R. Bajcsy. (1987) "Range Image Interpretation of Mail Pieces with Superquadrics," pp. 733–737. AAAI, Seattle, July.

Woods, D.D. (1986) "Cognitive Technologies: The Design of Joint Human-Machine Cognitive Systems," *AI Magazine* 6(4):86–92.

Designer's Toolkit

James Hennessey

Foreword

The subject of this report is the development of a *designer's toolkit.* It is based on a presentation of the toolkit concept to the faculty of the Technical University, Delft, for the purpose of obtaining comments and suggestions for its further development.

The designer's toolkit is intended to be a new computer aid to the field of industrial design. In this regard, a goal of this research was to avoid duplication of existing computer aids. Instead, the major emphasis was to investigate current computer aids and determine what aspects of the designer's work are lacking computer tools. This identification has led to a new and interesting development, a toolkit which distinguishes itself from other CAD systems in that it is specifically for the *conceptualizing* process of design. Additionally, it is the only system which allows for the development of product form in "creative" as well as "representational" techniques.

This report deals entirely with the development of the toolkit as a concept and is focused on the identification of this concept and on the framework of the toolkit, its methodological as well as systems approach. Specific attention is given to the specifications and requirements of the system, the system structure and the user interface. Later in this research, as many demonstration examples as time permits will be developed to show how the system might work.

The research is open-ended. At this point in the study it is clear that many more years would be needed for full implementation of the toolkit concept. A large task is the development of a final system architecture and the application of this architecture to different computers and systems. Another is the great number of software modules and refinements that will have to be created to obtain an operative concept. There is a great amount of interesting work beyond the scope of this study that needs to be accomplished by other researchers.

The initial idea for a toolkit was conceived as part of the research in "CAD for microcomputers" at the Technical University, Vakgroep Vormgiving. Particular thanks are given to Erik Jansen and Norbert Roozenburg for their inspiration and enthusiastic assistance. Hopefully the designer's toolkit concept will continue to be supported and realized. The project needs to attract corporate and financial support as well as students and researchers to continue after this short research term has ended.

Introduction

Computer-aided design has been a catchword in the design community since the early 1960s. At that time, designers first became interested in how the large and cumbersome machines might contribute to the design process. The pioneers of this era mainly used the computer as a non-graphic, numerical in/out device and their methodologies were implemented in the early stages of the design process. People like Bruce Archer (Great Britain) and later Charles Owen (United States) created sophisticated analysis-oriented programs to assist design teams in identifying and remembering attributes of large-scale problems. VTCON III, the Variable Threshhold Condensation Program developed by Prof. Owen at IIT, ran on an IBM-360 mainframe computer and required the laborious typing of hundreds of punchcards for both the program and the user input. Output (when the machine cooperated) consisted of pages and pages of numerical data, which then had to be carefully "decoded" and analyzed by the designer. It was no wonder that the average designer had no interest in these programs. Not only were they quite cumbersome to use but also the equipment was simply unavailable to all but the large university or research institutes.

The event to change all this was the introduction of minicomputers in the early 1970s. These stand-alone, interactive systems with graphic displays and easy to understand operating languages marked the beginning of a real interest on the part of designers. Soon afterward companies began to implement CAD systems and software. Indeed, there was a mad development of new equipment and software for this purpose. The development of CAD was initiated by two groups, engineers and programmers. If one were to look at the systems being created at that time, the lack of industrial design would be quite apparent. In this case, the "design" in "computer-aided design" really referred to the engineering process; the creation of machined parts with extensive material testing and highly toleranced mechanical drawings for production. This meant that designers had to learn to "intentionally misuse" them for the purpose of form development and aesthetics. Obviously, this was not a good practise as the software lacked many of the utilities required for form development such as easy input, fast three-dimensional rotation and color/shading enhancements. With the exception of better graphics through the introduction of color and perspective views, CAD was slow to be accepted by designers because of the inappropriateness of the processes used, the complexity of the systems and the high cost. While CAD systems did satisfy some needs for design, they were far from adequate as meaningful tools throughout the design process.

In the late 1970s small desktop computers took another meaningful direction. Graphics became all-important and screen imagery improved drastically. A new operating environment using symbols/icons and pull-down menus introduced structure and organization. Software development centered around tools for productivity and everything from word processing and desktop publishing to graphics tools and paintboxes began to appear. Additionally, the quality of graphics on these desktop machines improved through advances in technology and hardware. Small desktop computers could now do as much as the old mainframe systems. But, while the technology rapidly advanced, software development lagged far behind and sophisticated, usable design programs were not evident amidst the myriad of games and recreational programs being developed at that time. The small computer was perceived as a toy and, in some ways, that notion persists today.

Industrial designers have watched all this progress (and many have been involved in it from a product development point of view) and are now eager to purchase and use these new systems. But the average, money-conscious designer is not yet ready to embrace computers in his workplace until he can be shown that a system will be easy to use, time-saving, inexpensive and, above all else, appropriate. Of course, an industrial designer can use bits and pieces of existing CAD, graphics and art programs but his real needs cannot be completely satisfied this way. Additionally, there is no integration of these different systems and they all require different data formats and structures. Current CAD systems are designed for the production phase of product development. Computer aids for the conceptual, form generative phase of the process still need to be developed.

The designer's toolkit is intended to be the answer to the above problem. The purpose of this research is to develop a graphics-oriented, easy to use and inexpensive environment of computer utilities that is specific to the conceptual needs of industrial design.

The development of the designer's toolkit was divided into three phases: identification, specifications and examples.

The goal of the *identification* phase was to determine exactly what a designer's toolkit should be. In this regard, one should consider a "toolkit" as an operating environment for a desktop computer. It serves as a window to different utilities that the computer can provide to the designer. The way it appears on the computer screen can enhance the ease in which a designer relates to and learns the various tools. A great number of improvements in this area have been made in recent years and desktop systems with icons and pull-down menus are becoming a standard.

The means of identifying design tools took place through an abstraction of the design process and how it relates to computer usage. Through this analysis, obvious computer software modules emerged. In order to satisfy many points of view, a number of designers and design-related researchers were interviewed. Not surprisingly, each individual had a unique approach to design and relevant suggestions about how the computer could be implemented in their design strategies.

If a toolkit is going to be truly useful, it should be "design intuitive" so that a designer can achieve meaningful results without the need to change his design process. Fortunately, designers are visually oriented and can quickly recognize and understand icons and symbols. For this reason, the current use of "intuitive windows" in CAD workstations (Sun, Apollo, etc.) and in most of the new small computer systems (Amiga, Atari, Macintosh) make them ideal hosts for a designer's toolkit environment.

The goal of the *specification* phase was to determine the framework of the the toolkit system. How the components of the system would fit together to form a usable and interactive program had to be considered. Methods for enhancing the user interface and its understandability had to be developed. The assortment of software "modules" that would be important to the process of industrial design would have to be defined. And, to this, the better parts of CAD (engineering) systems as well as art, paintbox, animation, graphics and other existing utilities would be added.

The *example* phase allows a small amount of time to the creation of demonstration software. The time constraints of the research fellowship are not sufficient to enable real interactive programming. Therefore, software examples that only suggest how the toolkit operates will have to be created.

The scale of this research looked quite small at first. After a few months of development, however, its magnitude both in time requirements and importance became clear. The actual implementation of usable software will probably take some years of further research and experimentation. But the result should be a most meaningful tool for the conceptualizing process of design.

The Design Process

The best way to analyze the way designers work is to look at the design process, the systematic definition of problem-solving activity. For the purpose of this research, the seven-step process as outlined in the book *The Universal Traveler* by Koberg and Bagnall (1972) was adopted. Their first step, *acceptance*, was not considered as it usually is not a factor in a computer-assisted design process. This step involves whether the designer can *accept* the design task through an analysis of time, commitment, etc. For our purposes we assume that the project has been accepted. The remaining six steps, *analysis*, *definition*, *ideation*, *selection*, *implementation* and *evaluation*, were very appropriate and have been used to help define the types of activities a computer might assist within the context of industrial design.

Figure 1 shows the design process and its six steps. Below each step is a list of computer-related functions that provide input or output. The list is based on currently available computer software. For clarity, it is necessary to explain each part of the process and how these computer tools are used.

During the *analysis* phase, the designer relies on a great deal of research about the current project. He is required to study the past performance of the product he is designing through market tests and studies as well as other manufacturing evaluations. Usually this information is accessible in corporate databases and can be brought into the design process through a modem telephone link.

But the extent of information does not end with product testing. The entire range of market analysis techniques as well as psychological and behavioral studies can also be accessed. A good example is the wide range of computer-oriented research concerning product evaluation being done by the Vakgroep Bedrijfskunde and by the Vakgroep of Professor Gerda Smets at the Technical University, Delft. Based on current trends, new data storage structures will also include photographs and illustrations (very soon, in color) which can be downloaded from the modem. As more work is done in this area, the quantity of database information available to the designer will become overwhelming.

When the designer enters the *definition* phase, he has accumulated enough information about the project to be able to define the *essence* of the problem. As indicated in Fig. 1, the information obtained during the analysis phase leads to this accurate problem definition.

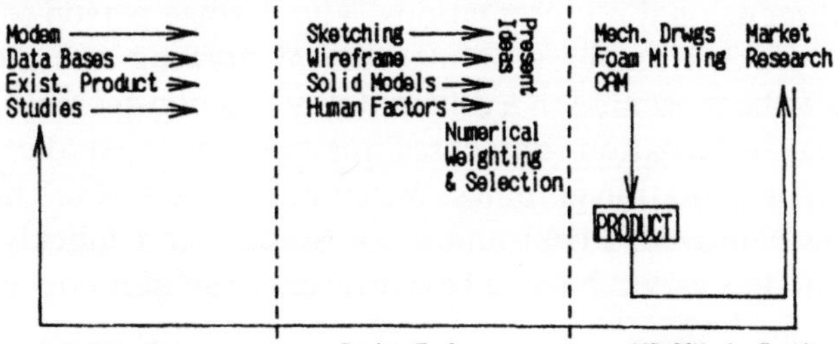

FIGURE 1. The design process.

It is the *ideation* phase that seems to offer the greatest possibilities for computer-designer interaction. The computer can provide quite a bit of specialized help during this phase, including different kinds of sketching and three-dimensional imaging. But the computer can also greatly enhance the conceptualizing and comparative evaluation of ideas and concepts. A particular source of inspiration has come from the work of Wim Muller, an instructor in the industrial design program at the Technical University, Delft. His approach to creative ideation through form manipulation (Fig. 2) shows how the relationship of product components can lead to a vast number of configurations and, ultimately, unique design concepts. Muller's technique is ideal for computer-conceptualized design because it uses elementary shapes which can be quickly and easily created and manipulated. The computer can enhance this process by providing the means of generating and rotating these views as well as the ability to capture them for later evaluation. It is a unique method because it presents a type of solid modeling in a sketching style which is very suitable to the designer. Through such a method, the possibility of developing a great number of form concepts is a pathway to innovative and creative ideas.

Renderings are also possible tools for ideation. And, since they allow for application of color, texture and material studies to product concepts, they are especially useful for presentation purposes to non-designers. The range of computerized tools can extend from very "manual" rendering using a computer paintbox with a designer's palette of markers and pens to the computerized generation of ray-traced images on an almost photographic level. Excellent examples of ray-traced images have been generated by the RAYMO computer program (developed by J. Van Wijk) at the Technical University, Delft.

Another important discovery of the research is the need to have design tools on varying levels, a suggestion that was made by Aad Bremer, an instructor in CAD at the Technical University, Delft. The need to have different levels of imagery is shown in Fig. 3, which focuses on the types of images that a designer might create and use for presentation to non-designers.

Simply put, non-designers respond most favorably to good graphics and three-dimensional representations. The average person cannot comprehend a complex database or mechanical drawing and these images would have to be presented in a different way to a non-technical audience. Much textual information (databases, methodologies, studies) would be converted to presentation graphics. Wireframe images would have to have hidden lines removed. Form and color studies and quickly generated geometric models would have to be converted to solid model images with texture and shading.

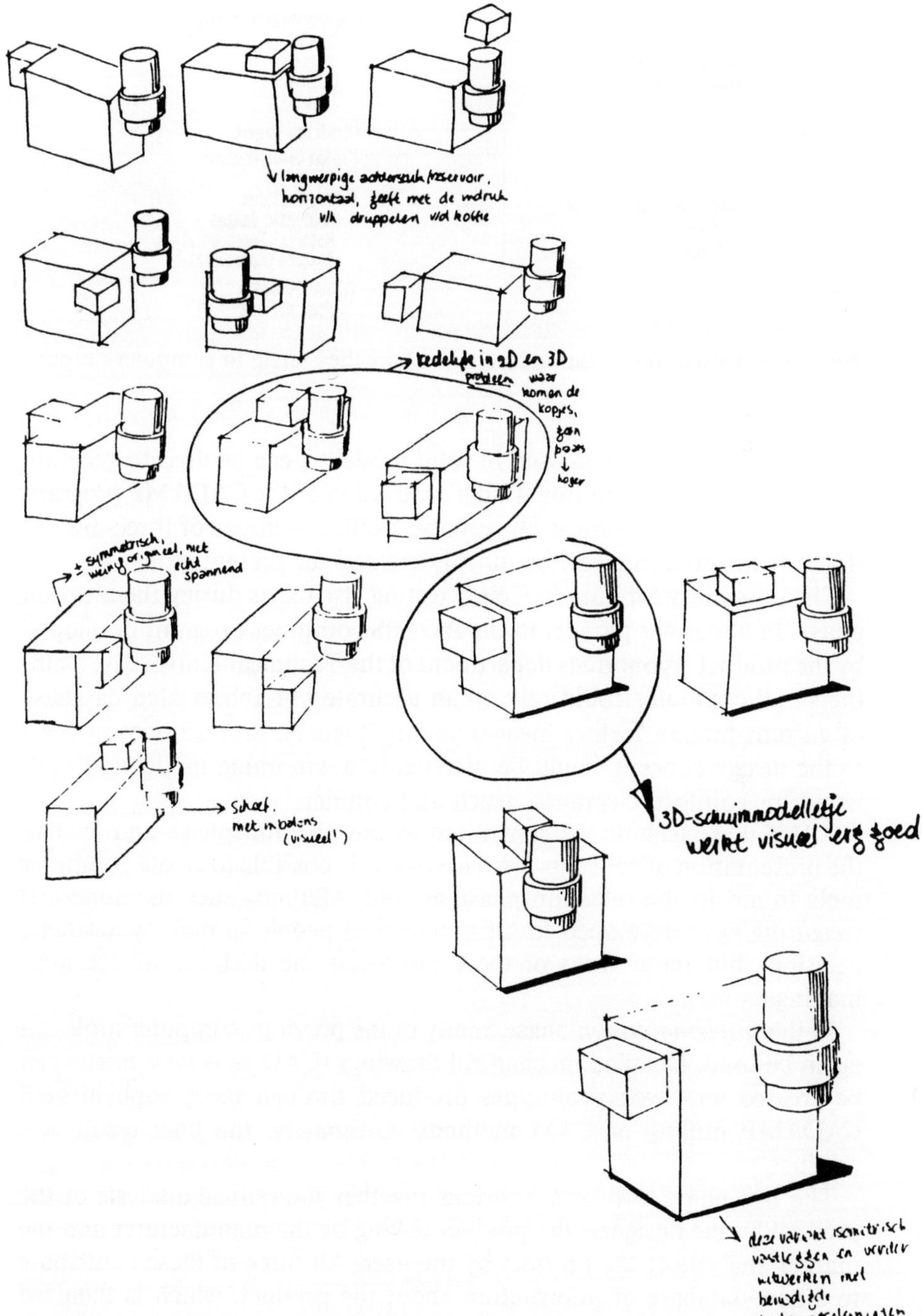

FIGURE 2. Idea generation through form relationships. Taken from an article by Wim Muller titled "Design Discipline and the Significance of Visuo-Spatial Thinking," *Industrieel Ontwerpen*, Rotterdam.

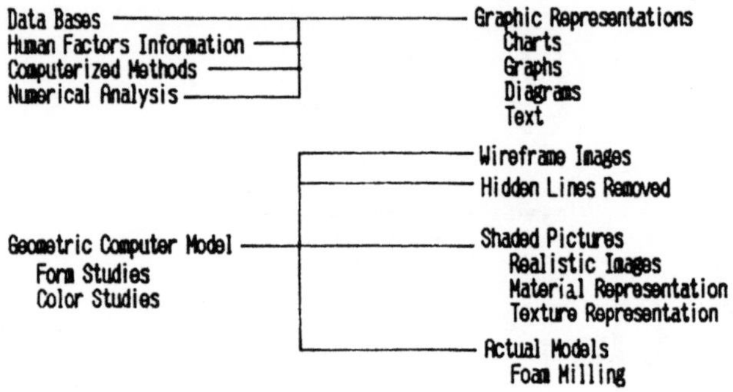

FIGURE 3. Design presentation levels and how they relate to computer output.

The same product data used in solid modeling can be used to generate computer-controlled milling. Using a variation of the CADAMP program developed at the Technical University, Delft, a number of three-dimensional foam models could be quickly created for presentation.

The possibility for human factors testing also exists during the ideation phase. In a manner parallel to the ADAPS computer program developed by the product ergonomics department of the Technical University, Delft, the small computer could rely on an accurate but abbreviated database of current human factors measurements. Figures, proportional in scale to the design concept, could be inserted in a wireframe model and evaluated for comfort, clearance, reach and conflict.

All of these techniques contribute to the ideation phase and lead to the presentation of concepts for *selection*. It is possible to create computer tools to aid in the selection phase as well. Methods such as *numerical weighting* were developed to assist technical people in making aesthetic decisions but these types of tools can assist the designer in decision-making as well.

In the *implementation* phase, many of the previous computer tools can again be used. Detailed mechanical drawings (CAD as it now exists) can be created and even prototypes produced through more sophisticated CADAMP milling or CAM methods. Ultimately, the final result is a product.

The last phase, *evaluation*, brings together the critical analysis of the product by the designer, the product testing by the manufacturer and the market analysis of the product by the user. All three of these contribute to a new database of information about the product, which is then fed back to the analysis phase of the next design generation.

The design process is a continuously evolving cycle which continues toward the goal of product optimisation. And, somewhere within this process, a designer's toolkit of computer tools should play an integral and important part.

The Toolkit Environment

The previous section has shown that there is a great variety of computer-oriented research possible within the structure of the design process. A large amount of research in this area is currently under development by various groups within the Technical University in Delft, for example. This great variety made it impossible to consider a single toolkit that could manage it all. It was necessary to analyze the design process more carefully in order to decide what part of it would be appropriate for a specialized toolkit environment.

A number of interviews with design professors and professionals were conducted and there was a great deal of discussion about the designer's workplace and habits. Trips to corporations (Philips and Nevesbo) provided insight into their concerns regarding designers and their role in industry. It became evident that the research phases of analysis and definition were well represented in database management systems and that the current CAD/CAM systems seemed to satisfy the production-oriented implementation and evaluation phases. But what emerged as an obvious need was the development of a toolkit for the *conceptual* aspects of design during the ideation and selection phases of the process.

The work of Wim Muller was again brought into consideration and it was decided that a toolkit environment could be created that was complementary to his concept. In keeping with this idea, one requirement of the toolkit should be to provide a level in which elements representing components of the product can be created and their relationships to each other explored.

Sketching was also introduced as an interactive feature of the toolkit environment. The designer needs to have the ability to apply free-hand drawing techniques for sketch development and rendering to his concepts. This particular idea is what distinguishes the toolkit from other CAD systems, in that it is unique to provide the designer with a sketching environment for creative form development as well as for solid modeling. This need became a major requirement of the system.

Through analysis of the design process a specialized activity called *the conceptualizing cycle* was identified (Fig. 4). This activity involves the creation of concepts, the comparison of these concepts and the selection of a particular idea. The idea is then fed back to the beginning for further refinement and the process started again. The entire process is defined

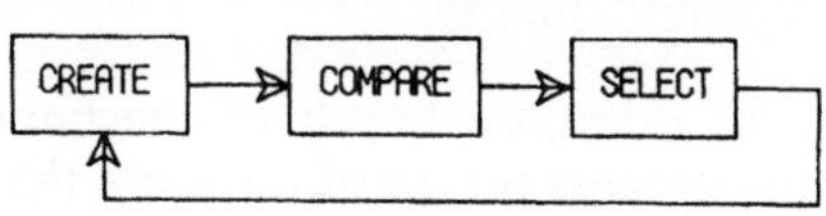

FIGURE 4. The conceptualizing cycle.

as a cycle in which the product is refined on each successive round until the designer is satisfied with the results. This cycle is the basis of the designer's toolkit environment.

An important strategy in the cycle is that of "deferment," in which a promising solution is set aside so that other combinations and types can be explored. Eventually all of the promising solutions can be compared for the ultimate selection. This deferring of a solution implies several toolkit requirements. There must be a way to store various ideas for later comparison, and the designer should be able to go backwards through his process in order to locate a decision point and pursue a new conceptual direction.

Having defined the process, the next step was to interpret it in a way that is compatible with both the designer and the computer.

The Toolkit Cycle

The cycle was interpreted to be a three step process:

1. A *create* step in which basic components are defined. This step would also be used in the cycle as a means to *refine* these basic components into more complex forms as the process continues.
2. A *combine* step in which the basic components are sized and grouped into representations of product shapes. All the shapes are presented in three dimensions and can be scaled or rotated by the designer. This step would also provide an *evaluation* function by presenting many product shapes at one time for comparison. Any shape can be selected and stored for further analysis.
3. A *sketch* step in which any selected product shape can be imported and improved through free-hand techniques. Two types of distinct activities can occur here. The more important is the use of sketching for creative form development and idea generation. The designer can actually begin the process with this step and cycle through a number of sketch developments before committing to the creation of solids. Sketching can also be applied as rendering for presentation and can be done by the designer using a *paintbox* of familiar tools (markers, airbrush, color pencils etc.).

   Enhanced sketches can then be returned to the create step for refinement by using the sketch as an "underlay" in the development of a more detailed set of elements to describe the product. Later, for a final concept perhaps, the designer may choose ray tracing of the product for near-photographic quality.

Figure 5 indicates this interpreted cycle of concept development. This type of conceptualizing process is typical for more than 90% of the products developed by industrial designers and, with some additional tools,

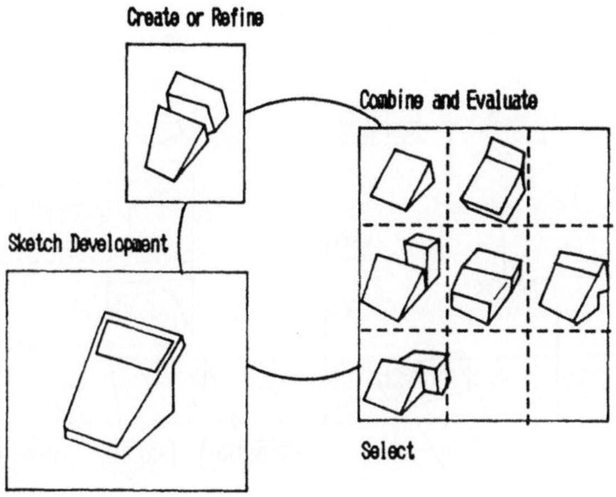

FIGURE 5. The toolkit cycle.

can be used for a great deal more. After establishing the basic process, more time was spent analysing the details of the system and determining what else might be added to enhance the toolkit environment. It was determined that a number of specialized tools would allow the toolkit to be used not only for the development of product concepts but for their presentation as well.

There should be some way to apply two-dimensional layouts to the surfaces of the product shapes, especially as the product is refined. This implies a *graphics module* which allows for the development of 2-D material such as control panel layouts, logos or text and converts it into a 3-D surface which can be "pasted" onto the product or wrapped around it. The graphics has to be defined in three dimensions so that it conforms to the product shape and rotates with it. The graphics module is related to the create/refine step because of the similarity and compatibility of operation.

In addition to a paintbox for rendering and sketching, there should be a video module which provides for the import and export of video information. *Video input* sources may illustrate a realistic background for a rendered product such as a kitchen scene for a kitchen-oriented product. *Video output* allows the designer to record any part of the process on videotape for record-keeping or presentation.

The *animation* module was added to allow the designer the means of recording a sequence of pictures for real-time playback. This is especially useful for ray-traced images since they take some time to be drawn. The animation module would draw and record the individual frames while allowing the designer to continue with conceptual work. The multi-tasking ability of computers like the Amiga would allow for simultaneous tasks like this to occur. This would be very useful for the analysis of a concept

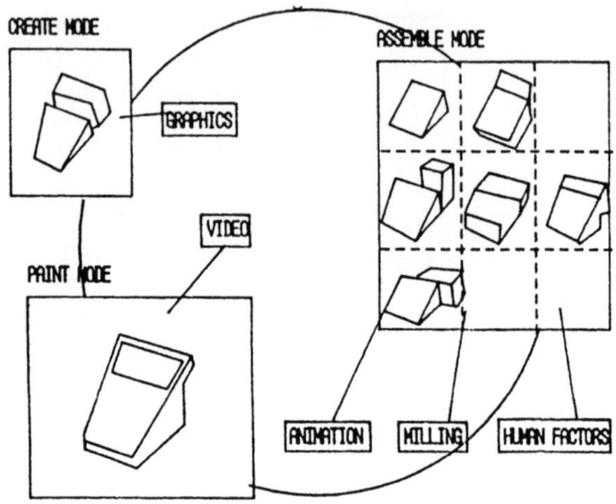

FIGURE 6. The revised toolkit cycle with the addition of specialized tools.

as well as its presentation to others because the resulting animation would have an extremely high image quality.

The work of the group that developed the CADAMP program is also very appropriate for this process. A *milling* module would provide for the quick generation of a three-dimensional foam study for any of the product shapes if the designer needs an actual model.

With the addition of these specialized modules, the designer's toolkit can provide for a very quick yet comprehensive development of concepts. By allowing for creative and innovative approaches to the conceptualizing process, this system can enhance and become an integral part of the designer's process (Fig. 6).

Implementation Software

The software requirements shown in Fig. 7 were established as a guide to the user interface. It is important to explain what the implications of these six steps are.

"Graphic oriented" (1) means symbolic, pictoral or photographic images are to be used as opposed to numbers and text. The term "graphic" should also imply that there is a sense of design to these images and that they relate to each other and to the design process in a meaningful way. If this goal is maintained in the software, the time needed to learn the system will be minimized.

"Modular and expandable" (2) is intended to imply interchangeability. The designer should be able to select software modules that are meaningful to his process and configure the system to his needs. Expandability suggests that modules can be added to the system at any time.

GRAPHIC	+ Image-oriented + Window environment + Short learning time
MODULAR	+ Same structure
INTEGRATED	+ Same Data Bases + Maintain screen image + Switch between applications easily
ICON DRIVEN MENU DRIVEN	+ Recognizable + Non-intrusive + Moveable
REVERSIBLE	+ Forward or Backwards through process

FIGURE 7. Software requirements.

"Integrated" (3) software is that which can be used together without conflict and which shares databases and structure. By keeping the software integrated, the designer can switch between applications to suit his process. Maintenance of the current image and its database is also important for consistency. For example, if the designer is working on a perspective drawing and switches from a wireframe to a shaded image, the scale, position and rotation of the image should remain constant.

"Icon selected" (4) software is a part of the normal "window" system of the computer but there are some important considerations in this development as well. Icons should never cover an image or substantially reduce the working screen. Some systems we have seen are so cluttered with icons and menus that it is difficult for the user to see important images and his overview of the process is obscured. Icons should be present when needed, positionable so that they do not obscure the main images and removable when unimportant. Also, they should be examples of good graphic communication so that the designer easily recognizes them and their intended purpose. "Menu-driven" software is also a component of the window environment and this development should follow the same rules as the icon. Menus, too, should be invisible until needed. They should also be organized in an intuitive sequence so that the designer can locate them easily.

"Reversible" (5) implies that the designer should have the ability to scan forward or backward through his process. A system for presentation, storage and retrieval of images in any succession is essential.

Based on these requirements and the application of the toolkit cycle (Fig. 6), the following software concepts were developed.

Create Mode

There has to be an easy way for designers to input three-dimensional shapes. The selection of primitive elements alone (cubes, cylinders, spheres and cones) would be possible but these shapes have limitations. Instead, the decision was made to use "sweep" and "spin" techniques for the creation of elements. These processes require the designer to draw a point-to-point profile of the element he wants. When he is finished, the computer shows the element as a three-dimensional flat plane. Thickness is added by "sweeping" the profile from one position to another, thus creating an extruded shape, or by "spinning" the profile around a centerline (Fig. 8). A great amount of variation can be created by having the sweep alter its size as it makes the transition (Fig. 9). The element can also be created by sweeping through an arc (Fig. 10). And, it is possible to sweep by twisting (spiraling) the profile (Fig. 11).

Spin works in a manner similar to sweep (Fig. 12). Any combination of these effects can be used to develop a tremendous variety of elemental form.

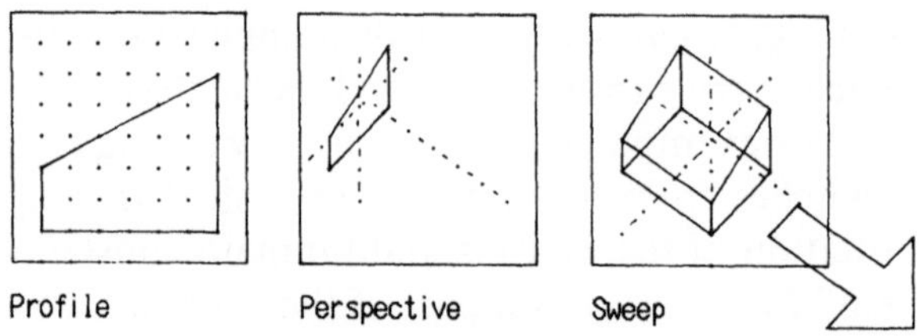

FIGURE 8. The sweep.

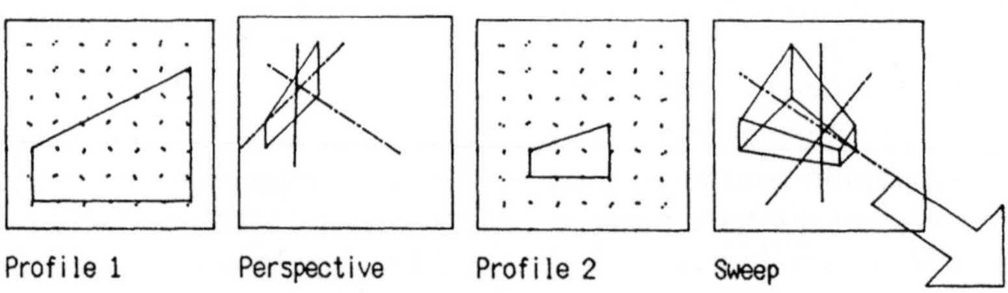

FIGURE 9. Modified sweep—altering size.

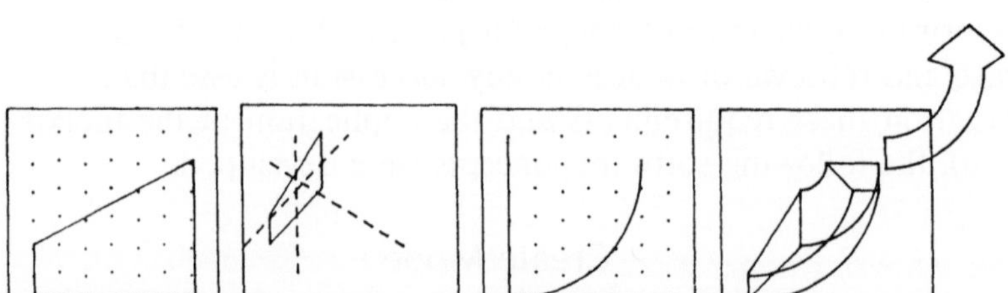

FIGURE 10. Sweeping through an arc.

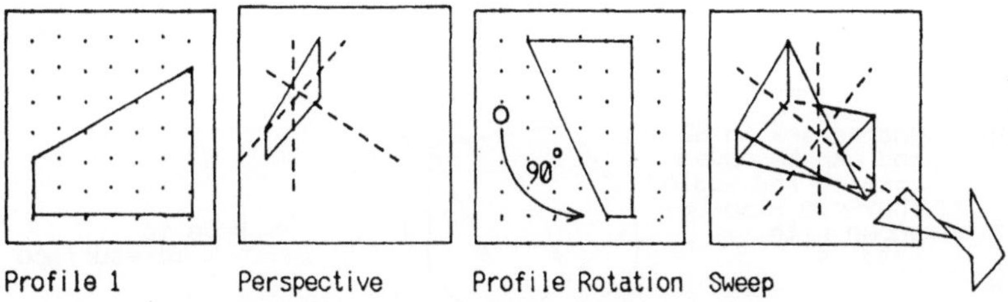

FIGURE 11. Sweeping through a spiral.

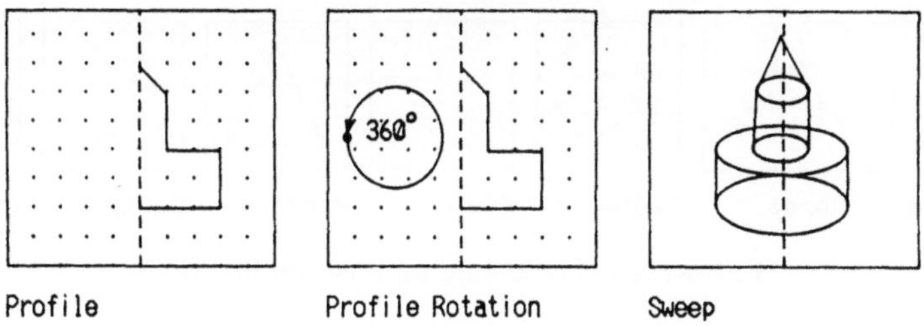

FIGURE 12. Spinning a profile.

Assemble Mode

As elements are created, they are assembled into meaningful concept shapes by the designer. The software would allow for the rotation, sizing and positioning of individual elements. For this purpose, a series of "movement" icons can be developed. Combined with the create mode, the assemble mode provides for the complete development of product concept shapes (Fig. 13). Once developed, they can be stored in a "sketchpad."

The Sketchpad

This mode provides for storage and retrieval of product images (Fig. 14). Using a standard window format, the sketchpad resembles its real counterpart. In addition to controls for sizing, moving and closing the sketchpad window, there would be a control for paging through the sketchpad either forward or backward. There would also be a page number for the current page as well as the total number of pages in the pad. One important systems implication is that the information on each page can be stored as a database representing the three-dimensional image. Not only does this conserve memory but it also allows any page image to be rotated, scaled or altered by using the movement icons. Actual sketchpad pages would be kept on a system diskette but the pages before and after the currently displayed page would be in memory for fast retrieval. This format also provides the designer with access to previously developed images so that prior concepts can be explored. Entire sketchpads can be given a name (usually that of the product being developed) and stored or retrieved as a disc file.

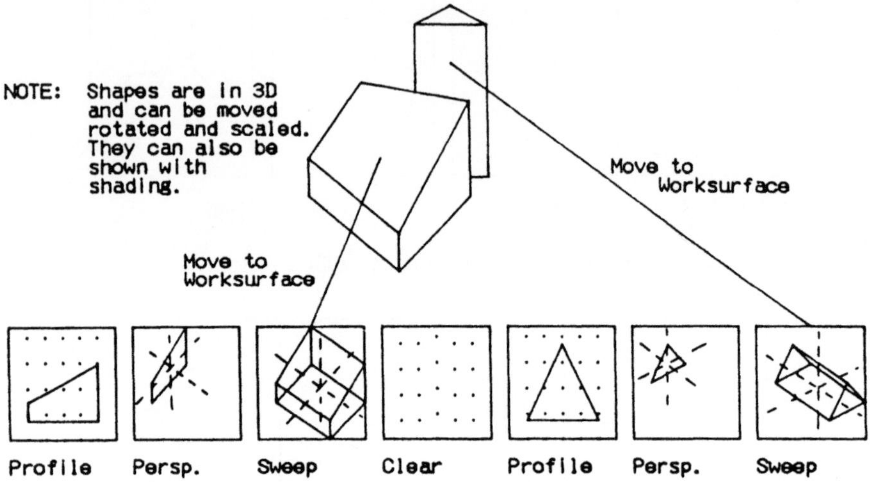

FIGURE 13. The create and assemble modes.

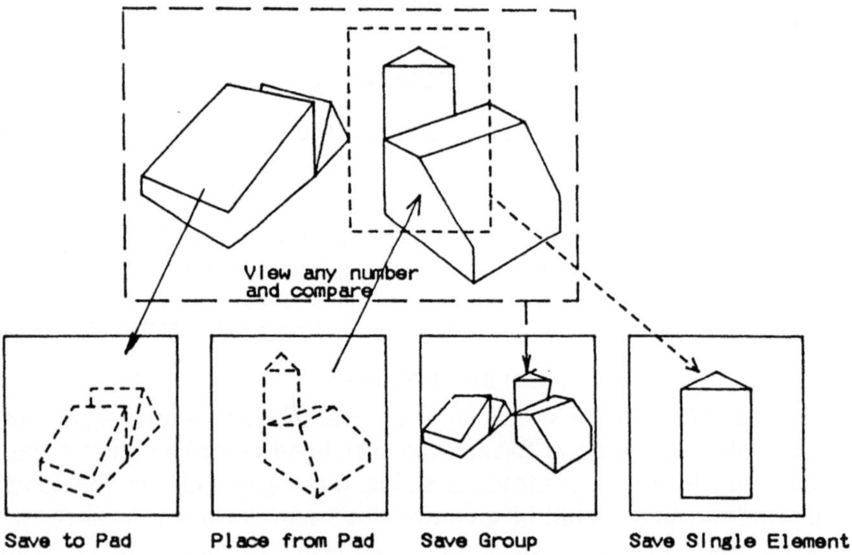

FIGURE 14. The sketchpad.

The Worksurface

The worksurface is a background screen or window that provides an area onto which any image can be placed. Images may be imported from the create mode or the sketchpad. Any number of concepts might be transported to the worksurface for comparison and evaluation. Product images can also be highlighted and viewed from different vantage points using movement icons or merged into one shape with fixed or rotatable axis. A selected image can then be exported to the paintbox for detailing or to the sketchpad for storage. The worksurface would be used primarily for the transfer of images from one part of the system to the other.

The Paint Mode

The paint mode is used to add details such as sketching, rendering with color and texture, hand-written comments, graphics or video backgrounds. It can also be used to create high-quality ray-traced images and send the results to a printer or video recorder. For the purpose of product refinement, the paintbox image can be sent back through the create mode and a new, more detailed, set of elements can be developed. It may be possible to store paint mode images on the sketchpad but, since these images are bit-mapped and use a large amount of memory, only a limited number of pages would fit on a diskette. It might be possible, however, to open up another sketchpad just for paint mode images in order to keep them separated from the 3-D images.

The Graphic Module

This module (Fig. 15) presents a grid on which the designer can lay out graphics or typography. The designer would use this module to create a control panel, label or other 2-D surface, which can then be scaled and applied to a perspective image. The surface of the graphic can be fit to the profile of the destination surface or it can be wrapped around or conformed to it in any way using surface-mapping techniques. When this mode is called, it would create its own window and icon set for two-dimensional input.

The Video Module

It would be exceptional to be able to import a video image into the bit-mapped screen of the paint mode. Realistic backgrounds and other product images could be combined with those being developed. There should also be the ability to export video information from both the paint mode and the animation module. The video icons allow for the control of video input and output at any time during the process. (See Fig. 16.)

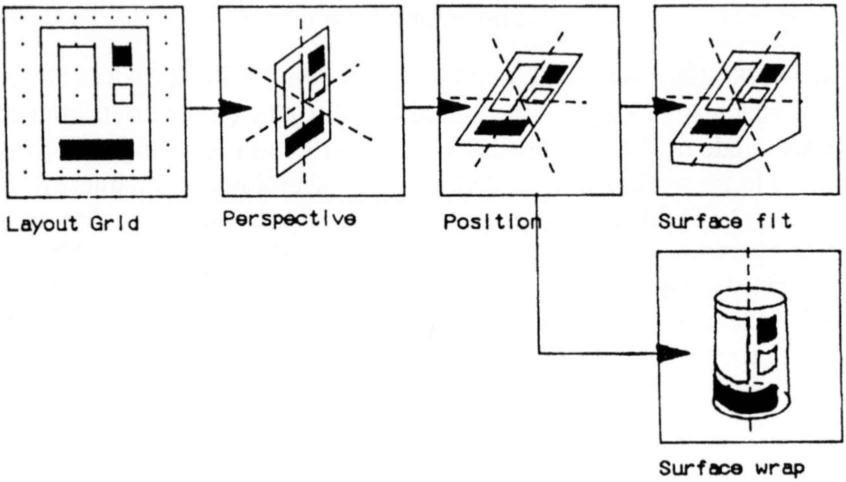

FIGURE 15. Graphic module.

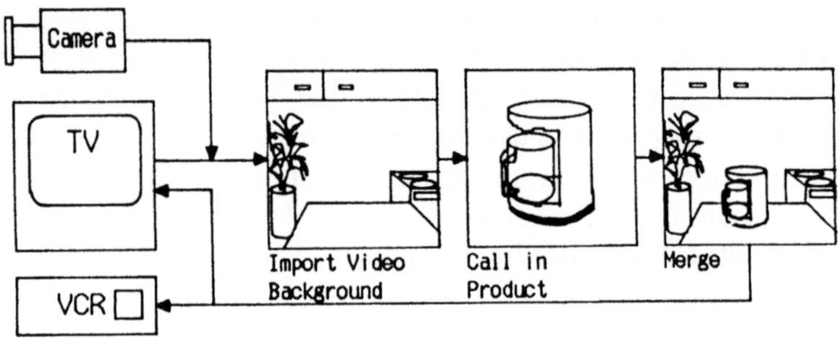

FIGURE 16. Video module.

The Animation Module

Calling this set of icons provides for storage and retrieval of a fixed number of bit-mapped screens from the paint mode (Fig. 17). These screens can show any kind of sequence such as rotation, scale, light source and shadow changes etc. They can then be played back by the animation mode at higher speeds. This is particularily important for ray tracing because of the time it takes to generate just one screen. Because of the multitasking environment available to some of the new computers, the animation module can be drawing and storing ray-traced images while the designer is busy doing something else with the system. For this reason, the animation module is a separate module from the paint mode or video module. However, recorded sequences from the animation module can also be sent to videotape through the video module. Since the number

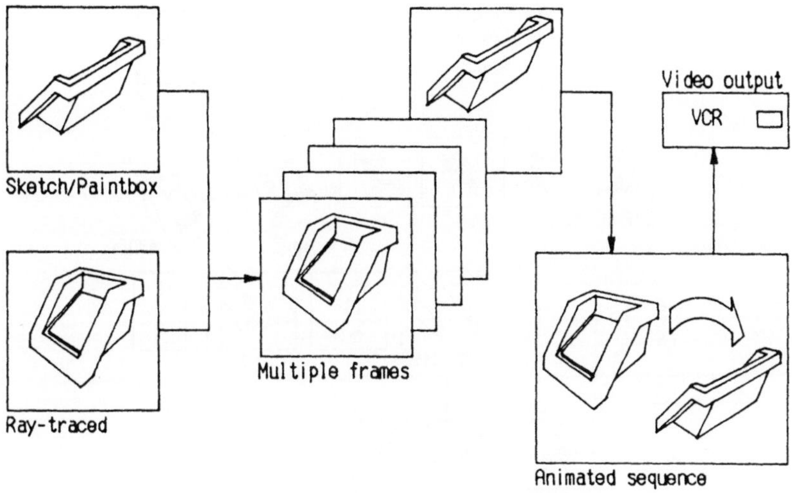

FIGURE 17. Animation module.

of screens is limited to the size of available memory, videotaping is the only way to achieve long animated sequences.

Foam Milling Module

A variation of the CADAMP foam milling program would be a convenient feature of the system. With this utility the designer could produce a series of foam studies for better human factors analysis or shape comparison. It should be quite possible to implement this software because of the compatible database structure.

Human Factors Module

A simplified database of accurate human factors information would be very valuable during the design process. A modified version of the ADAPS program would allow some testing of these factors during the conceptualizing phase. CADAMP and ADAPS are under development at the Technical University, Delft.

Summary

Since this is an interim report, the intention is to give an overview of the research that has been accomplished during the past three months and to provide insights into the direction of further development. The toolkit concept is now well defined (see Fig. 18) but much more detail is needed.

It is interesting to note that during the early part of this research, at least three other groups interested in this type of development have been

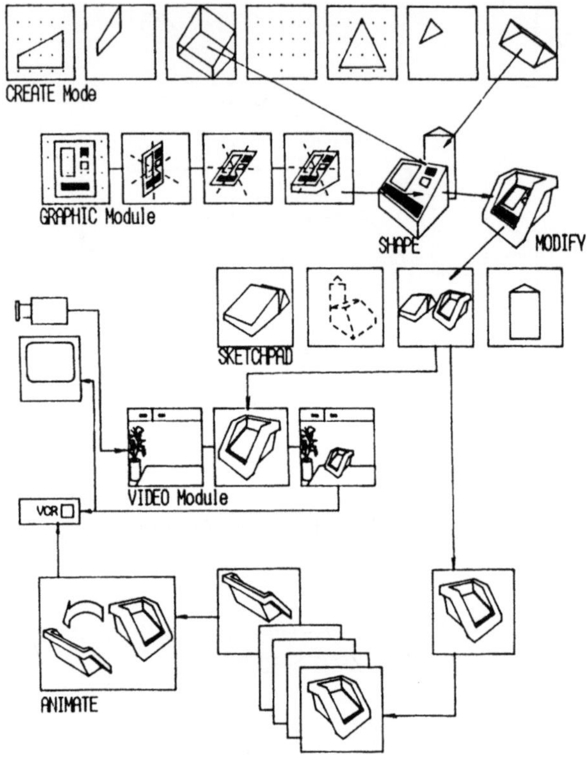

FIGURE 18. The toolkit system.

identified. Philips Corporation, Eindhoven, has one designer/student working in this area and plans to add an additional person to their staff in the Consumer Products Division in Drachten. The Technical University in Eindhoven has a student group working on a similar theme with an emphasis in sketch recognition. And there is an article (referred by Mick Van Ooy) about a group at the University of Edinburgh, Scotland, developing software for design that utilises artificial intelligence. It is encouraging that many prominent places are giving research priority to this type of project and it further establishes the recognition of a need for specific computer tools in design.

The greatest amount of work ahead lies in the identification and planning of a system framework for the toolkit. For example, the nature of the data structure involves using quite a bit of computer memory. A basic computer with 512K memory and a single disk drive would be economical for the designer but presents severe programming problems and insufficient memory for reasonable object development. An ultimate system with a 2-megabyte RAM memory and a hard disk with a 40-megabyte memory would be ideal for software development but too expensive for the average designer. Somewhere between these alternatives lies an alternative that satisfies both requirements. Issues dealing with the designer and the design process can be difficult to resolve and there will have to be compromises made in the development of a system framework.

Then, too, there is the myriad of different computers and systems currently available. Their system architectures differ from one to another, and it would be a challenge to design software that is transportable.

These issues are best left to those who will continue the toolkit research as it is far too complex to address them within this short time frame. Instead, the next phase of this work will be the development of demonstration images and software so that certain concepts can be displayed and evaluated. In this way, a designer's toolkit concept together with images to suggest its appearance and functionality will provide a well-established and tested base for the detailed work that will follow.

Computer Graphics and Animation for Interior and Industrial Designers

Peter P. Comninos

Introduction

Traditionally, designers communicate their ideas to other designers, architects, engineers and clients through drawings and models. Both these methods are reasonable compromises to having to build a prototype but are severely limiting and inflexible.

Representing a design by a set of drawings has a number of disadvantages. Designers, architects or engineers frequently have problems in understanding fully the three-dimensional implications of a design before a model is built or a prototype manufactured. Although they are all trained to think in three dimensions, their primary means of communication is in terms of two-dimensional orthographic projections, such as plans and elevations. Interpretation of such drawings is frequently ambiguous and thus may lead to expensive mistakes in the construction or manufacture process. When communicating a design to a client, a designer may resort to more realistic, but also more expensive, drawing representations such as axonometric, oblique or perspective projections. The latter appear to be the hardest to do for the designer but are the most useful to the client. Frequently the client may wish to view the proposed interior or product from a different angle or even a number of different angles or with a different degree of detail including alternative textures and finishes. In such a case new drawings must be made or commissioned at considerable cost in terms of time and money.

Constructing a prototype of the proposed product or model of the proposed interior again has a number of disadvantages. It is very costly, especially if the model has moving parts, and it is usually difficult to modify a part of the model without having to rebuild the entire model. Frequently models are unsatisfactory as they cannot be viewed at the appropriate scale, and in the case of interiors and buildings it is difficult, if not impossible, to move through them in order to understand and appreciate their architectural space and evaluate the spatial relationship of the design.

The majority of these problems can be overcome by the use of geometric modelling, computer graphics and computer animation techniques. With the orthodox approach the designer typically starts by quickly producing a first sketch or set of sketches and then proceeds with the more time-consuming task of producing a physical model. When using the computer-assisted approach, however, this process is reversed. The initial specification of the model to the computer system takes much longer than a quick hand-drawn sketch would and requires a lot more detailed information than would be present in such a sketch. Once this model specification stage is completed, the computer-assisted approach to design surpasses the traditional approach. At this stage the designer can easily assess the validity of the design, modify it and reevaluate the altered design in a progressive refinement cycle, with minimal effort. At any stage of this process the designer can satisfy himself that his model is valid. He can, through computer animation techniques, walk around a proposed product or interior, simulate the movement of any moving parts of the model, experiment with different colouring, texturing and lighting schemes, gradually perfecting the design, and finally produce presentation quality renderings and animated sequences demonstrating the functionality of the design. Data generated from the designer's model can be used as input to a computer-assisted manufacture system, thus integrating the processes of design and manufacture. This, however, is not always possible in a fully automated form with today's technology.

One of the criticisms often levelled at the computer-assisted approach to design is that the designer has to commit himself to too much detail, e.g., exact dimensions, at an early stage of the design process. This is due to the inability of the currently available geometric modellers to deal with sufficiently abstract parametric descriptions. This topic is still an active research area. Frequently, designers expect the computer system to act as a substitute for existing tools by mimicking their functionality and user handles. This, in my opinion, is an inappropriate use of the computer. The computer system should be seen as an alternative design tool which augments and supplements rather than replaces existing design tools.

This new approach to design poses a number of new problems but it also brings some undoubted advantages. It gives the designer a greater understanding and mastery of technology, it encourages an ease in communication between designers and engineers and it breaks down the artificial but often encouraged separation of tasks between design and manufacture. But above all, use of computer graphics tools allows the designer to experiment in the realm of perception and thus to apply his imagination to experimental design. In experimental design, the designer uses consciously or unconsciously the scientific method of hypothesis formation, testing, evaluation and reformation in a progressive refinement loop. The intermediate stages of this process may sometimes produce acceptable results and sometimes not. The actual process is as important to the designer as the finished product. It helps improve the designer's ability. Experimental design is made easier and cheaper with the computer as modifications of the geometric model are relatively easier than rebuilding a physical model. The computer improves the designer's ability in a qualitative as well as quantitative fashion and acts as an extension to his imagination. Thus one can say that the use of computers in the design process will give rise to tomorrow's designers.

At Teesside Polytechnic,* we take the view that to deny design students such an opportunity for self-improvement will be detrimental to their development. Because of this view, we have encouraged both interior and industrial design students of all years to use the computer creatively in the design process. Over the past few years we have experimented with commercially available as well as home-grown software. Our experience shows that off-the-shelf products either are not designed for designers or are prohibitively expensive. This leads to the development of home-grown state-of-the-art software designed with the needs and capabilities of the designer in mind. This approach provided us with the opportunity to do research in computer science and at the same time satisfy the computer graphics and animation requirements of the design students. Currently the main package that is being used by the design students is the CGAL animation system.

The CGAL 3D Animation Environment

CGAL stands for Computer Graphics and Animation Language. In 1976 the author started investigating the usefulness of high-level programming languages as a means of description for 3-D, still images and animated sequences. In the ensuing decade, two such languages were designed and implemented by him at Teesside Polytechnic. In 1979 the first language, called CGAL#0, was made available to the students of the design department (Comninos and Webster, 1980). In mid-1979 we produced our first computer-generated titles for a local BBC program. And by mid-1980 we produced our first shaded computer-animated sequence, which was filmed directly off the display screen with an 8-mm movie camera.

CGAL#0 was a command interpretive language and was found to be flexible enough for short sequences but it had all the disadvantages associated with command interpreters. The lack of variables, structure and other high-level language features was limiting and a constant source of frustration as far as long animated sequences were concerned. After experimenting with CGAL#0 for a number of years, the author decided that the only realistic solution to the afore-mentioned problems would

*When this paper was written the author worked at Teesside Polytechnic.

be achieved by the design and implementation of a procedural high-level language. This language is called CGAL#1 (Comninos, 1986). CGAL#1 includes all the features of modern structured languages, such as procedures, recursion, local variables, conditional statements, loops and intrinsic functions, as well as a number of more exotic features specifically designed to aid the animator. Because of the author's experience with command interpreters, when he was designing CGAL#1 he was not prepared to lose interactivity in his effort to gain structure. Thus the language was designed as a conversational language which is capable of operating in "command" and "program" mode in a fashion similar to BASIC-Plus, APL and LOGO.

The CGAL system provides the animator with a "work space" which remembers the state of the "CGAL universe." The CGAL universe consists of everything the system knows, such as objects, lights, camera, user programs, values of various system variables and switches. A work space exists even after the termination of a given user session and it thus provides continuity in the script development period. The animator may interact with a number of work spaces, which he can save and recall at will; thus it is possible for him to experiment with a number of alternative ideas at any given time. The system supports its own script editor, incremental compiler and interpreter. The animator is not required to submit his entire script at once; he may develop it incrementally. Portions of the script may be tried incrementally before they are incorporated in the script. Pencil tests of parts of the script or the entire script can be played back in real time, slowed down or speeded up.

In the author's experience, an animation script is very similar to a computer program in that it requires progressive refinement and debugging, but unlike most programs, as soon as it is debugged it will probably be used only once in the production of the animated sequence. It is this observation that led to the design of a system that makes the initial conception and debugging of the script as efficient as possible.

The CGAL#1 Language

The CGAL#1 animation language is similar to Pascal as far as its control structures are concerned, but it differs from Pascal in that it provides typeless variables and user-defined functions which only acquire a type at run time; thus it is an "attribute examining language." The language exists in a continuing state of development.

The animation language currently supports the following features:

1. *Named numeric constants.*

2. *Named typeless variables*, which must be declared before their use. A variable can at present be used to refer to a numeric value, a generalised polygon or a 3-D object. Future extensions will allow variables to refer

to flight paths, groups and assemblies of objects and arrays of any of the valid types. Although variables are typeless at declaration, the run-time system keeps track of the type referred to by each variable to prevent nonsense operations. A variable may change its type at run time through a direct or implied assignment.

3. *Recursive procedures and functions* with parameters. Procedures and functions may be nested. Forward procedures and functions are supported. Functions may be called as procedures. The way a parameter is passed, that is, by reference or by value, is determined at run time.

4. *All the Pascal control structures*, except GOTO, are supported in an extended form:

```
4.1 IF be THEN s1 ELSE s2
4.2 WHILE be DO s
4.3 REPEAT s;. . . ;s UNTIL be
4.4 FOR v:=ae1 TO ae 2 DO s
    Where ae1 ≤ ae2 step is +1.
          ae1 > ae2 step is −1.
4.5 FOR v:=ae1 TO ae2 STEP ae3 DO s
    Where the step may be +ve or −ve.
4.6 CASE ae OF
      ae1:s1;
      ae2. .ae3:s2; (* extension *)
      OTHERWISE s3; (* extension *)
    END;
4.7 NEXT jumps to the next iteration of
          a FOR, WHILE or REPEAT loop.
4.8 EXIT  jumps out of a FOR, WHILE or
          REPEAT loop.
4.9 RETURN terminates execution of a
           procedure, function or the
           program.

where: v  = variable
       s  = statement (simple or compound)
       be = boolean expression
       ae = arithmetic expression.
```

5. *Arithmetic expressions.*

6. *Boolean expressions.*

7. *Relational expressions.*

8. A comprehensive set of *intrinsic standard functions.*

9. A comprehensive set of *intrinsic inquiry functions*, which return information relating to various attributes of objects, light sources and the camera.

10. A set of *intrinsic time-variant functions*, which were designed to aid the animator; as they return different numeric values at different

instances in time they can be used to produce constant, accelerating, decelerating or oscillating rates of change. Their general format is

fn (sv , ev , sf , ef , pl)

where fn = function name
sv = start value
ev = end value
sf = start frame
ef = end frame
pl = list of parameters if any.

As an example consider the following statement, which may be placed in a script.

Set_Mid_x {ol} ctvf (10,25,35,70).

This statement will set the middle *x* coordinate of the object ⟨ol⟩ to the value returned by the "cosine time variant function" ⟨ctvf⟩. The object starts at rest on frame 35, gradually accelerates and eventually decelerates to rest on frame 70, having traveled 15 units along the *x* axis.

11. *Polygon expressions*, which when evaluated yield a generalized polygon. A generalized polygon consists of an outline contour and zero or more hole contours. Polygon expressions can be either a variable referring to a generalized polygon or the "define generalized polygon" ⟨dgp⟩ intrinsic function, which returns a generalized polygon. A call of ⟨dgp⟩ invokes the interactive polygon-editing subsystem, which is a sophisticated drafting tool with its own menu.

12. *Object expressions*, which when evaluated yield an object. These expressions can be a variable referring to an object or an object function. Object functions can be system or user defined. System-defined object functions allow the user to input object descriptions interactively or from a file; generate new objects by translational, rotational or general sweeps of a generalized polygon, by geometric and metamorphosis operations applied to existing objects. Objects may also be generated by skinning a number of generalized polygons and by invoking an interactive editor, such as the terrain generation subsystem.

13. An extensive set of *graphics instructions* allowing the user to:

13.1 Transform, deform and manipulate objects. Objects can be transformed relative to the object space origin, the eye space origin, their local origin and the local origin of another object.

13.2 Position and move the synthetic camera and its centre of interest; control the camera lens by changing its viewing angle, zooming factor and the lens distortion factor.

13.3 Control the lighting of the scene by selecting the light source type to parallel, point, spot-light or directed; changing the colour, intensity and decay characteristics of a light source; positioning, pointing a light source and switching it on or off; changing the colour of the background and the atmospheric decay factor.

13.4 Control the printing process by enabling or disabling various output devices; selecting the projection type, the output mode (wire-frame, hidden line and hidden surface) and the shading type.

13.5 Editing various object attributes such as the colour, transparency, translucency, surface reflection and texture characteristics.

14. *The SCRIPT and FROM statements.* The SCRIPT statement is a special type of loop. For every iteration of the loop and after the body of the loop has been executed a frame of animation is generated automatically. The format of the SCRIPT statement is

SCRIPT sf TO ef DO s

where sf = start frame (arith. exp.)
ef = end frame (arith. exp.)
s = statement (simple/compound).

The effect of this statement is to generate a number of frames starting at ⟨sf⟩ and ending at ⟨ef⟩. The SCRIPT statement increments the current frame counter, whose value can be accessed by the user via the "frame" intrinsic function. There may be more than one SCRIPT statement in a user program but they may not be nested.

Usually the body of a SCRIPT contains FROM statements. The format of the FROM statement is

FROM sf TO ef DO s

where sf = start frame (arith. exp.)
ef = end frame (arith. exp.)
s = statement (simple/compound).

Execution of the FROM statement is meaningful only inside the body of a SCRIPT statement. The effect of the FROM statement is that its body will be executed only if the frame counter is in the ⟨sf⟩ to ⟨ef⟩ range. FROM statements may be nested or performed in sequence. The SCRIPT and FROM statements not only allow for parallelism of operations between frames but also allow the user to determine the serial order of operations within one frame. An extended form of the FROM statement is

FROM sf TO ef EVERY cl LOOP ll DO s

where sf = start frame (arith. exp.)
ef = end frame (arith. exp.)
cl = cycle length (arith. exp.)
ll = loop length (arith. exp.)
s = statement (simple/compound).

an example of which is

```
SCRIPT 1 TO 150 DO
 BEGIN
  FROM 1 TO 100 EVERY 25 LOOP 10 DO
   RZ {ball} 1.5;
  ...
  END;
```

The above script will cause the production of 150 frames of animation. The FROM statement will cause the rotation of object ⟨ball⟩ in loops of 10 frames starting every 25 frames (i.e., between frames 1–10, 26–35, 51–60 and 76–85). The ball will be rotated about the z axis by 1.5 degrees for every one of those frames.

A number of FROM statements can be used to describe serial or parallel events. Non-overlapping frame ranges are used to describe serial events and overlapping frame ranges to describe parallel events. The following example illustrates how a set of complex object and camera moves can be expressed concisely by a set of serial and parallel events:

```
SCRIPT 1 TO 60 DO
 BEGIN
  MTX {ball} 0.25;                 (* event a *)
  RZ {ball} -3;                    (* event b *)

                                   (* event c*)
  CCP MID_X(ball), MID_Y(ball),MID_Z(ball);

                                   (* event d*)
  FROM 1 TO 50 DO
   CVP CTVF(10,15,1,50),CTVF(5,20,1,50),1.7;

  FROM 51 TO 60 DO TK 1;           (* event e *)
 END;
```

The above script will generate 60 frames. Events a, b and c occur in parallel on every frame. Event a translates the ball by 0.25 units (on every frame) along its local x axis. Event b rotates the ball by -3 degrees (on every frame) about the world origin. The net effect of these two events is to make the ball spiral away from the world origin. Event c changes the position of the center of interest of the camera so that it always targets the center of the ball. Mid_x( ), Mid_y( ) and Mid_z( ) are intrinsic enquiry functions which in turn return the middle x, y, and z coordinates of the ball. Event d occurs between frames 1 and 50, while event e occurs between frames 51 and 60. These two events are serial with respect to each other but parallel to events a, b and c. Event d gradually changes the position of the camera from point ⟨10, 5, 1.7⟩ to point ⟨15, 20, 1.7⟩ with ease-in and ease-out. CTVF is the cosine time variant function, which returns different numeric values at different instances in time. Event e tracks the camera towards the center of the ball by 1 unit on every frame for which it is active.

Conclusion

Over the past 6 years the CGAL animation environment has been used to train both interior and industrial design students in computer graphics and animation techniques. Some of these student become so proficient in the techniques that they become employed as experts by design and animation firms. A number of animation sequences have been designed by them (Comninos, 1985).

Over the past 2 years the CGAL animation environment has been used to produce nine computer-generated sequences for various television programmes which were broadcast or are to be broadcast on ITV, Channel Four and Tyne Tees television.

The system is currently used in the production of a computer-animated film depicting the manufacture of ammonia at the molecular level. This film is a co-production of ICI (UK) and Teesside Polytechnic.

In conclusion, the CGAL animation environment has proved to be a powerful, flexible and cost-effective tool for the production of 3-D colour animation for both commercial and educational applications.

References

Comninos, P.P. (1985) "Computer Animation in Interior and Industrial Design," *Computers and Graphics* 9(4):499–453.

Comninos, P.P. (1986) "The CGAL Animation Environment and Its Application in the Entertainment Industry," *Proc. International Electronic Image Week, Second Image Symposium*, pp. 324–332, Nice, April.

Comninos, P.P. and C.A.G. Webster (1980) "CGAL: Computer Graphics and Animation Language," *Proc. Eurographics 80 Conference*, pp. 113–126, Geneva, September.

Computer Graphics and Graphic Design: Too Costly, Too Complex, Too Cryptic

Gillian Crampton Smith

Introduction

I teach practising graphic designers computing. I enjoy my job. But I am unhappy with the kind and quality of computing which—with admirable exceptions—the computing industry offers graphic designers and which, I admit, graphic designers expect from the industry. The state of the industry's art, though remarkable, is not really improving the state of our art.

I believe the computing on offer is too costly, too complex and too cryptic. It is also too damn ugly.

What links my complaints is that the computer industry tends to offer graphic designers tools for *production*, not design. The present generation of computer tools enable designers to produce more quickly the work they used to do by hand—sometimes to do things they would not have contemplated before, such as tumbling logos or instantaneous news graphics. But these tools do nothing to help designers design better. On the contrary, they often make it more difficult.

Too Costly

My first concern is that, given the economics of the average design practice, available computer tools are far too costly.

Maggie Allison of the Moving Picture Company has complained publicly of the lack of imagination shown by designers using their facilities. But the cost of using most graphic design computer systems, I suggest, discourages the risky, experimental and playful frame of mind from which springs innovation. A designer who hired a paint system for the first time described his experience to me as like sitting in a taxi from London to Brighton—and getting caught in a traffic jam. When something went wrong he began to hear a meter ticking away.

At £100 an hour, or even £50, the spirit of adventure wanes. At this rate of expense designers will not be attracted to use computer tools, let alone use them imaginatively.

There is also a problem of pressure. The traditional process of design has built-in delays: the time taken to trace type, for instance, or make a photographic print. This allows time for the critical reflection required for good design. The high cost of computer equipment, however, means that designers are now expected to work long hours, often without breaks, at a regular and intense rate. Because work can be *produced* much faster, designers are pressed to *design* much faster.

Slavery is the enemy of quality. Really intelligent, reflective work cannot come from designers chained to workstations. For most purposes a design system needs to be cheap enough for each to have one on his desk and for no-one to worry if it stands idle.

Too Complex

This brings me to my second complaint: one reason for the high cost is that the tools are too complex, too clever.

Designers start a design at a very schematic level: thumbnail sketches of alternatives, thinking through drawing. They need a system that allows them to work initially very fast and flexibly but not in great detail. Only as the design progresses will they begin to test it more precisely—in their mind's eye and by drawing.

It is not that designers *can get by* without detail in the first stages, but that too much detail actively gets in the way. There are parallels in other areas of creativity. The mathematician Jacques Hadamard, for instance, in his book *On the Psychology of Invention in the Field of Mathematics*, notes how eminent mathematicians typically begin their speculations through visual images—visual images, what is more, *vague* enough, as he wrote, "to lead me without misleading me." Picasso, similarly, is quoted as saying that there nothing is as dangerous as a good idea—meaning, I suppose, that the seductive precision of a happy notion, stumbled upon too early, can discourage divergent exploration and channel it up a barren cul-de-sac.

Precision, moreover, is usually bought at the expense of speed. A designer needs to see quickly the result of changing the design, to flip between alternatives, to chase an idea quickly, to put in on "hold." So any tool must be interactive and work in real time, or something approaching it.

In 3-D animation, for instance, if you must wait for frames to be drawn you cannot get a feel for the final movement. This is what makes Computer FX's wireframe system or the Bosch FGS so attractive to designers—you can see the movement in real time.

But in the case of the Bosch system I question whether the provision of real-time shaded polygons is effort best spent. For its high cost means that designers cannot generally afford to use it as a design tool, only for production. If a designer understands how 3-D images are made, a wire-frame previewing facility is as good or better for the initial stages of animation. Roy Hall of Wavefront Technologies, for example, talking at Stirling last summer, showed how he initially works at a very coarse resolution when designing a ray-traced image. This greatly reduces the time taken to render it, but gives enough detail to show what it might look like. Similarly, a wireframe facility interfaced to a rendering machine would allow the user to check different aspects of the animation at varying levels of detail and there would be no need to render polygons in real time.

An ideal design tool has a hierarchy of complexity: a fast, flexible "front end" program working on cheap hardware which can, if necessary, be interfaced to more complex and costly systems for the later stages of the design process and eventually production.

A good example of a simple front end, linkable to a more complex system, is the Macintosh/Linotype desktop publishing combination. The Macintosh computer, at say £2500, with a page make-up program, at say £500, is used to work out page layouts. When finished, the layouts can be "translated up" for output on either a laser printer at 300 dots per inch, at say £4000, or a typesetter at 1200+ dots per inch, at say £40,000. So each designer need not be chained to tens of thousands pounds' worth of equipment. A hierarchy of complexity also means that systems are easier to learn to use. If you begin learning at the simplest end of hard- and software, you can afford to make mistakes. You are not, moreover, immediately deafened by the cacophony of bells and whistles emitted by the more complex systems.

Too Cryptic

This brings me to my third concern: most packages on offer are too cryptic in their presentation, too confusing.

There are of course the obvious follies. A recent software update of a well-known paintbox system, for instance, relocated the command positions on the graphics tablet so that what was SAVE is now ZAP! Less obvious is a failure to make systems correspond with intuitive, possibly innate, conceptual frameworks.

Learning and creating involve bodily conceptions, not just intellectual ones: the rhythm of a keystroke sequence, the choreography of a menu choice on the tablet, the physical consistency between *up* on an input device and *up* on the screen. Anything interrupting this subconscious ballet forces the user to switch from the more discursive, unfocussed way of thinking which favours invention into a more linear, arbitrarily coded mode.

So the user interface must be as intuitive and consistent as possible: commands used together should be grouped together, for instance, and you should not have to zip up and down trees of menus to carry out common sequences of commands, as many paint systems demand. In short, the system must suit the convenience of the user, not the programmer.

Avoidable obscurity, however, imports confusion into the *conscious* as well as the subconscious aspects of computer use. It is often difficult to get a clear and truthful view of what is going on within a package. The instructions tell you what buttons to press, but how the package then reacts, its principles of operation, is seldom expressed in either the design of the human interface or the documentation.

It is often argued, I know, that designers need not know about computers in order to use them. One drives a car without knowing how it works, it is said, so why not a computer? I think the driving analogy is misleading and prefer that of cooking. Anyone can cook by following a cookbook but if you do not understand the principles of cooking you are at the mercy of any slight deficiency in the recipe. If it says "add flour," in the insouciant way of the cookbooks, and you obediently dump in a cup of self-raising, you will get . . . a lumpy stodge.

If you wan to go further and invent new dishes, to assemble new combinations of ingredients, a grasp of culinary theory is essential: the effect on various foods of pressure, mixture, heat and so on. I do not say you need a BSc in food chemistry, simply a general idea of the principles.

It is correctly assumed that many computer users do not have a grasp of the operating principles. So many applications limit themselves to mimicking the operational principles of pre-computer technologies. The Quantel Paintbox, for instance, offers a type of mark that imitates chalk and a palette where colours are mixed as in a literal paintbox.

I find this patronising and artificially limiting. Designers, like everyone else, work the way they do because of the technology available to them. So new technologies mean new procedures and new possibilities.

It is said that if a new technology mimics its predecessor the user, feeling comfortably at home, can then gradually be weaned from the old ways. This might be true were the imitation exact, but it seldom is. Many paint systems, for instance, present a notional palette on which colours can be changed. But, having set up this essentially false model, they confound painterly expectations by allowing these changes to affect not only what is about to be painted but also what has already been painted. The user is left confused.

Furthermore, without a conceptual grasp of the fundamental operational principles shared by all computer tools, every newly encountered system or application appears strange, new and baffling.

To camouflage new technology, then, confuses. It also delays development. Car design, to take a well-known instance, never really took off until manufacturers and customers realised they were no longer horseless carriages but a different thing altogether. When computer systems imitate pre-computer procedures, similarly, they obscure their own logic from the user and thus dampen, or at least delay, customer demand for the most appropriate and efficient exploitation of technological innovation. My guess is that the most powerful innovations in computer-aided graphic design will be stunningly simple, spring naturally from the medium, and be invented not by computer scientists but by informed users who understand the basic principles.

Speaking of informed users, I can hardly as a graphic designer leave the question of clarity without mentioning documentation, just as much part of a system as the hardware and software. Writing and designing good documentation is a hard and laborious art, not often practised. It requires logical rigour to analyse what has to be put across and a sympathetic imagination to put oneself in the place of someone faced for the first time with a system. It is as difficult as designing the hardware and software themselves, and to the user just as important.

Documentation is frequently of an appallingly low standard. We must insist on documentation which approaches the package from several angles: how to get started, a tutorial, a detailed description of the commands, how to combine commands for common operations, a reminder card and so on. We must not tolerate jargon-laden, skimped, sloppily thought-out instructions which imply that the writer has no time for readers less well inducted into computing masonry than himself. And we should treat with incredulous contempt manuals for systems costing thousands of pounds which lack indexes or glossaries, say, or are presented as photocopied typewriting. If you buy a kitchen Magimix you get the machine, a recipe book, and a printed booklet showing how to use it, clean it and care for it—all for £70.

Too Ugly

Clearly, I am onto my final moan: ugliness. The computer industry seems to think that normal standards of grace and propriety need not apply to their products. But why should anyone, designer or not, share his office or living with something with as much elegance as a car battery? Why, when I sit at the counter of my local travel agent, should the thrown-together rear of his viewdata terminal confront me like a baboon's unlovely buttocks? Does no-one care?

As for the front end, how many people must spend each day with the appalling typefaces and gruesome colour screens of the IBM PC? IBM commissioned graphic designers to devise a beautifully and intelligently presented tourist-information system to run on their PCs at their New York headquarters. It was done there—why not everywhere?

Clearly, the computer industry on the whole, here and abroad, thinks that appearance doesn't *really* matter. But if it is tempted to ignore the graphic design industry as too negligible a fraction of the market to merit much attention, I say two things. First, increasingly in our time the visual image claims equality with the former dominion of the spoken or written word, and what the graphic designer needs from computing this morning is what all computer users will need this afternoon. And second, at many levels of computer equipment, appearances are *all* that matters: when, as with hi-fi, there are many systems offering broadly the same functions at similar prices, the look of the hardware, the manual and the screen will determine sales.

I am of course about to plug my profession. For what the computing industry might offer the graphic designer might be repaid by the skills the graphic designer can offer the computing industry.

One aspect of a graphic designer's work is to design things that delight or attract attention. But another is more fundamental: to devise efficient and vivid ways of transferring ideas from one person's mind to another's. It may be a persuasive idea: *buy OMO*; *vote SDP*. Or it may be information: *the 9:10 to Cambridge goes from platform 3*; *don't inflate your lifejacket until you get out of the aircraft*; *now put your disc in the disc drive*. If it is done well, you shouldn't notice it—which is perhaps why most people don't realise this is what graphic designers do.

Excessive complexity, obscurity and plain ugliness—evident in much computer software and documentation—are precisely what graphic designers are trained to deal with. How should the information be ordered? How is its inner structure best expressed? In what order should it appear to the user? How can colour be used on the screen to make information legible, comprehensible and pleasurable to look at?

At St. Martin's we are investigating these problems by having computer scientists work on projects with graphic designers. Our part-time postgraduate course in computers and graphic design, which has just finished its first year, aims to teach practising graphic designers enough about the principles of computers and computer graphics for them to be able to work efficiently and fruitfully with computer scientists, so that each may bring to a project his or her own particular expertise.

We hope that a closer relationship between graphic designers and computer scientists will develop tools that fit *our* purposes more closely. And we hope that computer scientists might use some of our skills and knowledge to design tools for others which are easy to learn and use. End of plug.

Let me sum up by saying that in computer-aided graphic design:

cheap is beautiful
simple is beautiful
clear is beautiful
and beautiful is beautiful.

Part 4 Animation

The Art of Simulation

John A. Vince

Introduction

In spite of the existence of automatic pilots and the sophisticated homing systems of modern offensive missiles, the role of the human pilot is still paramount in reassuring passengers that their lives are more secure under the guidance of a living brain rather than several million transistors. No doubt, one day we will all fly in pilotless aircraft, but until that time, the human guidance system must evolve and be maintained in peak condition to match the complex technology of modern aircraft.

In order to master the flying characteristics of an aircraft, pilots undergo rigorous training programmes which are both expensive and time consuming. Further, it would be impossible to employ real aircraft for this task, for obvious reasons of cost and the level of danger to which both pilot and public would be subject.

A flight simulator (Fig. 1) permits this training to be achieved from the relative safety of the ground, without the exorbitant operational expenses of aircraft and the possibility of its loss or damage. Nevertheless, flight simulators might still be considered expensive at a typical price of £6M, but they are normally expected to function 18 hours daily, without failure, and consequently are highly cost-effective.

Employing hardware which attempts to emulate the major characteristics of an aircraft under various dynamic conditions is not a trivial task. These systems must be capable of simulating the physical and visual sensations to a level of realism such that a pilot is totally convinced and absorbed during the training session. On more than one occasion, the author has nervously reached out for physical support during a rapid banking manoeuvre in a simulator working without motion; the visual cues are so convincing, one's brain is forced to accept that it is undergoing acceleration, in spite of the vestibular (organ for sensing spatial orientation located in both ears) system remaining in a non-excited state. The technology needed to configure such systems is highly complex, requiring

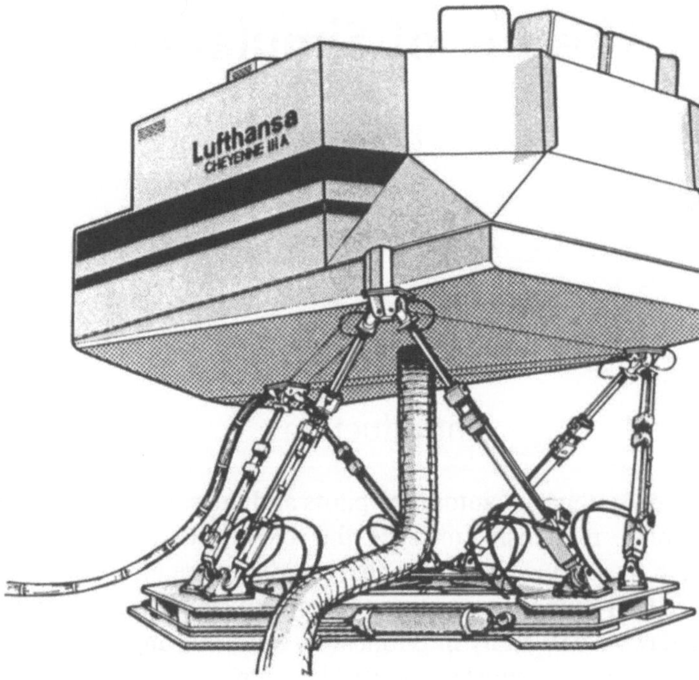

FIGURE 1

the integration of hydraulics, digital signal processing, computing, optics, electronics etc., not to mention major branches of mathematics.

Simulator Design

A typical simulator will comprise a motion system, a computer and an image generator together with its associated display system. The motion system dynamically orientates the training cabin—which is a replica of a specific plane or helicopter—in space with six degrees of freedom. Its hydraulic jacks are directly controlled by a computer, which solves in real time the equations of motion describing the flight characteristics of the simulated craft. The motion system can function only within a specific spatial envelope, being limited by the travel on the hydraulic jacks, and the motion cues are needed only to stimulate the pilot's vestibular system during times of acceleration, and even then, a compromise is necessary (Baarspul, Hosman and Van de Vaart, 1986).

In preventing a pilot's brain from receiving conflicting signals, and possibly causing motion sickness or other disturbing sensations (Kennedy et al., 1986), system response times must be minimal and as nearly syn-

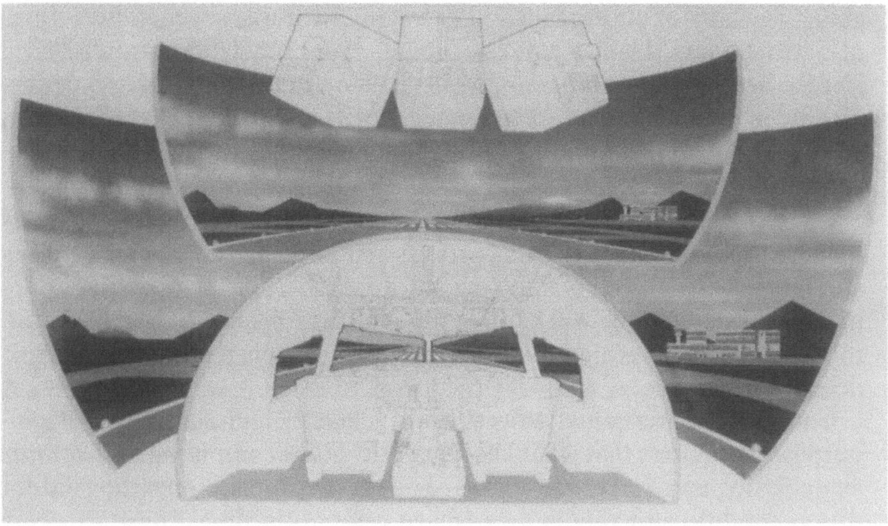

FIGURE 2. WIDE projection system.

chronous as possible. The real-time domain must be common to all system elements.

Rediffusion Simulation's WIDE (Wide-angle Infinity Display Equipment) display system, illustrated in Fig. 2, employs three or five RGB projectors to create a continuous image upon a translucent back projection screen. The projectors are capable of displaying a conventional raster image, which is overwritten caligraphically by approximately 5000 light points at 30 to 50 Hz (Fields). The light points are used to represent aeronautical beacons and the visual approach slope indicators (VASI) as well as decorating a night scene with hotel windows, terminal buildings, local landmarks and moving cars.

Surrounding the front of the simulator's aircraft cabin, and in the pilot's line of sight, is a large spheroidal mirror which reflects into the cabin a virtual image of the projection screen. The nature of this realistic image provides both pilot and co-pilot with a true 3-D visual sensation.

Each projector is driven by its associated CIG (Computer Image Generator) which provides raster and calligraphic signals in real time. The source of these signals is now covered in detail.

Computer Image Generation

The art of simulation is knowing how to balance the various features demanded of computer-generated images to create acceptable real-time scenes at realistic prices. For example, recent research has revealed the exotic imagery of photorealistic ray tracing with image generation times of 5 to 10 hours (Haines and Greenberg, 1986); fractal terrain-rendering images needing 6 hours/scene (Miller, 1986), and realistic seascapes requiring in excess of 10 hours to render 92,724 bi-cubic patches (Fournier, 1986)! Although it would be exciting to employ these images, their frame generation times are still a million times slower than real-time rates.

Consequently, real-time simulator images are achieved by selecting system features vital to the training process and implementing 3-D modelling and rendering algorithms that have ultra-fast solutions. Hopefully, future machine architectures will resolve the real-time display of fractal terrain models and sophisticated rendering schemes, but currently these systems do not exist.

Conventional computer animation is generally undertaken on general-purpose computers that would be equally at home computing VAT returns as rendering an object with Phong shading. But a price must be paid for this generality, and this is long image generation times. It is also very rare to be a single user on such machines; frequently an animation program is running alongside the company's COBOL payroll, apart from the omnipresent operating system ensuring that each request for a system resource is meticulously vetted and fairly distributed. Naturally, this is not an environment for real-time image generation; something much more specific and dedicated is needed to ensure that an uninterrupted real-time stream of images is output.

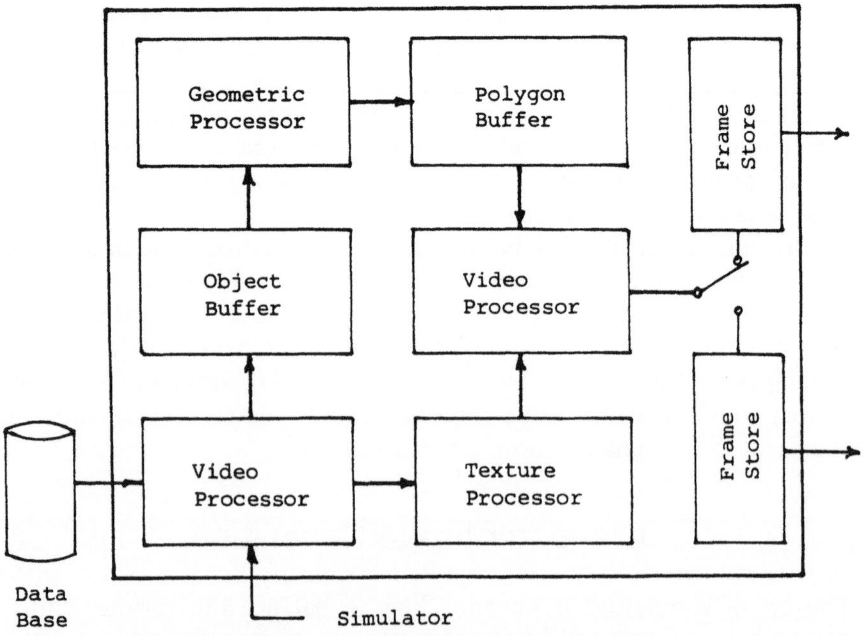

FIGURE 3. A hypothetical CIG system.

Although there is not one CIG architecture employed throughout the simulator world, it is possible to construct a block diagram which illustrates the major components of a hypothetical CIG system. Figure 3 illustrates such an architecture.

Database

CIG systems, like rendering programs, require a 3-D model to process. These are often stored on removable discs containing a specific airport and some surrounding terrain constructed from polygons and light points. Database modelling is an art, due to the constant compromise of keeping polygon density to a minimum without sacrificing realism. In general, one CIG channel is capable of processing 500 to 1500 polygons (depending on the system) without falling below the standard refresh rate. This polygon count is extremely low when compared to commercial computer animation models, which regularly contain several thousand polygons and occasionally one or two hundred thousand. Some supercomputer systems have even approached 750,000 triangles.

Because hidden-line and hidden-surface removal has always been a time-consuming aspect of computer graphics, a real-time solution requires that every component of a CIG system assists in making this possible. At the database level this is achieved by partitioning objects with separating planes which enable a binary tree to describe spatial relationships to clarify object occlusion (Schumacker et al., 1969). At a finer level, the binary space partitioning (BSP) approach proposed by Fuchs et al. (1979) uses object polygons as the separating planes. A traversal of the tree reveals a priority order sequence of polygons from any viewpoint in space.

Data are further partitioned on an area basis as shown in Fig. 4, providing a first level of 3-D clipping. These area blocks (approximately 25–100 square miles), together with the aircraft's position and direction, enable the viewing processor to distinguish between nonvisible and potentially visible zones.

As minimising the number of polygons displayed is so vital to achieving real-time update rates, objects may also be stored within the database at different levels of detail. Thus a distant detailed object is loaded only in its simplest form, with finer detail added as its distance decreases. To prevent this extra detail "popping" onto the image, the new polygons are introduced as transparent surfaces and made opaque during a brief finite period.

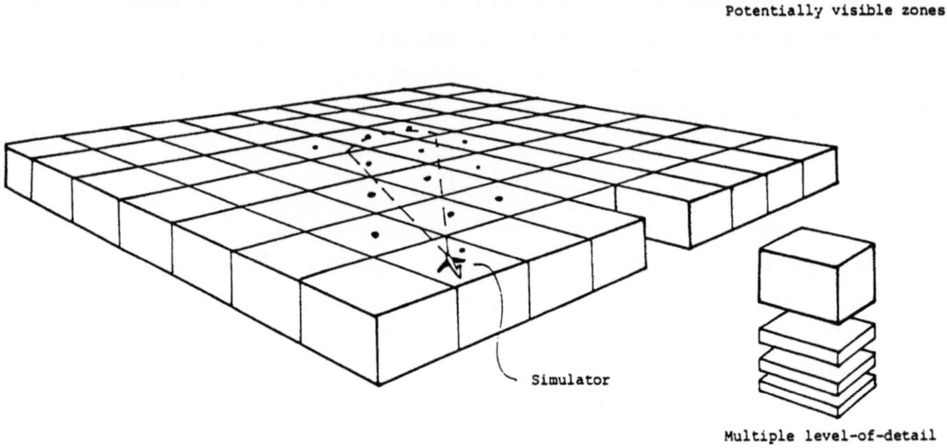

FIGURE 4. Space partitioning for first-level culling.

The Viewpoint Processor

The viewpoint processor is constantly updated with the 3-D position and direction of the simulated craft, which controls the area blocks and detail level loaded into the CIG. Back-face removal–which is vital to easing the hidden-surface process–is also undertaken at this stage.

Apart from polygonal data being loaded by the viewpoint processor, binary tree tables and information controlling the instancing of objects, light points, object colour and texture indices are also accumulated within a buffer feeding the geometric processors.

Geometric Processor

It was mentioned above that three or five projection systems are used to form the final image, creating a field of view of 120 to 200 degrees, with each projector driven by its own CIG. The viewpoint processor then supplies its data in parallel to the available image generators, which individually clip out their respective 3-D windows. The projection system electronically fades the left and right edges of a displayed image to provide a smooth transition from one projector to another.

Three-dimensional clipping is not a very difficult task to achieve in real time; in fact, Sutherland patented a device in 1972, and Silicon Graphics Inc. produced a geometry engine in 1982 which could clip and display 65K coordinates/second. More recently, several very large scale integration (VLSI)-based systems have appeared which are able to clip and render 10K polygons/second (Swanson and Thaye, 1986).

Apart from clipping, the geometric processor also undertakes perspective calculations computing eye and screen coordinates. Accurate perspective depth is very important within a flight simulation environment as the active range of objects is probably 20 feet to 25 miles; under these conditions the eye Z-coordinate is far more reliable but demands more computation.

The output from the geometric processors in this hypothetical system is a buffer containing visible polygons requiring rendering by a display processor.

Display Processor

Before the advent of cheap memories, a scan-line display algorithm was the most effective way of converting polygon boundaries into prioritised coloured areas. Video signals were created in real time as an edge buffer was scanned, which could cause overload problems if the system limit of edges was exceeded for any given raster.

More recently, with well-established frame stores and Z-buffer-based algorithms, new architectures are appearing, but unfortunately they bring with them a new range of problems.

The Z-buffer (Foley and Van Dam, 1982) resolves hidden-surface computations but cannot handle translucent polygons, which are so vital to fade level-of-detail and texture. Anti-aliasing, again very important, is not easily computed. However, the elegance of the Z-buffer cannot be ignored on the basis of these drawbacks.

Evans & Sutherland's CT5 CIG (Schumacker, 1980) introduces the concept of rectangular pixel spans storing parametric edge definitions, which can, with the aid of masking hardware, identify those sub-pixels covered by a polygon. Further hardware can anti-alias the spans using spatial filters for each pixel, removing "jaggies" and handling translucency.

Most CIG systems employ a Lambertian illumination model to flat shade polygons, and to increase image fidelity surface texturing adds the extra realism. Figure 5 shows a scene where the sky and ground are modelled by two parallel polygons suitably textured. The fields on the ground are individual texels, whilst the clouds are formed from detailed clusters of texels. The mapping of the texture is simplified by the fact that only two polygons are involved, and the inverse perspective calculations are trivial.

Although objects are flat shaded with the sun as a single light source, systems such as CT6 can provide for smooth shading and colour blending and also self-luminous surfaces. Phong shading, although vital to conventional computer graphics, fortunately is not needed in flight simulation images; however, I suppose the occasional glint of sunshine on a sea or lake or even windows would add that extra touch of realism, but the cost would be high.

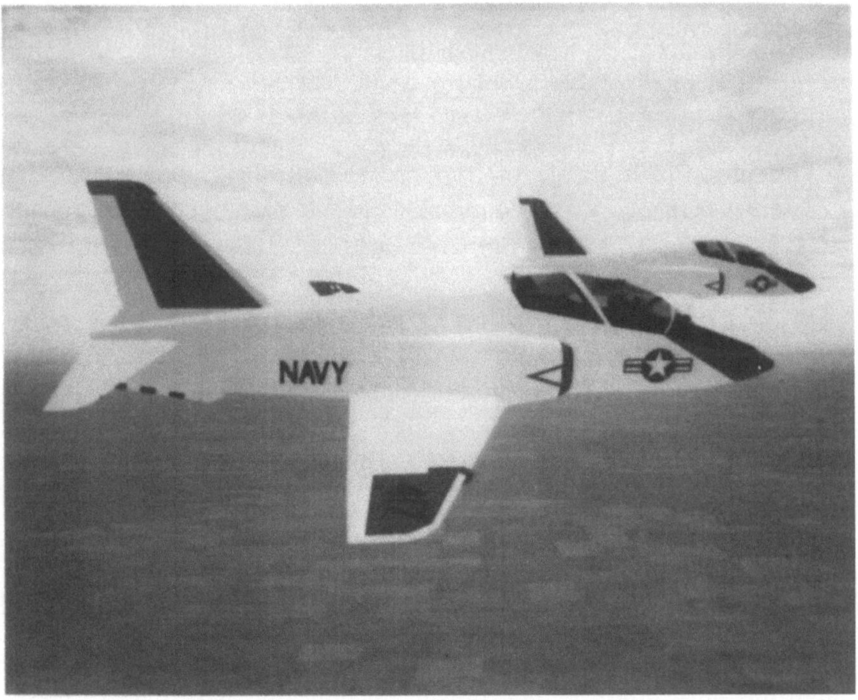

FIGURE 5. Rediffusion's SP-X family of computer generated image visual systems offers new levels of design-to-cost flexibility. (Courtesy of Rediffusion Simulation, Ltd.)

Shadows are vital spatial cues and are used continuously by the human visual system in processing object recognition, orientation and size. In spite of the fact that shadows are rarely found in commercial sequences, real-time shadows are possible by employing dark polygons moving along the ground synchronous with another object. They might not be geometrically accurate but nevertheless are useful.

Texture Processor

In Rediffusion Simulation and Evans & Sutherland's CT6 and SPX CIG systems, texture plays an increasingly important role in providing realism. It can be readily mapped on arbitrary surfaces such as trees and undulating terrain and, with the concept of transparency incorporated within the texture, creates detail without extra polygons. A system specification for CT6 is shown in Appendix 1.

Texture can be captured from paint systems or photographs, and dedicated high-speed hardware is necessary to compute the inverse perspective matrices and map subscripts for its real-time mapping on polygons.

Moving textured surfaces are a nightmare within any computer graphic environment, for causing aliasing artifacts, but again the art of simulation is concerned with solving problems with algorithms and fast hardware. Of course there are solutions, one being the use of pre-filtered MIPMAPS (Williams, 1983) and texture clamping (Norton, Rockwood and Skolmoski, 1982).

Apart from increasing surface detail, texture maps are used to mimic the wake of a ship, smoke from a tank and rotor blades of a helicopter, and an animated sequence of maps can create effective explosions for military applications.

Weather Effects

Fog and haze are real hazards for pilots and must be implemented as true phenomena; simply desaturating scene colours is not acceptable. A bank of fog must be treated as finite volume of space and the physics of light absorption implemented accordingly.

Distant lightning can be effectively simulated by momentarily increasing scene brightness, and local lightning strikes can be simulated by a suitable luminous texture pattern.

The clever use of colour and texture also resolves snow on ground surfaces, but the effect of flying through snow storms and rain still creates some problems, but perhaps not for long.

Conclusion

As one can see, there is no magic or mystery in achieving real-time images; a CIG system is designed specifically to function in a real-time mode, specific tasks being assigned to processors running in parallel with other system elements. Yet in spite of highly sophisticated technology, the act of creating 60 Mpixels/sec is still an art, as one is working in a branch of knowledge that changes daily, resolving yesterday's problems and revealing a new set for tomorrow.

Appendix 1: CT6 Specification Summary

Specifications

Modes	Day/dusk/night (continuous if required)
Eyepoints	Two (more for certain applications)
Channels	Up to 8 per eyepoint, 16 for two eyepoints
Field rate	50 Hz standard (60 Hz available)
Resolution	260,000 to 1,040,000 pixels per channel

Scan standards	Software programmable/switchable
Colors	Up to 6 software-selectable color maps per channel: full color or monochrome
Texture	Texture and modulation: minimum of 32 texture patterns on-line
Distortion correction	Non-linear image mapping (NLIM). Fits arbitrary mathematical descriptions
Database management	Whole world coverage; multiple level-of-detail management with fade blending and instancing
Overload management	Field time extension, dynamic level-of-detail range adjustment. Dynamic polygon perspective, size rejection
Moving objects	Up to 16 simultaneous dynamic coordinate systems (DCS). (Up to 24 for certain applications)
Animation	Up to 128 different representations per animated object
Collision detection	Reports ownship interference with all major objects in the database; 1 calculation per eyepoint
Height above terrain	Reports height of defined dynamic coordinate systems above the ground: minimum of 1 calculation per eyepoint
Laser range finding	Reports range from eyepoint to specific database features
Threat occulting	Reports if a pre-specified database feature is visible (not occulted)
Weather effects	Fog, haze, cloud, horizon, scud, lightning
Landing light illumination	Uniform and lobular representation
Surface effects	Shading: flat, smooth, fixed, color blending, transparency, self-luminous surfaces—all in combination with texture

Image Generator Capacities at 50 Hz

Per channel displayed	1,500 surfaces 4,000 light points*
Total displayed	7,500 surfaces for two eyepoints (expandable to 14,000 surfaces) 20,000 light points available*
Total database	500,000 polygons
Density displayed	500,000 surfaces per square mile available

*Lights trade with surfaces at 1 surface per 3 light points.

References

Baarspul, M., R.J.A.W. Hosman, and J.C. Van de Vaart (1986) "Some Fundamentals of Simulator Cockpit Motion Generation," *Advances in Flight Simulation—Visual and Motion Systems RAeS Conf. Proc.*, pp. 81–100.

Foley, J.D. and A. Van Dam (1982) *Fundamentals of Interactive Computer Graphics*, p. 560. Addison-Wesley, Reading, Mass.

Fournier, A. (1986) "A Simple Model of Ocean Waves," *Computer Graphics SIGGRAPH '86 Conf. Proc.*, pp. 75–84.

Fuchs, H., Z.V. Kedem, and B. Naylor (1979) "Predetermining Visibility Priority in 3-D Scenes," *ACM Computer Graphics* 13:175.

Haines, E.A. and D.P. Greenberg (1986) "The Light Buffer: A Shadow-testing Accelerator," *Computer Graphics and Applications* 6(9):6–16.

Kennedy, R.S., K.S. Berbaum et al. (1986) "Issues in Simulator Sickness," *Advances in Flight Simulation—Visual and Motion Systems RAeS Conf. Proc.*, pp. 227–237.

Miller, G.S.P. (1986) "The Definition and Rendering of Terrain Maps," *Computer Graphics SIGGRAPH '86 Conf. Proc.*, pp. 39–48.

Norton, A., A.P. Rockwood, and Skolmoski (1982) "Clamping: A Method of Anti-Aliasing Textured Surfaces," *Computer Graphics ACM* 16(3):1–8.

Schumacker, R.A. (1980) "A New Visual System Architecture," *Proc. 2nd Interservice/Industry Training Equipment Conf.*, pp. 94–101, November. Salt Lake City, November.

Schumacker, R.A., B. Brand et al. (1969) "Study for Applying Computer Generated Images to Simulation," AFHRL-TR-69-14, Air Force Human Resources Laboratory, Wright-Patterson AFB, Ohio, September.

Swanson, R.W. and L.J. Thaye (1986) "A Fast Shaded-Polygon Renderer," *Computer Graphics SIGGRAPH '86 Conf. Proc.*, pp. 95–101.

Williams, L. (1983) "Pyramidal Parametrics," *Computer Graphics ACM* 1983 17(3):1–11.

Computer Animation: A Personal View

Alexander King and Mike Stapleton

Introduction

Animation is a universal language and has already become part of our cultural tradition. It is a technique exploited by industry, government and education to inform, persuade and entertain. It is a versatile technique which allows the image maker to go beyond reality, to extrapolate an idea into the absurd, into fantasy or the unknown. We see space rockets entering uncharted areas of space, or a scenario where a character, run down by a steam roller, gets up and walks away although flattened like a piece of card.

All animation is made from a set of images slightly different from one another which, when filmed independently and projected at 24/25 frames per second, give the illusion of movement. This illusion is the result of a phenomenon known as *persistence of vision*. The human visual system, not capable of discerning individual images when presented with more than 10 per second, sees movement as a result of the images blending in with one another.

Movement is the essence of animation. Norman McLaren, a Canadian pioneer, talking of traditional animation said: "animation is movements which are drawn, not drawings which move." The artists working at Disney studios spent large amounts of time looking at the movements of animals and humans and also textured objects such as cloth. An important technique used in hand animation is that of *rotoscoping*, which involves live action filming, then replaying the film frame by frame and in turn drawing the outline of each individual object, which is its movement.

Much in hand animation concerns itself with repetition, a job for which computers are particularly well suited. In the late 1960s, computer graphics pioneers tried to use computers to carry out some of the drudgery involved with hand animation.

At first computer animators tried to emulate hand animation, with some notable achievements in early systems such as TWEEN and ANTICS (Catmull, 1979; Kitchen, 1973). The images produced by these systems sometimes lacked the flexibility of hand drawings and did not measure up to McLaren's axiom, "movements which are drawn, not drawings which move." Another area of development was in computer aids to hand animation; here digital techniques would be used to colour video digitised drawings and simple inbetweenings. It soon became clear that the main strength in the use of computers lay with the manipulation of 3-D objects in 3-D space. This offered computer animators a powerful new capability in a previously difficult area. Computer graphics did not remove the conceptual difficulties of working in unlimited 3-D space, but did remove many of the technical skills necessary and provided a framework in which animators could experiment.

A current view of computer animation would include such topics as:

Model building—the description of the objects to be animated.

Animation—the description of the movement of the objects, light sources and virtual camera.

Rendering—producing the images with whatever quality of rendition is required, from wireframe to texture-mapped solids.

Object transformation—whereby objects can be transformed from one form to another in a plastic fashion (Magnenat-Thalmann and Thalmann, 1985).

With the evolution of this model, computer animation became established as a new means of visual communication, different from its early beginnings and predecessors. We must remember that computer animation is very young. Computer animation dates from the 1960s, and the first film to win acclaim was *Hunger*, made by Peter Foldes in 1974 (Foldes, 1974). Although good work was being done at this time (Halas, 1974) computer animation has become a commercial force in this country only over the last 5 years. The completion in the United Kingdom of the Channel Four logo seems historically to be the point at which the media, seeing something different, something fresh, decided that this was the way to stay one step ahead of the competition.

Current research is particularly active in finding new techniques for modelling 3-D objects such as fractals, soft objects and new methods for rendering them such as texture mapping and ray tracing. Progress in this area has led to the concept of *digital scene simulation*, where reality can be faithfully reproduced and manipulated by a computer.

More experimentally we are seeing the use of artificial intelligence techniques in trying to develop and control the behaviour of complex systems, evolving hypothetical worlds (Zelter, 1985).

A Challenge

Looking at the computer animation scene as it exists today, a cynic may be forgiven for observing that computer animation has simply become a tool for the glossy markets of advertising and special effects. A decade's experience, increased technical sophistication and commercial pressure have resulted in a practice which requires a massive capital investment into massive machines running massive amounts of software producing more and more startling imagery, albeit a diet which solely supports the status quo, with bankruptcy (and disillusionment?) ever more frequent. No "vernacular computer animation" seems to have emerged, nor has it a platform.

Will computer animation ever become a simple means to process ideas, a technique which can be used by anyone, an alternative to our concept of animation (largely conditioned by the Disney school of anthropomorphic creatures) and a new form of popular culture? Is there any evidence that there is a larger role for it to play now that the ubiquitous micro has permeated our lives?

Other technologies which have become available such as the electric guitar, or more recently the synthesizer, have been readily exploited to create a new popular culture, in some cases by those who may not otherwise have been capable of doing so. In either case there is a learning process which allows for the use of the medium for expression and for those with a commitment to a technological appreciation who wish to explore the medium more fully. An example with more immediate relevance has been the rapid acceptance of computer-based paint systems. Recently these have been used to produce comics, both in digital form, with the computer as the medium, and published in print. Electronic publishing has been one of the success stories of the computer and has spawned the serious use of the micro.

Is computer animation any different from the above examples, any more difficult to get to grips with? Increasingly, computer animation is being taught in its own right, but how do we offer students a simple way into a subject as complex as this?

A Personal Approach

When one of the authors, Alex King, was first approached to teach computer animation at an art school, he looked around to see what was available and was presented with Hobson's choice: PICASO or nothing (Vince, 1983). The PICASO approach involved a massive learning curve for those new to computers: operating systems, editors, Fortran language files, data files, directories, compilers, syntax errors, run-time errors and screen modes were just some of the factors, and all of this with a user intimidated by a keyboard. It seemed that, although he had some successful students, this was not the best approach. How could the process of bringing people to computer animation be simplified?

In order to provide more rapid feedback in the learning process than was possible with a compile/link/load system, King decided to implement an interactive program for use by beginners without any technical background. What should the goals of such a system be?

The user interface had to be easy to use, and a traditional approach was taken, providing a set of menus, offering sensible defaults and providing a useful selection of the facilities of more ambitious systems.

A low-cost system would be unlikely to be able to provide sophisticated rendering and so perhaps should concentrate on aspects of movement and transformation in 3-D space. Thus the system should be able to move and transform objects in space and provide a movable *virtual camera* for viewing them.

Having made the decision to concentrate on movement and transformation rather than rendering, it was possible to adopt a simple data structure to describe objects and avoid the necessity for an elaborate model-building facility.

The next consideration was to ascertain a minimal set of functions necessary to produce computer animation. This should be rich enough to make worthwhile graphics possible while not raising a barrier by providing a daunting array of features. A useful starting point seemed to be the overlap between hand animation and computer animation: the technique of *key framing*. Here an initial and final version of the image are decided on, and a human operator or a computer draws the in-betweens. This seemed a simple model that was easy to grasp, familiar to hand animators, and one which had a proven track record (Burtnyk and Wein, 1971). This was used as the model for setting up the various transformations for the start and end positions of the objects.

The initial aim was to produce a program that would provide an introduction to computer animation for students from non-technical backgrounds, some of whom would go on to computer graphics programming using PICASO. A similar data structure to PICASO was used and the basic geometric transformations were provided. It was an early decision not to provide the wide range of shape generation and special-effects functions of PICASO. The program, at this point called ANI, for obvious reasons, was initially implemented in Fortran on a PRIME 850 at Bristol Polytechnic, where it became popular with a group of students in the art school.

After these early experiences, it became apparent that ANI was worth developing in its own right, to produce an entry-level system capable of being used to create interesting computer animation. Furthermore, if this were to become a worthwhile tool, it should eventually reach the widest audience. The program was converted to Pascal (under UCSD Pascal) to run on an Apricot micro. The latest stage in its evolution on MS-DOS/CPM machines uses Turbo Pascal and GXS as the standard interface between different micros and their graphic capabilities. At the Dorset Institute of Higher Education (DIHE) we have also developed a version running on the Apple Macintosh computers, using MacAdvantage Pascal and the Mac native graphics. These new versions go by the name IMP, for Imagè Manipulation Program.

IMP: The Image Manipulation Program

IMP allows a user to set the initial and final values for transformations for a group of objects interactively and thereby control the movement of the objects through space, over a time interval specified as a number of frames. These sets of transformations can be saved as files which describe sequences of transformations for one or more objects. These can be restored for subsequent editing or assembled to record a final set of images.

The user interface uses menus to access screens containing default values for the transformations. These are altered by a simple form-filling procedure.

Objects to be manipulated by IMP are described in the files containing lists of digitised X, Y and Z co-ordinates. These use the PICASO convention of EOL and EOS for end-of-line and end-of-shape markers.

When object data has been entered, IMP's main menu allows access to three sub-menus for viewing transformations, image manipulations and image generation as well as the possibility to restart and end an IMP session.

The viewing transformations menu gives the animator control of the "virtual camera" and allows camera movements to be specified in polar or Cartesian co-ordinates. The window size can be altered in accordance with the user's world co-ordinates. Parallel or perspective projection can be selected and the background colour/pattern set.

The image manipulations menu controls transformations of each object which occur over a specified selection of frames. The only transformations available to the user are scaling, stretching (differential scaling), rotation and shifting. The user does not have control of the order in which transformations are done. A fixed sequence of events is used within the program: objects are first scaled, then rotated, then shifted. This seemed to be the most intuitive approach. Users do not have the flexibility or the problems of selecting transformations in different orders to give different results.

An important facility in IMP, one that is essential for smooth animation, is that each transformation has a *fairing* parameter associated with it. This controls the rate of change of the transformation over the given number of frames, to enable acceleration, deceleration, acceleration then deceleration or change with constant velocity.

Three-dimensional clipping is always set. Optional rendering facilities allow for removal of back-facing polygons and the employment of the *painter's algorithm* to determine the priority in which objects are drawn. Using this and pattern or colour fill option, a simple solid rendering effect can be obtained.

The image generation menu allows the user to specify whether the image is to be generated on the screen or on a plotter. If the screen is selected, the user has a number of options to control the behaviour after each frame is displayed. One of these permits control of a camera. At DIHE we use a Super8 camera to film individual images direct from the screen.

Limitations of IMP

In terms of the model of computer animation developed above, IMP concentrates on the animation aspects. It has no model-building capabilities, but allows simple descriptions of both 2-D and 3-D objects. Its rendering is limited to hidden-line/surface removal and surfaces can be shaded, but this is controlled by the user and not by a lighting model. A limited range of camera movements is possible.

IMP restricts the theoretically possible flexibility or choice, concentrating the user's effort on the concept of 3-D space and prompting users to experiment while learning to think in terms of 3-D space. Its limitations are soon reached when trying to achieve anything which is not "sequential" in nature. For example, it is possible to rotate an object about three axes simultaneously, but the axes of rotation must have a common origin.

There is no "effects" menu, as this would present too easy an option for transforming one shape into another or moving between different sequences of images. IMP's strength and its weakness lie in its simplicity. This was a deliberate early decision, but a need that is increasingly felt is for some form of automatic inbetweening between objects of different shapes.

In common with all animation systems we have used, IMP suffers from Rudge's rule: The next piece of animation you wish to do will require a facility which is not yet implemented in your animation system. For this reason there should exist a "hook" between a basic setup such as IMP and the outside world to allow user-implemented routines.

Conclusions

Given that IMP is a fairly minimal 3-D computer animation system, how successful has it been?

So far IMP has been used as a hands-on tool for gaining acquaintance with computer animation techniques before moving on to more powerful systems. Students following the BA(Hons) in communication and media production at DIHE have all cut their teeth on it, and those pursuing the computer graphics option are all producing 3-D animation with it. These students represent an interesting set in that, although well qualified generally, few have an O level in art and even fewer an A level in art or a science subject, yet they are interested in using this technology to manipulate images and create animation.

The fact that these students are beginning to make use of and understand the medium offers support to the thesis that computer animation can become a popular means for expression and can become a vehicle for making certain statements by those who otherwise would not be able to do so.

It has always been a conviction of ours that computers offer the possibility of having a radical influence on our lives. We do not think the concept of art as a radical influence on our lives need be questioned. Therefore a combination of both would offer possibilities and be of benefit to anyone who feels they have something to say. We believe that technologists and artists ought to work to achieve this. Perhaps IMP and its future developments are a tiny step down this road.

References

Burtnyk, N. and M. Wein (1971) "Computer Generated Key-Frame Animation," *Journal of the Society of Motion Picture and Television Engineers*, March, pp. 149–153.

Catmull, E. (1979) "New Frontiers in Computer Animation," *American Cinematographer*, October. pp. 1000–1003, 1049–1053.

Foldes, P. (1974) *Hunger*, National Film Board of Canada. 12 minutes.

Halas, J. (1974) *Computer Animation*. Focal Press, London.

Kitchen, A. (1974) "Computer Animation; Some New Antics," *British Kinematography Sound Television Journal*, vol. 55, No. 12, pp. 372–386.

Magnenat-Thalmann, N, and D. Thalmann (1985) *Computer Animation Theory and Practice*. Springer-Verlag, Tokyo.

Vince, J. (1983) "The PICASO System," System Reference Manual, *CAMPUS*, October.

Zeltzer, D. (1985) "Towards an Integrated View of 3D Computer Animation," *Proc. Graphics Interface '85*, pp. 105–115.

Towards Autonomous Control for Three-Dimensional Facial Animation

Keith Waters

Introduction

It is evident that the face is one aspect of a complex articulated structure and the elements that compose facial expressions can be analysed in terms of muscle actions (Ekman, 1977). The subsequent task is to organize the multiple muscle actions into autonomous substructures for animation. At first glance this appears to be a simple exercise; however, to be of use to the animator, the animator-level interface requires the incorporation of all the features that are to be expected in a good programming language (Reynolds, 1982).

Methods for motion control have been established within the field of robotics, where the emphasis is on the control of manipulators and robot arms. Both robotics and three-dimensional computer simulation of articulated structures have common goals concerning motion trajectories, collision detection, path-planning, dynamics and kinematics. Consequently, procedures from robotics can be integrated with computer simulation and animation to produce the desired result.

The motional dynamics of synthetic faces have to mimic reality surprisingly closely to be convincing, as the synthetic images are susceptible to comparison with real life and any discrepancies can readily be identified. As a result, a multitude of parameters are required to create the correct motion attributes; however, a majority of these activities can be grouped together to form specified tasks.

The Synthesis of Three-Dimensional Faces

The facial structure can be successfully synthesized in three dimensions by creating a polygonal mesh to describe the surface form (Waters, 1986). It is evident that the facial structure cannot be easily encapsulated in a single generic mould, hence any motional characteristics must be independent of facial type (Waters, 1987a). Various models (Parke, 1975;

Bergeron, 1985) have used the most direct form of control by identifying and controlling key vertices on the topology. However, this becomes limited to the particular model in question. A more general approach is to formulate geometric transformations (Waters, 1987b; Sederberg, 1986) that are applicable to a free range of geometric objects.

This author's earlier research used synthetic images of real people's faces and was concerned with the frontal two-thirds of the head. Some 14 muscles were implanted into the model to represent the major muscles for facial expression; one was a sphincter-type muscle while the others were linear. Each muscle had parameters controlling tension, two influence zones and the contraction for any moment in time. The objective was to be able to create the six primary facial expressions (Ekman, 1977) using the facial action coding system as a source of reference. Consequently, for each frame some 56 parameters were required to control the model, and data files were used to control the activities. These files could be altered at will, but they were incapable of interacting with each other to self-regulate the environment. For example, all the muscles could be contracted at once such that impossible articulations were produced.

The increasing realism (Oka, 1987) and precise dynamics of flexible objects (Terzopolulos, 1987) including the face present additional problems for the animator as they present a multitude of parameters to be controlled and manipulated even for the shortest sequence. While parameter-driven models are highly desirable (Welsh, 1985), describing the control of the parameters becomes even more critical, as coherence between characteristics cannot be easily maintained. Therefore, further investigations are required to establish the nature of the control and the activities that can be grouped together. Two disparate models of control, robotic manipulators and human biological, can be combined to provide more realistic motion characteristics.

Motion Control

Methods of three dimensional motion control have been established within the field of robotics, where the emphasis is on the control of manipulators and robot arms. Here the objective is to specify, via a series of programmed instructions, the position of the arm (in particular the end tool-tip) in three-dimensional space (Paul, 1981). This can involve forward and inverse kinematics, dynamics, collision testing and path planning. With automated manipulators is necessary not only to reach a point in space but also to reach that point from any arbitrary direction. Roll, pitch and yaw describe the orientation of the manipulator, and the independent motions are referred to as the degrees of freedom (DOF). Six are required to reach almost any point at any orientation The human arm has exactly six, two at the shoulder, one at the elbow and three at the wrist, and as a result it is almost possible to reach any point in space in any direction. The limiting factor lies in the joints themselves; for example, the wrist is limited to approximately 60 degrees, rendering some orientations of the arm physically impossible, and the scenario is the same for the robot manipulator.

The mathematics of robot manipulators (Paul, 1981) concern the mechanisms for relating the location and orientation of one point to another. Homogeneous co-ordinates in the form of 4×4 matrices are used (Coulson, 1965). Basic matrices can be derived from roll, pitch, yaw and translation. These can then be concatenated to perform one operation on the joint angles. Frequently a Euler operation is described as a sequence of rotational operations such that:

$$\text{Euler}(\phi, \beta, ¥) = \text{Rot}(z, \phi)\, \text{Rot}(x, \beta)\, \text{Rot}(y, ¥)$$

The order in which these transformations are performed is critical, but they can be applied to produce one homogeneous matrix. The result is a general function for linked hierarchies of objects such that any joint angle can be established from the concatenation of lower orders.

The Three Levels of Animation

While industrial robotic manipulators have been developing with various levels of operation, animation techniques have been expanding with concurrent interests. Key framing was the earliest and remains the most common method of motion specification. The basic principles involve the explicit definition of positions and when they occur; then the successive frames are computed from interpolation. Interpolation often involves non-linear functions (Kockanek, 1984) to establish either velocity (first derivative) or acceleration (second derivative). Shape interpolation is an extension from the two dimensions, where there is a one-to-one correspondence between data points, and the intermediate frames are computed for each vertex. The advantage of this environment is that the user has complete specification ability over all the motions and all the objects. The disadvantage of this level of animation is that the animator has to specify all the actions of the model in advance, which is reasonable only if the environment is simple and contains no other interactions. However, because objects cannot interact or regulate themselves, they are locked into a single mode of operation.

Written scripts have been used as tools for animation. Some of the original developments (Reynolds, 1982; Chaung, 1983) permitted more flexibility than the key-framing approach and were not as complex to manage as a full programming language. The script usually includes a description of both the models and the animation sequence, and when fully notated the script can be edited and modified to create the desired effect. Finally, the script is interpreted by the animation system and the frames rendered, thus isolating the user from the intricate details of the software.

Various techniques have been developed to supply the user with even higher-level control (Badler, 1987; Korien, 1982). The concept of high-level control means that animator can outline the movement, and the animation system then fills in the details. As a result, the non-expert user can easily dictate motions.

It is evident from the three levels of animation that each environment has its own particular advantages, but with no one level constituting the ultimate mode of control. The face is not concerned with locomotion, nor with path planning or collision testing; as a result it partially simplifies the description of the system tasks. Research (Parke, 1982; Waters, 1986) has indicated that an open environment such that the animator can have explicit control over the facial topology (as in a guiding system) is necessary for the fine control required to distort the facial structure. Also, a level of scripting is required such that the low-level manipulations can be grouped and activated together. Finally, a more powerful task manager is required to remove the mundane activities of, for example, head tilting when the eyes track objects, and the more direct mode of control such as "smile, nod, wink, be happy, be sad."

Reflex Biological Control

The human biological motor system has evolved into an extremely complex structure capable of manoeuvring multi-linked forms with many degrees of freedom, through dynamic environments. The conscious decision of motion has been described as being built on a base of reflex processes (Evarts, 1979), or low-level motor programs regulated by high-level controllers.

These low-level motor programs, or local motor programs (LMP), have been identified as common principles for the control of walking in animals (Pearson, 1976) and may be the only economical method of controlling structures with multiple degrees of freedom. Zeltzer (1984) successfully based a system on the creation of low-level motor programs for the kinematic control of walking figures under high-level control, such that it was possible to describe gaits from the command "walk." This has since been developed by Maciejewski and Girard (1985) at Ohio State University with the PODA system. Here the animator is supplied with the computational model which facilitates the direct control of the functional dependence between different parts of the figure. The strategy allows the interactive design of the motion at various levels, with a focused attention on complex motor skills such as those found in dance and gymnastics.

The psychologists of non-verbal communication (Ekman, 1977) have established group activities of the muscles to form facial expressions. It is suggested that the expressions of happiness, anger, fear, disgust, sadness and surprise, are six grouped activities that can be defined as functional synergies. For example, Fig. 1 illustrates the expression of fear, which is controlled by individual muscle actions: The brows are curved and raised, the jaw is open, the angular depressors pull the corners of the lips down and the eyes are wide with the pupils dilated to display the expression of fear. Figure 2 shows six emotions that can be described as synergic functions.

The Hand as a Functional Synergy

A good example of a functional synergy is encapsulated in the prehensile activity of the hand (Warwick, 1973), where three grips can be described to have very distinctive characteristics:

The *power grip*, where the fingers are flexed around the object, with a counter pressure from the thumb. The purpose of the grip is to hold an object firmly, either to be wielded as a tool or weapon by the whole hand or to be worked on by the other hand.

The *precision grip*, where the activity is precise, with the main source of activity being the small movement of the digits. The object is usually gripped between the tips of the fingers and the thumb, such as holding a pen.

The *hook grip*, which is used to suspend or pull on objects or to elevate the body in climbing. The fingers are looped around such things as handles, straps, cords, branches etc. The thumb may or may not be

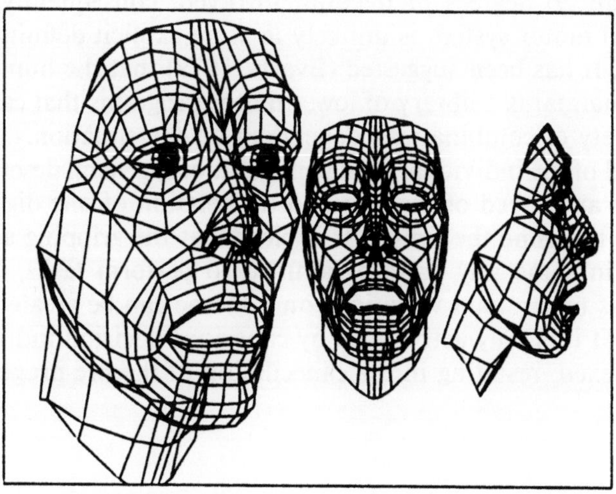

FIGURE 1. The expression of fear activated by 10 individual muscle actions.

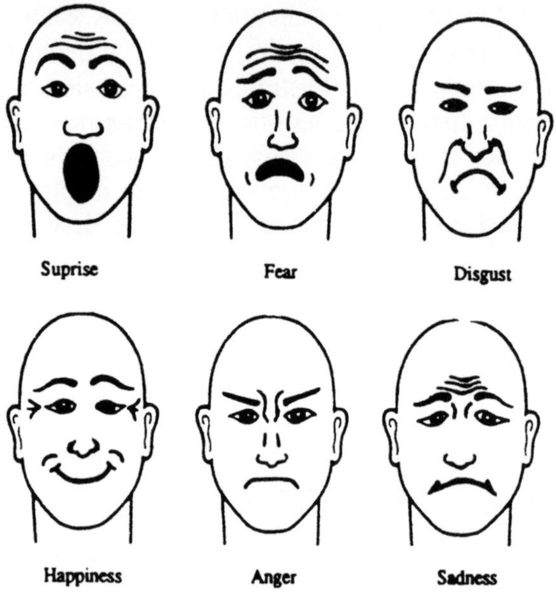

FIGURE 2. Six emotions that can be described as synergic functions or reflex actions.

involved, as it is a grip for the transmission of forces and not for skilled manipulation.

These three characteristics are not precise definitions of the individual mechanisms but the group action of the fingers and thumb, orchestrated to perform particular skills. Controlling all the individual joint activities for the hand requires an enormous amount of information, as there are more than 20 degrees of freedom involved; consequently, the human biological motor system is unlikely to store explicit definitions for these motions. It has been suggested (Evarts, 1979) that the human biological system maintains a library of lower motor programs that can be invoked in a variety of combinations dependent on the situation.

Instead of the individual joint configurations, general descriptions about the force and speed of the grip and the relation of one digit to the next are used to define the action. It is clear that the gripping activity of the hand is in some way pre-programmed to perform tasks, and once the activity is understood variations on a theme can be created. This is not to say that it is only activity, as by conscious decision individual fingers can be flexed, resulting in the cancellation of the pre-programed skill.

Modelling the Hand

The first task is the construction of the hand model. The hand comprises some 15 distal joints and a vast majority of the movement can be achieved by these alone. Each segment of the hand is treated as an object of the hand such that a data structure can be built up comprising distal objects. Each distal segment has an associated axis frame relating to its own origin, which is used in reference to the rotations with that joint. As a result, the model is built individually about the universal axes, with any applied rotations to the object maintaining the original starting axis.

The motion motor programs are at the heart of the system. Here information about linking of the hierarchy and the joint variables are described. It is necessary to have defined the objects and the model completely before this stage can be undertaken, as the information described in this section is passed to the data structure. Because the motion motor programs are required to be open (under user control), external file descriptions are used that can be altered at will. For the two hands (or however many hands are required) the description is most likely to be in the form:

```
#Define NOSFINGERS 5
typedef struct {
            lower_carpel;
            middle_carpel;
            upper_carpel;
            } finger;

typedef struct {
            finger fingers[NOSFINGERS];
            } hand;

hand lefthand;
hand righthand;
```

Here the finger is made of three components and the hand of five of the fingers. Once the components of the hand have been established, the next task is to create the linkage of the hierarchy, which can be achieved as follows:

```
start hand
            [2, thumb1, thumb2]
            [3,index1, index2, index3]
            [3, middle1, middle2, middle3]
            [3, ring1, ring2, ring3]
            [3, little1, little2, little3]
end hand
```

In this example the hand is a descriptor, and index2 = finger.finger[2].middle. This information is passed to the data structure and stored as an explicit definition for the hand. The final stage is the specification of the joint variables and the joint limits that can also be achieved via data files. It is assumed that the fingers have at most three degrees of freedom and can be referenced as

index1 [x 20.0, y 0.0, z 60.0]

The result is that the structure holds all the information on the explicit world coordinates, the hierarchy linking and the limits to each object's motion.

The Skill

Once the model has been described and the motion motor descriptions defined, the final task is the description of the skill. By skill, we mean the group activity of the fingers to form a defined synergy (see Fig. 3). With the system already set, the only manipulation remaining concerns the start positions of the fingers and the joint rotations per time step. Massaging the position of the fingers into the starting place does not disturb the data structure and is is a trivial task. The joints must then be given appropriate percentage motion during the grasp. This requires only 15 joint parameters to be manipulated and corrected to get the grasping motion to contain personal attributes. Consequently, what has been designed is a powerful abstraction for the complex motion with many degrees of freedom by the use of functional synergies.

The Synergies of the Head, Neck and Face

The face is not determined as a hierarchy of distal objects but rather as a flexible surface with multiple degrees of freedom for each vertex, which increases the complexity of the required control. The head, however, is supported by the neck, which is primarily a stack of cervical bones of the upper spine. Consequently, what is required is the description of the synergies that encapsulate the activities of the face, head and neck.

Previous models of the head and neck (Bergeron, 1985) used a hierarchy of multiple joint rotations to achieve the desired effect. While at first this appears to be the simplest solution, the fundamental drawback is that the user interaction and specification is limited to a list of limb segments with associated rotational angles. It is suggested that a more realistic approach would be to utilize muscle vectors in the form of contraction springs, such that the motions could be more clearly defined from muscle names and percentage contractions. Additionally, the head could have embedded characteristics to balance the head on the shoulders, as this is

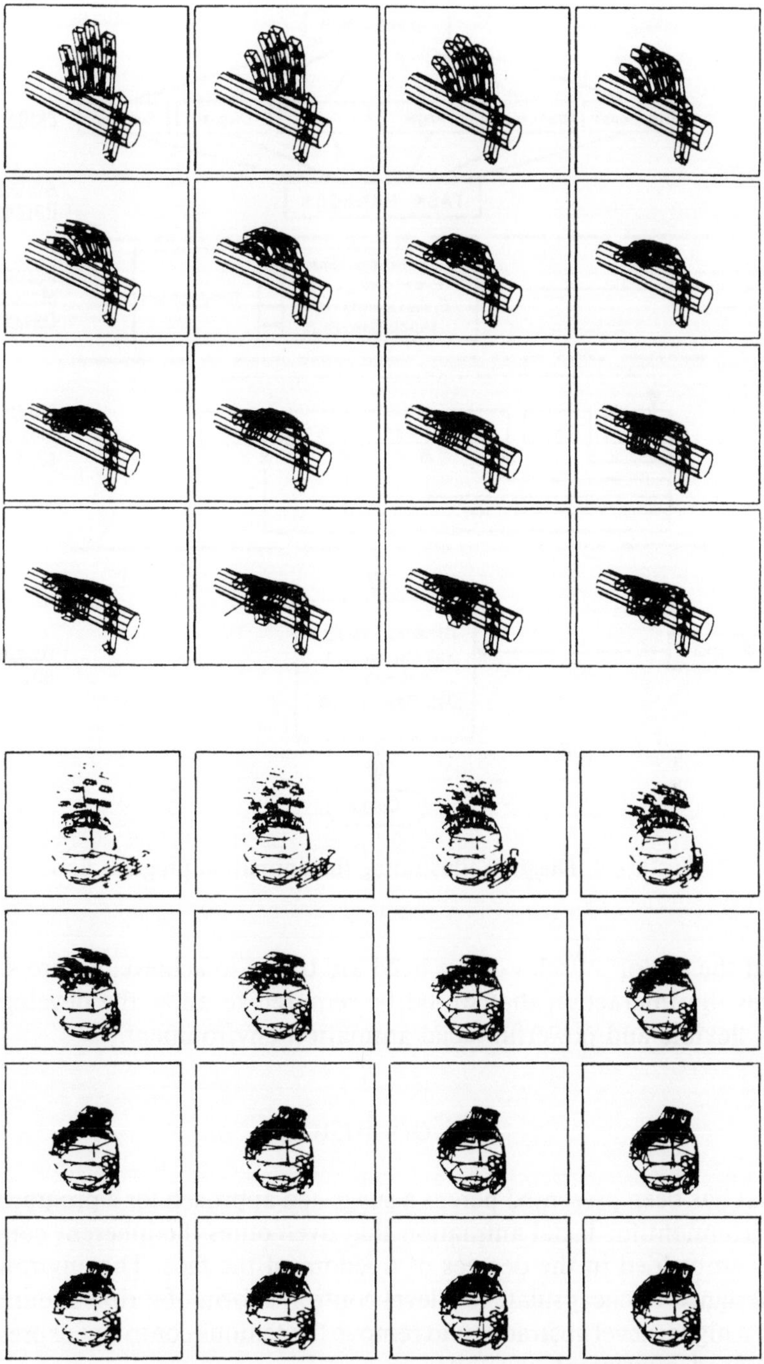

FIGURE 3. Two examples of the gripping activity as functional synergies: the hook grasp and the power grasp. The hand comprises five fingers with three distal joints per finger. Collision testing prevents the hand from passing through the objects and the motional attributes for the fingers are set up in data files.

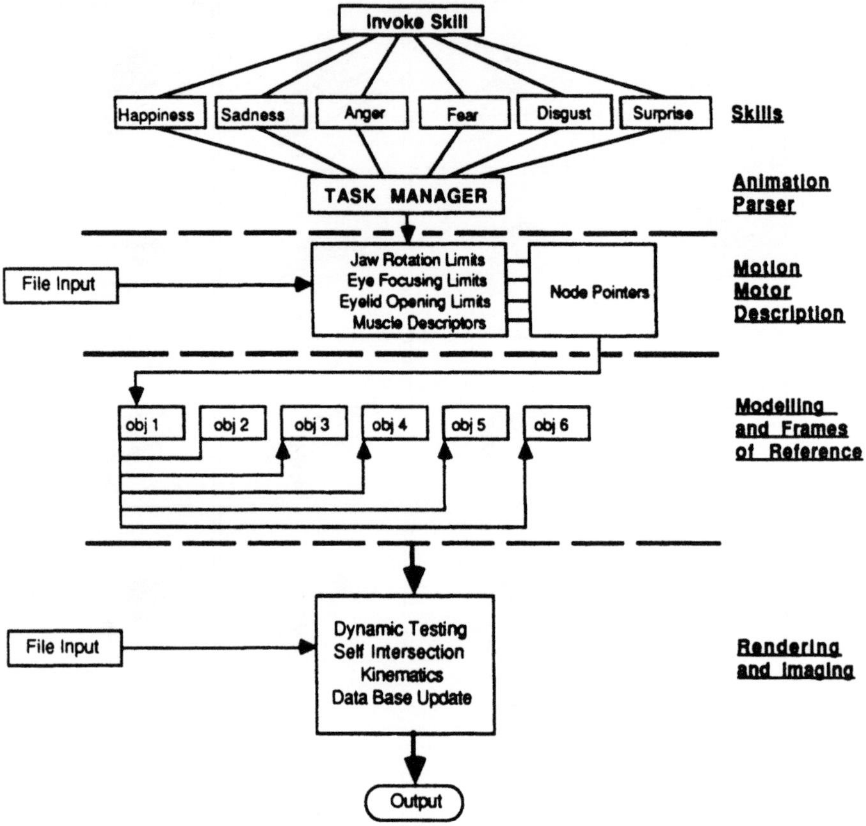

FIGURE 4. Diagram illustrating the animation program flow.

what the major muscles of the head are trying to achieve. Figure 4 illustrates the interaction that would be required to allow the development of a flexible and powerful facial animation environment.

Conclusion

What has been presented here is a suggested approach for a programming environment for facial animation that overcomes the inherent complexities embedded in the degrees of freedom of the face. The environment is designed to encapsulate low-level control, a form of scripted animation and a higher-level abstraction to remove the tedious control of expressions and head movement.

Additionally, the potential of a majority of head and neck motions could be initiated as local motor programs generic to humans. The consequence would be that individual idiosyncratic behavior could be formulated while governed by high-level controllers. Research into the nature of the motor programs governing such activities tends to be general and deficient in precise details useful for computer synthesis. However, provided the computer environment could be established as suggested here, it would provide a valuable tool for the visualization and subsequent analysis of motor activity.

References

Badler, N.I. (1987) "Articulated Figure Positioning by Multiple Constraints," *IEEE Computer Graphics and Applications*, June, pp. 28–38.

Bergeron, P. (1985) "Controlling Facial Expressions and Body Movement in the Computer Short Tonie de Peltrie," *Course Notes*, SIGGRAPH.

Chaung, R. (1983) "3D Shaded Computer Animation Step-by-Step," *IEEE Computer Graphics and Applications* 3:18–25.

Coulson, A.E. (1965) *An Introduction to Matrices*. Longman.

Evarts, V.E. (1979) "Brain Mechanisms of Movement," *Scientific American*, September, pp. 146–156.

Ekman, (1977) *Manual for the Facial Action Coding System. Consulting Psychologist Press*, Palo Alto, Calif.

Girard, M. (1975) "Computational Modelling for the Computer Animation of Legged Figures," *Computer Graphics Proc. SIGGRAPH* 19(3):263–270.

Kockanek, D. (1984) "Interpolating Splines with Local Tension Continuity and Bias Control," *Computer Graphics Proceedings SIGGRAPH* 18(3):24–41.

Korien, J.U. (1982) "Techniques for Generating the Goal-Directed Motion of Articulated Structures," *IEEE Computer Graphics and Applications*, November, pp. 71–81.

Oka, M. (1987) "Real-Time Manipulation of Texture-Mapped Surfaces," *Proc. Computer Graphics SIGGRAPH* 21(4):181–186.

Parke, F.I. (1982) "A Parameterized Model for Facial Animation," *IEEE Computer Graphics and Applications*, November.

Paul, P.R. (1981) *Robot Manipulators: Mathematics, Programming and Control*. MIT Press, London.

Pearson (1976) "The Control of Walking," *Scientific American*, December, pp. 72–86.

Reynolds, C.W. (1982) "Computer Animation with Scripts and Actors," *Computer Graphics Proceedings SIGGRAPH* 16(2)289–296.

Sederberg (1986) "Free-Form Deformation of Solid Geometric Models," *Proc. Computer Graphics SIGGRAPH* 20(4):151–160.

Terzopolulos, D. (1987) "Elastically Deformable Models," *Proc. Computer Graphics SIGGRAPH* 21(4)205–214.

Warwick, R. (1973) *Grey's Anatomy*, 35th ed. Longman.

Waters, K. (1986) "Expressive Three-Dimensional Faces," *Proc. Computer Graphics*, Online, Wembley.

Waters, K. (1987a) "A Muscle Model for Animating Three-Dimensional Facial Expression," *Proc. Computer Graphics SIGGRAPH* 21(4):17–24.

Waters, K. (1987b) "Animating Human Heads," *Computer Graphics*, Online, Wembley.

Welsh, (1985) "Report on Knowledge-based Picture Coding Research," British Telecom Research Dept. R16.4.3.

Zeltzer, D.L. (1984) "Representation and Control of Three-Dimensional Computer Animated Figures," PhD Thesis, Ohio State University.

A Stylised Model for Animating Bharata Natyam, an Indian Classical Dance Form

Sumant Narayan Pattanaik

Introduction

Bharata natyam is a classical dance form of India which has been practised for centuries in the southern region (Ayyangar, 1978). Natyam or dance is considered to comprise three elements: *nrutta*, *nritya* and *abhinaya*. Nrutta is primarily rhythm oriented. It involves intricate footwork with complementary movements of other limbs. Nritya is a step ahead of nrutta. It has an abundance of gestures expressive of themes, situations and emotions. Abhinaya is composite in character. It lays special emphasis on facial expression. However, the lines of demarcation between these three elements are never quite explicit. It is only the point of emphasis which distinguishes them.

India does not have any script for dance. Bharata natyam is described in ancient literature and is learnt and practised under the visual guidance and demonstration of the teachers. Even though the texts contain description of poses of movement and gestures, they do not reveal the exact manner in which time and space are to be utilised in a dance number. Many popular dance numbers have retained their form over centuries because they are learnt by rote. Over the last hundred years bharata natyam dance has continuously evolved, resulting in new dance movements and forms. But much of this has not been possible to record.

Even though there does not exist any notation, bharata natyam is a highly formalised dance as described in the ancient texts. The primary unit is a *karana* in Sanskrit, also termed *adavu* in southern India, and is a combination of body posture, limb movements and gestures. Originally 108 karanas were defined and these have given way to some newer ones. An *angahara*, a more complex unit, is an elegant, flawless, technically perfect movement of limbs with appropriate combination of karanas. To describe karanas, the human body is modelled somewhat hierarchically as consisting of *angas*, which are head, hands, chest, hips, sides, feet and shoulder; *pratyangas*, which are neck, arms, belly and back, thighs, wrists and knees; and *upa-angas*, which are eyes, eyebrows, eyelashes, pupils of eyes, cheek, nose, lips, teeth, tongue, chin, heels, ankles, fingers, toes and soles. Karanas are then described in terms of various positions and movements of these body components. This formalisation and structure–though not sufficient–does provide much help in the computational modelling of the human body and movement for animating bharata natyam dance. Over the past year we at the National Centre for Software Technology (NCST) have been working closely with a dance student who is also familiar with computing, with the aim of animating a few karanas. In this chapter I describe the work carried out and its relation to other similar work done for notating/animating Western dance. This work has been motivated by a number of factors, mainly potential assistance in teaching of bharata natyam dance, preservation in its pure form, the study of its evolution and, last but not the least, trying to derive computer-interpretable notations for it, if only partially.

Human Body Modelling

Computer animation can be defined as the specification and display of the movement of objects. Animation of any movement requires the modelling of the object for display and a set of actions which operate on the object to generate movement in terms of change in position in space. One requires three-dimensional modelling techniques to animate human movements by using physical laws. Such modelling techniques are slowly gaining popularity and are being used to produce sequences in a number of science fiction films. However, realistic modelling of both the human body form and the movement is extremely difficult and is still an open problem. The difficulties are largely due to

1. the necessity of modelling the human form itself with its elasticity, complex surface and joints;
2. the complexity of articulation of human body movement;
3. the increased expectation of realism when viewing human form; and most important
4. the fact that computer rendering of individual images has to be done in reasonable time.

A number of solutions have been proposed for modelling the human body. We discuss these briefly below.

Stick Figures

The limbs and joints of the body may be abstracted as stick figures. Several systems for the display of human movement use this simple model (Calvert and Chapman, 1982; Savage and Officer, 1978). Its limitations are that

1. stick figure displays are highly unrealistic and cause confusion in the perception of animated movement;
2. depths are difficult to judge as the body parts cannot hide each other;
3. it is impossible to generate those gestures and expressions in the body which are essential for dance.

However, stick figures still can be used to model the network of body segments and joints which articulate the body. Additional techniques may be used to remove the visual limitations associated with their use.

Sculptured Surfaces

The stick figure can be fleshed out by defining a surface over it. The body surface may be modelled by partitioning it into planar or curved patches (Fetter, 1964; Catmull, 1972; Platt, 1986). Movements which displace the surface are visible, and suitable hidden-surface algorithms provide the proper occlusion and depth effects. These models are computationally very expensive and hence may be generated off-line and stored for real-time display.

Volumetric Surfaces

The body segments are assumed to be instances of one or more primitive volumes, such as cylinders (Potter and Willmert, 1975), ellipsoids (Herbison-Evans, 1982), generalised cones (Marr, 1982) or spheres (Badler, O'Rourke and Toltzis, 1978). A few of these primitives can capture the information about the spatial distribution of the shape while retaining some of the simplicity and speed of the stick figure. Although the resemblance is quite stylised, the forms are very smooth and symmetrical, even cartoon-like. Specifying the simplest volumetric primitive requires just a location and a spatial extent and corresponds to a roughly spherical region in space. By adding a vector to this information a roughly cylindrical region can be specified whose length is indicated by the spatial extent parameter and whose diameter is indicated by the length of the vector. A second vector could indicate a rotational orientation about the first vector, making it possible to specify an elliptical cylinder whose cross section along the first vector is thicker than in the direction of the second vector. An additional vector could be used to specify the direction and magnitude of curvature in the axis of the cylindrical region.

Hidden-surface removal for cylinders can be extremely time consuming. Modelling with overlapping spheres as discussed in Badler et al. (1978) provides a better display.

The Bharata Natyam Body Model

We adopted the stick figure model to start with. However, we found it inadequate for depicting the various postures and movements. Hence a stylised volumetric model was evolved which could convey the position

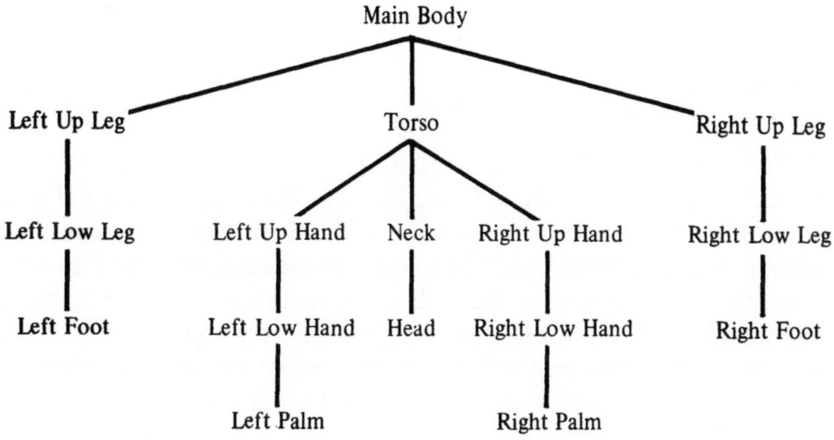

FIGURE 1. Bharata natyam body structure.

and movement without ambiguity. In this model, solid body segments are modelled in their local co-ordinate system. The information items retained are spatial extent (length of the segment) and two perpendicular vectors, whose lengths are width and breadth of the segment at one end. This information is used to construct a pyramidal solid. The base of the pyramid could be broken into as many sides as required to provide a smooth appearance to the body segment.

The stick figure joint structure is derived from the model of angas and pratyangas as described in the karanas. It is basically a hierarchical structure with over 15 joints. To keep the modelling aspects reasonably simple and the specification of the animated movement within our computational capabilities, we have modelled only the angas and pratyangas. The upa-angas, which model finer features such as eyes, pupils of the eyes, nose, lips, teeth, tongue and chin, have not been modelled at present. We would, however, like to emphasize that these are very important in the classical bharata natyam dance and play a very significant and aesthetic role in communication. We did attempt to model the palm and finger joints, so that the various *mudras* (palm and finger positions) could be depicted. However, the simple fleshed-out stick figure approach did not result in successful visual communication of the mudras.

By building object hierarchies, a much greater degree of local control is attained. All joints are modelled as spherical joints with constraints imposed on their extent of motion and with the implicit rule that transformation travels only down the hierarchy. At present, transformation effects up the hierarchy have not been modelled. The hierarchy has been defined as a tree structure with limbs as nodes (Fig. 1). Each node is a record with the following components:

1. name.
2. extent.
3. vector1, vector2.
4. number of children.
5. pointers to the children.

The vectors above are defined by endpoints. The length of vector1 is the width and that of the vector2 is the breadth of the wider end of the body segment. The co-ordinates are in a local co-ordinate system. The origin defines the connection with the node up in hierarchy. The system design is independent of the number of the limbs and the connection structure and size of the limbs and hence can be used to model any articulated system. The body model is provided to the system as an input file. Figure 2 shows a sample of the body model data actually used by the program for modelling the dance.

Animation System

The three components of the animation system are the object, the action, and the animation process. The action is procedurally defined over generic objects to result in geometrical changes following principles of kinematics. The animation process is merely the application of the action to objects.

Node Name	:	#1	("Left Upper Leg")
extent	:	25	
vector1	:	2.5, 0, 0	
vector2	:	0, 0, 2.5	
Children	:	1	(number of children)
		#2	(node number of "Left Lower Leg")
		0, −25, 0	(connecting point)

Node Name	:	#4	("Torso")
extent	:	30	
vector1	:	10, 0, 0	
vector2	:	0, 0, 2.5	
Children	:	3	(number of children)
		#5	(node number of "Left Upper Hand")
		−10, 30, 0	(connecting point)
		#8	(node number of "Neck")
		0, 30, 0	(connecting point)
		#10	(node number of "Right Upper Hand")
		10, 30, 0	(connecting point)

FIGURE 2. Node data structure.

We have broken down our system into basically four parts: specification or input, output or image synthesis, motion, and inbetweening.

Input

In this process we input the various karanas. There are a number of methods for input of dance forms. Dance notations exist for Western dance—Benesh (1956) and Laban (Hutchinson, 1970) notations, for example. These are graphical in nature. That is, basically these are meant for interpretation by dance experts or dance students. They are not meant for automated interpretation, except perhaps some time in the distant future when computer vision systems become a reality. There have been attempts at computerising these but not with much success (Savage and Officer, 1978, for example). The tools made available are essentially draughting tools and not tools for computer interpretation of a dance sequence. Indian dance does not have a notation. However, for several styles of dancing, specialised technical terms have been evolved that describe the movements and positions: *taiyum, tata, taiya,* and so forth. These utterances are currently the only method used by the dance teachers to get students to learn the dance numbers. However, the interpretation of these terms is quite context dependent and though this terminology is a potential candidate for computerisation, we have not yet attempted it. At the other extreme is the numerical description as an input process. Basically, the animator specifies every position and orientation of every part of the body for every single frame of animation. This method is aided by the use of goniometers, electromechanical devices, attached to the various parts of the body, which return position and orientation information (Hannah, 1980).

We adopted an intermediate approach of a simple command language interface which specified atomic movements of the human body and a macro facility to generate individual karanas by combining a number of suitable atomic movements. The command line has the form:

1. ⟨body segment⟩ ⟨action⟩ ⟨parameter list⟩

   For example, Left_Leg Rotate +45.0—to rotate the left leg outwards by 45 degrees. This results in an atomic movement and is the basis for constructing the poses and movements.

2. BEGINP primitive_name
[⟨atomic movements⟩. . . . . . .]
ENDP

   Primitives are incrementally constructed by the user through the sequence of command lines. The primitives are stored as a sequence of generalised transformation matrices. Currently we have restricted our primitives to leg and hand groups.

3. APPLYP
[⟨primitive_name⟩. . . . .]
ENDP

Primitives are concatenated to generate body poses.

The bharata natyam dance student who collaborated in this work provided the positional information necessary for the various body poses. She did this essentially by taking measurements from photographed dance poses of herself. She also visually verified the computer-produced stylised images with the photographs and fine-tuned the positional information. Though the precision of the input positional information was entirely dictated by our dancer co-worker, it was accepted as being fairly accurate by other dance experts. Within the system, positional judgement is assisted by providing views from front, back, left and right of the body.

Output

All body segments, except the head, are displayed as pyramidal objects. The head is displayed as a set of overlapping spheres. Literature abounds with techniques for image synthesis and we shall not go into details here. We actually implemented a full shading model with specular reflectance and hidden-surface removal (Rogers, 1985) but without texture. Plate I shows the various poses in an adavu sequence shot directly off the screen.

(The resulting picture of the human body is still very synthetic but without any ambiguity concerning the positions and orientations of the

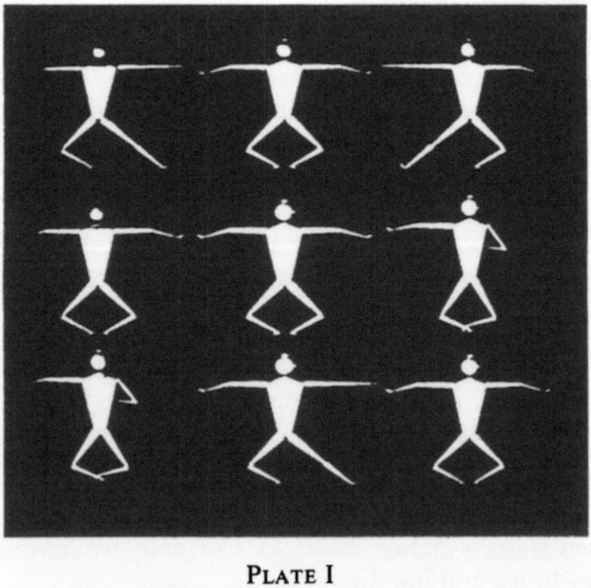

PLATE I

parts. For more realistic visual images, better body sculpting techniques are being planned.)

Kinematics

This is the principle used for generating changes in the body during the input process. The human body is thought of as a configuration of chains of rigid bodies interconnected by joints. The analytical study of the spatial configuration of these linked rigid bodies as a function of time without regard to the forces, moments that cause the motion, is called *kinematics*. This problem is being studied extensively in the field of robotics.

The kinematics problem has two subproblems: direct kinematics and reverse kinematics. If we consider a linear chain of rigid body segments connected through simple joints with one end fixed, the direct kinematics is to find the position and orientation of the free end with respect to a reference co-ordinate system, given the joint co-ordinates, the joint angles and the length of the link. The reverse kinematics problem is to find the joint parameters given only the position and orientation of the free link with respect to the reference co-ordinate system. Vector and matrix algebra is used to describe the location of the links with respect to a fixed reference frame.

The whole system is divided into two co-ordinate systems: the fixed reference co-ordinate system and a moving (translating and rotating) co-ordinate system, attached to each of the links on the chain. To describe the geometric relationship between these two co-ordinate systems, a 4×4 homogeneous transformation matrix is used. Homogeneous transformation matrices have the combined effect of rotation, translation, perspective and global scaling when operating on position vectors expressed in homogeneous co-ordinates $\langle x, y, z, \omega \rangle$.

If we consider two consecutive links on the chain, link $(i-1)$ and link (i), the link $(i-1)$ co-ordinate system is the reference co-ordinate system and the link (i) co-ordinate system is the moving co-ordinate system. Then

$$\mathbf{P}_{(i)} = \mathbf{TP}_{(i-1)}$$

where $\mathbf{P}$ is the position vector of a point in the ith link in homogeneous co-ordinates and $\mathbf{T}$ is the transformation matrix.

For a chain of three-links such as leg and hand, the position in the world co-ordinate system is represented by

$$\mathbf{P} = \mathbf{T}_1 \cdot \mathbf{T}_2 \cdot \mathbf{T}_3 \cdot \mathbf{P}_{(0)}$$

So calculating the positional information at any joint just involves matrix multiplication.

The reverse problem is much harder. One way to approach this problem is to consider the 4×4 homogeneous transformation matrix which contains sines and cosines of joint angles. For a three-link chain with the orientation and position specified for the distal end there are 12 unknowns and 12 equations to solve, all in sines and cosines. Basically, numerical methods are used to arrive at the solution.

Realistic and reasonably accurate animation is possible with kinematic simulation provided the body is always in contact with the ground and accurate kinematic descriptions are provided as input. The disadvantage is that a very large library of kinematic description must be built in if a variety of movements are to be handled at different speeds.

Inbetweening

For animation, motion is the important requirement. Given two poses, we have to find out the intermediate poses whilst taking into consideration speed, time and other subtleties. Currently we are working on motion planning. The requirements are

1. To define the trajectory followed by the articulated body. The trajectory may have to be provided by the animator or may be automatically computed.
2. Along the trajectory to solve for the data concerning articulated variables, that is, their co-ordinates and orientation.

The latter problem is solved by taking into consideration the various constraints such as

Spatial constraints like the presence of obstacles. (Ground is also an obstacle; feet must remain on or above the ground.)
Constraints associated with the deformation limit of the joints.
Timing constraints.

Hence a typical configuration may not have a solution, may have a limited number of solutions or may have an infinite number of solutions. If solutions exist, one has to choose the best.

Simple geometrical and kinematic models assume that for any configuration taken up by the articulated system, a state of equilibrium is achieved. These models become less representative as the speed increases and the inertial, centrifugal and coupling forces become significant. Therefore certain dynamic phenomena of the system should be considered (Coiffet, 1983).

Implementation

The entire system development has been carried out in C language on an HP9000 series computer with a high-resolution colour graphic processor.

Acknowledgments. I am grateful to Prof. R. Narasimhan and Dr. S. P. Mudur for their guidance and encouragement and to Ms. Ramya Sarma for her keen interest, indefatigable efforts in inputting a few adavus of bharata natyam and continuous feedback about the system during the development.

References

Ayyangar, R.R. (1978) *Sangeet Ratnakaram.* Wilko Publishing House, Bombay.

Badler, N., J. O'Rourke, and H. Toltzis (1978) "A Human Body Modelling System for Motion Studies," Movement Project Report 13, Department of Computer and Information Science, Univ. of Pennsylvania, July.

Benesh, J. and R. Benesh (1956) *Introduction to Benesh Dance Notation.* A.C. Black, London.

Calvert, T.W. and J. Chapman. (1982) "Aspects of the Kinematic Simulation of Human Movement," *IEEE Computer Graphics and Applications*, November, pp. 41–50.

Catmull, E. (1972) "A System for Computer Generated Movies," *Proc. Annual Conference*, vol. 1, pp. 422–431. ACM, New York.

Coiffet, P. (1983) *Robot Technology*, vol. 1, chapter 7. Prentice-Hall, Englewood Cliffs, N.J.

Fetter, W.A. (1964) *Computer Graphics in Communication.* McGraw-Hill, New York.

Hannah, R.E. (1980) "Interpretation of Clinical Gait Data," *Proc. Special Conference Canadian Society of Biomechanics–Human Locomotion*, London, pp. 80–81.

Herbison-Evans, D. (1982) "Real-Time Animation of Human Figure Drawing with Hidden Line Omitted," *IEEE Computer Graphics and Applications*, November, pp. 27–33.

Hutchinson, A. (1970) *Labanotation—The System of Recording Movements.* Theatre Art Books, New York.

Marr, D. (1982) *Vision.* Freeman, San Francisco.

Platt, S.M. (1986) "A Structural Model of the Human Face," MS-CIS-86-11, Univ. of Pennsylvania.

Potter, T.E. and K.D. Willmert (1975) "Three-Dimensional Human Model," *Computer Graphics* 9(Spring):102–110.

Rogers, D.F. (1985) *Procedural Elements for Computer Graphics.* McGraw-Hill, New York.

Savage, G.J. and J.M. Officer (1978) "Choreo:An Interactive Computer Model for Dance," *International Journal for Man-Machine Studies*, vol. 10, 1978, pp. 1–8.

Visual Modelling in Architectural Design

Tom W. Maver

Buildings on Their Site

For some years now, the visual impact of buildings on the landscape has been a contentious issue at many public planning inquiries. This reflects the underdeveloped state of objective visual appraisal, particularly in the clear presentation of the harmful and enhancing effects of building proposals on the local environment. Notably, the accuracy and realism of traditional visual assessment methods has been called into question.

The opening section of this paper is concerned with an established generation of computer-based models which predict, accurately and meaningfully, the visual impact of buildings and other constructions on their urban or rural environment. As such, they form part of the increasing repertoire of CAAD techniques which allow designers to appraise, and thereby select from, alternative design options at the conceptual stages of design.

Typical of the tools in everyday use by architects and planners are the programs VIEWER and VISTA. VIEWER (see References) is a highly user-friendly program designed to offer (inexperienced) users the capacity to generate virtually any perspective projection—monocular or stereo—of the built or natural environment. Figure 1 shows a general view of Strathclyde University Campus generated by VIEWER. Figure 2 is a view of Kurashiti, typical of the elegant images generated by similar software from Tee Sasada (1987) which represent the interaction of natural and man-made environments. Rather than generate the natural environment by computer, the photo-montage options of a program like VIEWER can be employed: the user specifies, for any site photograph, the camera position and direction, its focal length and the enlargement factor of the print in order to generate a computer image which can immediately by superimposed onto the photograph. Plate 1 shows a VIEWER photomontage of a controversial waste disposal plant proposed on a Norwegian fiord; in this case the wire line drawing has been hand-coloured.

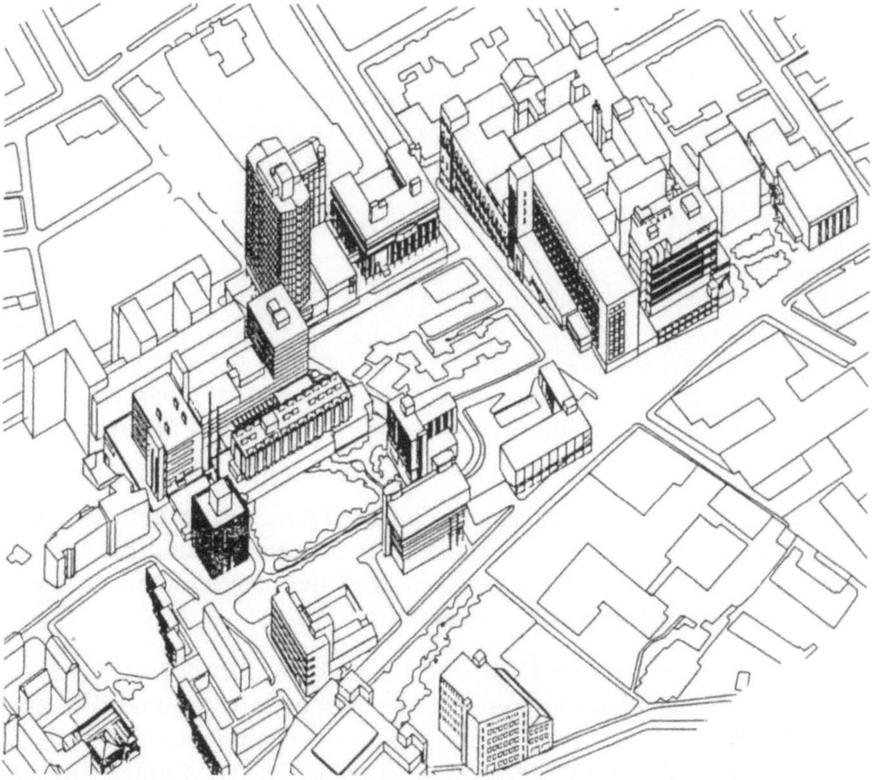

FIGURE 1. General view of Strathclyde University campus generated by VIEWER (see References).

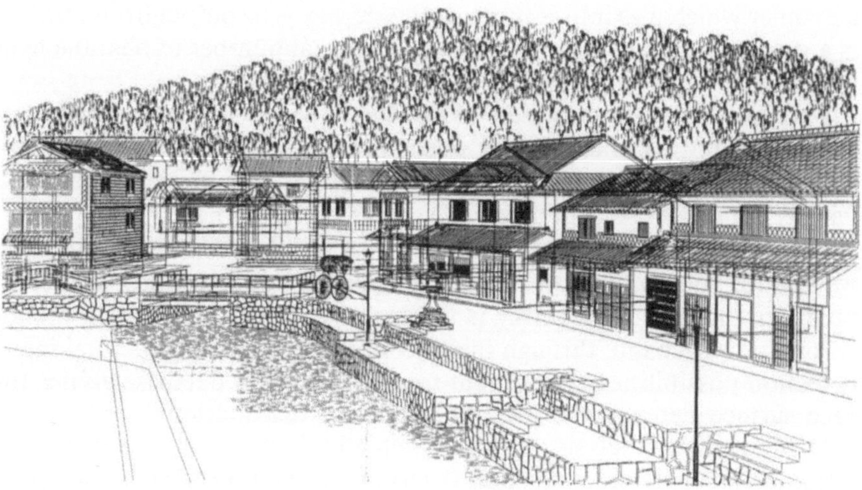

FIGURE 2. Cityscape of Kurashiti with trees represented by a light and shadow 2-D pattern (1987).

The alternative to hand colouring is to employ a program such as VISTA (see References). VISTA will generate coloured and textured images which are shadowed for sunny or cloudy conditions at any hour of any day in any latitude. Such images may be superimposed on site photographs (Plate 2) or, more commonly (Plate 3) merged on the screen with frame-grabbed images of real sky and vegetation.

Spaces Within Buildings

Exterior views of buildings are (now) relatively simple. There is only one light source—the sun—and it, being a long way off, illuminates all plane surfaces equally; inter-reflection—at least between the surfaces of man-made objects other than glass—is insignificant. When we attempt to model spatial interiors, we are dealing with phenomena which are an order of magnitude greater in complexity:

light sources may be point (spots), linear (fluorescent tubes) or planar (windows) and each has a complex intensity and spectral distribution

each surface of the spatial envelope and of the objects within it have a complex spectral reflective distribution.

The prototype software DIM (see References), currently being developed into a design aid by ABACUS and Philips International BV, takes a 'first principles' approach to these physical phenomena and seeks to provide a level of realism hitherto unobtainable. The DIM suite comprises four programs and three database modules (Fig. 3).

The first program module—DIMdis—accepts user data which describes a zone's topography and topology. The objective of DIMdis is to transform this continuous zone model to a discrete numerical equivalent in a manner which maximises numerical accuracy. The output from DIMdis is a data structure of rays representing the total number of possible light flowpaths.

The second program module of DIM is DIMray. This accepts the output from DIMdis and the user's specification of the positioning of luminaires extracted from DIM's fittings database. Luminaire photometric data is conceived as a number of vectors representing a fitting's three-dimensional intensity distribution, with a number of mono-chromatic wavebands superimposed to represent spectral characteristics. The computational mission of DIMray is to process each vector, for each monochromatic waveband, through the list of rays representing the total inter-reflection possibilities. The output from DIMray is a database giving, for each surface element, the spectral luminance distribution.

DIMout is the analysis module which allows the recovery and presentation of this performance data. It has two capabilities. The first allows the performance data to be integrated by fitting and by surface. This

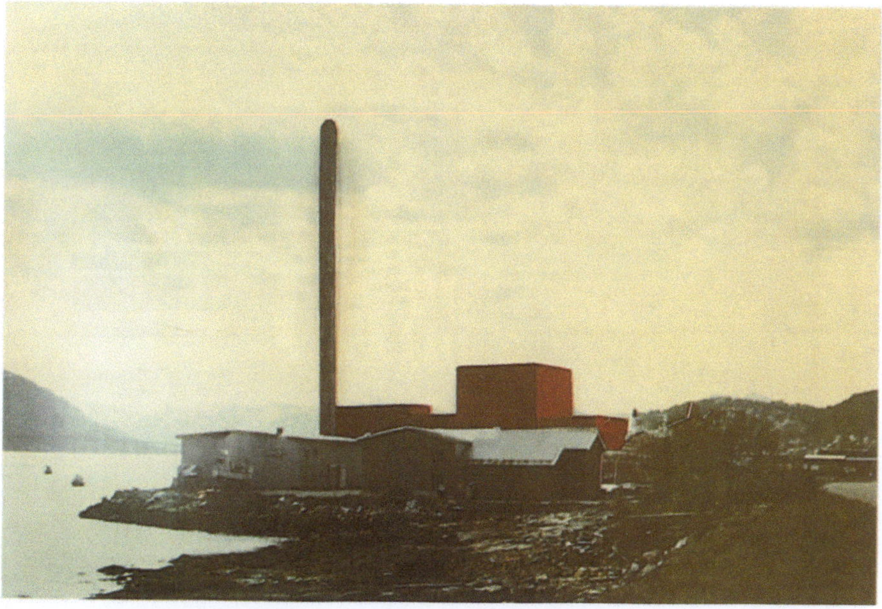

PLATE 1. Photomontage of a proposed waste disposal plant on a Norwegian fiord; the VIEWER wire-line image has been hand coloured.

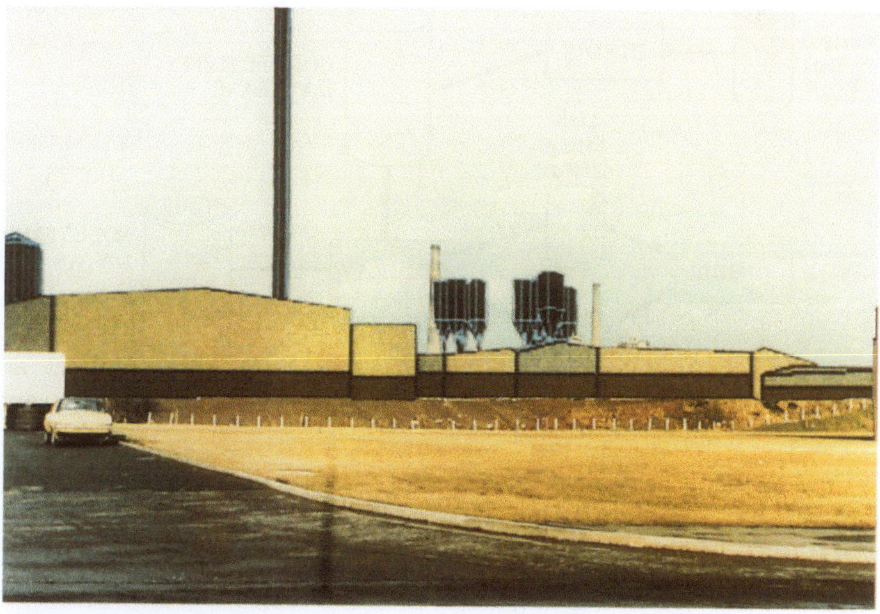

PLATE 2. Photomontage of a factory complex in Glasgow's east end; the colour image of the building has been generated by VISTA (see References).

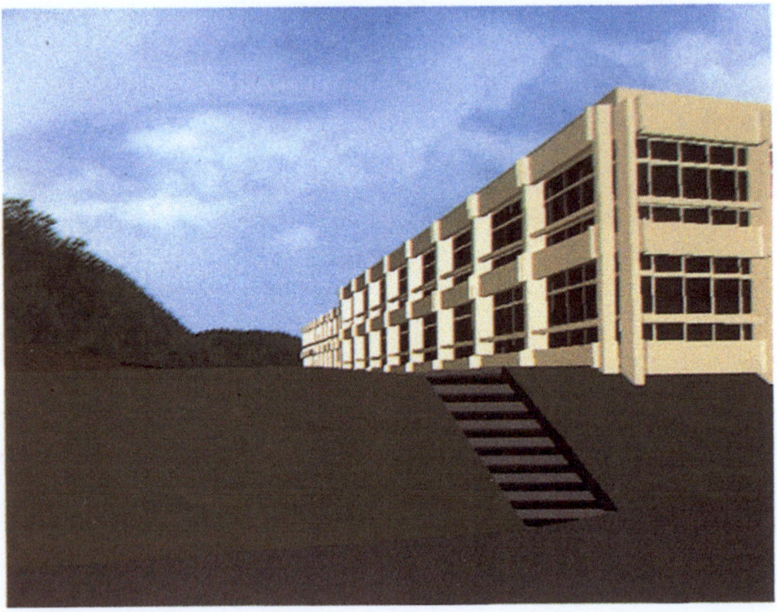

PLATE 3. VISTA image of proposed company headquarters in Brussels; the image of the building has been mixed with frame-grabbed images of sky and vegetation.

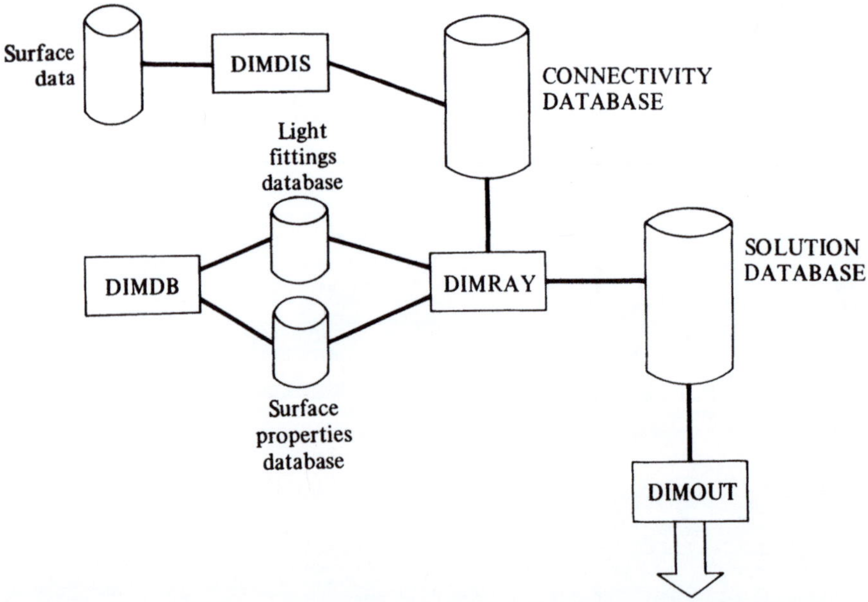

FIGURE 3. Structure of the DIM lighting software (DIM, see References).

yields, for any mix of fittings, surface illuminance or luminance. This is the performance data which can be transmitted to thermal energy models for investigation of the energy effects of various lighting control strategies. The second capability concerns the transformation to terminal RGB to enable, via a scan-cell algorithm, the production of an enhanced screen image.

The final module, DIMdbm, is a database manager for the luminance and surface property databases. It allows the display of existing entities and the insertion of new fittings and surface finishes as required.

Plate 4 illustrates DIM's current capability to model lit interiors of buildings.

Moving Through Space

John Lansdown has quite rightly pointed out (1988) that we perceive and appreciate the built environment not as an immaculate set of coloured, textured and lit 'stills' but as a more jumbled, fuzzy, dynamic sequence of impressions. Such a sequence has, until recently, been compiled by painstaking capture, frame by frame, of discretely generated images.

Recent advances in the technology of computer graphics offer a change in this scenario and hold out the prospect of a truly interactive dynamic interface with whosoever wishes to explore the environment—on foot, by

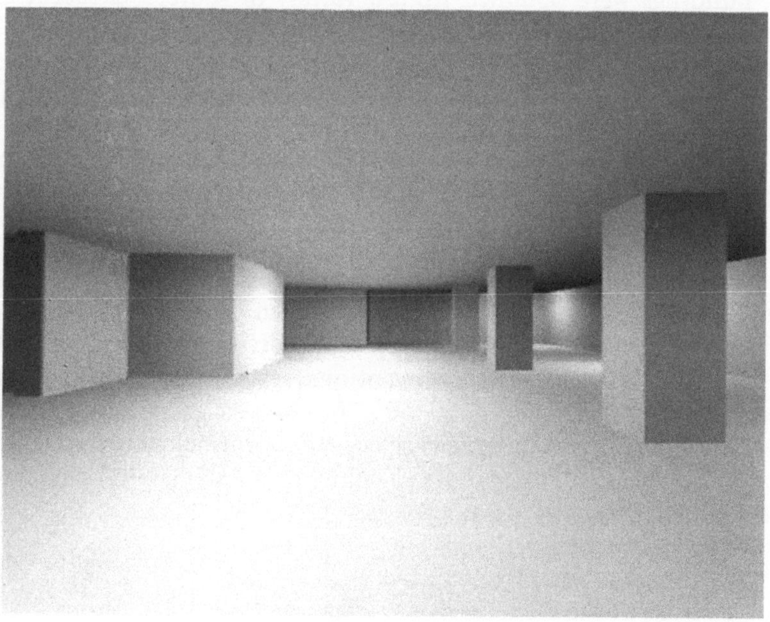

PLATE 4. Image of an artificially lit interior generated by DIM (see References).

bus or by helicopter. In the Spring of 1986 ABACUS was invited by the Rutherford and Appleton Laboratories to evaluate the relevance and efficacy of the Silicon Graphics Iris 2400 Colour Graphics Workstation to building design and urban planning. The Iris—similar in computer architecture to the new generation of 32-bit Unix CAD workstations such as those produced by Sun and Whitechapel, which are becoming increasingly common in CAD environments—has, in addition, a number of 'geometry accelerators' which automatically carry out, at great speed, perspective transformations of any 3-D data set.

Intent on demonstrating the relevance of this technological advance to urban design, ABACUS volunteered to build a model of Glasgow city centre within the Iris through which architects, planners, developers and others could 'fly' or 'walk.' Funding from Glasgow Action was sufficient to employ six architectural students over two summer months to capture the geometry of the city centre.

In effect, three databases were constructed: the terrain, the road network and the buildings:

Glasgow is a hilly city and it was considered necessary to model the topography; this was done by digitizing the contours at 1:10,000 scale over an area of 64 sq km.

The roads, over the central city area of 6 sq km, were digitized as if they existed on one plane; they were then 'floated' down onto the terrain model until they took on the 3-D shape of the landform.

The buildings required, by far and away, the greatest effort. The heights of buildings were obtained from a variety of sources—a recent architectural survey of the merchant city, a physical model owned by Glasgow District Council and the stereoscopic analysis of aerial photographs. These heights were entered onto the 1:1250 scale ordnance maps which were then digitized as 20 separate sections of the city. These 20 files were than 'floated' down onto the terrain and combined to give a database of some 2500 buildings extending over the 6 sq km of the city centre.

The databases of terrain, roads and buildings exist in a format which allows them to be viewed individually and in combination, in wireline or in colour, by the ABACUS programs VIEWER and VISTA. When accessing the database from a conventional graphic terminal the user can generate line perspectives from any chosen viewpoint using VIEWER (see Fig. 4); these can be displayed on the terminal screen and can be plotted to any scale; with access to a colour terminal, the user can generate shadowed and textured colour perspectives for any hour of the day and any day of the year.

It is the facilities offered by the Iris, however, which put computer graphics truly at the disposal of the urban modeller. Dynamic control of the viewing parameters are effected by the mouse and the keyboard, in-

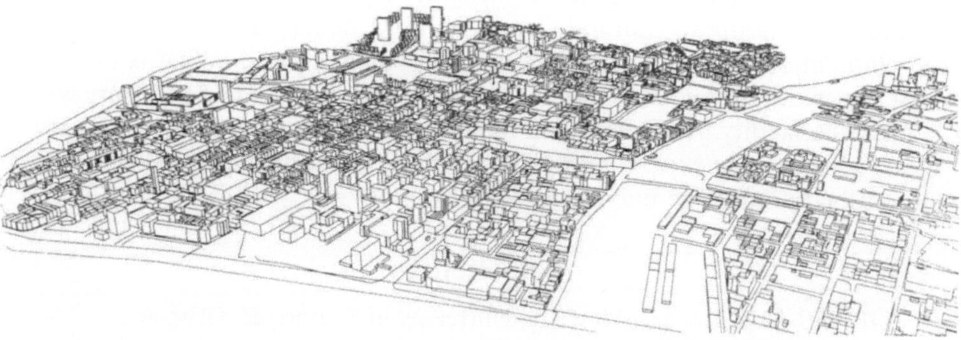

FIGURE 4. Perspective view of the Glasgow database through which it is possible to "fly."

dividually or in combination; the degree of control can be summarised under three headings: movement, image and viewpath. The three mouse buttons (L = left, R = right, M = middle) allow the following 'eye' movements:

L = turn left
M = move forward
R = turn right
LM = turn up
LR = move back
MR = move down
LMR = rotate.

The keyboard controls the following movements of the object:

q = move up
w = move down
< = move left
> = move right
z = zoom in
x = zoom out.

The image may be viewed in wireline or in surface filled colours; in either case, colours can be attributed to individual bodies within the data set. The thickness of the wireline vectors can be changed and the wireline images can be depth-cued over any range. In surface colour mode, the user can call for surface depth sort and for a horizon line.

Facilities exist to program any viewpath; it is thus possible to explore, interactively, a variety of viewpaths and then program a particular one for video recording.

Video output is possible for 60 Hz and PAL (phase alteration by line) monitors.

With the Glasgow Garden Festival in 1988 and Glasgow being honoured as European Cultural Capital in 1990, demands for extension and elaboration of the existing database can be anticipated. What is not yet clear is the serious use to which architects, planners and developers will put the facility. A crucial development is the link between the geometry database and an expanding alphanumeric database of archive information on the buildings of interest in Glasgow.

References

VIEWER User Manual. ABACUS, University of Strathclyde, Glasgow.

Sasada, T.T. (1987) "Drawing Natural Scenery by Computer Graphics," *Computer Aided Design* 19:(4).

VISTA User Manual. ABACUS, University of Strathclyde, Glasgow.

DIM. Preliminary Report. ABACUS, University of Strathclyde, Glasgow.

Lansdown, J. (1988) Computers and Visualisation of Design Ideas," *Proceedings of CAAD Futures 87*. Elsevier, Eindhoven.

Using Soft Objects in Computer-Generated Character Animation

Brian Wyvill and Geoff Wyvill

Introduction

Traditional animators often criticise 3-D computer-generated animation for the stilted way objects move. Computer-generated objects or *characters* tend to lack the subtleties in motion seen in traditional animation. Characters do not have to be humanoid; objects can be given character, such as the brooms in the Sorcerer's Apprentice sequence from Disney's *Fantasia*. In other words, they are anthropomorphic. The motion of such objects is controlled to a fine degree to characterise their movement. Characters tend to bend as they move. At times, they must conform to their surroundings: a figure sitting in a chair is an example, or flowing water. In computer animation, popular modelling techniques such as polygon meshes or spline patches do not lend themselves to the manufacture of objects which can be given this type of motion.

We favour the use of a different modelling technique, which we call *Soft Objects*. The intention is to let the animator design the skeleton of the character or object and then automatically *clothe* this skeleton with a surface. If the skeleton moves then the surface changes its shape smoothly to conform. If the skeleton undergoes metamorphosis to a totally different skeleton or inbetweens to a skeleton in a new position then a new surface is calculated at every frame. The surface is represented in such a way that it maintains nearly constant volume as the skeleton moves, thus providing convincing *character coherence*. This property of coherence is very important. Intuitively, it means that throughout metamorphosis the character remains recognisable as the same character.

Our experiments show that this approach may well provide a modelling technique that will allow computer-generated character animation to become very much more useful to the traditional animator. In this paper we present an overview of the mathematics that makes this technique possible and show some examples of the type of pictures that can be produced and how they may be animated.

Modelling Soft Objects

Our *soft* objects are represented by a surface of constant value in a scalar field. This is a logical extension of the idea of a contour map. In a contour map the lines connect the points of constant height. If you think of the field as a three-dimensional map of temperature where every point in the space can have a temperature value, then a soft object is a surface connecting points with a certain value. The skeleton of the object, which controls its shape and movement, consists of a structure of hot points, or wires, which affect the shape of the field. This method was first reported by Jim Blinn (1982) and our first implementation has been explained in detail (Wyvill et al., 1986a). Both of these descriptions concentrate on the use of a skeleton of control points to create the field, although Blinn does describe an extension to make the field asymmetrical about a point.

To construct the surface of a soft object, we have to calculate the field at many points in space, so it is important that the cost of calculating the field at any given point is not too large. To keep this cost low, we choose a field function which vanishes to zero beyond a certain distance from a control point. Thus the value of the field is not affected by control points further away than this distance. We call this distance the *radius of influence* of the control point. It then becomes possible to sort the control points in space and to use only the nearby points in calculating the field.

The main disadvantage of using simple points, or hot spots, to define the field is that a large number can be required for some fairly simple shapes. For this reason we use an extended notion of a control point which we call a *key*. In general, a key consists of three line segments at right angles representing the axes of an ellipsoid each of which has an associated radius of influence. A point which is within a radius of influence of more than one key has a field value equal to the sum of the values calculated for each key. This field determines the shape of the soft object because the surface of the object is an iso-surface of the field. The surface created by just one control point in the original model is a sphere. The surface created by a single key is an ellipsoid. Here we introduce the use of these ellipsoids.

Field Functions for Soft Objects

We want to construct a function which will enable us to represent arbitrary shapes when we plot the iso-surfaces. The function is therefore going to depend on a set of keys as defined above. We assume that the keys are independent. For our models we want the field to be continuous. Although the use of ellipsoids somewhat reduces the number of keys required, it is still important not to have to inspect every key whenever we calculate a field value. So our field function must decay smoothly to zero at a predictable distance from the key. The field function we use describes an ellipsoid, and the distance from the key at which the value falls to zero depends on the angular distances from the three axes.

Let **a**, **b**, **c** be vectors defining the ellipse and P be some point whose field is to be calculated defined by the vector **p** (distance r) from the origin of the ellipsoid. Let α, β, γ, be the angles made between **p** and **a**, **b**, **c**, respectively. The field at P is given by

$$f(r, \alpha\ \beta, \gamma) = 1 - (r^*r \cos^2(\alpha)/a^*a + r^*r \cos^2(\beta)/b^*b + r^*r \cos^2(\gamma)/c^*c\,.$$

In the special case where the magnitudes $a = b = c$ a sphere is obtained:

$$f(r) = 1 - r^*r/a^*a\,.$$

If r is greater than the largest axis of the ellipsoid or if the function is negative, then zero is returned. This serves to define the field due to single key. We make the field value due to many keys equal to the sum of the values due to each one. This is the very simplest way to combine the effect of many keys and we have found no reason to change it. The contribution at the position of the key itself will be some maximum value (we use 1.0).

Note that if a key has a negative contribution, this is treated as a scale factor of -1 when the contributions from all the keys are summed. Negative keys can be used to create flat areas or cavities as illustrated in Fig. 2; the train has been manufactured from eight ellipsoids on a base made from a further eight smaller ellipsoids. Various other small ellipsoids have been added to provide some details such as the chimney. The cab and top of the chimney have been flattened using negative ellipsoids with a large radius.

Blinn (1982) used an exponential function based on the known field of electron density around an atom. Originally, we used a cubic in r squared (Wyvill et al., 1986a); which produced a spherical field around each control point. The ellipsoid function, although slower to calculate, allows the designer more flexibility and spheres become a special case. The original function needed only three additions and five multiplications. In the special case where the axes have the same length, two multiplications, one division and subtraction are required but in general two dot products are calculated to find the cosine values. The difference in the results can be seen in Fig. 1. Two key points approaching one another are shown in Fig. 1a using the cubic function and in Fig. 1b using the function described above where the axes are equal in magnitude. It can be seed that the spheres join to form one surface more quickly with the ellipsoid function. We are also experimenting with other functions to obtain different shapes. A full account of rendering the surface is given in Wyvill et al. (1986a). The problem is to find the position of the surface. This is done by finding the field value at successive points along one axis

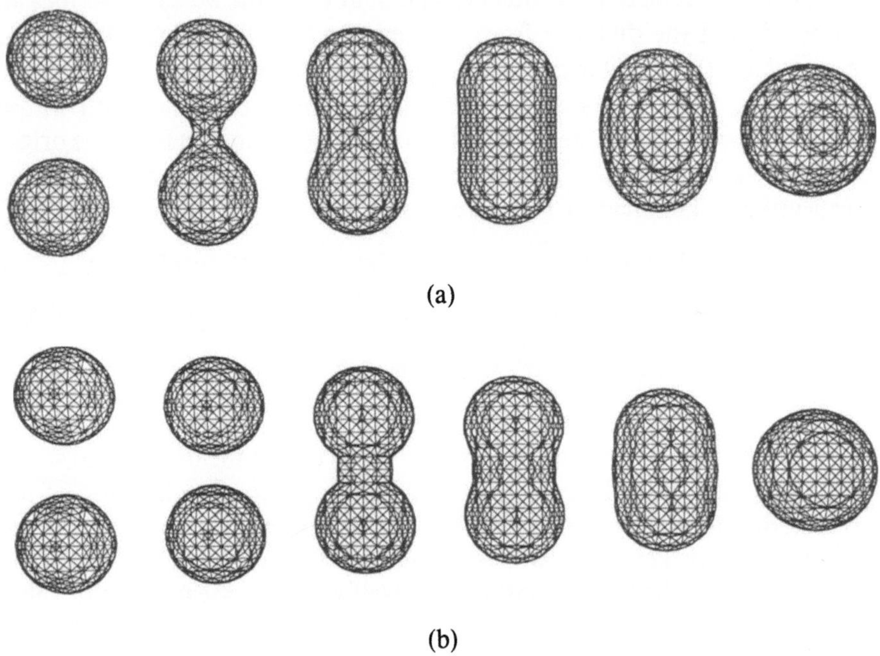

FIGURE 1. Merging key points using (a) original cubic field function and (b) field function for ellipsoids. (Axes are equal.)

(starting at a control key). Near the key the value will be greater than the iso-value (hot); when the field falls below the iso-value the surface has been crossed. At this point we erect a cube and find the field value at each vertex. It can then be ascertained if the surface cuts any edge of the cube by comparing the field value of each vertex to the iso-value. If the surface cuts a particular edge the adjacent cube is manufactured and the process repeated recursively until the entire surface has been covered by containing cubes. The surface can then be approximated by examining each cube and substituting polygons. Alternatively, we ray trace by firing rays at the cube, which gives an approximation to the intersection with the surface. An iteration technique is used to determine the actual intersection. The diagrams (Fig. 1) are plotted from the polygon mesh approximation; back-facing polygons have been removed.

Defining the Iso-surface

Having established a definition of the field, we must choose a field value for the iso-surface. Suppose we choose a function value, *magic*, and plot the iso-surface connecting all points whose field value equals *magic*. Now

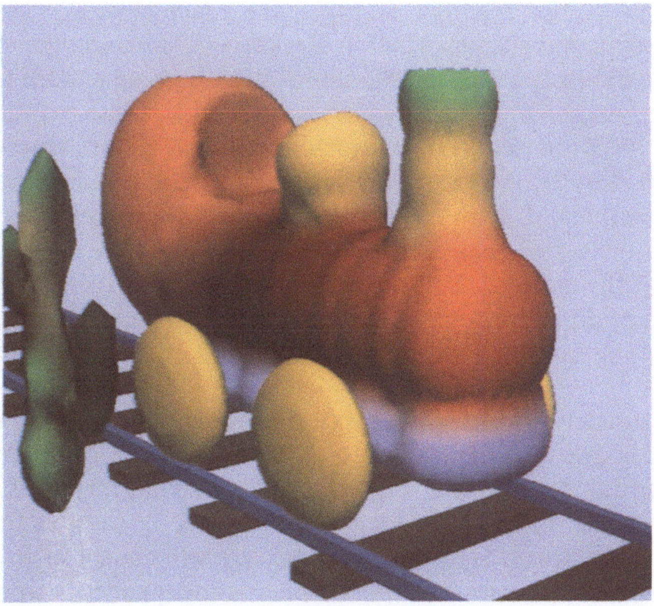

FIGURE 2. Engine built from soft ellipsoids.

consider the field due to two keys in the same place. If the magnitudes of the axes of the ellipsoid are equal the surface is symmetrical about the centre of the keys and an iso-surface for value *magic* in this field will be a sphere of larger radius than the iso-surface in the field due to one key. We have chosen *magic* so that this larger sphere has exactly twice the volume of the other.

This choice is intended to suit the modelling of liquids, to provide a reasonable effect when two droplets merge. It also helps to preserve the *character coherence* mentioned earlier, since the volume of merging objects will be approximately maintained. If a definite increase in volume is desired, this can be achieved by adding new keys or increasing the axes. Other choices are possible, as are other functions for the field. Finding functions appropriate to particular applications is a research project in its own right. For our purposes, the above is used throughout.

Colour and Texture

The colour at any point on the surface is defined as a weighted sum of the colours of those key points which influence the field at that point. The weights are the contributions to the field value of each key. This means that soft objects can exhibit smooth colour changes across their surface. We can alter the colour of keys as a function of time to produce special effects. For example, we can make a face blush.

Texture mapping is described in Heckbert (1986) and others. It is usually done by using some coordinates of position on a surface as input to a texture function or as selectors in a texture table. More recently Darwyn Peachey has proposed using a three-dimensional texture space (Peachey, 1985; see also Perlin, 1985). This has many advantages. For example, the surface textures of marble or wood-grain are a consequence of the way in which the surface has been cut to expose part of the continuous solid texture of the material. Soft objects may also have texture. For example, mixtures of differently coloured liquids may show a streaky surface, and softly oozing sand or mud retains the surface characteristics of sand or mud.

Unfortunately, ordinary solid texturing does not work with soft objects. This is because they have no natural centre, position or orientation. To understand this, imagine a marble object with solid texture. Suppose we move or rotate the object. If the texture space is the same as the physical space in which the object resides, its texture will change as it moves. To avoid this, we use a texture space which is independent of physical coordinates and yet provides us with the simplicity and continuity associated with the solid-texturing technique. We refer to this as an *abstract texture space*. This technique is fully described in Wyvill et al. (1987). Figure 3 shows a striped model in three different poses. In the first it is shown with horizontal stripes. In the second pose the model is rotated but the abstract space associated with each key point is stationary. If we want to regard the motion of a collection of key points as a rotation, then we must rotate the abstract texture space. Otherwise the texture behaves as if the object has merely transformed to the new shape by distortion. There is nothing wrong with Fig. 3. The animation represents a blob of soft material whose surface is changing (perhaps because of some internal flow of material). Only if we want to regard the motion as a rotation without distortion need we deliberately rotate the texture space as in the third pose. Figure 4 illustrates how a 2-D texture (the well known *Mandril*) may be used as a rectangular tile to cover the required area and then extruded into 3-D to produce a 3-D texture space.

Animating the Objects

The motion of a rigid object can be described as a sequence of geometric transformations which are applied uniformly to all the components of the object. This kind of description has proved very useful in engineering and it has been inherited by the discipline of computer animation, but it utterly fails with soft objects. We cannot conveniently separate the gross motion of an object from its changes of shape because some soft objects,

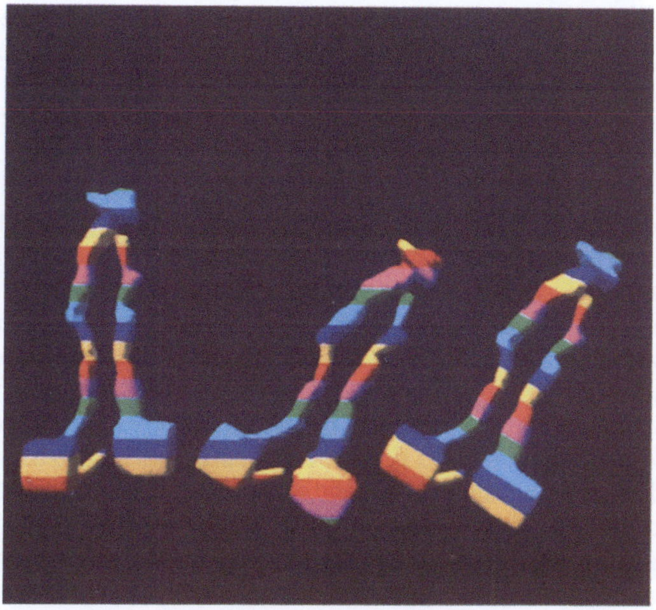

FIGURE 3. 3-D abstract texture space.

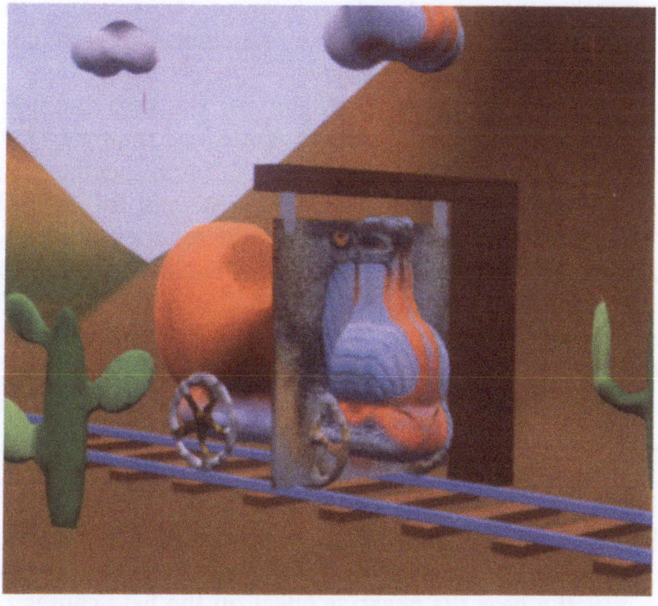

FIGURE 4. Traindril—Mandril textured onto soft train.

liquids for example, actually break into separate parts during their motion. The separate parts can then move independently. The problem centres on the unsuitability of traditional modelling techniques to describe these objects.

Polygon meshes are a poor choice for representing curved surfaces even if you are not trying to animate them. Spline patches, in particular beta splines (Barsky, 1981), provide an excellent way of forming a 3-D surface. But moving the object so that it changes shape requires careful management of a large number of control points to ensure that the patches remain as a closed surface and do not penetrate one another.

Soft objects may be represented by spline patches as still frames but often lose credibility when motion is attempted (Huitric and Nahas, 1985). Spline surfaces also require the animator to enter a large number of carefully chosen control points to model an object. This can become an immense task for large and complex closed surfaces. Bending could be achieved by moving the spline control points at different velocities and recalculating the spline surface at every frame.

Like a spline surface, a soft object is also defined by a set of key points. However, unlike a spline surface, the soft object control points form a skeleton of the model, which gives a better intuitive idea of the form of the object than can be given by the control points of many spline patches. Our initial experiments indicate that an equivalent model built using the iso-surface technique uses considerably fewer control points than are required to describe the same models by patches. This will, however, not be true in all cases.

Shape change can be achieved by moving the keys and adjusting the spatial relationship between them in a controlled manner. It is also possible to alter the elliptical axes of each key. Motion specification for these models is, naturally, more difficult to express than for rigid objects. To some extent this problem is offset, since our representation of these objects guarantees the formation of one or more closed surfaces, no matter how the control points are moved. This is illustrated in Fig. 5, where the train model has been made to bend. In this case the animation is controlled by a path. The centres of the railway sleepers (*ties* for North Americans) are used as control points and a beta spline curve is calculated as the path (after Kochanek, 1984). The centres of the ellipsoids are aligned in the un-bent train and made to follow the path keeping a certain distance apart to produce the bent train. Another example is shown in Fig. 6. The bears are constructed from soft ellipsoids. The ring is made from polygons but contains an invisible ring of negative keys. As the ring descends over the bear the negative effect on the field causes the bear to appear squashed. One problem is that the arms disappear. It can be quite difficult to work with soft-object models when negative keys are used. Our feeling at the moment is that some of the problems could be overcome with a good user interface which gives immediate feedback when the

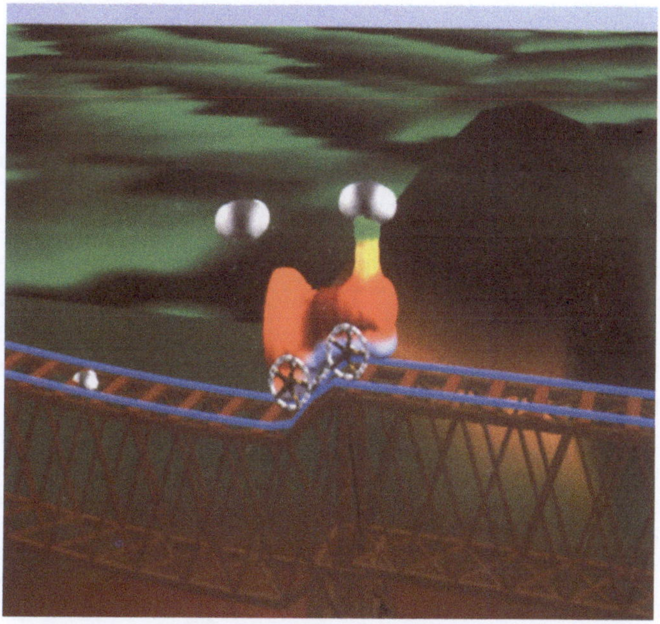

FIGURE 5. Bending the train.

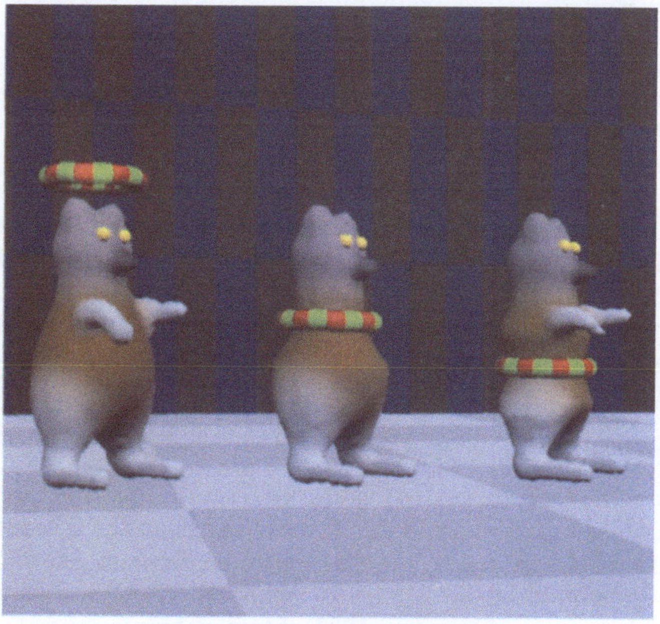

FIGURE 6. Squashing Pooh bear.

property of a key is altered. Our current system is not fast enough to do this.

Keyframe Interpolation

In hand animation an animator draws a character in some position, makes a second drawing of the character in a new position and then fills in the inbetween frames. The digital version of this technique that has been used extensively to represent complex motion in 2-D animation is generally known as "inbetweening." Technical difficulties, such as shape distortion and even loss of surface continuity, not to mention the expense of computation, encountered in this process are due primarily to the way in which the animated objects have been modelled. Soft objects remove or at least mitigate these problems. Moreover, soft objects are amenable to various techniques of inbetweening.

Best of all, they present a simpler model for the animator to work with. A simple form of inbetweening, suitable for two-dimensional (cartoon) models, would have the character drawn on a vector-oriented display in two positions and the inbetween frames interpolated by the system. The simplest way to do this is to interpolate each point of the first (source) object to a corresponding point on the second (destination) object. Difficulties arise if the number of points is different on source and destination objects. New points have to be created or several points have to collapse onto a single point. Even if the number of points is the same on the two objects, if they are distributed in a different way the image will be scrambled as each point is interpolated.

Inbetweening is not only used to show motion of a character from one position to another; it can also be used to show metamorphosis from one character to another. If the characters are very different in shape, the scrambling problem is difficult to avoid. Peter Foldes uses software by Burtnyk and Wein (1976) in the film *La Faim* and exploits this technique to advantage. However, to avoid scrambling is a difficult and tedious task which requires very careful design of the key points for inbetweening.

For inbetweening in 3-D, two methods of solving these problems have been tried. Both solutions require the definition of a set of keyframes, with the objects in their correct orientations.

The first method uses interpolation of a set of keys which are defined for each object. The interpolation usually works on the geometric transformations or the parameters of a parameterized model. Examples of this type of system would be BBOP or EM, both developed at the NYIT Graphics Laboratory (Sturman, 1984). More elaborate control of the motion is discussed in Steketee and Badler (1985). This system guarantees continuous acceleration while still having local control of key points and the ability to join motions.

The second method uses interpolation of the actual objects. A set of key points is defined either by the artist or by the system, and these key points are interpolated. Theoretically, systems for doing inbetweening of this type in 2-D can be extended to 3-D, although this may often be impractical. The technique of using moving point constraints (Reeves, 1981) may be unsuitable only because of the difficulty of specifying a natural user interface into the system, which would now extend over four dimensions (three space and time). In simple cases the problem of matching key points can be left to the system. More difficult cases arise when the objects change shape, or components are added or removed from the scene.

It is possible to combine the two types of system. The parameters of the objects could be interpolated to change location, and at the same time the source object could be inbetweened to the destination object to make some sort of shape change. Since the two systems work on different levels of detail this should not pose a problem.

The difficulty of inbetweening in 3-D is influenced by the choice of modelling technique. In the case of polygons, for example, the polygons and their vertices must be carefully matched from source to destination object Q, a difficult task to automate. The use of B-spline patches reduces the number of points that have to be inbetweened, but to manufacture a complex object would require many patches, and maintaining a closed surface demands the management of complicated constraints on the inbetween positions of the patch control points. With the soft object technique, however, a continuous closed surface is guaranteed; some kind of closed volume will be produced whatever the shape of the object in the inbetween stage. This will always produce a more desirable result than allowing the objects to collapse incoherently.

We have experimented with a number of different methods for matching keys on source and destination objects. Each method produces a different type of result, providing the animator with some alternatives for a particular metamorphosis problem. A paper describing these methods is in preparation. One method we call *surface inbetweening* or SIN. At each inbetween stage both source and destination keys are all present, but the keys are weighted. The weight of the source key changes from 1 to 0 as the weight applied to the destination keys changes from 0 to 1. The speed at which the weights change provides the animator with another way of controlling the appearance of the inbetween stages. Figure 7 shows a human figure undergoing a metamorphosis to a rabbit. The weight was applied to the radius of influence of the keys. The rate of change of the weights was controlled by sampling a cosine curve to obtain the source weighting (applied to the human shape) between 1 and 0 and a sine curve to obtain the weight between 0 and 1 to be applied to the rabbit. For further details on animating these objects please see Wyvill et al. (1986b).

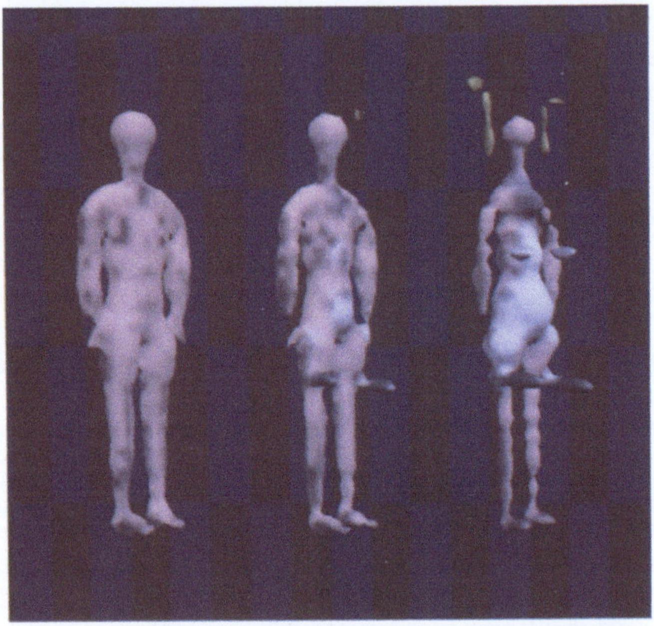

(a)

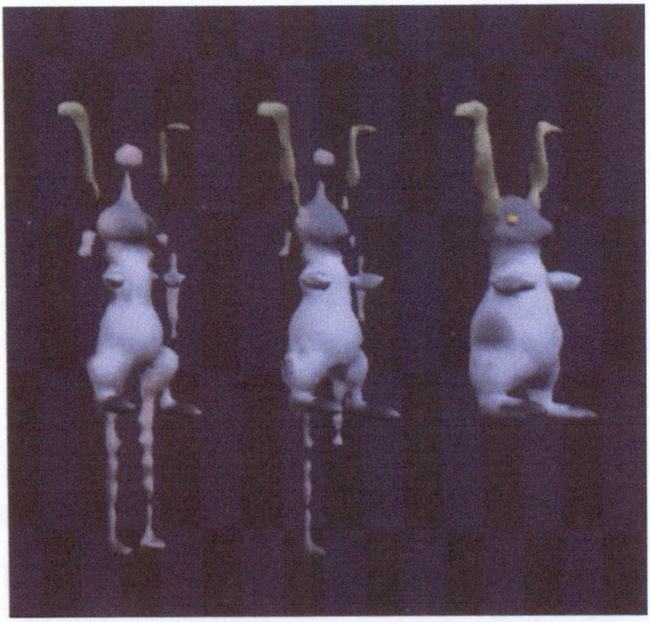

(b)

FIGURE 7. Metamorphosis of man to rabbit.

The Graphicsland Animation Project

The Graphicsland project group (Wyvill et al., 1986c) at the University of Calgary has developed an organised collection of software tools for producing animation from models in three dimensions. The system allows the combination of several different kinds of modelling primitive (Wyvill et al., 1986c). Thus polygon-based models can be mixed freely with fractals (Fournier, 1982) and particles (Reeves, 1983) in a scene. Motion and camera paths can be described and animation generated. Note that we do not include the use of a two-dimensional "paint" system. Our objective is always to construct views of a full three-dimensional model.

The kernel of Graphicsland is called *Groper*, a 3-D graphics language based on a hierarchical structure. Objects may be defined in terms of subobjects or recursive references to themselves, leading to some interesting 3-D objects akin to 2-D space-filling curves. Various special functions use the idea of limited recursion to produce results which are awkward or impossible to obtain from other systems. Constrained random transformations can be introduced to achieve a fractal-like effect.

Primitive objects may be made from a variety of types including particle systems, fractals, polygons and soft objects. An object can consist of all these types and all objects are rendered in a single pass.

Results

So far we have used soft objects in the production of a 2-minute animated sequence showing a bubbling liquid, a character deforming to a flight of steps, and then bouncing and squashing (*SOFT* shown at SIGGRAPH 86 Electronic Theatre in Dallas). We are currently engaged in a second sequence showing the soft railway engine (Fig. 2, 4, 5) which bends to its surroundings. Figure 8 was created by Gerry Hushlak, an artist working in the fine arts department at the University of Calgary. The model uses soft ellipsoids and was created as part of a design for a sculpture.

Conclusion and Future Work

We have presented a modelling technique with possible applications to computer-generated character animation. The models may be easily deformed whilst preserving the *volume* of the character. This method lends itself to various animation techniques such as inbetweening. The models can be given colour and texture. Although soft objects are useful for modeling and animation, there are several problems which have to be addressed. Firstly, keys which are near to each other will cause interference of the surfaces whether or not this is what the animator requires.

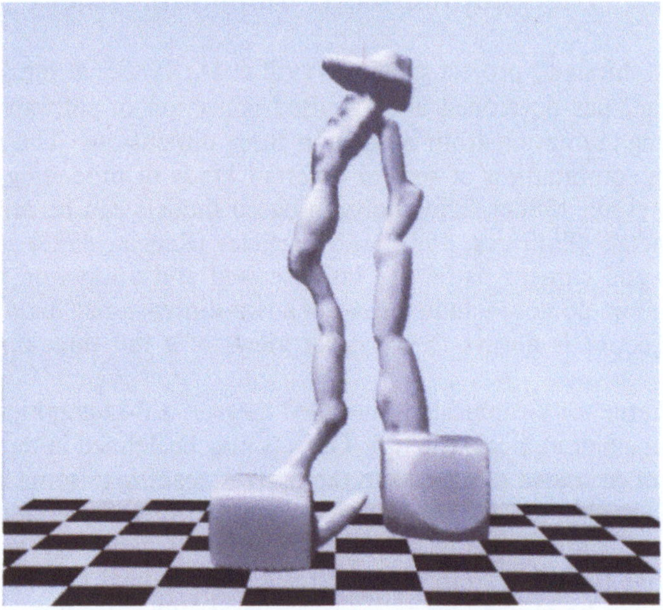

FIGURE 8. Design for a sculpture.

For example, it is easy to bend the arm of a human figure constructed from a set of keys. However, as the arm comes close to the body the fields attract and the arm could then merge with the body. We are trying to solve this problem by incorporating the object definitions in the Graphicsland hierarchy. Branches of the hierarchy can be given their own surface independently. Problems arise when two independent objects are required to inbetween simultaneously to a third. Soft objects can be used to design a complex surface with few control keys. It may be possible, given the right design tools, to use this technique for the design of complex surfaces with industrial applications. We are currently exploring the use of different functions to define the field and also interactive design tools for modelling and texturing these objects.

Acknowledgments. We would like to acknowledge the help of all the students and research staff who have worked on the Graphicsland project and soft objects, in particular Craig McPheeters, Angus Davis and the many graduate and undergraduate students at the University of Calgary who have contributed to the project. This research is partially supported by grants from the Natural Science and Engineering Research Council of Canada and Control Data Corporation.

References

Barsky, B. (1981) "The Beta-Spline: A Local Representation Based on Shape Parameters and Fundamental Geometric Measures," PhD dissertation, Dept. of Computer Science, Univ. of Utah.

Blinn, J. (1982) "A Generalization of Algebraic Surface Drawing," *ACM Trans. Graphics* 1:235.

Burtnyk, N. and M. Wein (1976) "Interactive Skeleton Techniques for Enhancing Motion Dynamics in Key Frame Animation," *Communications ACM* 19(10):564.

Heckbert, P. (1986) "Survey of Texture Mapping," *IEEE Computer Graphics and Applications* 6(11):56–67.

Huitric, H. and M. Nahas (1985) "B-Spline Surfaces: A Tool for Computer Painting," *IEEE Computer Graphics and Applications* 5(3):39–47.

Kochanek, D. (1984) "Interpolating Splines with Local Tension, Continuity and Bias Control," *Computer Graphics (Proc. SIGGRAPH 84)* 18(3):33–41.

Peachey, D. (1985) "Solid Texturing of Complex Surface," *Computer Graphics (Proc. SIGGRAPH 85)* 19(3):279–286.

Perlin, K. (1985) "An Image Synthesizer," *Computer Graphics (Proc. SIGGRAPH 85)* 19(3):287–296.

Reeves, W. (1981) "Inbetweening for Computer Animation Utilizing Moving Point Constraints," *Computer Graphics (Proc. SIGGRAPH 81)* 2:263–269.

Reeves, W. (1983) "Particle Systems—A Technique for Modeling a Class of Fuzzy Objects," *ACM Trans. Graphics* (April) 2:91–108.

Steketee, S. and N. Badler (1985) "Parametric Keyframe Interpolation Incorporating Kinetic Adjustment and Phrasing Control," *Computer Graphics (Proc. ACM SIGGRAPH 85)* 3:255–262.

Sturman, D. (1984) "Interactive Keyframe Animation of 3-D Articulated Models," *Proc. Graphics Interface*, pp. 35–40.

Wyvill, G., B. Wyvill and C. McPheeters (1986a) "Data Structures for Soft Objects," *Visual Computer* 2(4):227–234.

Wyvill, B., G. Wyvill and McPheeters (1986b) "Animating Soft Objects," *Visual Computer* 2(4):235–242.

Wyvill, B., C. McPheeters and R. Garbutt (1986c) "The University of Calgary 3D Computer Animation System," *J. Soc. Motion Picture and Television Engineers* 95(6):629–636.

Wyvill, G., B. Wyvill and C. McPheeters (1987) "Solid Texturing of Soft Objects," *IEEE Computer Graphics and Applications* 7(12):20–26.

Index

MIX
Papier aus verantwortungsvollen Quellen
Paper from responsible sources
FSC® C105338

If you have any concerns about our products,
you can contact us on
ProductSafety@springernature.com

In case Publisher is established outside the EU,
the EU authorized representative is:
Springer Nature Customer Service Center GmbH
Europaplatz 3, 69115 Heidelberg, Germany

Printed by Libri Plureos GmbH
in Hamburg, Germany